50% O..

Online DANB CDA Prep Course!

By Mometrix

Dear Customer,

We consider it an honor and a privilege that you chose our DANB CDA Study Guide. As a way of showing our appreciation and to help us better serve you, we are offering **50% off our online DANB CDA Prep Course**. Many DANB CDA courses are needlessly expensive and don't deliver enough value. With our course, you get access to the best DANB CDA prep material, and **you only pay half price**.

We have structured our online course to perfectly complement your printed study guide. The DANB CDA Prep Course contains **in-depth lessons** that cover all the most important topics, over **750 practice questions** to ensure you feel prepared, and more than **850 digital flashcards**, so you can study while you're on the go.

Online DANB CDA Prep Course

Topics Included:

- Evaluation
  - o Preliminary Examination
  - o Head, Neck, and Oral Cavity
- Patient Management and Administration
  - o Patient Management
  - o Oral Health Education
- Chairside Dentistry
  - o Transfer Instruments
  - o Bleaching and Whitening
- Dental Materials
  - o Impression Materials
  - o Operative Materials

Course Features:

- DANB CDA Study Guide
  - o Get content that complements our best-selling study guide.
- Full-Length Practice Tests
  - o With over 750 practice questions, you can test yourself again and again.
- Mobile Friendly
  - o If you need to study on the go, the course is easily accessible from your mobile device.
- DANB CDA Flashcards
  - o Our course includes a flashcard mode with over 850 content cards to help you study.

To receive this discount, visit us at mometrix.com/university/danbcda or simply scan this QR code with your smartphone. At the checkout page, enter the discount code: **danbcda50off**

If you have any questions or concerns, please contact us at support@mometrix.com.

Mømetrix
TEST PREPARATION

SCAN HERE

FREE Study Skills Videos/DVD Offer

Dear Customer,

Thank you for your purchase from Mometrix! We consider it an honor and a privilege that you have purchased our product and we want to ensure your satisfaction.

As part of our ongoing effort to meet the needs of test takers, we have developed a set of Study Skills Videos that we would like to give you for <u>FREE</u>. These videos cover our *best practices* for getting ready for your exam, from how to use our study materials to how to best prepare for the day of the test.

All that we ask is that you email us with feedback that would describe your experience so far with our product. Good, bad, or indifferent, we want to know what you think!

To get your FREE Study Skills Videos, you can use the **QR code** below, or send us an **email** at <u>studyvideos@mometrix.com</u> with *FREE VIDEOS* in the subject line and the following information in the body of the email:

- The name of the product you purchased.
- Your product rating on a scale of 1-5, with 5 being the highest rating.
- Your feedback. It can be long, short, or anything in between. We just want to know your impressions and experience so far with our product. (Good feedback might include how our study material met your needs and ways we might be able to make it even better. You could highlight features that you found helpful or features that you think we should add.)

If you have any questions or concerns, please don't hesitate to contact me directly.

Thanks again!

Sincerely,

Jay Willis
Vice President
<u>jay.willis@mometrix.com</u>
1-800-673-8175

Mometrix
T E S T   P R E P A R A T I O N

Secrets of the
CDA®

Exam Study Guide

**DANB® Test Review for the Certified
Dental Assistant Examination**

Written and edited by Mometrix Test Prep

Printed in the United States of America

This paper meets the requirements of ANSI/NISO Z39.48-1992 (Permanence of Paper).

Mometrix offers volume discount pricing to institutions. For more information or a price quote, please contact our sales department at sales@mometrix.com or 888-248-1219.

Paperback
ISBN 13: 978-1-5167-2287-7
ISBN 10: 1-5167-2287-6

DEAR FUTURE EXAM SUCCESS STORY

First of all, **THANK YOU** for purchasing Mometrix study materials!

Second, congratulations! You are one of the few determined test-takers who are committed to doing whatever it takes to excel on your exam. **You have come to the right place.** We developed these study materials with one goal in mind: to deliver you the information you need in a format that's concise and easy to use.

In addition to optimizing your guide for the content of the test, we've outlined our recommended steps for breaking down the preparation process into small, attainable goals so you can make sure you stay on track.

We've also analyzed the entire test-taking process, identifying the most common pitfalls and showing how you can overcome them and be ready for any curveball the test throws you.

Standardized testing is one of the biggest obstacles on your road to success, which only increases the importance of doing well in the high-pressure, high-stakes environment of test day. Your results on this test could have a significant impact on your future, and this guide provides the information and practical advice to help you achieve your full potential on test day.

Your success is our success

We would love to hear from you! If you would like to share the story of your exam success or if you have any questions or comments in regard to our products, please contact us at **800-673-8175** or **support@mometrix.com**.

Thanks again for your business and we wish you continued success!

Sincerely,
The Mometrix Test Preparation Team

> **Need more help? Check out our flashcards at:**
> **http://mometrixflashcards.com/DANB**

TABLE OF CONTENTS

Introduction

Thank you for purchasing this resource! You have made the choice to prepare yourself for a test that could have a huge impact on your future, and this guide is designed to help you be fully ready for test day. Obviously, it's important to have a solid understanding of the test material, but you also need to be prepared for the unique environment and stressors of the test, so that you can perform to the best of your abilities.

For this purpose, the first section that appears in this guide is the **Secret Keys**. We've devoted countless hours to meticulously researching what works and what doesn't, and we've boiled down our findings to the five most impactful steps you can take to improve your performance on the test. We start at the beginning with study planning and move through the preparation process, all the way to the testing strategies that will help you get the most out of what you know when you're finally sitting in front of the test.

We recommend that you start preparing for your test as far in advance as possible. However, if you've bought this guide as a last-minute study resource and only have a few days before your test, we recommend that you skip over the first two Secret Keys since they address a long-term study plan.

If you struggle with **test anxiety**, we strongly encourage you to check out our recommendations for how you can overcome it. Test anxiety is a formidable foe, but it can be beaten, and we want to make sure you have the tools you need to defeat it.

Secret Key #1 – Plan Big, Study Small

There's a lot riding on your performance. If you want to ace this test, you're going to need to keep your skills sharp and the material fresh in your mind. You need a plan that lets you review everything you need to know while still fitting in your schedule. We'll break this strategy down into three categories.

Information Organization

Start with the information you already have: the official test outline. From this, you can make a complete list of all the concepts you need to cover before the test. Organize these concepts into groups that can be studied together, and create a list of any related vocabulary you need to learn so you can brush up on any difficult terms. You'll want to keep this vocabulary list handy once you actually start studying since you may need to add to it along the way.

Time Management

Once you have your set of study concepts, decide how to spread them out over the time you have left before the test. Break your study plan into small, clear goals so you have a manageable task for each day and know exactly what you're doing. Then just focus on one small step at a time. When you manage your time this way, you don't need to spend hours at a time studying. Studying a small block of content for a short period each day helps you retain information better and avoid stressing over how much you have left to do. You can relax knowing that you have a plan to cover everything in time. In order for this strategy to be effective though, you have to start studying early and stick to your schedule. Avoid the exhaustion and futility that comes from last-minute cramming!

Study Environment

The environment you study in has a big impact on your learning. Studying in a coffee shop, while probably more enjoyable, is not likely to be as fruitful as studying in a quiet room. It's important to keep distractions to a minimum. You're only planning to study for a short block of time, so make the most of it. Don't pause to check your phone or get up to find a snack. It's also important to **avoid multitasking**. Research has consistently shown that multitasking will make your studying dramatically less effective. Your study area should also be comfortable and well-lit so you don't have the distraction of straining your eyes or sitting on an uncomfortable chair.

The time of day you study is also important. You want to be rested and alert. Don't wait until just before bedtime. Study when you'll be most likely to comprehend and remember. Even better, if you know what time of day your test will be, set that time aside for study. That way your brain will be used to working on that subject at that specific time and you'll have a better chance of recalling information.

Finally, it can be helpful to team up with others who are studying for the same test. Your actual studying should be done in as isolated an environment as possible, but the work of organizing the information and setting up the study plan can be divided up. In between study sessions, you can discuss with your teammates the concepts that you're all studying and quiz each other on the details. Just be sure that your teammates are as serious about the test as you are. If you find that your study time is being replaced with social time, you might need to find a new team.

Secret Key #2 – Make Your Studying Count

You're devoting a lot of time and effort to preparing for this test, so you want to be absolutely certain it will pay off. This means doing more than just reading the content and hoping you can remember it on test day. It's important to make every minute of study count. There are two main areas you can focus on to make your studying count.

Retention

It doesn't matter how much time you study if you can't remember the material. You need to make sure you are retaining the concepts. To check your retention of the information you're learning, try recalling it at later times with minimal prompting. Try carrying around flashcards and glance at one or two from time to time or ask a friend who's also studying for the test to quiz you.

To enhance your retention, look for ways to put the information into practice so that you can apply it rather than simply recalling it. If you're using the information in practical ways, it will be much easier to remember. Similarly, it helps to solidify a concept in your mind if you're not only reading it to yourself but also explaining it to someone else. Ask a friend to let you teach them about a concept you're a little shaky on (or speak aloud to an imaginary audience if necessary). As you try to summarize, define, give examples, and answer your friend's questions, you'll understand the concepts better and they will stay with you longer. Finally, step back for a big picture view and ask yourself how each piece of information fits with the whole subject. When you link the different concepts together and see them working together as a whole, it's easier to remember the individual components.

Finally, practice showing your work on any multi-step problems, even if you're just studying. Writing out each step you take to solve a problem will help solidify the process in your mind, and you'll be more likely to remember it during the test.

Modality

Modality simply refers to the means or method by which you study. Choosing a study modality that fits your own individual learning style is crucial. No two people learn best in exactly the same way, so it's important to know your strengths and use them to your advantage.

For example, if you learn best by visualization, focus on visualizing a concept in your mind and draw an image or a diagram. Try color-coding your notes, illustrating them, or creating symbols that will trigger your mind to recall a learned concept. If you learn best by hearing or discussing information, find a study partner who learns the same way or read aloud to yourself. Think about how to put the information in your own words. Imagine that you are giving a lecture on the topic and record yourself so you can listen to it later.

For any learning style, flashcards can be helpful. Organize the information so you can take advantage of spare moments to review. Underline key words or phrases. Use different colors for different categories. Mnemonic devices (such as creating a short list in which every item starts with the same letter) can also help with retention. Find what works best for you and use it to store the information in your mind most effectively and easily.

Secret Key #3 – Practice the Right Way

Your success on test day depends not only on how many hours you put into preparing, but also on whether you prepared the right way. It's good to check along the way to see if your studying is paying off. One of the most effective ways to do this is by taking practice tests to evaluate your progress. Practice tests are useful because they show exactly where you need to improve. Every time you take a practice test, pay special attention to these three groups of questions:

- The questions you got wrong
- The questions you had to guess on, even if you guessed right
- The questions you found difficult or slow to work through

This will show you exactly what your weak areas are, and where you need to devote more study time. Ask yourself why each of these questions gave you trouble. Was it because you didn't understand the material? Was it because you didn't remember the vocabulary? Do you need more repetitions on this type of question to build speed and confidence? Dig into those questions and figure out how you can strengthen your weak areas as you go back to review the material.

 Additionally, many practice tests have a section explaining the answer choices. It can be tempting to read the explanation and think that you now have a good understanding of the concept. However, an explanation likely only covers part of the question's broader context. Even if the explanation makes perfect sense, **go back and investigate** every concept related to the question until you're positive you have a thorough understanding.

As you go along, keep in mind that the practice test is just that: practice. Memorizing these questions and answers will not be very helpful on the actual test because it is unlikely to have any of the same exact questions. If you only know the right answers to the sample questions, you won't be prepared for the real thing. **Study the concepts** until you understand them fully, and then you'll be able to answer any question that shows up on the test.

It's important to wait on the practice tests until you're ready. If you take a test on your first day of study, you may be overwhelmed by the amount of material covered and how much you need to learn. Work up to it gradually.

On test day, you'll need to be prepared for answering questions, managing your time, and using the test-taking strategies you've learned. It's a lot to balance, like a mental marathon that will have a big impact on your future. Like training for a marathon, you'll need to start slowly and work your way up. When test day arrives, you'll be ready.

Start with the strategies you've read in the first two Secret Keys—plan your course and study in the way that works best for you. If you have time, consider using multiple study resources to get different approaches to the same concepts. It can be helpful to see difficult concepts from more than one angle. Then find a good source for practice tests. Many times, the test website will suggest potential study resources or provide sample tests.

Practice Test Strategy

If you're able to find at least three practice tests, we recommend this strategy:

UNTIMED AND OPEN-BOOK PRACTICE

Take the first test with no time constraints and with your notes and study guide handy. Take your time and focus on applying the strategies you've learned.

TIMED AND OPEN-BOOK PRACTICE

Take the second practice test open-book as well, but set a timer and practice pacing yourself to finish in time.

TIMED AND CLOSED-BOOK PRACTICE

Take any other practice tests as if it were test day. Set a timer and put away your study materials. Sit at a table or desk in a quiet room, imagine yourself at the testing center, and answer questions as quickly and accurately as possible.

Keep repeating timed and closed-book tests on a regular basis until you run out of practice tests or it's time for the actual test. Your mind will be ready for the schedule and stress of test day, and you'll be able to focus on recalling the material you've learned.

Secret Key #4 – Pace Yourself

Once you're fully prepared for the material on the test, your biggest challenge on test day will be managing your time. Just knowing that the clock is ticking can make you panic even if you have plenty of time left. Work on pacing yourself so you can build confidence against the time constraints of the exam. Pacing is a difficult skill to master, especially in a high-pressure environment, so **practice is vital**.

Set time expectations for your pace based on how much time is available. For example, if a section has 60 questions and the time limit is 30 minutes, you know you have to average 30 seconds or less per question in order to answer them all. Although 30 seconds is the hard limit, set 25 seconds per question as your goal, so you reserve extra time to spend on harder questions. When you budget extra time for the harder questions, you no longer have any reason to stress when those questions take longer to answer.

Don't let this time expectation distract you from working through the test at a calm, steady pace, but keep it in mind so you don't spend too much time on any one question. Recognize that taking extra time on one question you don't understand may keep you from answering two that you do understand later in the test. If your time limit for a question is up and you're still not sure of the answer, mark it and move on, and come back to it later if the time and the test format allow. If the testing format doesn't allow you to return to earlier questions, just make an educated guess; then put it out of your mind and move on.

On the easier questions, be careful not to rush. It may seem wise to hurry through them so you have more time for the challenging ones, but it's not worth missing one if you know the concept and just didn't take the time to read the question fully. Work efficiently but make sure you understand the question and have looked at all of the answer choices, since more than one may seem right at first.

Even if you're paying attention to the time, you may find yourself a little behind at some point. You should speed up to get back on track, but do so wisely. Don't panic; just take a few seconds less on each question until you're caught up. Don't guess without thinking, but do look through the answer choices and eliminate any you know are wrong. If you can get down to two choices, it is often worthwhile to guess from those. Once you've chosen an answer, move on and don't dwell on any that you skipped or had to hurry through. If a question was taking too long, chances are it was one of the harder ones, so you weren't as likely to get it right anyway.

On the other hand, if you find yourself getting ahead of schedule, it may be beneficial to slow down a little. The more quickly you work, the more likely you are to make a careless mistake that will affect your score. You've budgeted time for each question, so don't be afraid to spend that time. Practice an efficient but careful pace to get the most out of the time you have.

Secret Key #5 – Have a Plan for Guessing

When you're taking the test, you may find yourself stuck on a question. Some of the answer choices seem better than others, but you don't see the one answer choice that is obviously correct. What do you do?

The scenario described above is very common, yet most test takers have not effectively prepared for it. Developing and practicing a plan for guessing may be one of the single most effective uses of your time as you get ready for the exam.

In developing your plan for guessing, there are three questions to address:

- When should you start the guessing process?
- How should you narrow down the choices?
- Which answer should you choose?

When to Start the Guessing Process

Unless your plan for guessing is to select C every time (which, despite its merits, is not what we recommend), you need to leave yourself enough time to apply your answer elimination strategies. Since you have a limited amount of time for each question, that means that if you're going to give yourself the best shot at guessing correctly, you have to decide quickly whether or not you will guess.

Of course, the best-case scenario is that you don't have to guess at all, so first, see if you can answer the question based on your knowledge of the subject and basic reasoning skills. Focus on the key words in the question and try to jog your memory of related topics. Give yourself a chance to bring the knowledge to mind, but once you realize that you don't have (or you can't access) the knowledge you need to answer the question, it's time to start the guessing process.

It's almost always better to start the guessing process too early than too late. It only takes a few seconds to remember something and answer the question from knowledge. Carefully eliminating wrong answer choices takes longer. Plus, going through the process of eliminating answer choices can actually help jog your memory.

Summary: Start the guessing process as soon as you decide that you can't answer the question based on your knowledge.

How to Narrow Down the Choices

The next chapter in this book (**Test-Taking Strategies**) includes a wide range of strategies for how to approach questions and how to look for answer choices to eliminate. You will definitely want to read those carefully, practice them, and figure out which ones work best for you. Here though, we're going to address a mindset rather than a particular strategy.

Your odds of guessing an answer correctly depend on how many options you are choosing from.

Number of options left	5	4	3	2	1
Odds of guessing correctly	20%	25%	33%	50%	100%

You can see from this chart just how valuable it is to be able to eliminate incorrect answers and make an educated guess, but there are two things that many test takers do that cause them to miss out on the benefits of guessing:

- Accidentally eliminating the correct answer
- Selecting an answer based on an impression

We'll look at the first one here, and the second one in the next section.

To avoid accidentally eliminating the correct answer, we recommend a thought exercise called **the $5 challenge**. In this challenge, you only eliminate an answer choice from contention if you are willing to bet $5 on it being wrong. Why $5? Five dollars is a small but not insignificant amount of money. It's an amount you could afford to lose but wouldn't want to throw away. And while losing $5 once might not hurt too much, doing

it twenty times will set you back $100. In the same way, each small decision you make—eliminating a choice here, guessing on a question there—won't by itself impact your score very much, but when you put them all together, they can make a big difference. By holding each answer choice elimination decision to a higher standard, you can reduce the risk of accidentally eliminating the correct answer.

The $5 challenge can also be applied in a positive sense: If you are willing to bet $5 that an answer choice *is* correct, go ahead and mark it as correct.

Summary: Only eliminate an answer choice if you are willing to bet $5 that it is wrong.

Which Answer to Choose

You're taking the test. You've run into a hard question and decided you'll have to guess. You've eliminated all the answer choices you're willing to bet $5 on. Now you have to pick an answer. Why do we even need to talk about this? Why can't you just pick whichever one you feel like when the time comes?

The answer to these questions is that if you don't come into the test with a plan, you'll rely on your impression to select an answer choice, and if you do that, you risk falling into a trap. The test writers know that everyone who takes their test will be guessing on some of the questions, so they intentionally write wrong answer choices to seem plausible. You still have to pick an answer though, and if the wrong answer choices are designed to look right, how can you ever be sure that you're not falling for their trap? The best solution we've found to this dilemma is to take the decision out of your hands entirely. Here is the process we recommend:

Once you've eliminated any choices that you are confident (willing to bet $5) are wrong, select the first remaining choice as your answer.

Whether you choose to select the first remaining choice, the second, or the last, the important thing is that you use some preselected standard. Using this approach guarantees that you will not be enticed into selecting an answer choice that looks right, because you are not basing your decision on how the answer choices look.

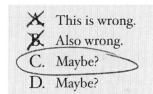

This is not meant to make you question your knowledge. Instead, it is to help you recognize the difference between your knowledge and your impressions. There's a huge difference between thinking an answer is right because of what you know, and thinking an answer is right because it looks or sounds like it should be right.

Summary: To ensure that your selection is appropriately random, make a predetermined selection from among all answer choices you have not eliminated.

Test-Taking Strategies

This section contains a list of test-taking strategies that you may find helpful as you work through the test. By taking what you know and applying logical thought, you can maximize your chances of answering any question correctly!

It is very important to realize that every question is different and every person is different: no single strategy will work on every question, and no single strategy will work for every person. That's why we've included all of them here, so you can try them out and determine which ones work best for different types of questions and which ones work best for you.

Question Strategies

☑ READ CAREFULLY

Read the question and the answer choices carefully. Don't miss the question because you misread the terms. You have plenty of time to read each question thoroughly and make sure you understand what is being asked. Yet a happy medium must be attained, so don't waste too much time. You must read carefully and efficiently.

☑ CONTEXTUAL CLUES

Look for contextual clues. If the question includes a word you are not familiar with, look at the immediate context for some indication of what the word might mean. Contextual clues can often give you all the information you need to decipher the meaning of an unfamiliar word. Even if you can't determine the meaning, you may be able to narrow down the possibilities enough to make a solid guess at the answer to the question.

☑ PREFIXES

If you're having trouble with a word in the question or answer choices, try dissecting it. Take advantage of every clue that the word might include. Prefixes can be a huge help. Usually, they allow you to determine a basic meaning. *Pre-* means before, *post-* means after, *pro-* is positive, *de-* is negative. From prefixes, you can get an idea of the general meaning of the word and try to put it into context.

☑ HEDGE WORDS

Watch out for critical hedge words, such as *likely, may, can, sometimes, often, almost, mostly, usually, generally, rarely,* and *sometimes.* Question writers insert these hedge phrases to cover every possibility. Often an answer choice will be wrong simply because it leaves no room for exception. Be on guard for answer choices that have definitive words such as *exactly* and *always.*

☑ SWITCHBACK WORDS

Stay alert for *switchbacks.* These are the words and phrases frequently used to alert you to shifts in thought. The most common switchback words are *but, although,* and *however.* Others include *nevertheless, on the other hand, even though, while, in spite of, despite,* and *regardless of.* Switchback words are important to catch because they can change the direction of the question or an answer choice.

☑ FACE VALUE

When in doubt, use common sense. Accept the situation in the problem at face value. Don't read too much into it. These problems will not require you to make wild assumptions. If you have to go beyond creativity and warp time or space in order to have an answer choice fit the question, then you should move on and consider the other answer choices. These are normal problems rooted in reality. The applicable relationship or explanation may not be readily apparent, but it is there for you to figure out. Use your common sense to interpret anything that isn't clear.

Answer Choice Strategies

⊘ ANSWER SELECTION

The most thorough way to pick an answer choice is to identify and eliminate wrong answers until only one is left, then confirm it is the correct answer. Sometimes an answer choice may immediately seem right, but be careful. The test writers will usually put more than one reasonable answer choice on each question, so take a second to read all of them and make sure that the other choices are not equally obvious. As long as you have time left, it is better to read every answer choice than to pick the first one that looks right without checking the others.

⊘ ANSWER CHOICE FAMILIES

An answer choice family consists of two (in rare cases, three) answer choices that are very similar in construction and cannot all be true at the same time. If you see two answer choices that are direct opposites or parallels, one of them is usually the correct answer. For instance, if one answer choice says that quantity x increases and another either says that quantity x decreases (opposite) or says that quantity y increases (parallel), then those answer choices would fall into the same family. An answer choice that doesn't match the construction of the answer choice family is more likely to be incorrect. Most questions will not have answer choice families, but when they do appear, you should be prepared to recognize them.

⊘ ELIMINATE ANSWERS

Eliminate answer choices as soon as you realize they are wrong, but make sure you consider all possibilities. If you are eliminating answer choices and realize that the last one you are left with is also wrong, don't panic. Start over and consider each choice again. There may be something you missed the first time that you will realize on the second pass.

⊘ AVOID FACT TRAPS

Don't be distracted by an answer choice that is factually true but doesn't answer the question. You are looking for the choice that answers the question. Stay focused on what the question is asking for so you don't accidentally pick an answer that is true but incorrect. Always go back to the question and make sure the answer choice you've selected actually answers the question and is not merely a true statement.

⊘ EXTREME STATEMENTS

In general, you should avoid answers that put forth extreme actions as standard practice or proclaim controversial ideas as established fact. An answer choice that states the "process should be used in certain situations, if..." is much more likely to be correct than one that states the "process should be discontinued completely." The first is a calm rational statement and doesn't even make a definitive, uncompromising stance, using a hedge word *if* to provide wiggle room, whereas the second choice is far more extreme.

⊘ BENCHMARK

As you read through the answer choices and you come across one that seems to answer the question well, mentally select that answer choice. This is not your final answer, but it's the one that will help you evaluate the other answer choices. The one that you selected is your benchmark or standard for judging each of the other answer choices. Every other answer choice must be compared to your benchmark. That choice is correct until proven otherwise by another answer choice beating it. If you find a better answer, then that one becomes your new benchmark. Once you've decided that no other choice answers the question as well as your benchmark, you have your final answer.

11

⊘ Predict the Answer

Before you even start looking at the answer choices, it is often best to try to predict the answer. When you come up with the answer on your own, it is easier to avoid distractions and traps because you will know exactly what to look for. The right answer choice is unlikely to be word-for-word what you came up with, but it should be a close match. Even if you are confident that you have the right answer, you should still take the time to read each option before moving on.

General Strategies

⊘ Tough Questions

If you are stumped on a problem or it appears too hard or too difficult, don't waste time. Move on! Remember though, if you can quickly check for obviously incorrect answer choices, your chances of guessing correctly are greatly improved. Before you completely give up, at least try to knock out a couple of possible answers. Eliminate what you can and then guess at the remaining answer choices before moving on.

⊘ Check Your Work

Since you will probably not know every term listed and the answer to every question, it is important that you get credit for the ones that you do know. Don't miss any questions through careless mistakes. If at all possible, try to take a second to look back over your answer selection and make sure you've selected the correct answer choice and haven't made a costly careless mistake (such as marking an answer choice that you didn't mean to mark). This quick double check should more than pay for itself in caught mistakes for the time it costs.

⊘ Pace Yourself

It's easy to be overwhelmed when you're looking at a page full of questions; your mind is confused and full of random thoughts, and the clock is ticking down faster than you would like. Calm down and maintain the pace that you have set for yourself. Especially as you get down to the last few minutes of the test, don't let the small numbers on the clock make you panic. As long as you are on track by monitoring your pace, you are guaranteed to have time for each question.

⊘ Don't Rush

It is very easy to make errors when you are in a hurry. Maintaining a fast pace in answering questions is pointless if it makes you miss questions that you would have gotten right otherwise. Test writers like to include distracting information and wrong answers that seem right. Taking a little extra time to avoid careless mistakes can make all the difference in your test score. Find a pace that allows you to be confident in the answers that you select.

⊘ Keep Moving

Panicking will not help you pass the test, so do your best to stay calm and keep moving. Taking deep breaths and going through the answer elimination steps you practiced can help to break through a stress barrier and keep your pace.

Final Notes

The combination of a solid foundation of content knowledge and the confidence that comes from practicing your plan for applying that knowledge is the key to maximizing your performance on test day. As your foundation of content knowledge is built up and strengthened, you'll find that the strategies included in this chapter become more and more effective in helping you quickly sift through the distractions and traps of the test to isolate the correct answer.

Now that you're preparing to move forward into the test content chapters of this book, be sure to keep your goal in mind. As you read, think about how you will be able to apply this information on the test. If you've already seen sample questions for the test and you have an idea of the question format and style, try to come up with questions of your own that you can answer based on what you're reading. This will give you valuable practice applying your knowledge in the same ways you can expect to on test day.

Good luck and good studying!

14

Evaluation (GC)

Transform passive reading into active learning! After immersing yourself in this chapter, put your comprehension to the test by taking a quiz. The insights you gained will stay with you longer this way. Scan the QR code to go directly to the chapter quiz interface for this study guide. If you're using a computer, simply visit the bonus page at **mometrix.com/bonus948/danbcda** and click the Chapter Quizzes link.

Preliminary Assessment

CHIEF COMPLAINT

The chief complaint is the reason the patient has come to the appointment. This is in the patient's own words and is often the first part of the documentation in the dental record for a specific visit. It is often abbreviated as "CC" for documentation purposes.

Examples of the chief complaint as part of the assessment include "tooth pain" or "jaw pain." More information is sometimes documented under the chief complaint section if the patient offers it as part of the reason they are being seen. Examples include "I have a cavity that has been bothering me for a month" or "I think I have an infection in a tooth on the left lower side." More information can be gathered and documented about the presenting problem, but the chief complaint should be the reason the patient is there in their own words. Often, the chief complaint is gathered at the time the appointment is made, but it should be verified during the patient's initial assessment at the office.

PATIENT'S HEALTH AND DENTAL HISTORIES

The patient's health and dental histories should be updated at least once per year, or whenever there is a change in their medical or dental health. Best practice is to ask the patient if there are any changes or updates to their medical or dental history at every appointment. This information can usually be provided by the patient themselves, if they are an adult. For minors, a parent or legal guardian should provide any updated health information for the dental chart.

It is important to update health information in a patient's dental record because there are many systemic illnesses, and medications, that may affect dental health. For example, patients with heart valve disease will require prophylactic antibiotics before dental procedures in order to decrease the risk of developing cardiac complications if a dental infection should occur. Patients with a seizure disorder may be placed on a medication called Dilantin (phenytoin), which can cause overgrowth of the gums. Updating the patient's medical and dental history is imperative to prevent any potential complications that can arise from dental care, whether it is routine preventive care or more complicated dental surgical procedures.

PERIODONTAL EXAMINATION

A periodontal examination consists of the history, radiographs, examination, measurements, charting, and assessment and scaling by the dentist. Good radiographs can show evidence of periodontal disease. Examination of the teeth includes assessment of tooth mobility with two instruments, inspection of the gingivae and supporting structures, and looking for and probing periodontal pockets. Periodontal probes standardized in millimeters are used to measure depths of six surfaces, the facial, lingual, distofacial, distolingual, mesiofacial and mesiolingual. The dental assistant logs the deepest pockets on the periodontal chart, along with pocket depths, furcations, mobility, exudates, and gingival recession. The dentist uses explorers to find calculus and assess the root, straight or curved scalers to get rid of supragingival calculus, and less blunt curettes to remove subgingival calculus.

15

EXTERNAL CLINICAL EVALUATION

For the external clinical evaluation, scrutinize the patient discreetly as he or she enters the room for indicators of abuse, nutrition issues, poor health, and aging. Focus on these issues that impact dental or orthodontic care: Exaggerated facial asymmetry; swelling (edema); speech problems; abnormal lip smacking; mouth breathing; and thumb sucking. Examine the lips for cracking or parching from dry mouth (xerostomia), which indicates underlying disease (e.g., thrush, vitamin deficiency, hypothyroidism, autoimmune diseases, or psychiatric drug use). Examine the smile line where the lips meet, the peripheral vermillion borderline, and the lip corners or commissures. Ask the patient to close his or her lips. Palpate the mandible and external floor of the mouth externally. Ask the patient to turn his or her head to the side. Feel the cervical lymph nodes between the ear and collarbone. To inspect the patient's temporomandibular joint (TMJ) externally, sit behind the patient. Palpate the tragus in front of the ear as the patient opens and closes his or her mouth. Listen for clicking (crepitus), watch for snagging, and ask if the patient feels pain.

INTERNAL CLINICAL EVALUATION

A certified dental or orthodontic assistant can legally perform both the external and internal clinical evaluation in most states. After examining the patient extraorally, perform an internal oral examination. Note mouth wounds, abscessed teeth, and abnormal mucosa colorations. Hold the mandible in one hand. Palpate the underside of the tongue and the floor of the mouth. Stand behind the patient. Examine the oral mucosa and frenum (fold) by pulling the lips outward. Use a mouth mirror to inspect the buccal (cheek) area and the tongue. Use gauze to pull the tongue to the side and upward for better vision. Instruct the patient to say "ah." Inspect the entrance to the throat and the oropharynx. In addition, the dentist uses a hand instrument to prod the hard surface of every tooth, and the assistant notes any findings in the patient's record.

NORMAL OCCLUSION AND FACIAL PROFILES

Occlusion is the relationship between upper and lower teeth when the mouth is closed. In normal occlusion, teeth in both dental arches are in maximum contact, without rotation or nonstandard spacing. The front teeth in the maxillary arch overlap the incisal edge of those in the mandible slightly, by about 2 millimeters. The maxillary posterior teeth are positioned one cusp further back than the mandibular posterior ones. Lastly, the mesial buccal cusp of the first permanent molar in the upper arch is in contact with the buccal groove of the first molar in the mandible. Normal occlusion should give a **mesognathic facial profile**, a straight line between jaws with only a slight projection of the mandible, relative to the upper part of the face.

LANDMARKS OF THE FACE

It is important to be aware of the following landmarks of the face and oral cavity during examination, in order to recognize and note any abnormalities:

- The first facial landmark is the outside edge or **ala** of the nose.
- Extending from the nose to the corner of the mouth is the **naso-labial groove**.
- The **philtrum** is the hollow between the bottom of the nose and the center of the upper lip.
- Lips have four landmarks: (1) the **vermillion zone**, the entire reddish part of the lips, (2) the **vermillion border** surrounding it, (3) the **tubercle of the lip**, the slight protrusion in the center of the upper lip, and (4) the **labial commissures**, the corners of the mouth. The lip vermillion zone is highly vascularized, which makes it pink or red in a healthy person, and blue in a cold, hypoxic, or dead person.
- The final facial landmark is the **labio-mental groove**, a horizontal depression in the middle between the lips and chin.

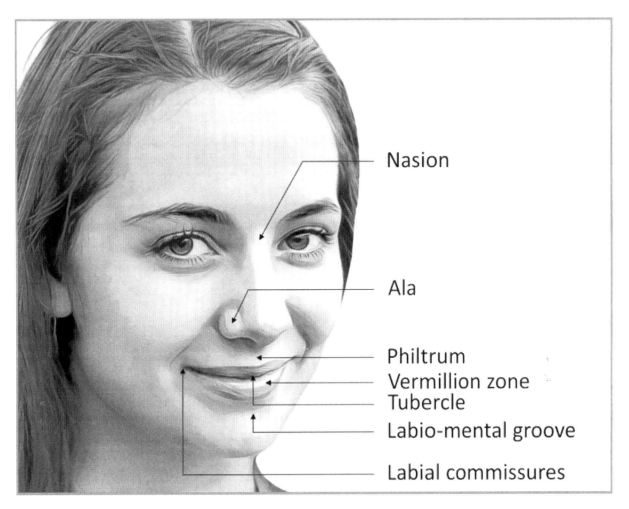

VITAL SIGNS

Temperature:

- Ideal: 98.6 °F (37 °C)
- Normal range: 97.8-99.0 °F (36.5-37.2 °C), typically lowest in the morning
- Hypothermia: <95 °F (<35 °C) from cold exposure or antipyretics
- Pyrexia: >98.6 °F
- Hyperpyrexia >107.6 °F (>42 °C)

Pulse:

- Normal adult is 60-100 bpm with a normal sinus rhythm, females typically have faster pulse
- >100 bpm in adults is tachycardia
- <50 bpm in adults is bradycardia; abnormal rhythm is arrhythmia
- Children (90-120 bpm) and neonates (~144 bpm) have faster pulses

Respiration:

- Adult normal is 12-20 breaths per min
- Tachypnea in adults is >20 breaths per minute; bradypnea is <12
- Children (15-35) and neonates (30-60) breathe faster

Blood pressure:

- Adult normal is 120/80 mmHg
- Hypertension is 140/90 mmHg
- Hypotension is 90/50 mmHg

MEASURING A PATIENT'S TEMPERATURE, PULSE, AND RESPIRATORY RATE

When taking a patient's vitals, first the General Chairside Assistant (GCA) must identify himself or herself and explain what they are going to do. Place a clean oral digital thermometer under the patient's tongue, and ask them to close their mouth for the duration of the measurement. Respiration rate indicates efficiency of oxygen intake and carbon dioxide output. Watch the patient's chest rise and fall. One respiration consists of an inhalation followed by an exhalation. Count respirations for 1 minute while holding the radial pulse (inner wrist on thumb side) with the fingertips, so the patient does not hold his or her breath. Do not feel a pulse with the thumb.

Record a baseline at the preliminary exam. Update TPR at subsequent visits. Document immediately, before the visit concludes. If the patient has no arms or the radial pulse cannot be felt, then palpate one of these pulses: carotid (neck groove beside trachea), brachial (antecubitum below elbow bend), or temporal (depression between eyebrow and ear).

MEASURING A PATIENT'S BLOOD PRESSURE

Blood pressure (BP) is controlled by the hypothalamus, medulla oblongata, and kidney. Pain, exercise, and fear increase blood pressure. Use either a stethoscope and a sphygmomanometer or an automated BP clip to measure BP. A thin adult needs a pediatric cuff. Use a thigh cuff on an obese patient's arm. A normal adult male's BP is 120/80 mmHg. Small women and children have lower blood pressures. Elders have higher blood pressure. **Hypotension** (low blood pressure) is below 90/50 mmHg. Hypotension leads to dizziness and fainting. **Hypertension** (high blood pressure) is above 140/90 mmHg. Hypertension leads to stroke and heart disease. The first Korotkoff sound heard ("lub") is the systole, when the heart contracts to pump oxygenated blood to the arteries from the left chamber of the heart. The second sound ("dub") is the diastole, when the heart relaxes as its right side fills with blood for subsequent oxygenation. BP is the ratio of systolic to diastolic pressure.

ABNORMAL FINDINGS OF THE PRELIMINARY ASSESSMENT
BENIGN ORAL TUMORS

Benign tumors are **not cancerous**, but can still cause pain, deformity, and loss of normal use. Some benign tumors have the potential for malignancy:

- **Squamous papillomae** are benign tumors that develop after human papilloma virus (HPV) infections, usually types 6 and 11. Projections of squamous epithelial tissue can be surgically removed.
- **Fibromas** are benign areas of hyperplasia; they present as pink, even, dome-shaped lesions, generally on the buccal surface.
- **Lichen planus** looks like a flattened, deep reed or violet bump. Often, lichen planus is found on the patient's leg or ankle. In the mouth, the buccal mucosa is usually involved, and lines know as Wickham's striae may be seen. The patient usually has soreness while eating. The dentist usually prescribes topical steroids. Its malignant potential is unclear.

ORAL LESIONS

The types of oral lesions observable on the surface flats of the oral mucosa include macules, ecchymosis, patches, petechiae, purpura, granulomas, neoplasms and nodules. The latter three may also present above the surface of the oral mucosa.

- **Macules** are irregular spots and patches that differ in texture and/or color from their surroundings. An example is white thrush, yeast that colonizes patients with depressed immune systems.
- **Ecchymosis** is bruised tissue.
- **Petechiae** is pinpoint hemorrhaging.
- **Purpura** is small red or purple spots, which include tiny petechiae, and larger areas of discoloration up to an inch in diameter, such as ecchymosis.
- **Neoplasms** are tumorous growths, either benign (noncancerous) or malignant (cancerous). The dentist refers the patient with a neoplasm to an M.D. for investigation.
- A **granuloma** is one type of neoplasm, in which chronic inflammation produces an area of granulation tissue.
- **Nodules** are small protuberances of either hard or soft tissue.

LESIONS ON THE SURFACE OF THE ORAL MUCOSA

Shallow lesions that appear on the surface of the oral mucosa include blisters, bullas, pustules, vesicles, papules, plaques, and hematomas. Shallow lesions are significant because they may be contagious, are painful, and can prevent the patient from obtaining proper nutrition.

- **Blisters** are thin-walled, fluid-filled sacs resulting from friction or viral diseases. Fluid accumulation occurs when blood vessels leak following trauma. Vesicles, bullas, and pustules are all variations of blisters.
  - o *Vesicles* are small blisters filled with fluid or gas and usually come from herpes or Varicella.
  - o *Bullae* are larger, with diameters larger than 0.5 inch.
  - o *Pustules* are infected blisters containing dead white cells and bacteria as pus.
- **Hematomas** are reddish lesions containing a semi-solid mass of blood from a ruptured blood vessel; hematomas commonly appear after application of oral anesthetic.
- A **plaque** is any elevated (or level) lesion in the oral mucosa.

DEEP LESIONS

Deep lesions that appear underneath the surface of the oral mucosa include abscesses, cysts, ulcers and erosions.

- **Abscesses** are pus-filled cavities resulting from bacterial infection and inflammation in the oral cavity. Most abscesses appear near the apex of the tooth or in the periodontal area. They require high dose antibiotic treatment (usually penicillin) to avoid bone loss, septicemia, and possible heart, kidney, and brain infection.
- **Cysts** are thick-walled cavities that contain fluid or a semi-solid, fluid mixture. Cyst formation usually occurs from duct blockage, but can result from other diseases.
- **Ulcers** occur when mucous membranes are damaged. Ulcers are reddened, painful, open sores.
- **Erosions** are indentations left after trauma; they have red and tender borders.

PHYSICAL CAUSES OF ORAL LEGIONS

Oral lesions can be caused by physical agents such as dental procedures, radiation injury, or trauma, which can be self-induced. Incorrect use of dental instruments can tear or bruise the oral mucosa. Incorrect removal of cotton rolls, used to dry tissue, can induce ulcers in the gums. Improperly fitted or worn dentures can also cause ulcers. Eventually, folds of extra tissue (hyperplasia) form. The palate develops red, swollen lumps. Particles of silver amalgam, used to fill caries, can catch in tissue and discolor it blue or gray. This phenomenon is called an amalgam tattoo, and it poses no health issue. Excess radiation therapy for head and neck cancer damages the teeth roots or ulcerates the target area. Self-induced traumas to the oral cavity include biting the inside of the cheek or contact with a dull object, such as mouth jewelry in piercings. Ask the patient to remove mouth jewelry before imaging.

<u>HORMONAL CAUSES OF ORAL LESIONS</u>

All of the following hormonal changes can result in bleeding at the gum unless good oral hygiene is maintained:

- According to the CDC, 60-70% of pregnant women develop **pregnancy gingivitis**, in which the gum tissues become inflated and inflamed secondary to the hormones secreted in pregnancy. Occasionally, tumors develop. Pregnancy gingivitis should subside when hormone levels return to normal.
- Another type of lesion often found in pregnant women is **pyogenic granuloma**. However, it can also affect nonpregnant women and men. Pyogenic granuloma is a rapidly growing, reddened, vascular mass of granulation tissue. It results from a combination of hormonal changes and local irritation.
- **Gingival swelling** can also occur during the hormonal changes associated with puberty, primarily in girls. Once hormonal balance is restored, the gingival enlargement should subside.

<u>HIV-ASSOCIATED ORAL LESIONS</u>

Human immunodeficiency virus (HIV) suppresses the immune response of acquired immunodeficiency syndrome (AIDS) patients, so they are susceptible to opportunistic infections unusual for adults in their prime. For example, oral thrush (Candida albicans) usually affects nursing babies, and Kaposi's sarcoma usually affects elderly Mediterranean men. HIV infection is transmissible by blood and is incurable, so wearing PPE is important. Good dental hygiene is imperative for AIDS patients because they are especially vulnerable to periodontal lesions due to bacterial and fungal infections. Chemotherapy or long-term antibiotic use trigger Candida in the oral mucosa. Assess for thick, white lines superimposed over red, inflamed areas, particularly on the tongue or cheeks. Give antifungals, like Nystatin. HIV-positive patients often have hairy leukoplakia or white patterns near the edges of the tongue. The vascular malignancy Kaposi's sarcoma presents as scattered bluish-purple lesions on the palate, nose, and arms that bleed. Low-dose radiation or chemotherapy are indicated.

APHTHOUS ULCERS

Aphthous ulcers are canker sores, painful oral ulcerations of unknown origin. Aphthous ulcers have lesions with yellow centers encircled by red halos. The yellow center is actually necrosis of epithelial cells. Aphthous ulcers do not appear to be contagious. Causative agents have not been positively identified. However, Streptococci are often found in these ulcers. Other factors that promote aphthous ulcer formation are stress, hormonal changes, and food allergies. Aphthous ulcers recur periodically when the patient experiences one of these triggers. Aphthous ulcers typically persist for 10-14 days. Soothe aphthous ulcers with topical anesthetics, e.g., Anbesol (contraindicated in children under the age of 2). Postpone oral procedures during exacerbations, as aphthous ulcers are very painful.

ORAL INFLAMMATION

Inflammation is the body's reaction to infection, allergy, or injury. Inflammation is characterized by redness, heat, swelling, and pain. Inflammation occurs because an injury, allergy, or disease causes immune cells to release histamine into the area. Histamine increases blood flow, manifesting as redness and heat. Histamine makes vessels leaky. Excess blood seeps from the capillaries into surrounding tissues, causing distension. Nearby nerve receptors register inflammation as pain. White blood cells (leukocytes) are recruited to the site to kill microorganisms. Fibrous connective tissue surrounds the area in a web. Be attuned to the signs and symptoms of inflammation because they represent an underlying disease process. Oral inflammation can be observed as a variety of lesions on the mucosal surface.

MISCELLANEOUS DISORDERS OF THE ORAL CAVITY

Additional miscellaneous disorders of the oral cavity include the following:

- **Geographic tongue**, in which smooth red patches bounded by yellow or white edges cover the back and sides of the tongue and filiform papillae (hairy extensions) are missing. Geographic tongue does not hurt and requires no intervention.
- **Acute necrotizing ulcerative gingivitis (ANUG)** often occurs in teenagers and young adults and is infectious. ANUG is characterized by oral cavity pain, infection, bleeding, and a foul odor. Clean and debride the affected area. Give antibiotics and hot water rinses.
- A **mucocele** is a mucus filled bump inside the mouth closed by trauma or obstruction of a salivary duct. The dentist may lance the mucocele to drain accumulated fluid.
- **Varices** are weakened and distended blood vessels in the mouth.
- **Bell's palsy** causes drooping features because of temporary paralysis of facial muscles on one side.

DEVELOPMENTAL ABNORMALITIES OF THE TONGUE OR ORAL CAVITY

One of the most common developmental abnormalities involving the tongue is **fissured tongue**, in which the tongue surface is deeply grooved and sometimes asymmetrical (unevenly shaped). A **bifid tongue** occurs when the sides of the front of the tongue do not fuse fully, and a tip of muscle is exposed at the end of the tongue. Usually, both of these conditions are left untreated. **Ankyloglossia** is the connection of the lingual frenulum close to the tip of the tongue, impeding its movement, and preventing the speaker from making certain sounds clearly. It can be corrected with a simple surgical procedure that cuts the frenulum. The vast majority of affected patients also have an abnormality called **Fordyce's spots or granules**, sebaceous oil glands close to surface epithelia in the oral mucosa.

CONGENITAL CONDITIONS

Congenital conditions are genetically inherited states. Nine common congenital abnormalities found in the oral cavity include:

- Cleft lip (hare lip) or cleft palate.
- Unusually large teeth (macrodontia).
- Unusually small teeth (microdontia) often associated with Down syndrome or congenital heart disease
- Amelogenesis imperfecta and dentinogenesis imperfecta, which hereditary conditions that thin the enamel, discolor it (amelogenesis), or make it opalescent (dentinogenesis) and prone to caries and enamel wear
- Congenitally missing teeth (anodontia).
- Extra teeth (supernumerary), present at birth and quickly shed
- Fusion of two or more teeth.
- Ankylosis, the fusion of a tooth, cementum, or dentin to the alveolar bone.
- Gemination, in which a tooth bud cannot fully divide.
- Twinning, the development of two distinct teeth from one tooth bud.

CLEFT LIP AND CLEFT PALATE

Both cleft lip and cleft palate are developmental failures of tissues in the oral cavity to fuse properly.

- **Cleft lip** occurs when maxillary processes in the head do not fuse with the medial nasal process, resulting in a notching or more pronounced indentation from the lip to nostril. It can be unilateral (on one side) or bilateral (on both sides).

- **Cleft palate** occurs when the palatal shelves do not fuse with the primary palate or each other. It can be found alone or in combination with cleft lip. There are different types of cleft palate, depending on the fusion failure. The least severe is cleft uvula, in which only the uvular flap at the back of the soft palate fails to fuse. More serious variations include: bilateral cleft of the secondary palate; bilateral cleft lip, alveolar process, and primary palate; bilateral cleft of the lip, alveolar process, and primary palate; bilateral cleft of the lip, alveolar process, and both primary and secondary palates; unilateral cleft lip, primary palate, and alveolar process.

The infant with a cleft lip or cleft palate requires maxillofacial surgery.

ORAL TORI AND EXOTOSES

Oral tori are benign, boney extensions into the oral cavity covered with fine layers of tissue. Extensions developing from the maxillary hard palate are called torus palatinus. They occur in about 20% of adults and are usually near the midline. Torus mandibularis, outgrowths in canine or premolar areas of the mandible, are less common but more bothersome, because food fragments imbed there. Both oral tori can cause tenderness during oral radiography. They should be surgically excised if dental appliances are necessary.

Exostosis is the swelling or nodular outgrowth of the lamella bone on the facial side of the maxillary or mandibular palates. It is very similar to oral tori.

PERIODONTAL DISEASES

Periodontal diseases involve the periodontium, the tissue that surrounds and holds up the teeth. Periodontal diseases can lead to tooth loss through lack of support. Most periodontal diseases start as inflammation resulting from the buildup of plaque, bacterial colonies sticking to teeth or areas of the gingivae. Mineralized plaque on teeth is called dental calculus. Caries can develop from plaque when sugars are converted into acids by the bacteria. Periodontal disease can also result from hormonal disturbances or other oral problems. Risk factors include diabetes, poor oral hygiene, osteoporosis, stress, certain medications, HIV/AIDS, irritation from dental appliances, and malocclusion. One type of periodontal disease involves the gums (gingivae). The presence of inflamed and bleeding gums is called gingivitis. If the bacterial infection spreads to the underlying supporting alveolar bone, periodontitis results.

ABNORMAL BITES

Abnormal bites include:

- A **cross-bite** is an atypical relationship between single teeth or groups of teeth in one dental arch, relative to the other. With a cross-bite involving anterior teeth, the incisors in the maxilla are lingual to the opposing ones in the mandible. Posterior cross-bite presents similarly, with maxillary back teeth closer to the tongue than the mandibular teeth, the opposite of that expected with a normal bite.

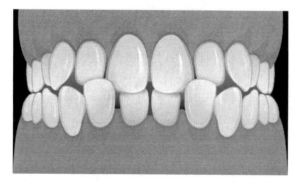

- An **open bite** is one in which there is a lack of occlusion between the mandibular and maxillary teeth.

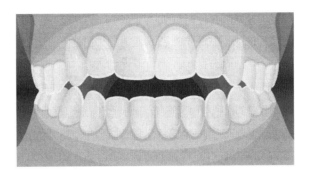

- A **deviated midline** is one in which the lines between the upper middle teeth and lower middle teeth are not in alignment.

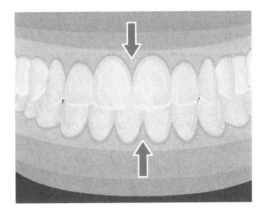

OVERBITE AND OVERJET

Overbite and overjet are two types of malposition between groups of teeth that result in malocclusion. Both are teeth overlaps.

- An **overbite** is a greater than normal vertical overlap between anterior maxillary and mandibular teeth. An overbite means the upper incisors extend over more than one-third of the front teeth in the mandible.

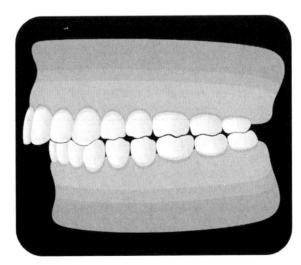

- An **overjet** is horizontal overlap, with an unusually large horizontal distance between the outer surface of the anterior mandibular teeth and the inner face of the maxillary anterior teeth.

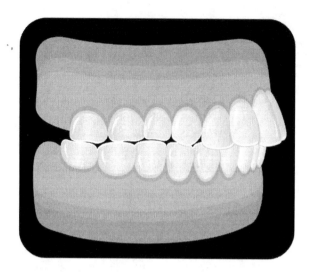

- A person can also have an **underjet**, where the front teeth in the mandible project significantly in front of the maxillary anterior teeth.

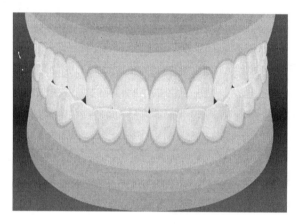

TMJ DYSFUNCTION

TMJ (temporomandibular joint) dysfunction is a lack of coordination in the structures associated with the TMJ. It can present as: pain near the ear that often extends into the face, soreness in the chewing muscles, popping or clicking noises when opening or closing the mouth, crepitus (grating), tinnitus (ringing in the ears), headache or neck pain, and the inability to adequately open the mouth (trismus) or move the lower jaw.

Diagnosis of TMJ dysfunction or disease is based on a combination of medical and dental history, physical examination, evaluation by tomographic radiography or magnetic resonance imaging, and casts of the teeth to replicate the movements of the jaws. In particular, ask the patient about grinding or clamping the teeth, bite issues, injuries, diseases, and stress when taking the history. The clinician examines the area by palpation, takes note of characteristic sounds while the jaw is opened and closed, and quantifies how wide the patient can open his or her mouth.

TREATMENT

Some treatment options for TMJ dysfunction are relatively minor, such as: Stress management; rotating heat and cold application; resting the jaw; and NSAID pain relievers, muscle relaxants, antibiotics, mood enhancers, and anti-anxiety drugs. Physiotherapy and massage are often helpful. If minor treatments do not alleviate pain, the dentist progresses to steroid injections into the intra-articular area. The dentist may apply occlusal splints to alleviate spasms or pressure. Often, TMJ disorders are treatable with orthodontia and other restoration. For extreme cases that do not respond to conventional treatments, several types of surgery can be attempted by a maxillofacial surgeon. TMJ surgeries include arthroscopic removal of adhesions, coupled with insertion of anti-inflammatory agents, and open joint surgery, in which the joints are actually reconstructed.

DIAGNOSTIC DATA

DENTAL X-RAYS

Dental x-rays enable the dentist to more thoroughly evaluate dental health. These images use low levels of radiation to produce images of the inside of the teeth and gums. Different types of dental x-rays can identify different types of dental problems:

- **Bitewing x-rays** are images of the upper and lower teeth that identify cavities between the teeth, missing fillings, damaged crowns, or problems with the roots of the teeth.
- **Periapical x-rays** are images of the upper and lower teeth that are used for identifying problems in the roots of the teeth or in the surrounding bony tissue of the jaw.
- **Occlusal x-rays** are images of the upper and lower teeth. These images are larger and enable the dentist to visualize development and placement of the teeth.
- **Extraoral x-rays** are not used to identify cavities or other problems within the teeth. These images are used to visualize the jaws and skull surrounding the teeth to evaluate tooth placement, tooth impactions, and the bony development of the jaws in relation to the teeth.

PHOTOGRAPHS

Intraoral and extraoral photographs have several uses in dental practice.

- Obtaining photographs upon the initial assessment of a patient provides the **baseline** at which a patient started before undergoing any dental treatments or procedures. These should be stored in the patient's chart and can be used to compare the appearance of dental structures before and after undergoing dental work.
- Dental photographs are useful for **patient education** purposes to clearly show specific dental problems that are identified. Images of corrected dental problems can be used to compare a patient's current dental health to expected outcomes following a specific procedure.
- **Changes** in dental hygiene can be visualized with dental photographs. Showing the patient images of their gum disease before and after treatment is performed can help them to visualize the benefits of treatments and preventive measures that have been implemented.
- A library of images can be used for **marketing** purposes for the practice to show before and after pictures of dental work that has been completed. These can show the success the dentist has in treating various types of dental disease.

INTRAORAL VS. EXTRAORAL PHOTOGRAPHS

Intraoral photographs enable the dentist to visualize areas of the oral cavity that are not easily visualized with the naked eye. Digital photographs can allow the dentist to enlarge images of the teeth to closely examine the condition of the tooth surface and enamel. Images of the surrounding gums and soft tissue can be enlarged to more closely examine any sites of potential dental disease. Enlarging the intraoral images enables the dentist to closely examine any cracks or imperfections in the surface of the tooth, early stages of gum disease, or irritation that would not otherwise be seen until the condition progresses. These images can also be shared with patients so they can clearly see any potential problems within the mouth.

Extraoral photographs are taken to capture the alignment of the mouth and jaw as they relate to all of the facial structures. Images of the patient's face while it is at rest and while smiling are helpful for viewing before and after images to show improvement after orthodontic work or after treatments to help realign the jaws.

DIAGNOSTIC CASTS

A diagnostic cast is a positive mock-up of the teeth and surrounding structures created by filling in the impression with model plaster or dental stone. Model plaster is the weaker material and is more easily trimmed. It is related to plaster of Paris. Dental stone is more robust and is the material of choice for retainers and custom trays. Both model plaster and dental stone contain gypsum, but a higher proportion of water is added to set model plaster than dental stone, or its stronger relative, high-strength stone. Setting time is affected by the type of gypsum, the water-powder ratio, length and speed of mixing, water temperature, and ambient humidity. Reduce setting time with a lower water-powder ratio, long or intense mixing, water temperature above room temperature, or on a humid day. Use the double-pour, box-and-pour, or inverted-pour methods. Trim and finish using a model trimmer. The end-product has two portions: an anatomic part showing the teeth, mucosa and muscle attachments (2/3), and an art portion or base (1/3).

ARTICULATORS

Articulators are frames symbolizing the jaws. They are attached to study models to keep the models in occlusion and to move them. They are useful for examination of malocclusion. One of the most common types is the **Stephan articulator**, which is designed to demonstrate both up-and-down and sideways movements. It has hinges corresponding to the temporomandibular joints. A wax bite is placed temporarily to determine correct occlusion. The base of each model is scored, and then they are connected to bows on the device with additional impression plaster.

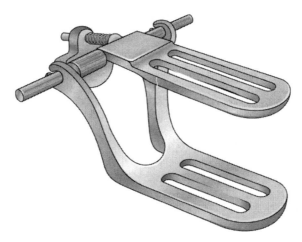

TRIMMING DIAGNOSTIC CASTS

When trimming diagnostic casts or study models, first don safety glasses. Wet the dry models in flexible mixing bowls. Ensure the base is parallel to the counter and occlusal plane. If not, trim it with the model trimmer. Apply even pressure on the trimming wheel, while supporting the hands on the trimmer table. Set the maxillary and mandibular models together in occlusion to further examine for parallelism. Once the two are parallel, draw a pencil line behind the retromolar area on the model. Trim the back of the model off perpendicular to the base. Reposition the two models in occlusion. Hold the two halves in place and cut off the untrimmed model at a right angle to its base, at the same spot as the opposing model. Draw lines as guides for trimming off the side areas, anterior cuts, and the heel portion. Trim the tongue area with a laboratory knife. Plaster fills the holes. Smooth with wet sandpaper. Apply model gloss, polish the model, and label it.

For **side trimming**, mark lines and make cuts on both models about 5 mm from and parallel to a line between the edge of the model and center of the premolars for the mandible, or the cuspids for the maxilla. Make anterior cuts on the maxillary model along a line from the midline to the area between the canine and cuspid on each quadrant. The line may need to be protruded outward, if teeth are in the way. For the mandibular model, make the anterior cuts back to each cuspid area in a more curved fashion. Heel cuts are small trimmed edges in the back on either side of each model that extend toward the center of the back.

CHARACTERISTICS OF A GOOD TRIMMED DIAGNOSTIC CAST

Diagnostic casts are shown to the patient to explain treatment. They should be trimmed to specifications and look professionally prepared. Approximately two-thirds of the model should be the anatomical portion (1 inch) and the other third the art portion or base (½ inch), for a total depth of 1½ inches. Displayed in occlusion, the total height should be 3 inches. Each model should be **symmetrically cut,** using the angles described elsewhere. Casts placed in occlusion should be capable of maintaining that relationship when placed on their ends together. If they fall apart, they are not trimmed properly.

Head, Neck, and Oral Cavity

TOOTH ANATOMY AND MORPHOLOGY
DECIDUOUS AND PERMANENT DENTITION

There are **20 deciduous teeth** (10 in each arch, 5 in each quadrant). Starting at the midline and extending backwards, each quadrant contains: (1) central incisor (cutter); (2) lateral incisor (cutter); (3) canine or cuspid (tearer); (4) first molar (grinder); and (5) second molar (grinder).

There are **32 permanent teeth (16 per arch, 8 per quadrant),** and they function similarly to primary teeth. The permanent teeth in each quadrant, extending from the midline to the back of each arch, are: (1) central incisor; (2) lateral incisor; (3) canine; (4) first premolar; (5) second premolar (bicuspids choppers); (6) first molar; (7) second molar; and (8) third molar (grinder). The anterior teeth in the front of deciduous and permanent dentition are the central and lateral incisors and canines. Anterior teeth have single roots and a distinct incisal edge. Posterior teeth, behind the anterior teeth, have more than one root and cusp (grinding surface).

ERUPTION AND EXFOLIATION SCHEDULE OF PRIMARY DENTITION

Children's deciduous or primary teeth begin erupting around four to six months of age. Most children have a complete set of primary teeth by 32 months of age. The eruption schedule is similar for both the maxillary and mandibular arch. Central incisors erupt first, followed by the lateral incisors, the first molars, the canines, and lastly the second molars. Primary teeth are shed from the oral cavity or exfoliated in approximately the same order. Exfoliation generally starts at age 6-7 years, beginning with the central incisor. Exfoliation should be complete by 10-12 years of age. The canines and second molars shed last.

ERUPTION SCHEDULE FOR PERMANENT DENTITION

From about ages 6-12 years, a child has mixed dentition. Permanent teeth begin to erupt during this period before all primary teeth are shed. The permanent teeth that eventually replace the deciduous central incisors, lateral incisors, and canines are succedaneous (they succeed deciduous teeth). Molars are not succedaneous. The first molars are generally the first permanent teeth to come into both arches at about age 6-7 years, followed by the central incisors and lateral incisors. The other teeth may come in differently for the two arches. The second and third molars are the last teeth to appear (usually at ages 13 and 21, respectively).

MORPHOLOGY OF THE DECIDUOUS MANDIBULAR TEETH
- The **mandibular deciduous central incisor** is very similar to its permanent replacement, except its crown is wider and both lingual and labial surfaces are curved, while the sides are flat.
- The **mandibular deciduous lateral incisor**s are slightly longer and broader than the central incisors; they have a prominent cingulum, distal and mesial ridges, and a deeper fossa. Their roots bend distally at the bottom.
- **Mandibular deciduous canines** have smaller roots and less prominent crown ridges than their maxillary counterparts.
- **Mandibular deciduous incisors** and canines have single roots.
- The **mandibular deciduous first molars** have four cusps (mesiobuccal is the biggest), relatively long buccal facades, and bifurcated roots on the mesial and distal sides.
- **Mandibular deciduous second molars** look like permanent mandibular first molars, but are smaller. The mesiobuccal and distobuccal cusps are about the same size. Mandibular deciduous second molars have two roots; the mesial root is bigger than the distal.

MORPHOLOGY OF THE DECIDUOUS MAXILLARY TEETH

- **Deciduous (primary) teeth** have relatively long roots compared to their crowns, more prominent cervical ridges, and are very white, due to thin enamel and dentin, but more pulp). Deciduous teeth are smaller than permanent teeth.
- **Maxillary deciduous central incisors** have distinct cervical lines, are wider than their height, have no mamelons, and their labial sides are convex.
- **Maxillary deciduous lateral incisors** are smaller, longer, and more curved than central incisors.
- **Maxillary deciduous canines (cuspids)** have pointed incisal rims, ridges on the mesial and distal sides, and prominent cingula. Maxillary deciduous cuspid roots are more elongated than the incisors. All of these anterior teeth have single roots.
- The **maxillary deciduous first molars** have four cusps, transverse and oblique ridges, and three roots. The mesiolingual cusp is the most prominent.
- **Second molars** have four or five main cusps, and three widely separated roots.

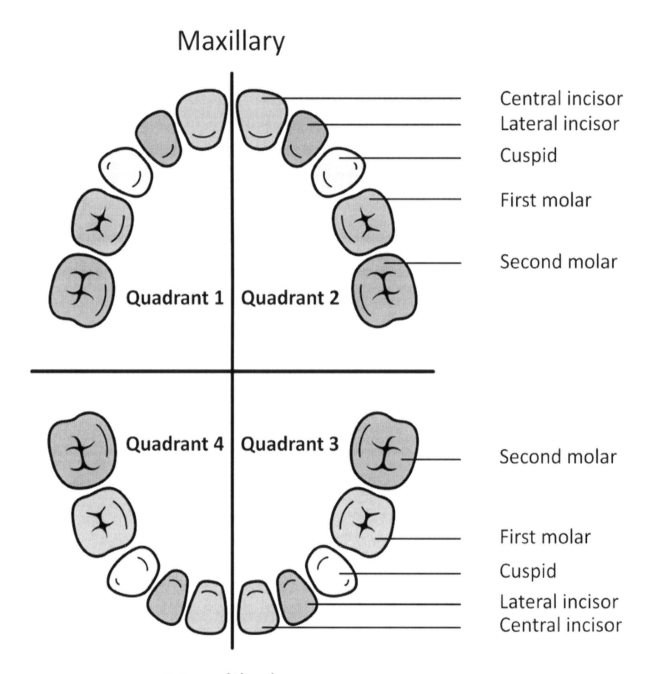

Maxillary

Central incisor
Lateral incisor
Cuspid
First molar
Second molar

Quadrant 1 | Quadrant 2

Quadrant 4 | Quadrant 3

Second molar

First molar
Cuspid
Lateral incisor
Central incisor

Mandibular

MORPHOLOGY OF THE PERMANENT POSTERIOR MAXILLARY TEETH

- **Maxillary first and second premolars** (bicuspids) are posterior to the canines. Premolars have crowns with two cusps. The facial cusp is larger than the lingual cusp. The difference is more pronounced in the first premolar. Maxillary first premolars have two bifurcated roots, whereas maxillary second premolars have single roots.
- Proceeding posteriorly are the **maxillary first molars**, which are almost square and have five cusps: mesiobuccal, distobuccal, mesiolingual, distolingual, and the cusp of Carabelli on the mesiolingual cusp. There is a buccal groove between the mesiobuccal and distobuccal cusps, and buccal and lingual pits, a central fossa, and oblique and transverse ridges. Maxillary first molars have trifurcated roots.

- **Maxillary second molars** are slightly smaller and have only four cusps (minus the cusp of Carabelli). They have trifurcated roots.
- **Maxillary third molars** are slightly smaller than the second molars and have more grooves on the occlusal surface. Their root structure varies. Third molars may be absent or fail to erupt, in which case they must be removed.

MORPHOLOGY OF THE PERMANENT ANTERIOR MAXILLARY TEETH

- **Maxillary incisors** have sharp incisal edges but no cusps. They have single roots up to twice the length of their crowns. The *maxillary central incisors* near the midline are slightly larger (both crown and root) than the adjacent maxillary lateral incisors. When central incisors initially erupt, they display three bumps on the incisal surface, called mamelons, which wear down to a flat edge. Incisors have imbrications, or faint overlapping lines and developmental depressions, on the labial surface near the gums. The labial surface of the crown is convex, while the lingual side is concave. Incisors are essential for producing certain speech sounds. *Maxillary lateral incisors* often vary from the expected.
- The **maxillary canines** (cuspids) have the longest roots in the maxillary arch, making them the most secure. The labial surface of the crown is convex with a vertical ridge. The incisal edge ends in a tip. The lingual side has two hollow fossae, separated by ridges. Canines contain more dentin (calcium-containing material) below the enamel, making canines darker than incisors.

MORPHOLOGY OF THE PERMANENT POSTERIOR MANDIBULAR TEETH

- The **mandibular first premolar** (bicuspid) has two cusps on the crown: a prominent buccal cusp and a smaller lingual cusp, with an occlusal groove between. There are mesial, distal, and transverse ridges. Mandibular first premolars have short, single, straight roots.
- The **mandibular second premolar** has up to three short lingual cusps and one buccal cusp. Three grooves and ridges are on the occlusal surface. Mandibular second premolars have one distally angled root.
- The **mandibular first molars** are the biggest teeth. They have five cusps, meeting on the occlusal face in a central fossa, with grooves in between cusps. The crown is concave on the mesial side but straight distally. This pattern reflects in the two root structures (mesial and distal). The mesial root has two separate pulp canals.
- The **mandibular second molar** is smaller than the first, with four cusps meeting on the occlusal surface, and buccal and lingual grooves that terminate in pits. Second molars usually have bifurcated roots.
- **Mandibular third molars** are smaller, with multiple roots and furrowed surfaces.

MORPHOLOGY OF THE PERMANENT ANTERIOR MANDIBULAR TEETH

- Contrary to dentition in the maxillary arch, the **mandibular central incisor** is smaller than the adjoining lateral incisor. Mandibular central incisors have single, very straight, pointed roots. The crowns are very slender and sharp at the edge. Initial mamelons wear off. Mandibular central incisors have convex labial and concave lingual surfaces and a cingulum. The only differences in the lateral incisors are larger crowns, with relatively smaller distal sides, and smaller single roots that may have concave surfaces.
- The **mandibular canines** (bicuspids) have single roots with deep depressions; they may be shorter than those of the maxillary canines in the upper arch. The crowns of mandibular canines have steeping sloping distal cusps and smaller mesial cusps.

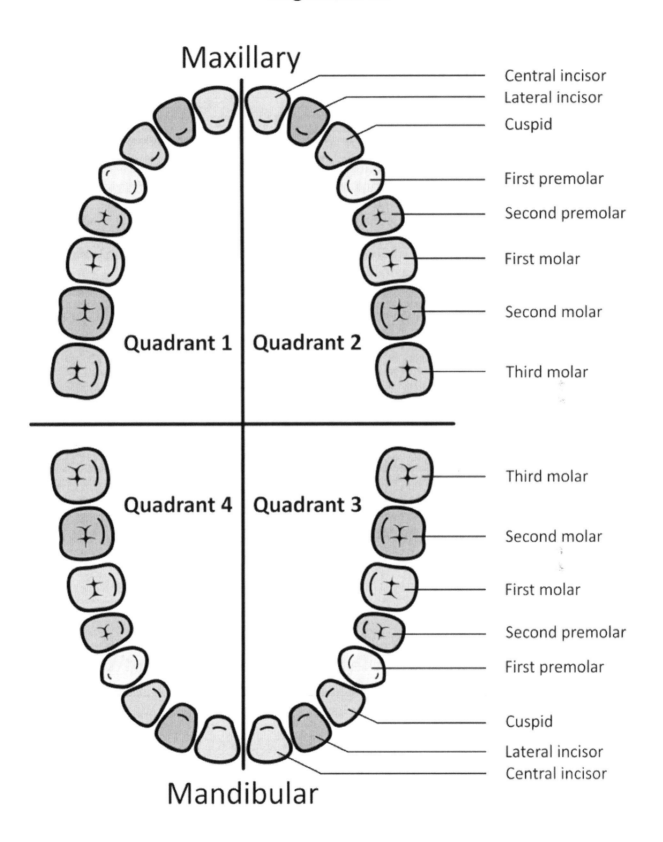

Maxillary

Central incisor
Lateral incisor
Cuspid

First premolar
Second premolar
First molar
Second molar

Quadrant 1 | Quadrant 2

Third molar

Quadrant 4 | Quadrant 3

Third molar

Second molar

First molar
Second premolar
First premolar

Cuspid
Lateral incisor
Central incisor

Mandibular

31

ANATOMICAL LANDMARKS OF TEETH

Anatomical landmarks of the teeth include the following:

- **Bifurcation or trifurcation:** 2 or 3 roots emerge from the tooth's main trunk. The dividing spot is the furcation.
- **Grooves or depressions**: The 3 types are buccal grooves, developmental grooves on the occlusal surface, and supplemental grooves emanating from the developmental type. Fissures are imperfectly united developmental grooves. Pits are areas where fissures meet.
- **Ridges**: Ridges are elevated sections of enamel. There are 4 types: marginal, oblique, transverse and triangular. Only marginal ridges are found on anterior teeth. All 4 types are observed on molars.
- **Fossa**: These are relatively superficial rounded or angular depressions
- **Apex**: The apex is at or near the terminus of the root. The apical foramen is an opening at the apex through which nerves and blood vessels come into the tooth.
- **Cusp**: Most molars have multiple cusps, or mounds on the crown. First molars may also have a fifth cusp on the mesial lingual surface, known as the Cusp of Carabelli. Lobes are united partitions that form teeth (usually equivalent to cusps for molars).
- **Cingulum**: This is the convex space on lingual surface of front teeth.
- **Mamelons**: Mamelons are the 3 protuberances on incisal edge of new central incisors.

DENTAL ARCHES AND DENTAL QUADRANTS

Dentition is the normal arrangement of teeth in the mouth. Teeth grow in one of two **dental arches**. Teeth set into the maxilla (upper jawbone) comprise the maxillary arch, which is affixed to the skull and has no flexible sideways movement. Teeth set in the mandible (lower jawbone) comprise the mandibular arch, which is flexible and can move sideways and up and down. Adjoining teeth that are correctly positioned touch each other. Maxillary arch teeth contact and slightly overlap those in the mandibular arch when the patient closes his or her mouth.

Dental quadrants are areas of dentition defined by the arch they are in (to the right or left side of the midline of the face). Thus, there are four dental quadrants: maxillary right quadrant, maxillary left quadrant, mandibular right quadrant and mandibular left quadrant. There are 20 primary or deciduous teeth grown initially, so children have 5 teeth in each quadrant. There are 32 permanent teeth developed in adolescence, with 8 in each quadrant.

TOOTH FUNCTIONS

Primary teeth, or "baby" teeth, help children to chew, speak, and smile. They support the lips and surrounding oral mucosa. They hold spaces in the jaws through which the permanent teeth will erupt. They also make it easier for the tongue to form words by serving as a brace against which the tongue can push when forming certain letter sounds. The function that primary teeth play in speech development is extremely important at a young age.

Permanent teeth, or "adult" teeth, help primarily with chewing food, but they also serve a role in articulating speech. Depending upon the type of permanent teeth, they are responsible for biting, tearing, crushing, and grinding food to aid in digestion. Correct placement of the permanent teeth is imperative for proper speech development and word formation. The correct placement of permanent teeth is also necessary for forming normal occlusion of the teeth to prevent tooth decay and gum disease.

FUNCTIONS OF SALIVA

Saliva performs four main functions:

- **Cleanses the mouth.** Saliva keeps the mouth moist and aids in washing bacteria and food off the teeth and oral mucosa. This can help to prevent gum disease and tooth decay. It also helps to prevent halitosis, or bad breath.

- **Dissolves food chemicals.** Saliva helps to dissolve the chemicals in food to improve taste, such as breaking down salt and other seasonings. This can help to stimulate the appetite and ensure adequate intake of calories for overall health.
- **Moistens food.** The saliva helps to compact the chewed food into very small pieces so that it can be formed into a bolus. Once the bolus is formed, the food can be more easily swallowed to travel through the rest of the digestive system.
- **Breaks down food.** Saliva contains enzymes that begin the digestive process of certain foods. Carbohydrates are the first food group to be broken down and this process begins within the mouth due to enzymes that breakdown starches.

OCCLUSION AND MALOCCLUSION

OCCLUSION

Occlusion is the relationship of the upper and lower teeth to each other when they are touching, such as when eating or at rest. Maintaining normal occlusion of the dental structures is important to prevent further problems. Occlusion can become abnormal from missing teeth, crowded teeth, crooked teeth, poorly fitting crowns or other prosthetics, or abnormal jaw growth.

If these problems are not corrected early in life, they can go on to cause serious problems with oral health. These problems include weakened ligaments, muscles, and tendons of the jaw that can impact the ability to speak and eat. The patient can develop pain through the teeth. The teeth can also become excessively worn down or can fall out if the malocclusion is severe enough. The gums can also be affected with recession of the tissue at the gum line due to poor occlusion of the dental structures. Chronic pain can develop in the temporomandibular joint due to problems with occlusion.

MALOCCLUSION AND ANGLE'S CLASSIFICATION

Malocclusion is any divergence from normal occlusion. In 1890, Edward Angle described a classification system for grading the degrees of malocclusion. These degrees are based on the relationship between the mesiobuccal cusp of the maxillary first molar and the buccal groove of the mandibular first molar.

Class	Characteristics	Result
Class I: Neutroclusion	Occlusion is essentially normal, except that individual or groups of teeth are out of position and the facial profile is still mesognathic.	A minor overbite that is often corrected for cosmetic purposes.
Class II: Distoclusion	The buccal groove of the mandibular first permanent molar is behind the mesiobuccal cusp of the corresponding maxillary molar. Distoclusion can be Division 1 or 2, due to either outward protrusion of the maxillary teeth or backward sloping of the mandibular teeth. Both produce a retrognathic facial profile, where one or both jaws are recessed.	This causes a severe overbite and can contribute to tooth decay, gum disease, and worn tooth enamel.
Class III: Mesioclusion	The buccal groove of the mandibular first permanent molar is mesial to the mesiobuccal cusp of the corresponding maxillary molar. The facial profile is prognathic, meaning the jaws project beyond the upper part of the face.	This can cause a severe under bite and can contribute to tooth decay, gum disease, and worn tooth enamel. This can also lead to TMJ syndrome.

CAUSES OF MALOCCLUSION

Malocclusion is caused by one of three factors:

- **Inherited genetic factors** can contribute to formation of extra or supernumerary teeth, missing teeth, atypical relationships between the jaws, or between teeth and the jaw, and deviations such as cleft palate.
- **Exposure to systemic diseases or nutritional deficiencies** during the formative years can interrupt the normal developmental pattern of dentition.
- **Particular habits or localized trauma** can produce malocclusion. These include mouth breathing, thumb or tongue sucking, thrusting of the tongue, nail biting, and bruxism. Bruxism is the unconscious grinding of teeth during sleep or stressful situations.

MALPOSITION OF INDIVIDUAL TEETH CONTRIBUTING TO MALOCCLUSION

Individual teeth can exhibit the following variations and contribute to malocclusion:

- Teeth that are mesial, distal, or lingual to their normal position are examples of **mesioversion**, **distoversion** and **linguoversion**, respectively.
- **Torsoversion** is the rotation or turning of a tooth from the expected position.
- **Buccoversion** or **labioversion** is the inclination of a tooth toward the cheek or lip. If the crown of an individual tooth is outside the normal line of occlusion, it exhibits either **supraversion** (above) or **infraversion** (below).
- Finally, a tooth may appear in the wrong position or order of the dental arch, a variation called **transversion** or transposition.

ANATOMY OF THE TONGUE

The **dorsal (top) side of the tongue** has several types of papilla or projections in its anterior two-thirds, bearing the taste buds. The dorsal tongue has a groove, called the median sulcus, dividing the front portion in half, and another groove in the back, called the sulcus terminalis. Large circumvallated papillae are located in front of the sulcus terminalis. Hair-like protrusions, called filiform papillae, appear further forward. Redder, fungiform papillae appear near the front of the tongue. Tissue creases on the sides of the tongue are foliate papillae.

The **ventral (underside) of the tongue** has a central line of tissue, termed the lingual frenum, which continues into the floor of the mouth. There are lingual veins on its sides, and tissue creases, called fimbriated folds. At the point of attachment where the lingual frenum meets the floor of the mouth, there are tissue folds called sublingual caruncles. Sublingual folds branch from the caruncles. There is a sublingual sulcus close to the dental arch.

BLOOD VESSELS IN THE HEAD AND NECK

Blood is supplied to the head and neck from the subclavian arteries and the carotid arteries. The external carotid artery branches into the superior thyroid artery, lingual artery, facial artery, occipital artery, and posterior auricular arteries. The external carotid then divides into the maxillary and temporal arteries. The maxillary artery provides blood for the teeth, gums, jaws, cheek, nose, and eyelids. The temporal artery provides blood for the surface areas of face and scalp as well as the parotid glands. The internal carotid artery divides into the anterior and middle cerebral arteries, which supply blood to the brain. The ophthalmic artery is a branch of the internal carotid artery.

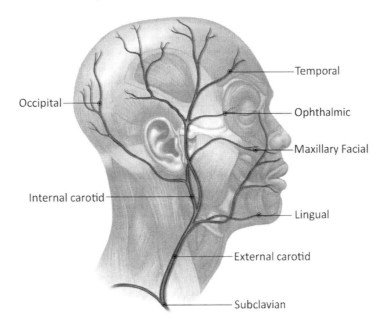

BONE STRUCTURE
MAXILLA AND PALATE

The maxilla (upper jaw) is the biggest facial bone, extending from the eye sockets and nasal cavities to form the roof of the oral cavity. The maxilla has two segments of bone, held together in the middle by the median suture. The maxilla develops from four bony outgrowths or processes: Frontal, zygomatic, alveolar, and palatine. The infraorbital foramen opens beneath the eye sockets. Sizeable maxillary sinuses open near the roots of the top molars, and there is a rounded area in the back, called the maxillary tuberosity. The palatine bones fuse at the midline along the palatine suture. The nasopalatine nerve connects to the palatine bones near the front at the incisive foramen. There is a horizontally located transverse palatine suture near the back of the hard palate. Posterior to it on each side are three other openings, one greater palatine foramen, and two more diminutive, lesser palatine foramen.

MANDIBLE

The only facial bone that can move is the mandible **(lower jaw).** It curves in front in the horizontal plane (following the dental arch), with vertical wings at the back, called rami. The rami are capped by two projections, the condyloid process in the back (which connects to the temporal bone to form the temporomandibular joint) and the sharper coronoid process, anterior to it. From the ramus area going forward, are the mandibular and mental foramen on the outside, and the lingual foramen on the tongue side. The latter has characteristic ridges. The front of the mandible is distinguished by a depression in its center, where the symphysis bones meet. The apex of the chin is the mental protuberance.

CRANIUM AND FACE

Cranial bones enclose and protect the brain, and produce some red blood cells. There are two temporal bones at the lower sides and base of the skull and one frontal bone in the forehead. There are two parietal bones on the top and upper sides of the head. The occipital bone lies at the rear and base of the skull. The sphenoid bone is in front of the temporal area. The ethmoid bones create part of the nose, eye sockets, and floor of the cranium. Various processes and sinuses make the cranium light.

There are eight types of facial bones: A set of nasal bones constituting the bridge of the nose; one vomer bone inside, forming part of the nasal septum that separates the two nasal cavities; inferior nasal conchae inside the cavity that warm and filter air; two lacrimal bones that are part of the orbit of the eye; zygomatic bones create the cheeks and are also part of the maxilla or upper jaw; two maxilla; the palatine bones; and the mandible.

TEMPOROMANDIBULAR JOINT

The temporomandibular joint (TMJ) is a junction formed by the glenoid fossa, and articular eminence of the temporal bone, and the condyloid process of the mandible. The temporal bones on either side of the face are cranial bones. The TMJ is immersed in synovial fluid, and its bones are enclosed by cartilage and supported by ligaments. The condyloid process or condyle is padded with fibrous connective tissue, called the articular disc or meniscus. When the mouth is closed, the meniscus is in close contact with the glenoid fossa of the temporal bone and the articular eminence further forward. The meniscus and glenoid are separated by cavities bathed in synovial fluid. As the mouth opens, a hinge motion develops, as the condyles and discs move forward. Then the condyles and discs move further forward, as the mouth opens more in a forward gliding joint movement. If the meniscus gets trapped or dislocated, TMJ disease manifests as a clicking noise and jaw pain.

SALIVARY GLANDS

Salivary glands secrete saliva, a digestive fluid, into the oral cavity. Saliva moistens food and tissues in the oral space, facilitates chewing and ingestion, aids digestion of starches, and normalizes water balance. Saliva is a transparent liquid, normally of slightly alkaline pH. Saliva contains water, mucin protein, organic salts, and ptyalin enzyme. Saliva is secreted from three pairs of salivary glands and their adjoining ducts, which drain the saliva into the mouth. The parotid glands are located ahead of the ear; their parotid or Stensen's ducts empty into the area around the maxillary second molars. The submandibular glands are located in the rear of the mandible; their Warton's ducts drain into the sublingual caruncles. The sublingual glands are positioned on the floor of the mouth and can empty either right into the mouth via the ducts of Rivinus, or indirectly via the ducts of Bartholin into the sublingual caruncles.

MUSCLES OF THE HEAD AND NECK

The epicranius covers the upper part of the skull and has two parts, frontalis and occipitalis, which are connected by a tendinous membrane. When the epicranius contracts, the forehead wrinkles and eyebrow raise. The orbicularis oculi surround the eyes and allow them to open and close and control the flow of tears. The orbicularis oris opens and closes the mouth. The buccinator muscle in the cheek helps to hold food next to the teeth for chewing. The zygomaticus major and minor allow the mouth to smile while the platysma helps lower the mandible and pulls the mouth down. The temporalis, which helps to raise the jaw, and the masseter, which also raises the jaw, are muscles of mastication along with underlying medial and lateral pterygoid muscles.

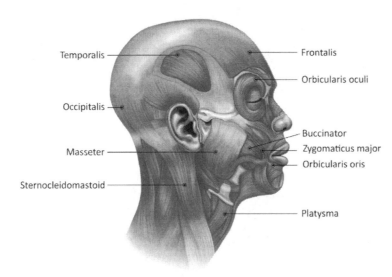

36

CRANIAL AND FACIAL NERVES
CRANIAL NERVES

Cranial Nerve	Name	Function
I	Olfactory	Smell
II	Optic	Visual acuity
III	Oculomotor	Eye movement/ pupil
IV	Trochlear	Eye movement
V	Trigeminal	Facial motor/ sensory
VI	Abducens	Eye movement
VII	Facial	Facial expression; Taste
VIII	Vestibulo-cochlear (Acoustic)	Hearing; Balance
IX	Glosso-pharyngeal	Pharynx motor/sensory
X	Vagus	Visceral sensory, motor
XI	Accessory	Sternocleidomastoid and trapezius (motor)
XII	Hypoglossal	Tongue movement

FACIAL NERVES

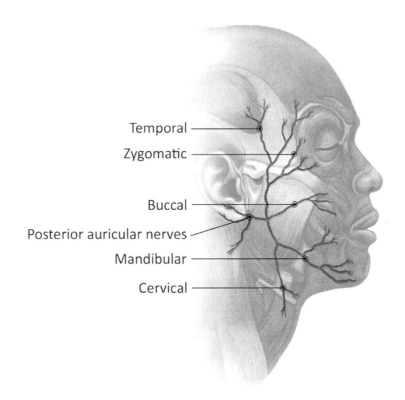

Temporal

Zygomatic

Buccal

Posterior auricular nerves

Mandibular

Cervical

LANDMARKS OF THE ORAL CAVITY

The oral cavity has a vestibule or mucobuccal fold, the pouch where the soft cheek and gums meet. Its continuous border is the vestibule fornix. The mucosa (moist linings) in the oral cavity are:

- The **labial mucosa** on the inside of the lips.
- The **buccal mucosa** on the interior of the cheeks.
- The looser, redder **alveolar mucosa** encasing the alveolar bone, shoring up the teeth.

On the labial mucosa, near the corners of the mouth, are Fordyce's spots, minute yellow glands. The **buccal mucosa** has two characteristic features: an elevated white line where teeth meet, called the linea alba, and a piece of skin across from the maxillary second molar, known as the parotid papilla. Another landmark is the **gingiva**, which are pink, fibrous gum tissue surrounding teeth. The oral cavity has two types of **frena** (restraining folds of tissue): The labial frena (the major ones between the central incisors in either jaw) and the buccal frena. Frenulum and frenum are both correct singulars of frena.

PALATE

The palate is the roof of the mouth, interior to the maxillary teeth. The front or hard palate is comprised of a bony plate, enveloped with pink keratinized tissue, and the back or soft palate, made of muscle.

Hard Palate Landmarks	Soft Palate Landmarks
Incisive papilla (an elevated area behind the top central incisors), ridges that run either down the center toward the back.	Uvula, an outcrop of tissue at the entrance to the throat.
A single palatine raphe, running horizontally across the hard palate posterior to the incisive papilla, the palatine rugae.	Anterior tonsillar pillars that arch toward the tongue, and posterior tonsillar pillars extending behind the soft palate into the oropharynx.
Torus palatinus, a bony protuberance in the center of the palate.	Palatine tonsils located between the posterior pillars at the rear of the oral cavity in the fauces, the entrance to the pharynx.

Charting Conditions of the Oral Cavity

DESCRIPTIVE CHARTING TERMS

Some basic charting terms that are descriptive include:

- **Abscess**: A deep, limited, infected pocket filled with pus.
- **Diastema**: The gap between two teeth, usually used to describe that between maxillary central incisors.
- **Drifting**: Movement of tooth position to occupy spaces formed by removal of another, also called over eruption.
- **Incipient**: Areas of developing decay where enamel is still intact, appearance is chalky due to initiation of decalcification.
- **Mobility**: Movement of a tooth within the socket quantified in millimeters; generally, results from trauma or periodontal disease.
- **Periodontal pocket**: Excessive space (more than 3 mm) in a gum sulcus, due to periodontal disease.
- **Overhang**: Presence of too much restorative material.

CHARTING SYMBOLS

- Red indicates **caries** that have not yet been restored; blue indicates caries that were restored. Either fill in the affected surface on the chart, or encircle it with the appropriate color.
- Chart **amalgam restorations** by both outlining and filling in. Show composites with outlining only.
- Indicate **recurrent decay** of previously restored teeth by outlining the existing restoration in red.
- For **enamel sealants** that have been used to deter decay, place an "S" over the area.
- **Temporary restorations** are indicated with blue circles.
- For **crowns**, draw diagonal lines across the whole area involved if gold, or encircle if porcelain.
- For **fixed bridges**, draw an "X" through the root(s) of missing teeth; the area for the bridge is either outlined (porcelain) or indicated by diagonal lines (gold).

- Show a **Maryland bridge**, which has wings on the pontic, with curves.
- Indicate **veneers** by outlining.
- For **dentures**, place "X"s over all involved root areas, and show the corresponding crown areas by either a large circle (full) or dotted lines (partial).
- Indicate **future dental work** in red on a chart.
- Indicate completed dental work in blue.
- Place an "X" through **missing teeth** on the chart. If all the teeth in an arch are missing, encircle and place an "X" over it.
- Draw supernumerary (extra) teeth on the chart.
- Show drifting or over-erupted teeth by drawing arrows in the direction of the drift.
- Circle impacted or unerupted teeth.
- Place a red slash through **teeth requiring extraction**.
- Indicate **diastema** with two vertical lines at the gap.
- Show **tooth rotation** with a directional arrow on the side.
- Indicate **mobility** with two small lines.
- Draw jagged lines to indicate **tooth or root fracture**.
- If a tooth needs a **root canal**, draw vertical red lines through it. If the root canal procedure has already been performed, draw blue vertical lines through it.
- Show **gingival recession** or furcation involvement with wavy lines and dots.
- A small red circle drawn near the root indicates an **abscess**.
- Arrows between roots indicate **periodontal pockets**.

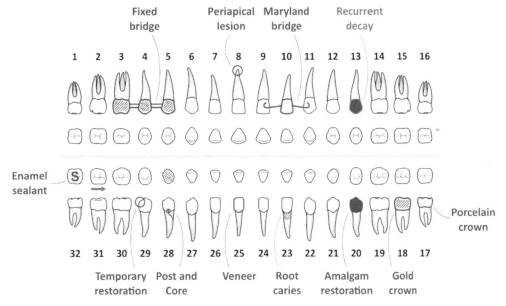

Tooth Diagrams and Coding Systems

Tooth diagrams are either anatomic or geometric. An anatomic diagram has pictures that look like real teeth, including the roots. A geometric diagram uses divided circles to represent each tooth. The circle's divisions signify different tooth surfaces. Each chart has positions for all 16 upper and 16 lower teeth.

Several different numbering systems may be used. The most common in the USA is the Universal/National System. Other countries use the International Standards Organization System more often. The teeth are shown as if one is looking into the patient's mouth. Indicate completed dental treatments in either blue or black on the chart. Note newly detected or incomplete treatments in red. Use Black's classification system to mark cavities (caries) on the diagram as Classes I to VI. Dental offices may use a variety of symbols or short forms to describe conditions or materials used in the patient's mouth. Ask the office manager for a copy of acceptable abbreviations to avoid confusion.

TEETH NUMBERING SYSTEMS
UNIVERSAL/NATIONAL SYSTEM

The Universal/National System is sanctioned by the American Dental Association and is the most common system used to number teeth in the United States. Children's primary teeth are lettered from A to J in the maxilla (upper jaw) from the right second molar to the left second molar. Children's mandibular (lower jaw) teeth are lettered from K to T starting with the left second molar and ending with the right second molar. Adults' permanent teeth are designated numbers from 1-32. Number 1 starts on the maxilla at the upper right third molar, and proceeds consecutively along the top to tooth #16 on the upper left third molar. Numbering of the lower teeth starts on the mandible at the left third molar as tooth #17 and ends at tooth #32 or the lower-right third molar.

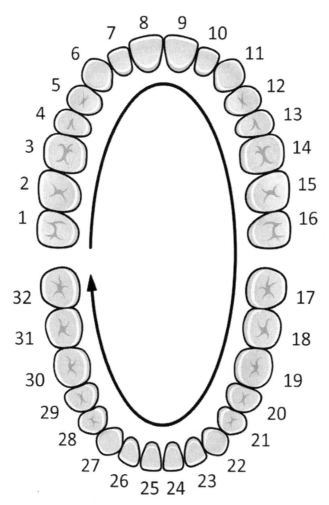

ALTERNATIVE NUMBERING SYSTEMS

Most foreign countries use the **International Standards Organization System/Fédération Dentaire Internationale (ISO/FDI).** Two digits identify each tooth: The first is the quadrant and the second is the tooth. Start numbering in the center of the mouth for adults and children. The first digit is the adult's right maxillary quadrant, 2 is left maxillary, 3 is left mandibular, and 4 is right mandibular. The second digit for permanent teeth in each adult quadrant runs from 1-8, starting at the incisors. Number children's quadrants from 5-8 for primary teeth. Children's second digits extend from 1-5 because they have fewer teeth. Pronounce digits separately, e.g., "One one", rather than "Eleven."

The UK uses **Palmer Notation (Military System).** Bracket symbols indicate the quadrant. The digit, representing the tooth, proceeds from the center. Number permanent teeth from 1-8. Number primary teeth from A to E.

PALMER NOTATION METHOD FOR ADULTS

The Palmer notation method (for adults) uses symbols (variations of the capitalized letter "L") to distinguish the tooth's quadrant followed by a number to identify its location from the midline.

- In this system, the mouth is divided into four sections called quadrants. The numbers 1 through 8 and a unique symbol are used to identify the teeth in each quadrant. The numbering runs from the center of the mouth to the back.
- In the upper right section of the mouth, for example, tooth number 1 is the incisor (flat, front tooth) just to the right of the center of the mouth. The numbers continue to the right and back to tooth number 8, which is the wisdom tooth (third molar.)
- The numbers sit inside an L-shaped symbol used to identify the quadrant. The "L" is right side up for the teeth in the upper right. The teeth in the upper left use a backward "L." For the bottom quadrants, the "L" is upside-down. The quadrants may also be identified by letters, such as "UR" or "URQ" for the upper right quadrant.

CHARTING DIVISIONS AND SURFACES OF TEETH

Each tooth has:

- A **crown** enclosed by enamel.
- A **root** faced with a thin layer of bony tissue called cementum.
- A **cervical line** (the cementoenamel junction) dividing the two.

Anatomical surfaces describe the actual covering material of crowns and roots. Clinical surfaces refer to the visible portion of the crown and root.

- **Anterior teeth** have 5 crown surfaces: (1) mesial, facing the midline; (2) distal, facing away from the midline; (3) labial, exterior opposite the lips; (4) lingual or palatal, interior facing the tongue; and (5) incisal or cutting edge.
- **Posterior teeth** also have five coronal surfaces: (1) mesial; (2) distal; (3) lingual; (4) buccal, exterior toward the cheek; and (5) occlusal, the top chewing surface.

Another term for labial or buccal surfaces is facial. Surfaces can be convex (curving outward), or concave (curving inward), or flat. Any combination of surfaces can be found on the same tooth.

CHARTING CAVITIES

Cavities are charted in terms of whether they involve one, two, three, or more surfaces that have been or need to be restored. A simple cavity restoration involves only a single surface. Simple cavity restorations are described by a letter standing for the surface involved: I (incisal); M (mesial); D (distal); B (buccal); O (occlusal) or F (facial). Compound or two-surface restorations use a combination of two letters that illustrate the two facades involved. Thus, typical compound cavity restorations are described as: OB (occlusobuccal); MO (mesio-occlusal); MI (mesioincisal); DO (disto-occlusal); DI (distoincisal); DL (distolingual); or LI (lingual-incisal). Complex cavity restorations involve at least three surfaces and the abbreviations for them incorporate all facades involved, for example MOD for mesiooccluso-distal.

CAVITY PREPARATION

Cavity preparation creates walls, lines and angles within the tooth. Walls are any side or floor of the preparation. They are described in terms of the nearest tooth surface, for example distal, buccal, pulpal (over the pulp), axial (parallel to the tooth's long axis), or gingival (perpendicular to the long axis). Lines are created when two surfaces converge. Preparation is described in terms of the line angles that result, for example, the buccopulpal line angle or mesiobuccal line angle. When three surfaces converge, they form point angles, for example, the mesiobuccopulpal point angle or distobuccopulpal point angle. Another angle is the cavosurface margin, which is the angle between the preparation and untouched tooth surface. It is important to seal these surfaces. In any cavity preparation, there are numerous line and point angles. Cavities are described in terms of depth. An ideal depth is shallow enough to retain the restorative material, a moderate depth is a slightly deeper one that does not invade the pulp, and a very deep preparation very nearly or actually exposes pulp.

CLASSIFICATIONS OF DENTAL CARIES

Dental caries (cavities) are classified from Class I to Class VI based on the teeth and surfaces they are formed in. Classes I to V were described by a pioneer in the field of dentistry, G. V. Black, and Class VI was included later. They are as follows:

Class	Characteristics
Class I	Developmental caries in pits and fissures, including occlusal surfaces of back teeth, buccal or lingual pits on molars, and lingual pits on maxillary incisors. Restore with tooth-colored composite resins.
Class II	Cavities on proximal surfaces of premolars or molars. Restore with tooth-colored resins, silver amalgam, gold or porcelain.
Class III	Cavities on interproximal surfaces of incisors or canines. Restore with composite resins.
Class IV	Similar to Class III except incisal edge is also involved. Restored with composites, and if considerably decayed, porcelain crowns.
Class V	Caries only near the gum line on either facial or lingual surface. Restore with composites for front teeth and silver amalgam for posterior teeth
Class VI	Cavities on occlusal or incisal surfaces formed by erosion. Various restoration materials are appropriate.

CLASSIFICATIONS OF PERIODONTITIS

In 2018, the American Academy of Periodontology and the European Federation of Periodontology agreed to adopt an updated classification system for periodontitis that reflects the complexity of the disease. These changes were agreed upon at the 2017 World Workshop on the Classification of Periodontal and Peri-Implant Disease and Conditions. The updated classification system incorporates a staging and grading process that reflections the multidimensional view of periodontitis.

The **staging process** examines the severity (combining an assessment of interdental CAL, radiographic bone loss and tooth loss due to periodontitis), complexity (maximum probing depth and bone loss) and extent/distribution of the disease (described as either local, generalized or molar/incisor pattern). A stage (I-IV) is the applied to the disease based on these factors. This stage applies to the full mouth rather than just one region or zone of the mouth. The condition is then **graded** based on progression (indirect or direct evidence), which is influenced by grade modifiers (risk factors such as smoking or diabetes). Grading is as follows: Grade A (slow rate of progression), Grade B (moderate rate of progression), and Grade C (rapid rate of progression).

This system is meant to specify the diagnosis and guide treatment of the disease.

Charting Periodontal Conditions

Excessive **dental plaque** leads to periodontal disease. Indicate plaque on the chart by placing a squiggly line above the tooth. Indicate periodontal pockets with an arrow and number indicating depths. A full periodontal chart enumerates the periodontal pocket depth for each tooth on both the facial and lingual sides. The dentist or hygienist "walks" the probe around the tooth and takes six distinct sulcal measurements (mesiobuccal, midbuccal, distobuccal, distolingual, midlingual, and mesiolingual). Classify **tooth mobility** as normal (0), slight (1), moderate (2) or severe (3). Note areas of exudate or pus. Show gingival recession by drawing a dotted or colored line along the gum line, to illustrate root exposure. Note furcation involvement for the molars only.

Treatment Documentation

Documenting Pre- and Post-Treatment Instructions

As part of the patient's right to be informed of their care, they also have the right and responsibility to prepare for and recover from their treatment appropriately in order to maximize the effectiveness of the treatment. It is the responsibility of the dental team to provide **pre- and post-treatment instructions** to the patient, both in person (orally), and through written instructions to ensure that the patient understands their responsibilities and has a reference to those instructions at home. The in-person/oral instructions allow the patient the opportunity to ask questions and for the dental team to assess understanding. In the case of patients that may have barriers in this process, accommodations should be provided, such as an interpreter and instructions in the patient's primary language, brochures with images to support the instructions, or access to a digital video with subtitles. As patients may not be best equipped to receive post-treatment instructions immediately following their treatment, both pre- and post-treatment instructions should be provided to the patient at the same time, at the appointment prior to the treatment.

Charting Terms for Completed Work

Basic charting terms referring to completed or suggested dental work include:

- **Bridge**: A prosthesis that replaces missing teeth, held in place on attaching sides (abutments), or sometimes just one side (a cantilever bridge). The middle area is termed the pontic.
- **Crown**: Permanent, custom-made or manufactured temporary tooth covers. Crowns are available in a variety of materials and combinations, including gold, porcelain, stainless steel, and plastic. A crown covers either the full tooth or ¾ of the tooth.
- **Denture**: A complete (full arch) or partial set of artificial teeth attached to a plate.
- **Restoration**: Materials used to fill caries or replace missing tooth structure, including silver amalgams, composite resins, and gold.
- **Root canal**: A procedure in which the dentist removes the tooth pulp and replaces it with a filling material.
- **Sealant**: A resin used to seal pits and fissures in the tooth enamel to deter decay.
- **Veneer**: A thin material bonded only to the facial aspect of the tooth, usually for cosmetic improvement.

Documenting Acceptance, Refusal, and Compliance with Treatment

Documentation must always be done during patient care or immediately afterward to ensure that no important information is forgotten or overlooked. The certified dental assistant should make objective observations as opposed to subjective:

- **Subjective**: Patient states he is "in severe pain from toothache."
- **Objective**: Patient moaning and holding right side of face.

All encounters (in-person, telephone, email) must be documented. Patient's acceptance of treatment should be documented, explaining the treatment and the patient response. Compliance or lack of compliance with the treatment regimen must be documented at each visit and contact. When appropriate, a consent form must be signed, witnessed, and entered into the permanent record. If a patient refuses treatment or refuses to follow through with advice, this information must be documented along with the patient's reason, and the patient must be asked to sign the statement as well if utilizing a paper record. In some cases, the patient may be asked to sign a "Refusal of Medical Advice" document, which is stored in the permanent record.

Conditions That Can Cause Medical Emergencies

NEUROLOGICAL CONDITIONS

Neurological diseases can affect dental health through disorders of nerves in the head and oral cavity, as well as through the inability to perform daily oral hygiene activities due to lack of nerve and muscle control.

- Conditions such as **strokes or neurologic trauma** can impair a person's ability to perform appropriate oral hygiene to prevent tooth and gum disease due to paralysis.
- **Parkinson's disease** affects a person's ability to maintain adequate control of mouth movements, which can lead to difficulty in providing adequate oral hygiene. The spasticity associated with Parkinson's disease can also lead to teeth grinding and disorders of the temporomandibular joint.
- Patients with **epilepsy or other seizure disorders** can suffer broken and cracked teeth during seizure activity.
- Dental abnormalities are also seen in patients with **multiple sclerosis**. The loss of muscle control and the spasticity associated with this disease can impair a person's ability to maintain adequate oral hygiene through brushing and flossing.
- Patients with forms of **dementia** may not be able to perform personal hygiene, which can lead to tooth decay and gum disease.

EPILEPSY

Epilepsy is a brain disorder, in which disorganized electrical impulses hop the hemispheres in a "storm." Epilepsy can occur through head injuries, drug withdrawal, high fever, and metabolic imbalances. Tonic/clonic seizures (formerly called grand mal seizures) are convulsions. The patient jerks and twitches, becomes unconscious for up to 5 minutes, followed by incontinence and exhaustion. Prolonged convulsions are status epilepticus, which is potentially fatal. Call EMS in the case of status epilepticus. Absence seizures (formerly called petit mal) are brief periods of blank staring and withdrawal. During partial seizures, an epileptic either retains consciousness (simple) or loses consciousness (complex). Both forms manifest as involuntary twitching; the main difference is recall ability. Absence and partial seizure do not require treatment. If a seizure occurs during a procedure, stop the procedure. Remove all instruments from the mouth. After the seizure, place the patient on the right side with the airway open.

STROKE

A stroke (cerebrovascular accident or CVA) is a sudden stoppage of blood flow to the brain. Strokes occur because a blood clot causes blockage (known as a cerebral embolism), or a blood vessel in the brain bursts (known as a cerebral hemorrhage). Vessel tissues in the brain die and cause a cerebral infarction. Signs and symptoms of stroke include severe headache, speech loss, dizziness, weakness or paralysis on one side of the body (hemiplegia), and loss of consciousness. If a patient experiences a stroke in the dental office, terminate the procedure. Remove all instruments from the mouth, raise the patient's head slightly, and call EMS. Give oxygen by mask and check vital signs until EMS arrives. Cardiopulmonary resuscitation may also be necessary.

SYNCOPE

Syncope is fainting, loss of consciousness from decreased blood flow to the brain and blood pooling in the extremities. Syncope is caused by stress, pain, shock from massive infection or drug reactions, or standing for too long. The patient faints because lying down restores blood flow to the brain. The patient feels dizzy or nauseated, initially. Lower his or her head to increase blood flow to the brain. If the patient becomes unconscious but is still breathing normally, place him or her in the Trendelenburg position (lying back with slightly elevated feet), so blood streams back to the brain. If the patient does not breathe well, open the airway by inclining the head and raising the chin. Remove restrictive clothing (scarves or ties) or jewelry at the neck. Dispense oxygen, using an oxygen tank, mask, and tubing. If breathing does not resume in 15 seconds, remove the oxygen mask. Apply spirits of ammonia under the patient's nose with a gauze sponge for a second or two. The unpleasant fumes should stimulate the person to take in air and oxygen and revive within a minute. Call an ambulance and start CPR, if necessary.

ALLERGIC REACTIONS

An allergic reaction is a response to exposure to a foreign agent (antigen). The patient's immune system develops antibodies to the antigen. Subsequent exposures to the antigen set off an allergic or hypersensitivity response, in which large amounts of histamine and other chemicals are released. Mild allergic reactions include skin reddening (erythema) and hives (urticaria). Remove the irritant and dispense antihistamines. Chronic allergy produces eczema. Asthma is a moderate allergic response in the airways. Anaphylactic shock is a possibly fatal allergic reaction. Allergens in the bloodstream stimulate histamine release, causing an immediate depression in blood pressure, airway constriction, swelling of the throat and tongue, and stomach pain. Give epinephrine immediately with an Epi-pen in the thigh muscle and call 911. Administer oxygen, if required. The patient needs hospital follow-up within 20 minutes.

RESPIRATORY CONDITIONS

ASTHMA

Asthma is a respiratory disease. It is often triggered by allergies or exposure to cold air, and is characterized by breathlessness and wheezing upon expiration. Asthma attacks are most likely to occur in the morning. A patient with asthma has narrowed bronchioles (small airways) in the lung. During exhalation, the lung collapses and bronchiole narrowing is exacerbated further, making it increasingly difficult to breathe. Administer antihistamines, such as albuterol, using an inhaler. The patient exhales first, then inhales the bronchodilator drug through the device's mouthpiece, while depressing the canister portion. Bronchodilators expand the bronchioles to enhance airflow. Usually, two inhalations of bronchodilator will allay an attack and improve breathing in about 15 minutes. If not, dispense oxygen and call emergency services (911). Status asthmaticus is prolonged bronchial spasms, which can be fatal.

HYPERVENTILATION

Hyperventilation is deep and rapid breathing, usually as a result of anxiety. The patient who hyperventilates for a prolonged period becomes faint, loses feeling in the extremities, and cannot take complete breaths. Alkalosis (high blood pH) further exacerbates the anxiety and rapid breathing. In the case of hyperventilation, terminate the procedure and sit the patient erect. Allay the patient's anxieties. Instruct the patient to hold his or her breath a few seconds before exhalation, which reverses the alkalosis by getting more carbon dioxide and less oxygen into the blood. Alternatively, have the patient breathe into a paper sack or their hands.

The converse is shallow breathing or hypoventilation, which can result in CO_2 accumulation in the blood and needs supplementary oxygen by mask.

FOREIGN BODY AIRWAY OBSTRUCTION

A dental patient is reclined, anesthetized, and likely has slippery objects in the mouth, so there are many opportunities for foreign body airway obstruction (FBAO) to occur. The universal distress signal for FBAO is clutching of the throat with both hands. If the patient does this, suspend treatment immediately. A choking patient cannot speak. Breathing is difficult or absent and the mouth may be blue (cyanotic). Ask the patient to sit up and cough. If he or she cannot force out the foreign body independently, call for help. Perform the Heimlich maneuver to open the blocked airway. If the patient is conscious, stand behind him or her and wrap your arms around the abdomen. Make one hand into a fist and grasp the other hand firmly over it. Deliver a

series of swift subdiaphragmatic thrusts, until the airway is clear or the patient falls unconscious. The patient needs follow-up medical treatment in case the airway was damaged.

<u>INTERVENTIONS</u>

If a patient with foreign body airway obstruction (FBAO) becomes **unconscious** during the standing Heimlich maneuver, call Emergency Medical Services (EMS) immediately. Brain death occurs in 4-6 minutes. Place the patient on his or her back and don gloves. Lift the tongue and jaw to check if the foreign body is visible. If so, attempt to remove the foreign body manually. A blind finger sweep is no longer recommended, therefore if no foreign body is visible, open the airway by tilting the head, lifting the chin, and pinching the nose. Insert a resuscitation mask into the mouth. Blow two slow breaths into the airway. Repositioning of the head may be required. If the airway remains obstructed, then landmark the xiphoid process. Straddle the patient's thighs and position the heels of both hands just below the xiphoid notch at the base of the sternum, with one hand on top of the other. Apply 5 abdominal thrusts, pressing toward the diaphragm. Continue thrusting until the airway is unblocked or EMS arrives to take over.

CARDIOVASCULAR CONDITIONS

ANGINA PECTORIS

Angina pectoris is chest pain. It indicates arterial damage and may lead to a heart attack if left untreated. Arteriosclerosis is hardening and narrowing of the arteries from plaque buildup, resulting in decreased blood flow to the heart. The patient may complain of chest pressure, or tightening, or a heavy weight behind the sternum. Pain may radiate up the neck or down the arms. If an episode of angina pectoris occurs in the dental office, stop the procedure. Check for increased blood pressure and pulse rate. Allow the patient to take sublingual nitroglycerin pills or spray to open up the coronary arteries and supply the heart with more oxygenated blood. Give the patient oxygen by mask. The patient can take up to three doses of nitroglycerin, spaced 3-5 minutes apart, before it is considered a myocardial infarction (heart attack) and 911 must be called.

MYOCARDIAL INFARCTION

A myocardial infarction (MI) or heart attack is an event in which a portion of heart tissue dies rapidly (necrosis), due to severe blockage or narrowing of the coronary arteries. The symptoms of MI are angina pectoris, ashen skin color, blue lips and ear lobes, and copious sweating. Unlike angina pectoris, chest pain from myocardial infarction cannot be assuaged with nitroglycerin administration. If an MI occurs in the dental office, terminate the procedure. Call 911. Reposition the patient with his or her head slightly raised. Administer oxygen and nitroglycerine. Alleviate the patient's stress.

MI is more prevalent in males, smokers, people older than 40, and diabetics. Heart disease can be controlled somewhat through diet, exercise, and lowering stress and blood pressure.

CONGESTIVE HEART FAILURE

Congestive heart failure (CHF) is eventually terminal. The heart is unable to pump sufficient blood to meet the needs of all organs. CHF affects five million people in the USA. Older adults are most at risk. Causes of CHF include previous heart attack, hypertension, coronary artery disease, cardiomyopathy, congenital heart defects, valvular disease, cardiotoxic drugs, myocarditis and endocarditis. Signs and symptoms are shortness of breath (SOB) when at rest or with exertion, chronic fatigue, edema, lung crackles and distended jugular veins. CHF patients need frequent bathroom breaks because they use diuretic drugs to increase urinary output and decrease fluid buildup and swelling.

BACTERIAL ENDOCARDITIS

Bacterial endocarditis is inflammation of the lining of the heart caused by a bacterial infection. Patients with a history of congenital heart disease or rheumatic fever are very susceptible to bacterial endocarditis. People who have had heart valve replacements, joint replacements, or organ transplants are also predisposed to development of bacterial endocarditis. An individual with a heart murmur is at risk for endocarditis. Insertion of dental implants also puts patients at risk. Any patient with one of these risk factors should be given a broad-

46

spectrum antibiotic prior to dental treatments or procedures to avoid infection. The recommended standard prophylactic course of therapy is as follows:

- **Adults**: Pre-procedure oral amoxicillin (2 g 1 hour before). If unable to take medications orally, then 2 g ampicillin or 1 g cefazolin is recommended (either intramuscularly [IM] or intravenously [IV]).
- **Children**: Medications recommendations are the same for children as adults, but the doses are weight-dependent: 50 mg/kg amoxicillin (oral), or ampicillin or cefazolin/ceftriaxone (IM or IV).

Of note, clindamycin is no longer recommended for dental prophylaxis.

ENDOCRINE CONDITIONS
HYPOGLYCEMIA

Hypoglycemia is too low a concentration of blood glucose (less than 70 mg/dl). It is caused by fasting, overexertion, stress, and drug reactions. Its symptoms are irritability nervousness, shaking, weakness, cold sweats, and hunger. If hypoglycemia occurs, stop the procedure. Give 8 ounces of orange juice, a glucose drink, 6 glucose tablets, or 10 Lifesavers candies immediately. A delay may cause the patient to become unresponsive and require glucagon injections, or hospital treatment for acidosis. If the patient loses consciousness, call EMS (911) and apply a tablespoon of sugar to the buccal mucosa. Excess amounts of insulin can produce severe hypoglycemia and a critical drop in blood sugar, called insulin shock; in this case, intravenous glucose is indicated.

DIABETES MELLITUS

Type I (juvenile) diabetes mellitus is a hereditary condition in which beta cells in the pancreas cannot produce insulin, a hormone that regulates glucose levels in the blood. Type I diabetics are insulin-dependent, meaning they must receive frequent injections of insulin to regulate blood sugar levels. Too much glucose in the blood is hyperglycemia, causing thirst, frequent urination, confusion, nausea, vomiting, abdominal pain, drunken behavior, and snoring. Too little glucose is hypoglycemia, with irritability, shaking, sweating, and loss of consciousness. Stop the procedure. Give the Type I diabetic his or her insulin pen or portable pump to prevent diabetic acidosis and possible coma. Type II diabetes mellitus patients have decreased sensitivity to insulin, with high blood glucose, obesity, and fatigue. Type II diabetes is probably not hereditary and tends to occur in adults. Type II diabetics can control their condition through diet and oral hypoglycemics. All diabetics have difficulty healing wounds.

ADDITIONAL MEDICAL CONDITIONS
Additional medical conditions that may cause dental concerns include:

Condition	Dental concerns
Emphysema, COPD	Patient may need to sit upright to relieve shortness of breath and may use pursed-lip breathing, making it difficult to keep the mouth open. Rubber dams should be avoided. The patient may cough and expectorate frequently and may have an infection, therefore dental personnel may need to wear masks. Treatments may need to be done intermittently at short intervals. If the patient has severe shortness of breath, an upper respiratory infection, and/or oxygen saturation level of <91%, the appointment should be rescheduled.
Hypertension	The patient's blood pressure may increase with the stress of dental care, so it's necessary to provide a calm environment and to reassure the patient. Any medications the patient is on should be noted as they may affect the dentist's choice of treatment. The blood pressure should be monitored with any complaint of headache or dizziness.

Condition	Dental concerns
Rheumatic fever	Preventive antibiotics are no longer recommended for patients with a history of rheumatic fever unless they have had infective endocarditis or other heart complications. Otherwise, routine care is indicated.
Hypotension	Hypotensive patients may experience a further drop in blood pressure with anxiety, causing the patient to faint or experience dizziness; but hypotension may also indicate an allergic reaction or other medical complication, such as a heart attack, so for patients who report hypotension, the blood pressure should be monitored carefully.
Pregnancy	Pregnancy and the weeks of gestation must be noted as some medications and treatments must be avoided because of danger to the fetus. Gums may be prone to bleeding due to pregnancy gingivitis. X-rays should be avoided if possible but any taken should be done with thyroid collar and lead apron. In later stages of pregnancy, the patient may become hypotensive if placed in supine position. Elective dental care is usually avoided during the first trimester.
Respiratory infection	Patients may expose others to infection through coughing, so infected patients should be rescheduled if possible. If not, then the dental personnel should all wear facemasks and carry out careful hand hygiene.

DENTAL EMERGENCIES

LOOSE CROWNS

In addition to the anatomical and clinical definitions of crown, the term also refers to prostheses that cover the coronal surface of a tooth with broad decay or other problems. There are full-cast crowns that enclose the complete coronal surface and partial crowns that cover up to three tooth surfaces. They are usually made of porcelain, gold, stainless steel, or a combination of porcelain and metal. **Loss of a permanent or temporary crown** is a dental emergency. A temporary fix is to use petroleum jelly or orthodontic wax to keep the crown in position. The individual must be careful during meals not to dislodge the crown. As soon as possible, the crown should be recemented in place with the appropriate type of cement.

LOSS OF A DENTAL PROSTHETIC

The loss of a dental prosthetic is considered a dental emergency because of the effect it can have on speech and eating. Repair or replacement of a broken or lost prosthetic is considered as important as the loss of a tooth.

The process of replacing a dental prosthesis depends upon the type of prosthesis being used. These can be removable appliances, such as dentures, or fixed prosthetics, such as dental implants. In either case, a mold of the patient's oral structures is taken to ensure the prosthesis will fit properly within the mouth. Once the prosthetic is created based upon the patient's existing oral structures, a final fitting is performed with alterations made as necessary for a replacement prosthesis. This ensures that a denture, for example, will fit properly without being too loose or too tight. Dental implants are replaced through oral surgery involving the placement of a post within the jaw bone that will hold the artificial tooth, or teeth, in place.

FRACTURED TEETH

Broken teeth are addressed according the amount and type of breakage, the degree of discomfort, and age. The dentist usually gives a child with a broken tooth pulp treatment and a temporary restoration, with a follow-up assessment several months later. **Tooth fractures** involving the enamel alone need their rough edges smoothed. If the fracture involves both enamel and dentin, then the exposed dentin is covered with glass ionomer, calcium hydroxide, and a bonding agent for composite restoration. If the break extends down into the pulp, then pulp capping or removal is indicated. If the crown is cracked with exposure of pulp, then a root canal supplemented by posts and casts in the crown for stabilization and protection are probably necessary.

HARD TISSUE DAMAGE

Hard tissue is calcified tissue, such as bone, teeth, enamel, dentin, and cementum. The cause of damage to this material is most often traumatic. This can include a broken tooth from chewing on a hard substance or from a traumatic blow to the mouth. Tooth decay leads to breakdown of the enamel on the surface of the teeth. Beneath the enamel, is a substance called dentin which can be damaged when enamel is broken down. Cementum is a hard substance that covers the roots of a tooth and this can be damaged when a tooth is broken off or the roots are disrupted.

The most common symptom associated with hard tissue damage in the oral cavity is pain. When a tooth breaks, the inner nerves can be exposed which produces significant pain. Damage to a tooth can be visible if the exposed surface is broken. Damages to the root of the tooth can cause significant pain, swelling, and redness at the gum line.

TRAUMA

Trauma to the hard tissues of the oral cavity is considered a dental emergency. If the trauma is to a primary tooth, rather than a permanent tooth, the tooth will not be splinted or re-inserted. If the trauma is to a permanent tooth, the following steps should be taken:

- **Loose or displaced teeth**: Splinting is usually performed to reposition the tooth into its proper alignment. If the tooth is completed removed from its socket due to the trauma, it should not be handled by the roots. The tooth should be placed in milk until the dentist can evaluate. Reinsertion of the tooth is most successful if no more than 60 minutes has passed since the injury occurred.
- **Broken teeth**: If a primary tooth is broken, the tooth will likely be extracted. If a permanent tooth is broken, any fragments should be kept in milk until the dentist can evaluate the patient. The fragments may be viable to reattach to the permanent tooth.

SOFT TISSUE INJURIES

Soft tissue injuries to the oral-facial area can occur easily during dental procedures because the oral cavity is damp and slippery, the patient may shift, or equipment can be dislodged. Soft tissue injuries to the area can also be caused outside the office by any contact with a sharp or dull object, electrical burns, or sports injuries. A situation unique to children is **traumatic intrusion**, the forcing of freshly erupted teeth back into their sockets after a tumble. Traumatic intrusion is treated by either permitting the teeth to re-erupt, or by moving them and using a splint across adjacent teeth for support. If traumatic intrusion occurs to primary teeth, the extent of damage to emergent permanent teeth underneath cannot be fully ascertained until they erupt.

ABSCESSED OR AVULSED TEETH

Abscesses are pus-filled, inflamed cavities from bacterial infection. Abscessed teeth are hot and painful due to pressure and edema. Untreated infection spreads into the surrounding tissues, producing a fistula (passageway) leading from the oral cavity, which alleviates some of the pressure. The danger is infection of the meninges around the brain. Treatment is root canal therapy, removal of necrotic pulp, opening the pulp chamber, and antibiotic therapy.

If the patient is conscious, wrap an avulsed permanent tooth in wet gauze and insert it between the teeth and lip. If the patient is unconscious or incapable, put the loose tooth in milk. Take patient and tooth to the dental office at once. The dentist then reattaches the tooth in the socket, using adjacent teeth to shore it up. Primary avulsed teeth are not reattached because infection or ankylosis (fusion of bone and cementum) can result. Primary teeth displaced to the side or loosened are repositioned and secured with a temporary splint as soon as possible.

DENTAL PULP VITALITY TEST

The dental pulp vitality test is used to assess the pulp, dental nerve, and blood flow of the pulp and roots of a tooth. It can be used to evaluate whether there is a dental abscess present, whether the pulp is necrotic, or if the tooth is normal.

An electric or thermal (hot or cold) stimulus is applied to the tooth to be evaluated. The stimulus is slowly increased until the patient feels sensation within the tooth. The neighboring teeth are also usually tested, along with the contralateral tooth. If the patient does not notice a change in sensation as the stimulus is increased, there is usually necrosis (death) of the pulp or a dental abscess present. If the patient experiences an immediate sensation when the stimulus is applied, inflammation of the pulp is usually present which may lead to necrosis. If the stimulus elicits a change in sensation that is equal to the neighboring teeth, the tooth in question is usually healthy without any disease present.

ALVEOLITIS

Normally, a blood clot forms over the socket where a tooth has been extracted. The clot protects the nerve endings and discourages infection. Alveolitis is a dry socket, where there is no blood clot formation, or the clot is rinsed out of the socket. Nerve endings are exposed and the extraction area is susceptible to infection. The therapy for alveolitis is cleansing with saline and stuffing the socket with a gauze strip or sponge drenched in the antiseptic iodoform to relieve pain. Analgesics may be used for palliation, such as ibuprofen. Medicated dressings are usually replaced in a day or two. In a surgical setting after extraction, anesthesia may be administered prior to alveolitis treatment.

Chapter Quiz

Ready to see how well you retained what you just read? Scan the QR code to go directly to the chapter quiz interface for this study guide. If you're using a computer, simply visit the bonus page at **mometrix.com/bonus948/danbcda** and click the Chapter Quizzes link.

Patient Management and Administration (GC)

Transform passive reading into active learning! After immersing yourself in this chapter, put your comprehension to the test by taking a quiz. The insights you gained will stay with you longer this way. Scan the QR code to go directly to the chapter quiz interface for this study guide. If you're using a computer, simply visit the bonus page at **mometrix.com/bonus948/danbcda** and click the Chapter Quizzes link.

Patient Management

THERAPEUTIC COMMUNICATION
PSYCHOLOGY, COMMUNICATION, AND LISTENING SKILLS

Psychology is the study of the mind and people's characteristic mental makeup. Each person brings an acquired belief system (paradigm) to his or her interactions with others. Patients have preconceived ideas about dental practices. Many are apprehensive about pain. The dental assistant must understand paradigms and employ good communication and listening skills to facilitate successful patient interaction and management.

Communication is the exchange of information. Good communication consists of skillful interpretation of the message by the sender (in this case the dental professional), interpretation of the message by the receiver (the patient), and establishment of a connection, as indicated by feedback. Active listening on the part of both sender and receiver enhances good communication.

VERBAL VS. NONVERBAL COMMUNICATION

Any type of communication between people that does not involve words **is nonverbal communication.** Up to 93% of successful communication depends on nonverbal cues. Remember that a dental patient is unable to speak during a procedure and is likely apprehensive. Watch the patient's facial expressions, gestures, posture, and position. Tight posture and/or crossed arms and legs suggest resistance. Conversely, relaxed posture and uncrossed appendage suggest openness. The dental assistant's posture affects the patient. Sit close to the patient, rather than towering directly over them in an intimidating manner. Maintain the proper social distance (territoriality) between oneself and the patient during discussions (~3 feet). A patient feels more comfortable when he or she is well-informed beforehand and the professional works from the side.

MULTICULTURAL COMMUNICATION

Different cultures have different value systems, and the dental professional must be aware of these to ensure a successful practice. Realize that social distance, eye contact, and use of first names versus surnames differs among cultures. For example, people from Arabic cultures usually find a social distance of 2 feet best, people from Asian cultures often find direct eye contact rude, people from Israel tend to talk on a first-name basis, and for people from Hispanic cultures the oldest male family member may speak for the patient. Familiarize oneself with the demographics of the area and take diversity training. Know where to find interpreters who understand dental terminology. Book the interpreter at least a day before the procedure. Speak slowly while facing the patient and do not address the translator first. Try to get more than perfunctory feedback from the patient during the communication.

PATIENT EDUCATION

Key topics in patient dental education include:

- **Pediatrics:** Children should be shown how to brush their teeth, how often, and for how long (usually at least 2 minutes) and shown how to use dental floss. They should also be advised to brush or drink water after eating sweets and to chew sugar-free gum. Older children should be instructed about the importance of a mouthguard when playing sports. Children who will have braces need to understand how the braces align the teeth, how the braces are applied, and how to care for them.
- **Adult:** In addition to the above, adults need to be educated about the effects of aging on dental health and ways to prevent gum disease. They should be advised regarding various options for dental care, including whitening and other cosmetic procedures as well as the importance of routine teeth cleaning. More specific information should be provided for any dental procedures, such as root canals.

PATIENTS WITH SPECIAL NEEDS

All patients with special needs require empathy and individual attention from the dental professional. The nausea that usually accompanies pregnancy presents problems related to oral hygiene. Acid regurgitated from the stomach during bouts of nausea promotes decay, the act of tooth brushing often causes gagging, and pregnant women commonly have bleeding gums. Advise pregnant patients that these circumstances may occur, and suggest they perform dental hygiene when they are not nauseated. Cancer patients commonly experience xerostomia (mouth dryness), widespread caries (including the roots), gum bleeding, and deficient muscle function. Approaches to oral hygiene issues include use of topical fluoride and/or extra-soft or foam toothbrushes. Patients with heart disease experience similar problems. Patients with arthritis may need to use special large toothbrushes or floss holders.

PAIN AND ANXIETY CONTROL FOR DENTAL PROCEDURES

Before, during, and after dental procedures, the dentist administers some type of pain and anxiety control to the patient. The dental assistant preps the supplies. The dentist can alleviate pain and anxiety by psychological methods, such as hypnosis and biofeedback, by chemicals, or by physiologic agents. The dentist can prescribe five types of pain relief:

- **Antianxiety drugs** that relieve apprehension (e.g., diazepam).
- **Local or topical anesthetic** that dulls pain (e.g., lidocaine).
- **Inhalation sedation** that induces a state of calm drowsiness (e.g., nitrous oxide N_2O).
- **Intravenous sedation** (e.g., midazolam, a benzodiazepine).
- **General anesthesia** by Jorgensen technique, which induces unconsciousness (e.g., pentobarbital sodium, a barbiturate, mixed with meperidine, an opioid, and scopolamine, an anticholinergic).

NUTRITION

SOURCES OF ENERGY IN THE DIET

All food consumed by an individual is his diet. Nutrients are dietary chemicals, essential for growth, maintenance and healing. There are six classes of nutrients, three of which are energy sources: carbohydrates, fats, and proteins. The other three classes are vitamins, minerals and water. Carbohydrates (sugars, starches, and fibers) provide energy, so at least half of the diet should be carbs. Fats and lipids are water-insoluble and contain fatty acids. Fat insulates, transports vitamins A, D, E and K, and provides energy when sugars are inaccessible. Proteins are linked amino acids. Proteins derive from plant and animal sources, and are vital for cell growth and repair. Of 20 possible amino acids, 10 are manufactured by the body and 10 are essential and must be provided in the diet. Animal proteins (eggs, milk, and meat) contain all essential amino acids and are complete. Plant sources do not contain all essential amino acids and are incomplete. Different incomplete foods eaten in the same meal are complementary (e.g., beans and rice) and provide complete nutrition.

CALORIE CONSUMPTION AND CALORIE EXPENDITURE

Consumed calories provide energy. Carbohydrates supply 4 Calories (cal) per gram consumed, fats 9 cal/g, and proteins 4 cal/g. A person's rate of metabolism is the relationship between bodily changes and energy expenditure. Everyone has a resting or basal metabolic rate (BMR). BMR is higher in children, thin people, and expectant women. The primary energy source is carbohydrates, while fats are also utilized when sugars are inaccessible. Conversely, if calories are not used, they are converted to fat and stored. Both carbohydrates and fatty acids comprising fats are made of the elements carbon, oxygen and hydrogen, in different configurations.

MAJOR DIETARY MINERALS

Minerals are elements that cannot be broken down chemically. Seven major elements and a few trace elements are required to sustain life. Minerals with negatively or positively charged ions are electrolytes.

- Two major minerals, **calcium and phosphorus**, are important for development of bones and teeth and are necessary to prevent osteoporosis. Calcium is involved in muscle contraction, conduction of nerve impulses and blood clotting. Phosphorus is involved in energy transfer and pH balance. Milk and cheese are good sources of calcium and phosphorous.
- **Sodium and potassium** are complementary major minerals that maintain fluid balance in the blood. Sodium, found in table salt and processed foods, causes high blood pressure in excess. Table salt also contains the mineral chlorine, which helps pH balance.
- **Sulfur** is important because it is a necessary component of protein and plays a role in metabolism of energy.
- **Magnesium**, found mostly in green vegetables and whole grains, also affects energy metabolism.

DIETARY TRACE MINERALS

Some minerals are found in the body in small or trace amounts. Fluorine, which is necessary for strong teeth and to avert osteoporosis, is considered a trace element. Numerous trace minerals facilitate metabolic processes, including iodine, copper, chromium, selenium, manganese, and molybdenum. Iodine is unique in that is concentrated in the thyroid gland. The trace mineral iron is a carrier of oxygen in blood; a deficit of iron can cause anemia. Cobalt is also necessary for red blood cell maintenance. Zinc is required by the immune system and promotes tissue growth.

CARIOGENIC FOODS

Carbohydrates contain the chemical elements carbon, hydrogen and oxygen, and are comprised of sugars, starches and fibers. Carbohydrates from natural sources include fruits, grains, and legumes. Most naturally-occurring carbohydrates are not broken down to simple sugars until they arrive at the stomach. Cariogenic foods are converted to simple sugars right in the mouth, where bacteria change them into acids. The acid demineralizes the enamel, predisposing the teeth to caries (decay). Manufactured sweets, such as candies and soft drinks, and naturally-occurring raisins and sticky fruits are cariogenic. The dental assistant should evaluate the patient's diet for use of cariogenic foods. Explain the possible consequences to the patient. The acid from cariogenic foods can be somewhat neutralized if they are eaten with foods that stimulate saliva production. Conversely, eating cariogenic foods late at night, when saliva production is low, enhances potential decay. New teeth in infants are susceptible to nursing bottle syndrome, which is rampant decay due to liquid sweets, such as fruit juice.

WATER-SOLUBLE VITAMINS

Vitamins C complex and B complex are water-soluble. Vitamin C (ascorbic acid) is found in all citrus fruits and vegetables, like tomatoes and broccoli. Vitamin C is a necessary component of collagen, needed in connective tissue. It prevents scurvy, aids in wound healing, and helps tooth development. Vitamin B complex includes:

- **Thiamine (B$_1$),** essential as a coenzyme in the oxidation of glucose and to avert the degenerative nerve disease beriberi.
- **Riboflavin (B$_2$),** which aids growth, energy release from food and protein production.

53

- **Niacin (B₃)** or nicotinic acid, needed for ATP synthesis and maintains the gastrointestinal and nervous systems.
- **Pyridoxine (B₆),** which plays a role in antibody, nonessential amino acids, and niacin production.
- **Biotin (B₇)** and **pantothenic acid (B₅),** which help with energy metabolism.
- **Folate (B₉),** which is involved in RBC production.
- **Cobalamin (B₁₂),** which synthesizes red blood cells (RBCs) and maintains myelin sheaths.

FAT-SOLUBLE VITAMINS

Nutrients that carry out essential functions but are not energy sources are vitamins. Four vitamins are fat-soluble and retained in the liver and other fatty tissues, Vitamins A, D, E and K. Vitamin A is available as carotene in dark leafy vegetables and orange or yellow fruits, and from dairy products and liver. It is essential for maintenance of mucous membranes, bones, skin (epithelial tissue), and vision. Vitamin D or cholecalciferol is necessary for good bone and tooth growth. It is available in animal sources, such as eggs, liver, and fortified milk. It can also be produced in the body after ultraviolet ray or sun exposure. Vitamin E or alpha tocopherol is obtained via plant sources, such as avocadoes, wheat germ, almonds, and fortified margarine. It is an antioxidant that prevents other nutrients from breaking down. Vitamin K is found in green leafy vegetables and animal products, like milk, liver, and egg yolks. Its primary function is to stimulate the formation of prothrombin, which is involved in blood clotting and coagulation.

CONSEQUENCES OF DEFICIENT OR EXCESSIVE VITAMIN INTAKE

All vitamins in proper amounts have beneficial effects. Vitamin A deficiency causes night blindness and inadequate bone growth. Vitamin D deficiency causes rickets, osteomalacia, and inadequately developed teeth. Vitamin B₂ or B₆ deficiencies cause mouth fissures and inflammation of the tongue. Vitamin C deficiency causes scurvy with tooth loss and muscle cramps. Vitamin E deficiency causes RBC destruction. Vitamin B₁₂ deficiency causes pernicious anemia.

Conversely, fat soluble vitamins, C, B₃ and B₆ are toxic if consumed in excess. Too much Vitamin A causes stunted growth and termination of menstruation. Vitamin C or D toxicity results in kidney stones. Vitamin E toxicity causes hypertension. Vitamin K toxicity causes hemolytic anemia or jaundice. Excess niacin causes rash and liver damage. Excess B₆ damages nerves. High amounts of other water-soluble vitamins are not toxic because they are excreted in the urine every four hours.

DENTAL CONDITIONS CAUSED BY AN IMPROPER DIET

The most common oral conditions caused by improper diet are angular cheilitis and glossitis.

- **Angular cheilitis** is due to a shortage of Vitamin B complex. It presents as a lesion of both the mucous membranes and skin near the corner of the mouth, thus changing the vertical dimension of the face. Saliva accumulates at the corners and microorganisms proliferate there, particularly opportunistic infections like Candida albicans. The deficiency must be corrected and antifungal drugs are prescribed. Angular cheilitis can also develop if the person often licks the corners of his or her mouth, or a reduction in the vertical dimension of his or her face. This reduction is commonly seen in the elderly population (due to tooth loss or alveolar ridge recession) and results in drooping at the corners of the mouth.
- Vitamin B complex deficiency is probably also the cause of **glossitis** or bald tongue, in which the tongue is inflamed and filiform papillae are lacking.

SYSTEMIC DISEASES

IMPACT ON HEALING

Any systemic disease that increases overall inflammation within the body and decreases tissue perfusion can have an adverse effect on oral health. For example, diabetic patients are much more likely to experience gum and periodontal disease due to circulatory impairment. Decreased tissue perfusion due to vascular changes associated with diabetes can increase the risk of developing oral disease. Heart disease also affects vascular

flow, which can interfere with adequate perfusion through the gums. The increase in inflammatory markers due to chronic heart disease also increases the risk of inflammation within the oral cavity, which can increase the risk for periodontal disease and impaired healing.

Patients with chronic disease and associated inflammation will also have impaired healing. Decreased tissue perfusion and decreased blood flow interferes with the body's ability to fight infection by limiting the number of immune cells present in the area. Often, an oral antibiotic will be prescribed to the patient to take before undergoing any dental procedures to decrease the risk of oral infection.

ORAL MANIFESTATIONS OF SYSTEMIC DISEASE

Oral health does not exist in isolation, and often can serve as an indicator of the patient's overall well-being. Many systemic diseases present with oral manifestations that the GCA must be familiar with:

- **Dehydration**: Prolonged dehydration results in decreased saliva production, dry mucus membranes, and dry tongue. Over time, these deficiencies can lead to an increase in dental caries. Any signs of dehydration that manifest orally should be investigated, as they may indicate chronic dehydration, which can be representative of a more serious underlying condition.
- **Anemia**: Iron-deficiency anemia manifests with pale gums and a smooth tongue (atrophic glossitis). The patient may also complain of a burning sensation of the tongue, gums and lips, a condition called angular cheilitis.
- **Systemic lupus erythematosus**: An autoimmune disease, SLE presents with oral manifestations in as high as 45% of its patients. These oral manifestations are most commonly oral lesions in the form of ulcers, erythematous, or hyperkeratosis.
- **Thrombocytopenia**: When thrombocytopenia is secondary to hematologic malignancy, it may first manifest in the oral cavity. Manifestations include petechiae or, when serious, hematomas or hemorrhagic bullae lesions. Minor trauma, such as probing the gum line, can also cause excessive bleeding in these patients.

IMPACT OF EATING DISORDERS

Anorexia nervosa is an eating disorder characterized by unrealistic fears of consuming food and weight loss of at least 15%. **Bulimia** is an eating disorder distinguished by uncontrollable binge eating followed by self-induced vomiting. Eating disorder patients can die from electrolyte imbalance and heart attack. The appearance of the oral cavity changes due to vomiting accompanying bulimia. The lingual surfaces of the front teeth lose calcium, enamel wears away, and the occlusal faces of back teeth also erode. If the patient had restorative work, the fillings fail. Eating disordered patients tend to have many caries and enlarged parotid glands. Good oral hygiene is imperative, particularly after vomiting. Recommend toothpaste for sensitive teeth to eating disordered patients.

FLUORIDE

Fluoride is a mineral derivative of the element fluorine. Fluoride is primarily absorbed via the gastrointestinal tract, and is found in low amounts in normal bone and dental enamel. Fluoride incorporated into tooth enamel forms fluorapatite crystals. Optimal fluoride exposure should be between 0.7 and 1.2 ppm, giving the teeth a gleaming, white, unblemished appearance. Average fluoride levels are lower in teeth with caries. If high amounts of fluoride are ingested during tooth development, the child's teeth acquire a mottled appearance, known as fluorosis. Excessive fluoride causes either chronic or acute fluoride poisoning. Chronic fluoride poisoning occurs from habitual ingestion, usually through a fluoridated water supply. Teeth mottle with a fluoride content up to 1.8 ppm. Enamel hypocalcifies at 1.8-2.0 ppm of fluoride, so teeth are chalky, with discolored bands, flecks, cracks, and pits.

BENEFITS

Fluoride can reduce dental caries because it binds to the bacteria in plaque, thus retarding acid production and decay. Fluoride can remineralize soft areas and reverse very early tooth decay. Dentists and hygienists administer gel or foam fluoride in trays to reinforce children's teeth once or twice yearly. Topical fluoride only accesses the outer enamel layer.

Systemic Sources of Fluoride	Topical Sources of Fluoride	
Fluoridation of the water supply with 0.7-1.2 parts sodium fluoride per million parts water.	2% Sodium fluoride	Professionally applied
Ingestion of meat, cereals, and citrus fruits.	8% Stannous fluoride	
Prescription tablets, drops, lozenges, or vitamin preparations given to children up until their second molars erupt.	1.23% Acidulated phosphate fluoride	
	Dentifrices (toothpastes)	Self-applied
	Polishing pastes	
	Mouth rinses	

ORAL HEALTHCARE HABITS
PREVENTIVE DENTISTRY

Good preventive dentistry is multifaceted. It involves daily brushing and flossing for removal of plaque and bacteria. Teach the patient correct techniques for brushing and flossing at the initial visit. It is advisable to use a disclosing agent at regular intervals to see how successful the removal has been. Children who are still developing dentition should undergo a fluoride program, including treatments at the office and in the home. A healthy patient should see the dentist every six months. Routine visits should include an examination, cleaning, and dental procedures, if indicated. In addition, good nutrition and adequate exercise have a positive impact on general health, including teeth and bones.

IMPACTS OF TRAITS OF INFANT AND CHILDREN ON ORAL HEALTHCARE HABITS

The oral health of **infants** is the responsibility of the parent or guardian. The adult removes the infant's plaque with an infant toothbrush or cloth while the child reclines. Instruct parents to bring the child to the dentist at **age 3**. Preschoolers respond to visual instruction but they also have a short attention span. Role-play to teach the child oral hygiene habits. Tell the parent to oversee or perform tooth brushing at bedtime. **Children ages 5-8** have a longer attention span and are eager for knowledge. They can be taught good oral hygiene techniques with visual aids, like short videos or pictures. **Children ages 9-12,** have an even longer attention span, greater curiosity, and the ability to brush and floss effectively on their own. They also have unique issues, such as peer group acceptance and dealing with mixed dentition, which the dental assistant should keep in mind when providing instruction.

IMPACT OF TRAITS OF TEENAGERS AND ADULTS ON ORAL HEALTHCARE HABITS

Peer pressure and concern about personal appearance motivate all teenagers.

- **Thirteen to fifteen-year-olds** have poor coordination (due to growth spurts) and bad eating habits. Thus, they often have trouble with flossing. The decay rate in this age group increases dramatically. The dental assistant should give individualized instructions and encouragement to motivate young teenagers.
- **Sixteen to nineteen-year-olds** question authority and have busy schedules. The assistant needs to act more as a friend. Explain the processes involved in plaque and caries formation.
- Approach **young and middle-aged adults** on an individualized basis.
- **Elder older than 60** have age-related concerns, such as tooth retention, disease-specific difficulties, maintaining oral hygiene with poor sight, or use of drugs that interfere with oral health. The professional needs to give advice based on each specific case.

PLAQUE CONTROL

Dental plaque is a tacky, bacteria-containing mass found on teeth that have not been brushed thoroughly. It looks like a soft, white, sticky accumulation. It is concentrated near the gingiva. The bacteria feed off consumed sugar and convert it to acid. The acid, in turn, damages the tooth enamel by causing demineralization. The content of the minerals calcium and phosphate is depressed. Demineralization on enamel surfaces looks chalky and white. Demineralization is often a problem found in patients who have had orthodontic appliances removed where the brackets were previously situated. Eventually, plaque that is not removed leads to tooth decay.

PLAQUE DISCLOSING AIDS

Plaque disclosing aids are used to identify areas on the surface of the teeth that contain plaque. It is usually a solution or a tablet that is given to the patient. After the disclosing aid is used, areas of the teeth will be stained a different color to identify the plaque. Plaque has the ability to absorb the stain readily, which causes it to become discolored when the disclosing aid is used.

Plaque disclosing aids are useful to assist the dental professional in locating the specific areas that will require more care during a dental cleaning. They plaque in these areas can then be removed through a thorough dental cleaning. Patients may be given the plaque disclosing solution or tablets to use at home in order to evaluate the thoroughness of brushing and identify the areas of the mouth that may require more attention. This can also be used to motivate patients and allow them to see the progress they are making when performing their own dental care at home.

ORAL HYGIENE AIDS

Oral hygiene aids include disclosing agents, dentifrice, toothbrushes, flosses, mouth rinses, chewing gum, and a variety of interdental aids. Dentifrice is another term for toothpaste, used by the patient with a toothbrush or floss. Dentifrice products earn the ADA Seal of Acceptance if they are deemed both safe and effective. Toothpastes contain abrasive materials, and often fluoride for decay prevention, or other ingredients (for example whiteners or calculus inhibitors). Mouth rinses are designed to be swirled in the mouth to dislodge debris or temporarily get rid of halitosis, as adjuncts to brushing and flossing. Some have ingredients (alcohol) that eradicate microorganisms. Special oral hygiene gums chewed after eating carbohydrates encourage saliva production and loosen debris. Interdental aids clean between the teeth and stimulate the gums. They include the interproximal brush, dental stimulators, floss holders and threaders, and irrigators.

INTERDENTAL AIDS

Interdental aids help clean between the teeth. Available forms include:

- **Interproximal brushes** consist of a handle (often bent) attached to a small, nylon-bristled brush. They reach into interproximal areas, open bifurcations and trifurcations, and under orthodontic brackets.
- **Dental stimulators** activate soft tissues in interproximal areas and get rid of plaque. Some toothbrushes have rubber tipped stimulator ends. Wooden dental stimulators made of balsam wedges have plastic handles with toothpick tips attached; moisten both before use.
- **Floss holders** are "Y" shaped to hold floss for easy access to interproximal areas. Shift the floss up and down on the sides of the tooth and into the sulcus.
- **Floss threaders** are rigid plastic, shaped into a large loop at one end, through which floss is threaded. Insert the straight end into one side of the space. Pull it out the other for removal, leaving the floss for elimination of plaque and debris.
- A **water irrigation device** uses pulses of water to remove debris. Irrigators are for cleaning orthodontic brackets and prostheses and are ineffective against plaque.

FLOSS

Dental flossing removes plaque and fragments from proximal tooth surfaces. Traditional dental floss comes as a thread that is either waxed or unwaxed. Waxed floss glides more easily and is less likely to tear or snag. Flosses can be flat tape, finely textured, colored, or flavored. Flossing requires 18 inches of floss. Secure the ends around the middle and ring fingers of each hand. Grasp a short section (about an inch) between the thumb and index finger of each hand. Draw the floss into each proximal space, using a gentle back-and-forth motion. In the maxilla, use both thumbs or a thumb and finger. For the mandible, use the two index fingers. The floss should be wrapped around the proximal surface and into the sulcus. Move the floss up and down along the surface for plaque removal. Transfer it to the proximal surface of the adjoining tooth, and repeat the action. Use a new section of floss for each space. Include the distal surface of the last molar.

TOOTHBRUSHES

All toothbrushes fall into two main categories:

- **Manual toothbrushes** have a head containing the bristles, an indented shank adjacent to the head, and a long handle. There may also be a rubber dental stimulator on the end. The head has a toe end at the exterior and a heel end at the interior. Bristle configurations differ on various brushes; they are usually spaced or multi-tufted. Manual toothbrushes with soft, nylon bristles are best because they are durable and will not wear away the teeth or gums.
- **Mechanical toothbrushes** are attached to a recharging unit or are battery operated. Their heads t can move in various directions: Reciprocating (back and forth), vibratory (quick back and forth), orbital (circular), arched (in a semi-circle), elliptical (oval rotation), or a combination of movements. Mechanical toothbrushes may also include sonic action.

TOOTHBRUSHING TECHNIQUES

BASS AND MODIFIED BASS TECHNIQUES

The main objective of tooth brushing is the thorough cleaning of every surface of all teeth. Manual brushing should take 2-3 minutes. Manual brushing techniques include the Bass, modified Bass, Charter, modified Stillman, rolling stroke, and modified scrub-brushing techniques. Dentists most often recommend the Bass or modified Bass techniques because they are effective at removing plaque near the gums.

- **Bass technique:** Hold the toothbrush bristles slanted at 45° to the teeth, toward the gingival sulcus. Sequentially brush small areas, each for a count of 10, with small back and forth movements. Apply the toe bristles to the lingual surfaces of the front teeth.
- **Modified Bass technique**: Essentially the same, except after each area has been cleaned, bring the bristles up over the crown toward the biting surface.

CHARTERS AND MODIFIED SCRUB BRUSHING TECHNIQUES

Charters and modified scrub brushing techniques are effective for plaque removal and gum stimulation.

- With the **Charters brushing technique**, the toothbrush head is pointed toward the end of the root. The brushes touch the gingiva, centered between adjacent teeth, and are aimed toward the teeth. Small areas are sequentially brushed for a count of 10 each, with small back and forth movements. Front teeth are brushed with the sides of the toe bristles and the brush parallel to the teeth.
- The **modified scrub brushing technique** uses back-and-forth movements centered initially between the gum and tooth. The brush is held perpendicular to the tooth surface. This is repeated until all teeth have been cleaned.

<u>MODIFIED STILLMAN AND ROLLING STROKE BRUSHING TECHNIQUES</u>

Modified Stillman and rolling stroke-brushing techniques are effective for plaque removal and gingival stimulation. In both, the initial position of the bristles is toward the apex of the tooth.

- The **modified Stillman method** also positions the handle level with the biting surface. The bristles are brushed downward simultaneously, with a back-and-forth action, to cover the complete surface of the tooth for a count of 10. The patient performs a minimum of 5 sequences before continuing to the next tooth and repeating the sequence.
- With the **rolling stroke brushing technique**, the toothbrush is held parallel to the tooth, with the bristles toward the apex. The bristles are rolled from the gums down toward the teeth, including the biting surface. Each tooth is brushed in this manner 5 times before moving to the next one. A similar motion is applied on the lingual surfaces of the front teeth, using either the toe or heel portion.

EVALUATING RESPONSE TO HOME CARE THERAPY

The GCA can evaluate the patient's response to home-care therapy through subjective and objective information.

- **Subjectively**, the patient can describe their symptoms. If they were having dental pain related to a specific problem before, it is hoped that their pain has decreased. It is important to ask the patient whether they have been having any difficulty with performing any interventions at home to help their problem. Identifying any obstacles the patient is having to complete home-care therapies can help to increase compliance and improve outcomes.
- **Objectively**, the oral exam can provide information on how a specific problem appears. If the home-care therapies are being performed appropriately, there should be improvement in the appearance of the problem. Referring back to oral photographs that were taken before treatment started can provide a "before and after" reference to visualize improvement. These can also be shared with the patient so they can see the improvement they have attained through the treatments they have performed at home.

SPECIAL DENTAL HEALTH NEEDS

There are many physical disabilities that must be accommodated in the dental office. Accommodations are discussed below:

- **Hearing impaired:** Assess the level of hearing impairment and the patient's preferred method of communication (hearing aid, writing notes, sign language, lip reading, etc.). For lip readers, be sure that the mouth is visible when speaking, and sit in a position that the patient can easily read lips. Lightly tap the patient to notify them that you are speaking. Use written explanations if there is any confusion. For sign language, utilize medical interpreter who is able to communicate all relevant information to the patient. Look at the patient when speaking, not the interpreter. Patients with hearing aids may choose to turn it off during treatment so be sure to allow them to make that decision.
- **Visually impaired:** Assess level of visual impairment. Slowly acquaint the patient to the dental office and dental treatment room. Utilize a Tell-Feel-Do technique to demonstrate and prepare patients for ongoing procedures. Avoid sudden movements or loud noises that may startle the patient.
- **Wheelchair bound:** The Americans with Disabilities Act (ADA) Standards for Accessible Design (2010) requires that dental offices offer a barrier-free environment for individuals that are wheelchair bound. Guidelines require reserved parking spots for patients in wheelchairs, sidewalks that are 3 feet wide, at least one entrance that is wide enough to accommodate wheelchair entrance and is on ground level or accessible by ramp, dental treatment rooms that can accommodate wheelchair entrance and storage in addition to the personnel and equipment required, and a dental chair that can be lowered to 19 inches above the ground for easy transfer to and from the chair.

- **Non-English speakers:** The most recommended accommodation when treating patients that are non-English speakers is the use of a professional interpreter. Dental offices with high levels of non-English speaking patients may have an onsite interpreter or access to interpreters by phone. Other alternatives in non-emergent situations include visual models and diagrams, videos, and brochures.

REMOVABLE APPLIANCES AND PROSTHESES

Removable dental appliances or prostheses come in the form of dentures, which can be partial or complete. Cleaning and caring for the appliance are the same regardless of whether it is partial or complete.

- After eating, rinse the dentures with water to remove any pieces of food.
- Be careful to avoid dropping the dentures because they can break. Placing a towel on the counter or in the sink when cleaning will help to protect them in case they are dropped.
- After removing dentures, a soft toothbrush should be used to gently clean the gums, oral mucosa, and tongue.
- Dentures should be brushed daily using a denture cleaner. If a denture adhesive is used, be sure to completely remove the adhesive when cleaning.
- In order to help dentures maintain their shape, they should be soaked in water overnight. A mild denture cleaning solution may be used, depending upon the manufacturer's recommendations.
- Rinse the dentures well before inserting them, especially if a denture cleaning soak is used overnight.

NON-REMOVABLE APPLIANCES AND PROSTHESES

Care of the two most common types of non-removable dental appliances, dental bridges and implants, is similar to caring for natural teeth:

- A **dental bridge** is a dental appliance that replaces missing teeth. It is anchored to existing teeth to fill in a gap where there are missing teeth. Every day, dental floss or a specialized small toothbrush should be used to clean under the artificial teeth. This will help to remove any food or debris that is stuck underneath the bridge. Regular brushing should be performed twice daily to clean all of the teeth.
- **Dental implants** can be cared for the same as natural teeth. In order to prevent plaque build-up, a soft toothbrush should be used at least twice daily to brush the teeth. This is especially important after meals. The implants should also be flossed, the same as natural teeth.
- **Regular dental checkups** are imperative to have non-removable appliances and prostheses examined for any cracks or chips. The fitting of these devices should also be assessed to ensure there is not crowding from the surrounding teeth.

PROSTHODONTICS

Prosthodontics are artificial parts (*prostheses*) created in the dental laboratory to replace missing teeth or tissues. They can be fixed or removable. Fixed prostheses are designed to integrate into the natural dentition and are maintained through regular brushing and flossing. The purposes they serve include restoration of chewing ability, prevention of teeth movement by providing underlying support, speech improvement, promotion of oral hygiene, and aesthetics. Crowns, inlays, outlays, bridges, and veneers are examples of fixed prosthodontics. The two categories of removable prosthodontics are partial dentures, which replace one or more teeth in an arch, and complete or full dentures, which take the place of all teeth in one arch. Partial dentures are held in place by underlying tissues and other teeth, while full dentures are supported by gingival and oral mucosal tissues, alveolar ridges and the hard palate.

MAINTENANCE

Fixed prostheses are maintained by brushing and flossing. Toothbrushes selected should be soft, multi-tufted, and small enough to access all areas. Bridges can be cleaned by using a bridge threader to insert dental floss underneath. Interproximal brushes and tips are also available. Dental implants, which are titanium devices or screws that fuse with bone tissue by bonding (osseointegration), should be brushed with a similar type of brush and a specialized type of floss that is wider and designed to be wrapped around the implant (such as

Proxi-Floss). Other maintenance measures include use of a plastic interproximal brush, water irrigators for plaque and debris removal, antimicrobial rinses, and a variety of plastic cleaning instruments. Removable prostheses or dentures are brushed with a special denture toothbrush and mild soap or toothpaste. Tissue under the denture should also be brushed. Dentures are removed and placed in cleaning agents to get rid of stains. Orthodontic devices should be maintained with specially designed toothbrushes, water irrigation, and an interproximal brush.

PRE- AND POST-TREATMENT INSTRUCTIONS

Patients should be provided with clear pre- and post-treatment instructions including the following details:

- **Pre-treatment instructions**: For surgery, advise the patient to remove contact lenses and wear loose clothing that allows for monitoring blood pressure and to avoid taking aspirin for a week prior to surgery, other NSAIDS for 2-3 days, and alcohol for 12 hours before surgery. If the patient is to be sedated, the patient must have an adult to drive them to and from the appointment.
- **Post-treatment instructions**: For cosmetic restoration, advise the patient to expect some difficulty speaking and increased saliva for a few days. With crowns, advise the patient to return to the office if the crown loosens or comes off. Following extractions, advise the patient to keep pressure (gauze plug) on the site for 30-40 minutes or longer if bleeding persists and to notify dentist for prolonged or severe bleeding. Once a clot forms, the patient should avoid drinking from straws, smoking, and rinsing forcefully or brushing teeth around the extraction site for 72 hours. After fillings, advise the patient to avoid eating or drinking hot liquids until numbness subsides.

RESTORATIVE MATERIALS/PROCEDURES

Restorative materials and procedures in dentistry are performed to correct structural problems with the teeth. This can include composite fillings, crowns, bridges, dentures, and implants.

The main advantage of restorative procedures is to maintain the structure of the tooth, or teeth, to prevent impairments of eating or speech. This can also help to maintain gum health and prevent gum disease. Repair or replacement of a tooth may also help to decrease pain, which can improve the quality of life.

A disadvantage of restorative materials or procedures is the risk of malfunction or damage to the device. Crowns can come off and require the creation of a new crown. Dentures can break or become ill fitting, which may require repair or refitting of them. Implants are also subject to falling out and would need to be replaced. This requires a dental procedure with associated pain and expense. Even simple fillings can become loose and fall out, which would require they be replaced.

Administration

LEGAL RECORD MAINTENANCE
ESSENTIAL COMPONENTS OF A PATIENT RECORD

A patient record is a legal document containing pertinent information related to the individual and his or her care. Patient records should be retained for at least seven years from the last visit and kept confidential. On the left, attach the registration form for demographics such as: patient name, address, phone numbers, employer, spousal or parental information, payer, insurance (photocopy the insurance card), and chief complaint. On the right side, attach a Medical History, including: Prescription, over-the-counter, and street drugs; exposure to radiation and toxins; medical conditions (e.g., diabetes, epilepsy, pregnancy, bleeding disorders, or rheumatic fever); allergies marked with brightly-colored alert stickers; and height and weight to calculate anesthetic dose. The dentist authorizes the Dental History form. The patient or guardian signs and dates Consent to Treatment and Release of Information forms, for legal coverage and continuity of care. Keep the patient record in reverse chronological order, with the most recent treatment record on top and the oldest at the bottom.

LEGAL COMPONENTS OF A PATIENT RECORD

A patient's dental record must be correct and current because it is a subpoenable court document that may be reviewed by a judge, prosecutor, defense lawyers, and privacy commissioner. The dentist may be required to appear in court to explain their documentation. Document all care and payments legibly in ink. If a mistake is made, never use correction fluid or an eraser to fix it. Strike through the original entry with one line. Write the correct information above it. Initial and date the change. Keep records for at least seven years from the last service date. Most dentists keep them indefinitely because of variations in the statute of limitations, the time period for local legal action. Place a signed informed consent in the chart for any surgical procedures. The dentist must explain the procedure, risks, expected results, alternatives, and perils associated with denying treatment before asking the patient to sign the informed consent form. Implied consent is an implicit contract between dentist and patient whenever the latter allows work to be performed.

FORMS INCLUDED IN THE PATIENT RECORD

If the patient has any conditions that require the dentist to consult with the physician, then ask the patient to sign a **Release of Information form.** Before subsequent visits, ask the patient's doctor to complete a **Medical History update form**. Include laboratory reports for communicable diseases. The diseases of concern are hepatitis and human immunodeficiency virus (HIV/AIDS). Give the patient (or his or her guardian) a written description of the right to privacy under the Health Insurance Portability and Accountability Act (HIPAA). Keep these signed forms for at least 7 years from the last visit. Document the examination, dental charting, and oral radiography. The dentist reports suspicious lesions or other medical conditions (e.g., suspected heart disease) back to the physician.

DENTAL RECORD MANAGEMENT

Keep dental records in color-coded file-folders. File cabinets must be locked when unattended to comply with privacy laws. The most popular type of file cabinet used in dental offices is the open-shelf lateral file cabinet, in which files can be pulled out. Vertical file cabinets are often used. Files must be sorted alphabetically, starting with the last name, proceeding to the first name, and lastly the middle name. Patient information sent via computer or fax machine must be protected from hackers. Keep records indefinitely. Microfilm records older than seven years. Keep a tickler file containing index cards with tasks that should be completed by a certain time. Alternatively, set a computer reminder to perform the tasks.

STORING PATIENT RECORDS

Patient records should be stored based on the type of record contained and the manner in which it was recorded:

- **Images:** If electronic records are utilized, the x-ray system is usually synced with the records to allow images to be downloaded into the patient chart. If hard copies of x-ray films are being stored, they should be kept in a climate-controlled area that will minimize damage to the films. Digital photographs should be downloaded into the patient's electronic health record if this is available.
- **Histories:** The dental and medical history should be gathered from the patient at their initial appointment and at least annually after that. Generally, at every visit, the patient should be asked if there has been any change to their medical history or medications. This information should be documented in the patient's chart.
- **Correspondence:** Correspondence from specialists that may be utilized for referrals should be kept in its own section of the chart so it can be found easily. Any correspondence to the patient regarding their care should also be included in the patient chart. Documentation pertaining to billing or account delinquency should not be kept in the medical chart.

MANAGING SECURITY RECORDS FOR CONTROLLED SUBSTANCES

Rules and regulations for the proper documentation and storage of controlled substances in the office are established by the Drug Enforcement Administration (DEA). These include:

- Maintain records for the purchase and wasting of all controlled substances. These need to be kept for 2-5 years depending upon state requirements.
- Controlled substances should be stored in a locked metal cabinet or safe within a locked room or closet, and bolted or cemented to the wall/floor so it cannot be removed. Access to the locked site should be limited to only a couple of personnel.
- Federal law requires a full drug inventory every 2 years, though it is advisable to keep a log book that records intake and output of any controlled substances in the office.
- Documentation should be thorough in the patient's chart pertaining to the administration of any controlled substances. Any documentation in the chart should be able to be verified through documentation in a written drug inventory log that lists the patient's name, patient identifier, drug name, and quantity given.
- When wasting a controlled substance, DEA form 41 must be completed before the drug is destroyed. Preferably, a reverse-distributor should be used.

SHARING MEDICAL RECORDS

Sharing of medical records: Under HIPAA regulations regarding privacy and security, a patient's records cannot be shared with other dental offices or healthcare providers without the permission of the patient, who must sign a release form indicating which records are to be shared and with whom. The patient should be advised of the method of sharing (paper, electronic) and the reason for sharing.

REFERRAL FOR ORAL SURGERY

There are several reasons why a dentist would refer a patient to an oral surgeon:

- Impacted teeth that require cutting into the gum tissue or the bony tissue of the jaws.
- Insertion of the post that is rooted into the jawbone for dental implants (the dentist will affix the artificial tooth onto the post after it is healed).
- Decreased bone mass in the jaws or the need for strengthening of the jaw.
- Decreased bone mass in the upper jaw can be corrected by an oral surgeon in order to prevent sinus complications from dental implants.
- Jaw disorders resulting from infection, trauma, or TMJ disorders.
- Repair of broken or lost teeth due to trauma, along with treating associated trauma to the gums.

When referring a patient to an oral surgeon, the patient's face sheet, insurance information, and progress notes from their dental office visit should be forwarded to their office. Any x-ray images or dental photographs should also be included. The dentist may want to include additional correspondence explaining the purpose for the referral or any concerns they may have.

PROFESSIONAL REGULATIONS
AMERICAN DENTAL ASSOCIATION'S CODE OF PROFESSIONAL CONDUCT

There are 17 pledges that members of the American Dental Assistants Association (ADAA) subscribe to in their **Code of Professional Conduct**. The pledges are primarily related to ethics. Many of these relate to the relationship between the dental assistant and the ADAA, such as the dental assistant will:

- Abide by the bylaws and regulations.
- Maintain loyalty to the ADAA.
- Follow ADAA objectives.
- Respect members and employees, serve, and act cooperatively with them.

- Refrain from spreading malicious information regarding the ADAA.
- Utilize sound business principles related to the organization.
- Serve the ADAA and instill public confidence in it.
- Uphold high personal standards of conduct.
- Hold separate personal opinions from those endorsed by the ADAA.
- Refrain from acceptance of compensation from other members.
- Try to influence relevant legislation in a legal and ethical way.

ETHICS IN DENTISTRY

Ethics are moral principles or values indicative of the times. The American Dental Association's Principles of Ethics outlines the values that dental care providers must adopt to stay in practice. The main ethical concerns relate to advertising, professional fees and other charges, and the responsibilities and entitlements of the dentist relative to the patient. Dental advertising is presently considered ethical, providing it is truthful. Up until the 1980s, advertising was considered crass. Ethical behavior related to professional fees and charges means the firm's billing must conform to what other local dentists charge, the charges must be correct, and insurance dealings and missed appointments can be charged. Current ethics dictate that the dentist cannot refuse to see a patient based on discrimination against race, religion, or HIV status. HIV-infected dentists must limit their work to procedures and techniques that will not infect others. It is unethical for the dentist to be swayed by financial gains.

DENTAL PRACTICE ACT

Every state has a Dental Practice Act, which outlines the legal constraints and controls, which the dental team members must follow. Each state has a board that administers the Dental Practice Act, usually the State Board of Dental Examiners or the Dental Quality Assurance Board. The state board issues a dentist, a hygienist, and usually a dental assistant, a license to practice in that state only if they meet certain minimum qualifications. These requirements include educational qualifications, moral requirements, and successful completion of a written examination. A license to practice can be used in another state if the two states have a reciprocity agreement. The board defines reasons for suspension or revocation of a license. The Dental Practice Act and the corresponding board define which expanded functions a dentist can delegate to a dental assistant. Most often, the doctrine of respondeat superior is invoked, making the dentist ultimately responsible, but leaving the employee accountable, too.

LEGAL REGULATIONS
AMERICANS WITH DISABILITIES ACT

In 1990, the federal Americans with Disabilities Act (ADA) was passed by Congress. It mandates that people with disabilities cannot be discriminated against in terms of employment and access to public services, accommodations, and goods. ADA provided more sophisticated telecommunication services to facilitate the hearing and speech impaired. ADA requires dental offices to have ramps, entryways, and treatment rooms that provide access and accommodate the needs of the disabled. The office must have at least one accessible room where patients in wheelchairs can be positioned for dental procedures. Technically, ADA applies to facilities with more than 15 employees, but all dental offices should strive to comply with ADA.

OSHA STANDARDS

There are currently no specific OSHA standards for dentistry, however, there are several OSHA standards for general industry that can apply to dental practice. These include:

- **Blood borne pathogens:** Prevention of exposure to blood and body fluids.
- **Hazard communication**: On container labels and safety data sheets.
- **Personal protective equipment**: Including gloves, gowns, masks, or face shields.
- **Medical services and first aid**: Available to employees in case of injury.
- **Ionizing radiation**: Protection against exposure to radiation at work.

- Maintenance, safeguards, and operational features for exit routes.
- Sanitation.
- **Occupational exposure to hazardous chemicals in laboratories:** Establishes a Chemical Hygiene Plan that educates employees in protecting themselves from hazardous chemicals in the lab.
- **Formaldehyde:** Educates employees on the potential hazards when working with formaldehyde, protective measures that can be taken to decrease the risk of exposure, and steps that should be taken in case of a formaldehyde exposure.
- **Forms/documentation:** Businesses that employ more than 10 employees must report any serious work-related injuries to OSHA.

CDC Guidelines for Infection Control in Dentistry

The CDC guidelines for standard precautions should be used to comply with infection control and prevention requirements.

- **Hand hygiene:** Wash hands with soap and water if they are visibly soiled. Otherwise, an alcohol-based hand rub may be used. Hands should be cleaned after touching instruments that may be contaminated, before and after treating each patient, and before and after wearing gloves.
- **Personal protective equipment (PPE):** Wear gloves when there is risk for contact with blood or other body fluids, mucous membrane, skin that is not intact, or contaminated equipment. Wear protective clothing when there is risk of clothing being soiled by blood or other body fluids. Wear a mask, face shield, and eye protection when there is risk for splashing of blood or other body fluids. PPE should be removed before leaving the work area.
- **Sharps safety:** Never recap needles using both hands. Use a one-handed scoop technique or syringes with retractable needles. All sharp objects should be disposed of in a sharps container that is labeled as a biohazard risk.
- **Sterilization/disinfection of instruments:** Always follow manufacturer guidelines to properly disinfect and sterilize reusable dental instruments.

HIPAA

HIPAA is the federal **Health Insurance Portability and Accountability Act of 1996**. Congress ratified HIPAA to safeguard electronic healthcare communications, including claims, funds transfers, eligibility and claims status inquiries and replies. HIPAA directed the Department of Health and Human Services (HHS) to implement national standards for clerical and financial electronic transmissions related to healthcare. Dentists and all other healthcare providers and health plans must comply with HIPAA's privacy standards by protecting health information and the patient's rights. To find out the latest guidelines for dental offices, parameters related to use and disclosure, enforcement and preemption, visit www.hipaa.org.

Protected Health Information

Protected health information (PHI) is any patient identifier, such as name, Social Security number, birth date, or address. Cover all records in the reception area, so they cannot be seen by patients and visitors. Lock up unattended records. Play quiet background music to blur phone conversations, and be discrete. Place computer screens and fax machines out of patient viewing areas. Disguise names with bar codes, so the individual cannot be identified, before open transmission. Each dental office appoints a **privacy officer (PO)** who is responsible for informing patients about their privacy rights. HIPAA grants patients the right to access and copy their own dental information. Each dental office must have a written PHI policy, including requirements for use and disclosure of patient information and procedures for handling grievances. Information released to third parties must be preauthorized by the patient and kept to a minimum. Violations of PHI under HIPAA are punishable by up to $250,000 in fines and 10 years imprisonment.

MINIMUM REQUIREMENTS FOR THE DENTAL STAFF MANUAL

The staff manual must include HIPAA's minimum requirements:

- Table of contents.
- Identify the privacy officer (PO) in charge of informing patients about their privacy rights.
- Job descriptions of all personnel, to establish who has access to patient's information.
- Privacy policy statement.
- HIPAA training plan with training schedule.
- Copies of HIPAA forms regarding compliance, documentation, and the scheme for reporting violations.
- Confidentiality agreements between the dentist and patient.
- Agreements between the office and business associates, such as dental laboratories, computer services, records shredder, temporary employment agencies, and trash removal company.
- Contingencies for change.

COMPUTERIZATION OF THE DENTAL BUSINESS

Most dental business office systems are at least partially computerized. Networked personal computers (PCs) are connected to a secure server that complies with HIPAA. The computer programs most used are for word processing, x-ray imaging, spreadsheets, accounting, and database management. ABLEdent, Dentrix, and DentiMax are examples of common dental office software. Database management is particularly important in a dental office because these programs store vital patient contact and insurance information and track and analyze data. The practice needs an Internet Service Provider (ISP), antivirus software, a firewall, and an e-mail account regularly monitored by the receptionist.

SAFETY ISSUES RELATED TO COMPUTER USE

Dental office computers must comply with HIPAA regulations. Safeguard against computer viruses and hackers with regular antivirus and firewall updates. There must be an audit trail or another way to ensure only authorized personnel access patient records. Back up data daily to disc or external hard drive. Off-site storage is safest, in case of fire or flood. Computer operators must practice good ergonomics to avoid repetitive strain injuries, like carpal tunnel. Position the monitor with the top just below eye level and at a slightly backward incline. Position the keyboard at a height that allows for relaxed shoulders and flat wrists. Sit in a chair with lumbar supports, armrests low enough that they are not used during keyboarding, and a shallow seat to permit leaning backwards. Sit with thighs at or just above the knees, feet firmly planted on the floor, and head directly over your shoulders. Protect from eyestrain with an anti-glare screen and by looking away from the computer for 10 minutes every hour.

FDA LAWS RELEVANT TO DENTISTRY

The Food and Drug Administration (FDA) controls drugs. Drug laws relevant to dental practice are the 1906 Pure Food and Drug Act, the 1938 Federal Food, Drug, and Cosmetic Act, and especially the Comprehensive Drug Abuse Prevention and Control Act of 1970, which divides drugs into five schedules, based on their potential for abuse:

- **Schedule I drugs**: Great potential for abuse and no established medical benefit, such as heroin.
- **Schedule II drugs**: Great possibility of abuse and dependence but with some known medical benefit, e.g., narcotics, opiates, some barbiturates, and amphetamines.
- **Schedule III drugs**: Less potential for abuse and established medical utility; includes other barbiturates, stimulants, strong depressants, and combinations, including many drugs used in dental practice.
- **Schedule IV drugs**: Some potential for abuse, with established medical utility, and little possibility of addiction; includes sedatives, anti-anxiety drugs, and certain depressants.
- **Schedule V drugs**: Slight potential for abuse; dispensed over-the-counter.

LEGAL CONCEPTS

Legal concepts that the dental assistant should be familiar with include the following:

- **Jurisprudence** is the legal system set up and enforced at various governmental levels. Laws that pertain to dentistry are referred to as dental jurisprudence. There are both civil and criminal laws. Civil laws are more often invoked in the dental setting, as they pertain to either contracts or torts.
- A **contract** is an enforceable covenant between two or more competent individuals. An agreement between a dentist and his or her patient is a contract. It can be an expressed contract, with written or verbal terms, or it can be an implied contract, where actions create the contract.
- **Tort law** governs the other branch of civil law. Torts relate to standards of care and wrongful actions that cause injury to a patient. Criminal laws speak to crimes that endanger society in general. There are occasions when criminal law may apply to dentistry, usually resulting in fines, incarceration, and discipline by the state dentistry board.

STANDARD OF CARE

Standard of care is covered by tort laws. Dental specialists are expected to provide due care, the accepted reasonable and judicious care. Malpractice is professional misconduct, resulting in failure to provide due care. Most malpractice lawsuits are related to professional negligence, the failure to perform what is considered standard care. Tort laws pertain to unethical or immoral behavior by the professional, resulting in harm to the patient. Examples are defamation of character, invasion of privacy, fraud, and assault and battery. Defamation of character harms an individual's character, name, or reputation through untrue and malicious statements, either written (libel) or spoken (slander). Invasion of privacy is unsolicited or unauthorized exposure of patient information. Fraud is intentional dishonesty for unfair or illegal gain. Assault is declaring one's intent to touch a patient inappropriately. Battery is the actual act of inappropriate touching. People who provide unpaid assistance to the injured in emergency situations are protected from assault and battery charges under the Good Samaritan Law.

CONTRACT LAW

There is an expressed or an implied contract between the dentist and patient. The dental assistant or other personnel are the dentist's agents. The dentist is ultimately responsible for breach of contract under the doctrine of respondeat superior. Nevertheless, the assistant's words or actions regarding care are legally binding upon the dentist. Breach of contract is failure to fulfill and complete the terms of the contract. There are **four situations where a contract can be legally abandoned**:

- The patient releases the dentist by failure to return for treatment. Ideally, the patient sends the dentist a certified letter of discharge, but this is not required.
- The patient/guardian does not comply with specific instructions from the dentist regarding care.
- The patient no longer requires treatment.
- The dentist formally withdraws from the case by sending a certified letter to the patient explaining the situation, to preclude any charges of patient abandonment.

THREATS OF MALPRACTICE

Legal issues related to dentistry include threats of malpractice. If a patient threatens malpractice, it's important to avoid arguing or making excuses. In order to prove malpractice, the patient must be able to show that he or she suffered an injury of some type as the result of dental care. The certified dental assistant should listen patiently and should carefully document any specific complaints that the patient makes, using quotations and including the date and time and any witnesses. If the patient is angry, sometimes simply being allowed to vent may solve the problem, but if the patient is in a public area, the certified dental assistant should suggest a more private area and should advise the patient to discuss the matter with the dentist. Because malpractice is a legal issue that is generally handled by attorneys, the practice may have an established protocol for dealing with complaints, and that protocol should be followed exactly.

PATIENT'S RIGHTS

RIGHT OF REFUSAL

There are times when a patient will refuse to consent to recommended dental care. This may be routine procedures or complex surgical procedures. Even if a treatment is highly recommended or could prevent the patient from suffering serious consequences, the patient may still choose to refuse treatment.

For the patient to make an informed decision regarding their dental treatment, the treatment should be clearly communicated. The steps of the procedure should be explained, along with expected outcomes and the probability of a positive outcome. The risks of the procedure should be clearly explained, as well as the risks of potential complications if the patient does not want to have a procedure performed.

If a patient refuses treatment, it is important to clarify the reasons for making this decision. The decision may be financial and the office may be able to offer a reduced cost or payments may be set up to help with affordability. More education can be given if the patient is scared of the procedure and is worried about pain or other side effects from the procedure. Nonetheless, the patient has the right to refuse recommended care and the dental assistant should not carry out treatment without patient approval.

RIGHTS IN THE DENTIST-PATIENT RELATIONSHIP

According to the **ADA's Dental Patient Rights and Responsibilities Statement**, patients should be given the following rights in the dental office:

- The right to choose their dentist and appointment time.
- The right to be informed of the dentist's training and education.
- The right to arrange to see their preferred dentist for each treatment (per state policy).
- The right to be granted the time to ask questions and get answers regarding dental treatment and conditions.
- The right to be informed of the dentist's opinion in terms of optimal treatment, and to be informed of alternative options.
- The right to informed consent, with a detailed explanation of the purpose, likely results, alternatives, and possible risks involved with dental procedures.
- The right to be informed of continuing health care needs.
- The right to know the cost of treatment prior to the procedure.
- The right to refuse treatment.
- The right to make reasonable arrangements for emergent dental care.
- The right to receive respectful and confidential treatment by the dental team.
- The right to expect proper infection control measures to be utilized by the dental team.
- The right to inquire about processes for mediating disputes about treatment.

INVENTORY MANAGEMENT

BACKORDERS AND ROTATION

The aim of supply and inventory control is to have adequate supplies on hand but to avoid oversupplies with a goal of 8-12 inventory turns per year with shelf lives no longer than 3 months for expendable (consumable) supplies. For that reason, expiration dates must be considered when managing inventory because outdated supplies, including medications, must be disposed of. New supplies should be placed behind those already stocked so that the supplies are rotated according to expiration date. Backorders can pose a problem if orders are placed at the last minute, resulting in the need to order from different suppliers or to substitute other supplies. A record of backorders should be maintained to determine if there are patterns in the types of backorders and the timing of backorders. Critical supplies should be maintained at a higher inventory level than those used less frequently. All shipments received should be checked for completeness and inspected for damage. The projected life expectancy of nonexpendable supplies (equipment) should be factored into purchases.

REORDERING SUPPLIES

Two common methods of reordering supplies are the red flag reorder tag system and the electronic bar code system. In the red flag reorder tag system, a tag is affixed to an item in inventory at the previously identified reorder point. At minimum, the name of the supply is on the tag. When the product reaches the reorder point, the tag is removed and put in a specified area for reordering. Every type of supply has an index card with information needed for ordering. The tag is attached to the upper-right corner when the item should be ordered, the left-hand corner after ordering, and removed upon receipt. New inventory is placed in the back of the pile and the red tag reaffixed at the new reorder point. With an electronic bar code system, supplies that must be reordered are identified by a specific bar code that is kept in a book. The assistant sweeps a bar code wand over the appropriate code, inputs the number of items needed, and the order is sent directly to the supplier via computer.

EXPENDABLE VS. NON-EXPENDABLE SUPPLIES

The dental assistant usually orders supplies because he or she has clinical knowledge and surveys the stock daily. Supplies are either expendable (disposable and quickly consumed) or non-expendable (enduring and purchased rarely). The assistant must consider:

- Shelf life (expiration date) and rate of use.
- Storage space and special requirements (e.g., ice, dark, dry, fume hood).
- Single item price, unit price for grouped items, bulk price (cut-rate price for ordering a minimum number of units), and price break (the smallest number of units needed to obtain a bulk price).
- Lead time between ordering and delivery, which determines the reorder point at which a supply needs to be bought in order to ensure continued availability.

RECEIPT AND STORAGE OF SUPPLIES

Examine all supplies received for damage. Look for inaccuracies and backorders on the packing slip enclosed with the shipment. If there is any damage or discrepancies, contact the supplier. Regular suppliers do not enclose a statement of payment due; it is sent separately to the practice on a monthly basis. A backorder is an item not immediately available; the supplier gives an estimated shipment date. If any units are returned, the supplier should issue the practice a credit slip, indicating there will be no charge. After receipt, the dental assistant should transfer the supplies to a well-organized storage area. Place older items in front to be utilized first. In a dental office, certain items are stored in a refrigerator or in a dark, dry spot. Controlled substances must be in a locked cabinet. Remember that thieves target dental offices for gold and addicts look for narcotics and syringes.

STORING STERILE SUPPLIES AND GASES

Sterile supplies should be placed in a storage area maintained at 65-72 °F with 35-50% humidity and at least 10 air exchanges (positive to adjacent areas) per hour. Supplies should be placed on shelves or in cabinets or carts and be at least 8 inches above the floor, 18 inches from the ceiling, and 2 inches from outside walls, taking care not to crush or puncture the outside wrappings. Sterile supplies should never be stored under sinks or where they may be exposed to liquid (such as near water or sewer pipes).

Nitrous oxide (NO2) and oxygen (O2) cylinders should be safely secured so that they cannot fall in a non-public storage area and away from all grease and oil because of the potential for explosion. In the United States, NO2 cylinders are blue and O2 tanks green. Tanks should be protected against temperature extremes. The storage area should contain a sign indicating that the gases are present and no smoking or open flames are allowed.

EQUIPMENT/INSTRUMENT MAINTENANCE

GENERAL DENTAL INSTRUMENT CARE

Most dental instruments are made of stainless steel, or occasionally aluminum or high-tech resins. Clean them promptly after use by immersion in an ultrasonic bath or instrument washer. Instruments that cannot be cleaned right away should be presoaked temporarily. Separate the blades of all instruments. Ultrasonic solution should cover all the instrument parts. Instruments that have hinges (e.g., scissors and forceps) should be sanitized first and later sterilized in the open position. Remove instruments from the ultrasonic bath, hold them under running water, dry, and then sterilize them. Sterilization techniques include liquid chemical disinfectants, ethylene oxide, hot glass bead, dry heat, chemical vapor, and steam autoclave sterilization. Dry the instruments well prior to storage. Some instruments have different or additional maintenance requirements. For example, burrs and handpieces must be scrubbed first, and since handpieces are attached to a power source via tubing, they need initial flushing and lubrication.

ROTARY INSTRUMENTS, TRAPS, AND SUCTION LINES

Rotary instruments: The central console and hand piece should be wiped down with a soft cloth dampened with disinfectant. The hand piece cartridge nut, heat shield, heat pluggers/thermal response tips, and entire motor should be autoclaved. The cartridges are for single patient use and should be cleaned or sterilized after use.

Traps: Chemical cleansing compounds are usually used to clean the traps to remove organic materials. There are microbiology-based cleaning bacteria, also, that provide a less caustic and more natural way to clean debris from traps. These cleaning products contain bacteria that actually breakdown the organic matter. Cleaning should be done according to the guidelines provided by the manufacturer of the evacuation system.

Suction lines: Should be disinfected daily with a compound that is compatible with the evacuation system. Buildup of tissue and debris within the lines can lead to low pressure through the lines. If patients close their mouths tightly around the suction tip, it can create a backflow and any debris in the lines can be recirculated back to the patient's mouth.

DENTAL LABORATORY EQUIPMENT

All dental laboratory equipment must be decontaminated and maintained in safe condition or retired. A dental laboratory technician may perform maintenance of complex equipment at the office, but often it is the dental assistant's responsibility. Much of the equipment is for taking impressions, creating trays, or making casts. These include the gypsum vibrator, extruder guns, lathes, model trimmer, hydrocolloid conditioning unit, soldering and welding equipment, and vacuum former. Most of these ship with explicit manufacturer-provided instructions, or you can obtain a copy of the instructions from the sales person. Instruments that must be cleaned between uses and checked for wear include spatulas, laboratory knives, reusable impression trays, flexible rubber bowls, and measuring devices.

EMERGENCY PREPAREDNESS

The role of each person in the dental office during an emergency should be clearly identified in the job description and rehearsed. For example:

- The **front desk receptionist** phones EMS, notifies the dentist, directs traffic, and reschedules patients
- The **assistant** obtains the crash cart, provides first aid, and assists the dentist with life support
- The **hygienist** provides first aid, and contacts the patient's next-of-kin and physician
- The **dentist** leads two-person CPR and administers resuscitation drugs

Staff must cross train in various roles during routine practice drills, in case of absences or multiple casualties. Clearly post these emergency telephone numbers at Reception and in each treatment room: Emergency medical services (EMS), fire department, police, nearest hospital Emergency Room, oral surgeon, nearby doctor, Public Health, and the morgue. The universal emergency number is 911, except in some rural areas.

DENTAL OFFICE EMERGENCY KIT

A dental office emergency kit should be maintained and updated in every dental office. Each treatment room should have a self-contained oxygen inhalation unit (with a green oxygen tank) or a wall-piped system for nitrous oxide gas and oxygen. Test the oxygen tank(s) weekly. The dental office emergency kit should contain: Plastic or metal airways; tracheotomy needles; masks for cardiopulmonary resuscitation; tourniquets; sterile syringes; antihistamines to counteract allergic reactions; an Epi-pen (epinephrine); vasodilators like nitroglycerin to increase blood flow and treat high blood pressure (hypertension); a vasopressor, like Wyamine, to treat low blood pressure (hypotension); anti-convulsants, like Diazepam; atropine to block the vagal nerve and increase the pulse rate; and analgesics (pain relievers). Check the medications monthly for expiration dates. Replace when needed.

MAGILL INTUBATION FORCEPS

Small dental tools and debris may dislodge in the patient's mouth during a procedure, causing obstruction. Intubation means placement of a tube into the airway to supply oxygen when the patient is unable to breathe independently due to obstruction. The dentist passes a long, curved Magill intubation forceps into the windpipe for endotracheal intubation and retrieval of objects obstructing the airway that are still visible. The assistant must be present to suction the mouth. Do not allow the patient to sit up during retrieval, as movement can result in further injury and force the object farther down the throat. If only one professional is present, or if the airway is partially obstructed, then tell the patient to bend his or her head down over the side of the chair and try to cough it free. Call 911. If full obstruction occurs, perform the Heimlich maneuver.

CARDIOPULMONARY RESUSCITATION (CPR)

Cardiopulmonary resuscitation (CPR) is an emergency technique to revive a person whose heart has stopped beating. The process of CPR follows an ABC (and often D) pattern:

- "A" represents the **airway**, which must first be opened up to allow air flow.
- "B" signifies **breathing**, which the rescuer must observe and work to re-establish if the patient is not breathing by using rescue breathing or bag-mask ventilation.
- "C" stands for **circulation**, which the rescuer must check using the carotid pulse; if there is no pulse, then chest compressions interspersed with slow breaths are used to re-establish a pulse. Chest compressions should be at a rate of 100-120 compressions per minute at a depth of about 2 inches in adults. The compression to breaths ratio in adults is 30:2.
- "D" refers to **defibrillation** using an automated external defibrillator (AED) unit, if available. Follow the AED's automated prompts to safely utilize this intervention.

Dental assistants are legally required to recertify in CPR with the American Red Cross or the American Heart Association every two years at the Healthcare Provider Level.

ADULT WITH SINGLE RESCUER

The dental assistant or dentist performs **CPR** on patients with cardiac arrest. The patient must be unresponsive, with no pulse or breathing.

1. Call emergency medical services (911) before beginning.
2. Don gloves, if possible.
3. Place the patient supine on the floor.
4. Look, listen, and feel for the patient's pulse and breathing. If there is no breathing but a pulse is palpated, open the patient's airway by inclining the head back and raising the chin. Place a resuscitation mouthpiece patient's mouth. Pinch the nose closed. Inflate the lungs with two breaths. Observe the chest's rise and fall. Rescue breaths should be provided at a rate of 1 every 6 seconds if a pulse is palpable.

5. Check the carotid pulse for no more than 10 seconds. If there is no pulse and no breathing, compressions should be initiated prior to rescue breaths. To administer chest compressions, kneel beside the patient.
6. Landmark the xiphoid process.
7. Place the palms over the breastbone. Compress 30 times, followed by two breaths.
8. After four cycles, check the carotid pulse again.
9. Continue until the patient breathes or emergency services arrive.
10. Discard the mouthpiece.
11. Document CPR in the patient's chart.

AUTOMATED EXTERNAL DEFIBRILLATION FOR CARDIAC ARREST

An automated external defibrillator (AED) can revive a person in cardiac arrest if it is applied within four minutes and damage is not extensive. Continue CPR while the device is being applied. The patient must be on a flat, dry surface. Connect the electrodes of the AED to the patient, as illustrated on the unit. Hold chest compressions and press the "analyze" button to allow the device to determine the patient's rhythm. If a shock is not needed the device will instruct for chest compressions resume. If a shock is warranted, continue chest compressions while the device charges. Next, announce, "Stay clear of the patient." The unit indicates by tone or light that it is ready to shock the patient. Make sure that everyone is clear of the patient, and press the appropriate "shock" button on the AED. The AED display shows when defibrillation occurs. Resume CPR immediately after the shock is administered. Check the pulse after the third shock, or follow the AED's instructions if a pulse is detected. If there is a pulse, check the airway and breathing circulation and move the patient into recovery position. If there is no pulse, perform CPR for one minute before rechecking the pulse. If there is still no pulse, defibrillate again. Press the analysis button. Nine defibrillations can be performed. The unit indicates when to stop defibrillation.

RESCUE BREATHING

Rescue breathing in emergency situations may be performed by the dental assistant, hygienist, nurse, or dentist if the patient is orally unresponsive. Call emergency medical services (911) before beginning. Gloves are suggested but not required. If the patient is not breathing, tilt the head back and raise the chin to open the airway. Look, listen and feel for breathing. If there is none, insert a resuscitation mouthpiece into the patient's mouth. Pinch the nose closed. Provide two breaths to make the patient's chest rise. If it does not rise, assess the airway. If there is a visible source of obstruction, remove it, but do not do a blind sweep, as this risks pushing an object further into the airway. Check the carotid pulse in the neck, using the middle and forefingers. Perform rescue breathing while there is still a pulse, one slow breath every five seconds for a minute, followed by a pulse check. Repeat the sequence until breathing is re-established or a more qualified person takes over. If the pulse stops, begin CPR. When the incident concludes, throw the mouthpiece into a biohazard container. Document the incident.

OXYGEN ADMINISTRATION

The dental assistant can administer oxygen in emergency situations. A crash cart contains a green oxygen tank, masks, airways, a defibrillator, and resuscitation drugs. One crash cart should be available per floor; remember where it is located. Tell the receptionist to call an ambulance (911) and notify the dentist. Place the patient in the supine position, lying on their back. If the patient is in true distress, place them on the floor, if possible, as this position is safest and most effective for CPR. Position the oxygen mask over the patient's nose and mouth, with tubing to the side. Fasten the mask firmly. Administer oxygen without delay, at a rate of 2-4 liters a minute. If the patient is still conscious, help reassure the patient and encourage them to take slow deep breaths. Try to calm and comfort the patient. Cover the patient with a blanket to help prevent shock. The dentist or registered nurse intubates the unconscious patient and administers resuscitation drugs.

AMBU-BAG

An Ambu-bag is the proprietary name for a portable manual resuscitator or bag-valve-mask (BVM) device. Anytime a patient has an emergency involving respiratory failure or arrest, it is essential to deliver positive pressure oxygen to increase the relative amount of oxygen in the lungs, blood, and ultimately the brain. The preferred method is delivery of oxygen from a pressurized oxygen tank via a hose and mask. Emergencies occurring where an oxygen tank is unavailable can be addressed with an Ambu-bag, which has a self-inflating bag that fills up with air (and sometimes additional oxygen attached to a flexible mask), and seals to the patient's face. Positive pressure ventilation is delivered when the rescuer compresses the valve joining the bag and mask. Another portable method of resuscitation is a pocket mask, where the rescuer inflates the patient's lungs using exhaled air.

Chapter Quiz

Ready to see how well you retained what you just read? Scan the QR code to go directly to the chapter quiz interface for this study guide. If you're using a computer, simply visit the bonus page at **mometrix.com/bonus948/danbcda** and click the Chapter Quizzes link.

Chairside Dentistry (GC)

Transform passive reading into active learning! After immersing yourself in this chapter, put your comprehension to the test by taking a quiz. The insights you gained will stay with you longer this way. Scan the QR code to go directly to the chapter quiz interface for this study guide. If you're using a computer, simply visit the bonus page at **mometrix.com/bonus948/danbcda** and click the Chapter Quizzes link.

Four Handed Dentistry Techniques

PREPARING THE TREATMENT ROOM

The dental assistant is responsible for preparing the treatment room between patients. This includes cleaning, disinfecting, and placing barriers on all areas (including charts) that may be touched. The Infection Control (ICE) exam covers appropriate procedures. The assistant pulls the rheostat, chairs, and mobile carts out of the patient's pathway, and lifts up the dental light. The dental chair should be about 15-18 inches above the floor, with the arm positioned for patient access. The dental assistant reviews the chart and sets out any needed radiographs, trays or lab work.

EQUIPMENT IN THE DENTAL TREATMENT AREA

The following equipment should be available for the treatment room:

- A comfortable, supportive dental chair with arm supports and an adjustable headrest and controls. The chair must accommodate upright, supine and sub supine positions.
- Ergonomic chairs or stools for both operator and assistant. The operator's (dentist's) chair should have 5 castors, an adjustable seat and back, and a broad base. The assistant needs a chair with a foot bar for support.
- Track-mounted, iridescent operating light to illuminate the oral cavity.
- An air-water syringe to provide streams of water and/or air.
- An oral evacuation system that includes a saliva ejector and a high velocity evacuation (HVE) device.
- A curing light, an electronically-controlled blue light-emitting wand that polymerizes resins and composites.
- Various handpieces operated by a foot-controlled rheostat or resistor attached to the dental unit.
- If restorations are performed, use an amalgamator to make the materials.

PREPARING TREATMENT TRAYS
CRITERIA FOR A CUSTOM TRAY

A custom tray is fabricated to make an accurate impression. Therefore, the tray must be durable enough to hold the material during positioning and removal. It should be smoothed and shaped to the patient's arch. Ideally, it should allow the impression material to fill with consistent thickness in all regions of the arch. The tray should be adaptable to any type of dentition, from an edentulous condition to full dentition, and any other type of unusual area. Trays that have stops in the spacer to grip the impression material are a good design and provide greater accuracy for the impression.

TYPES OF MATERIALS FOR CUSTOM TRAYS

Custom trays are made from acrylic, resin, or a thermoplastic substance:

- **Self-curing acrylic tray resin**: This system combines a polymer powder with a liquid catalyst or monomer, initiating polymerization and exothermic release of heat. Complete setting to a very hard state takes about a day.
- **Light-cured acrylic tray resin**: Similar to self-curing acrylic, but remains malleable until a special curing light is activated, which initiates the polymerization and sets much faster.
- **Vacuum-formed custom trays:** These use heavy, stiff sheets of plastic resin. The resin is hung within a special unit and heated until soft. The sheet is then released onto the model, as vacuum pressure is applied.
- **Thermoplastic materials:** Beads or buttons are softened and made pliant through exposure to heat, usually warm water. After shaping, hardening occurs as heat disperses.

OUTLINING THE MARGINS AND PREPARING THE CAST FOR A CUSTOM TRAY

When outlining the margins and preparing the cast for a custom tray, first the dental assistant adapts a working plaster or stone cast. The assistant draws a blue line in the deepest area of the entire margin. The assistant draws a red line for wax spacer placement 1-2 mm above the blue line. The red mark corresponds to about 2-3 mm below the tooth margin or above the lowest point of the vestibule, if edentulous. Spacers are made of pink baseplate wax, a special molding material, or wet paper towels. The assistant plugs any recessed undercuts in the model. The spacer material is heated, shaped, and trimmed to the red line with a laboratory knife. Stops or holes are cut at intervals on the top edges of the spacer to permit impression material through. The assistant drapes the top of the spacer with aluminum foil, if self-cured resin is being used to dissipate heat and facilitate removal of wax at the end of the procedure. Sometimes, the assistant paints a separating material over the spacer.

MIXING RESIN AND CONTOURING A SELF-CURED ACRYLIC RESIN CUSTOM TRAY

The dental assistant mixes the self-curing resin components, the powder polymer and the liquid catalyst, in a wax-lined paper cup with a wooden tongue blade, until the mixture is uniform. Follow the directions from the manufacturer. The initial set or polymerization takes about 2-3 minutes. Apply petroleum jelly to the palms and the cast. The dental assistant takes the malleable resin and manipulates it into a doughy patty or roll for a maxillary or mandibular arch. A little is reserved to make a handle later. The resin patty or roll is inserted over and extending slightly beyond (1-2 mm) the wax spacer. For the maxillary tray, this means inclusion of the palatal area. The assistant manually contours it with a rolled edge. Use of the laboratory knife is permitted, but less desirable. The handle material is molded and attached to the front of the tray, near the midline, using a drop of the monomer catalyst liquid.

MAKING A VACUUM-FORMED ACRYLIC RESIN CUSTOM TRAY

The dental assistant prepares the previously-made cast by immersing it in warm water for up to 30 minutes to remove surface air bubbles. Add spacers, if specified. Outline the outer margin. Place the cast on a vacuum-forming unit with a platform. Secure the unit between two frames with acrylic resin sheets. These hang above the platform. One of the frames contains a heating element. Turn it on to cause the resin sheet to droop downward. When the resin hangs down about an inch, the operator pulls the frames down over the cast, using the handles on the sides. Activate the vacuum right after the resin drops over the cast. Turn the heat off. Keep the vacuum on for a minute or two. Once the tray cools, take it off the frame. Release it from the model, and trim it to the preferred form with a laboratory scissors. Cut a handle and attach it using a torch. Clean, disinfect and label the tray.

FINISHING A SELF-CURED ACRYLIC RESIN CUSTOM TRAY

Finishing a self-cured acrylic resin custom tray:

- Don safety glasses.
- Remove the custom tray from the model and wax spacer after 8-10 minutes of setting.
- Remove the wax by melting or using a spatula, hot water, and a toothbrush.
- Trim the outside edges of the tray later, using an acrylic burr.
- Ensure the material is completely set (about 30 minutes).
- Clean disinfect, and label the tray.
- Before taking the impression, paint two thin coats of impression adhesive onto the inside of the tray and along the margins.
- Further secure the impression material by making holes in the tray with a round burr.

COMPONENTS OF A DENTAL BLEACHING TRAY

Teeth whitening is the most common cosmetic dentistry procedure performed. There are several home products and methods for whitening the teeth, but in-office teeth whitening is generally considered the safest and most effective method. The components of the dental bleaching tray will vary depending upon the manufacturer, but generally, the following supplies will be included:

- **Cheek retractor:** Holds the mouth open and cheeks away from the teeth to expose the teeth that are visible during smiling.
- **Liquid rubber dam or hardening resin**: Brushed onto the gum tissue to prevent irritation.
- **Bleaching gel:** This is a hydrogen peroxide-based gel that is applied to the teeth for 15-30 minutes. This is rinsed off and reapplied at least one more time for another 15-30 minutes.
- **Light:** Some products include a light that is used to illuminate the treated teeth during the whitening process. It is unclear whether this step increases the outcome of the whitening process.
- **Whitening outcome measure:** This measures the shade change to compare the color of the treated teeth before and after the procedure.

PREPARING THE DENTAL PATIENT FOR TREATMENT

After preparing the treatment room, the assistant then greets the patient by name in the reception area and escorts the patient to the treatment room. The assistant illustrates where to put personal items. The assistant offers mouthwash, tissues for lipstick removal, a lip lubricant, and a drink of water to the patient and then seats him or her in the dental chair. The dental assistant puts the bib apron on the patient and gives them safety glasses to wear. The assistant asks about changes in the medical history, and inquires whether the patient has any questions. The assistant places the most recent radiographs on the view box. The assistant positions the patient supine for treatment, with the headrest supporting the head. The assistant adjusts the rheostat, operator's chair, assistant's stool, and lamp. The assistant dons a mask and protective eyewear. After washing his or her hands, the assistant dons gloves, then sets up trays, saliva ejector, air-water syringe, evacuator, and handpieces.

DENTAL UNIT AND DENTAL HANDPIECES

The dental unit is the center from which dental handpieces and other essential equipment, such as the oral evacuator and air-water syringe, are controlled. The unit is set up to deliver instruments to the dentist from the rear, on the side of the dentist, or transthorax (over the patient's chest). There are at least two high-speed and one slow speed handpiece and an air-water syringe connected to the unit. Slow-speed handpieces are straight and are used for decay removal, fine finishing, and polishing. Accessories are attached to the end, depending on the intended use. Slightly bent contra-angle attachments hold either friction-grip (FG) or latch-type (RA) burrs. The prophylaxis angle holds the polishing cup or brush. Low-torque, high-speed handpieces have curved ends. They are used with hard carbon steel burrs or diamond stones to remove the greater part of

76

tooth structure for restoration before refinement. The friction generated necessitates use of a cooling water spray. The assistant is responsible for evacuation.

INSTRUMENT TRANSFER TECHNIQUES

PRINCIPLES OF THE FOUR-HANDED DENTISTRY TECHNIQUE

The four-handed dentistry technique is one in which the dental assistant and operator (dentist) are seated on either side of the patient and work together as a team. Using the clock face as a frame of reference, the patient's head is at 12. If, for example, a right-handed operator is on the right side and the dental assistant is on the opposite side, the operator zone is between 8 and 11 and the assistant's zone is between 2 and 4. A left-handed operator may have a slightly wider operator zone, and the operator may sit at position 12 for some procedures. The transfer zone where instruments are passed (under chin, over chest) and received is from 4 to 8. The static zone is from 11 to 2. The dental assistant should sit close to and facing the patient at a level about 6 inches above the dentist. During instrument transfer, the assistant should use minimal motions, and the operator should keep eyes on the treatment site.

SINGLE-HANDED AND TWO-HANDED INSTRUMENT TRANSFER TECHNIQUES

The assistant should transfer instruments within the transfer zone over the patient's chest. Both operator and assistant wear gloves. Transfer instruments with minimal motion. Keep the working end pointed toward the tooth being repaired. Keep the handle available for the dentist to grasp.

- In the **single-handed transfer technique**, the clinical assistant picks up the instrument from the tray, using the thumb and first two fingers of the left hand. The assistant holds the handle end or the side not required and places it into the transfer zone, near the implement in use. Exchange the instruments by using the last two fingers of the left hand for retrieval of the used one. Fold the used instrument into the palm. Simultaneously, put the new tool into the operator's fingers. Return the used instrument to its correct position in the setup tray.
- In the **two-handed technique**, grip the new instrument similarly in the right hand. Recover the used implement with the left hand and return it to the tray by releasing the palm grasp. Give the new instrument to the dentist with proper orientation of the working end.

SITUATIONS REQUIRING UNIQUE INSTRUMENT TRANSFER TECHNIQUES

The operator uses the mouth mirror and explorer for examination at the beginning of the procedure. These are transferred from the assistant to dentist at the same time, using the two-handed technique. Most instruments are gripped by the dentist in a pen, palm, or palm-and-thumb grasp. The assistant holds pliers and forceps over their hinges and puts the handles directly into the dentist's palm or over his or her fingers. To transfer using cotton pliers, squeeze the beaks together to avoid dropping the cotton. Transfer dental materials much closer to the chin than instruments. The dental assistant can either give amalgam to the dentist or, if allowed by state law, directly insert it into the tooth. Transfer impression materials and cements delivered via syringes directly to the dentist, with the tip facing the arch where he or she is working. Convey cements and liners on mixing slabs, along with the applicator device. The assistant uses his or her right hand to hold the slab. The left hand wipes off any excess with gauze.

FOUR ZONES IN THE DENTAL FIELD OF OPERATION

Team or four-handed dentistry requires four distinct zones in the treatment area:

- A **static zone** right behind the patient, where the dental unit and a moveable cabinet are located.
- The **operator's zone** is the largest segment, to the left or right of the static zone, where the operator (dentist/hygienist/nurse) sits and moves around. Placement depends on whether the dentist is right-handed or left-handed.
- The **assistant's zone** is directly opposite the operator with the instrument cart and dental materials.
- A **transfer zone** next to the assistant is over the patient's chest, where assistant and operator exchange dental materials and instruments.

These four operating zones are often described in terms of a clock face with 12 divisions: The static zone occupies 2 portions; the operator occupies 5 portions; and the combined assistant and transfer zones making up the remainder (5 portions).

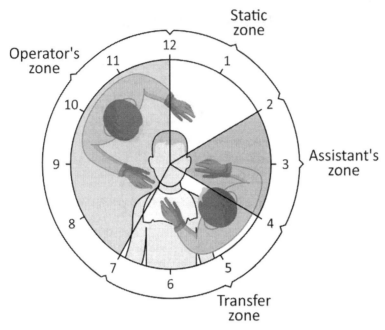

Right-Handed Dentist

PROPER SEATED POSITIONS FOR INJURY PREVENTION

The dental operator (dentist, hygienist, or nurse) sits with a straight back, feet planted on the floor, and knees slightly below hip level. Adjust the chair height level so the patient's mouth is level with the operator's elbows. The operator should be relaxed, with eyes directed downward toward the patient.

The assistant sits 4-5 inches higher than the operator to permit greater visibility and access. Sit up straight, with the abdominal bar or chair back in a supportive position. Place feet on the base platform, not the floor. Keep hips and thighs parallel to the floor, level with the patient's shoulders.

Dental operators experience shoulder, neck and back pain. Pain in the shoulder and neck is due to extended strain or flexion. Pain in the neck and back is due to prolonged extension or lifting of the arm. Low back pain is due to prolonged twisting. Carpal tunnel syndrome is a repetitive strain injury from prolonged wrist flexion and extension, as when keyboarding.

MAINTAINING THE FIELD OF OPERATION

IRRIGATION

The GCA is responsible for **irrigating** the dental operative site as necessary during a procedure. Irrigating the oral cavity when necessary allows small pieces of tooth material, blood, and debris to be washed loose so they can be removed via suction. This allows for a cleaner operative site that is easier to visualize.

The GCA can use a hand tool to perform irrigation, but additional irrigation is usually necessary to remove all of the material. Some dentists may not want to use the hand tool for irrigation during certain procedures. Frequently, the GCA will be responsible for operating the 3-way syringe which has a rotating tip to perform irrigation, aspiration, or apply air to the operative site. Depending upon the manufacturer guidelines, the tip is usually removable for sterilization. The GCA may also use a syringe with normal saline or sterile water for irrigation. This is performed with a bulb-type or Luer syringe. Following irrigation, the fluid and debris is suctioned from the operative site.

RETRACTORS AND MOUTH PROPS

Retractors redirect tissue, so the dentist can see clearly during procedures. Retractors are for oral surgery, but have other applications, too. There are tissue, cheek and lip, and tongue retractors. Tissue retractors have small jagged edges on the working end to grasp tissue, and resemble forceps or cotton pliers. Cheek and lip retractors are large metal or plastic tools that fit into the mouth to pull the cheeks or lips outward, expanding the viewing region. Tongue retractors are spoon-shaped or lengthy blades that displace the tongue. Place tongue retractors between the rim of the tongue and the lingual surfaces of the teeth, or adapt them for cheek retraction by positioning them on the buccal mucosa. Hemostats and needle holders are forceps with jagged beaks and locking handles, usable for retraction. Insert mouth props when the patient's mouth must be open for a long period. They can be stainless steel, silicone, plastic, or hard rubber, and come in various sizes. The locking Molt mouth gag is an example.

CRITERIA FOR OPTIMIZING ACCESS AND VISIBILITY

The purpose of four-handed dentistry is not just to assist the dentist, but to also efficiently perform dental procedures in a way that will decrease physical stress. In order for true four-handed dentistry to be practiced, the clinical assistant should be in charge of the transfer of all instruments and all of the equipment should be within reach of the assistant. In order to have optimal access and visibility, the following criteria should be met:

- Excess motion should be minimized with ergonomically-designed equipment.
- The patient should be in the supine position.
- The procedure team and patient should be situated comfortably in ergonomically-designed furniture.
- The personnel necessary for the procedure should be seated as close as possible to the patient. The assistant should be sitting with his or her legs parallel to the patient chair.
- Use as few instruments as possible and have them arranged in order of use to increase efficiency.
- All materials used during a procedure should be placed in the appropriate area before the procedure to increase efficiency.

MOUTH RINSING METHODS

The dental assistant is responsible for both mouth rinsing and oral evacuation during dental procedures. Use either a saliva ejector or a more powerful high-volume oral evacuator (HVE). Perform limited-area rinsing often during pauses in the procedure to eliminate debris. Perform a complete mouth rinse at the end of the procedure. Grip the air-water syringe in the left hand and the saliva or HVE in the right hand. For a limited rinse, point the tip toward the desired area and direct air and water to the site. Suction out fluid and debris. Dry the site by compressing the air button. The patient should be facing the dental assistant during the final full-mouth rinse. Direct the HVE or saliva ejector tip into left part of the oral cavity (without touching tissues). Direct the air-water syringe first from right to left, along the maxillary arch, and then right to left along the mandibular arch. Place the suction tip in the back of the mouth to remove the fluid and extracted debris.

ORAL EVACUATION METHODS

Moisture control and maintenance of a clinical field are paramount during dental procedures. A **saliva ejector** is a small flexible tube attached to a bulb, used for oral evacuation of minute quantities of saliva or water. A **high-volume oral evacuator (HVE)** is needed for large quantities of saliva and water, or for blood, pus, and vomitus. The HVE is essentially a vacuum with a sterile tip attached. Tips can be made of plastic or stainless steel. Tips are either straight or slightly angled, and the working end is slanted. Hold the evacuator with either a pen or thumb-to-nose grasp in the same hand as the dentist uses. Use the other hand to operate the air-water syringe or for instrument transfer. The patient's tongue and cheek must be isolated from the evacuation site with the HVE tip or the mouth mirror. There are several techniques for HVE tip placement, including on the lingual or buccal surfaces, slightly behind the prepped area, or on the opposite side of the tooth.

PLACEMENT OF THE HIGH-VOLUME ORAL EVACUATOR

When using an HVE (high-volume oral evacuator) in posterior areas, position the beveled edge of the tip as near to the tooth being prepared as possible, and parallel to either the buccal or lingual surface. The upper edge of the tip should reach a bit beyond the occlusal surface. Place a cotton roll under the tip for comfort when mandibular areas are being controlled. For anterior or front teeth, position the HVE tip parallel to the opposite surface and somewhat beyond the incisal edge of the tooth being prepared. Lingual and facial preparations require vacuum extraction from the facial and lingual sides, respectively.

DRY ANGLES

Dry angles are triangular-shaped, absorbent pads that may be used during oral procedures in the back areas of either dental arch. Position the angles on top of Stensen's duct, on the inside of the cheek, near the maxillary second molar. One type of salivary gland, the parotid gland, leads to Stensen's duct. Therefore, the main purpose of dry angles is to obstruct the saliva flow into the area. The pads also preserve the oral tissues. Replace dry angles that become saturated with saliva. Moisten them further with the air-water syringe before removal.

COTTON ROLLS

Cotton rolls isolate and control moisture in a working area during an oral procedure. For maxillary placement, the patient faces the assistant with his or her chin elevated. The assistant uses cotton pliers to grasp and convey the cotton roll to the mucobuccal fold nearest the working area of the patient's mouth. For mandibular placement, the patient faces the assistant with his or her chin lowered. The assistant picks up the cotton roll with the cotton pliers and transfers the roll to the corresponding mucobuccal fold. Place a second cotton roll on the floor of the mouth, between the operational field and the tongue. Ask the patient to raise his or her tongue to facilitate placement. Bend cotton rolls used in anterior regions before positioning. Take rolls out before the final full-mouth rinse, using cotton pliers. Very dry rolls can stick to the oral mucosa causing tissue damage. If a roll sticks, moisten it with water from the air-water syringe before removal.

RUBBER DAMS

Rubber dams, sometimes referred to as dental dams, are commercially-available barriers used to isolate areas during oral procedures. The dam improves access for the dentist and assistant because it retracts the lips, tongue and gums. It also enhances visibility of the area by providing color contrast. Dams come in latex or latex-free materials in various sizes, colors and thicknesses. Dams are divided into sixths, with holes punched for placement in the upper or lower middle portion for maxillary or mandibular treatments, respectively. Employ rubber dams for involved procedures requiring local anesthesia. The patient is less likely to accidentally inhale or swallow materials when a dam is used. A rubber dam provides infection and moisture control. It inhibits contact with debris and dental materials. In some states, the dental assistant may legally place the rubber dam.

EQUIPMENT USED WITH A RUBBER DAM

The rubber dental dam is held in a three-sided, plastic or metal dam **frame** for positioning. A dam **napkin** is a cotton sheet placed between the dam and patient to absorb moisture. A rubber dam **punch** is a specialized type of hole-puncher to tailor holes in the dam exactly where the teeth need to be isolated. Punches come in five **ascending sizes**, and are specific to the type of tooth involved:

- No. 1 for mandibular incisors.
- No. 2 for maxillary incisors respectively.
- No. 3 for canines and premolars.
- No. 4 for molars and bridge abutments.
- No. 5, the largest, for the anchor tooth chosen to hold the dam clamp securely.

Rubber dam **clamps** are made of stainless steel in the shape of the crown; they come in cervical, winged and wingless conformations, and have a bow, jaws and forceps holes. The rubber dam **forceps** are for dam

positioning and removal, adding lubricant, and a dam stamp. The latter is an ink-pad stamp made like a dental arch, which serves as a guide to indicate teeth to be punched out on the dam.

PREPARATION

Before inserting a rubber dam, the dentist administers local anesthetic, with the help of the dental assistant, who must note any misaligned or malposed teeth at that time. If a tooth is abnormally positioned, punch holes in a corresponding spot in the dam. Note the width of the arch for possible accommodations. Apply lubricant to the patient's lip with a cotton roll or applicator. Use a mouth mirror and explorer to find a suitable location for dam placement. If there is any debris or plaque in the area, brush the teeth or apply coronal polish prior to dam positioning. Floss all regional contacts to avoid tearing the dam. Mark a dam stamp to identify the teeth for isolation in the correct arch. Using this template, punch the dam with the correct size of dam punch. Make a hole for the anchor and the tooth for isolation. Lubricate holes that stretch over tight contacts with water-soluble lubricant on the underside.

PLACEMENT

When placing a rubber dam, attach the correct clamp to both a floss safety line and a locked dam forceps. Fit the dam over the anchor tooth, initially over the lingual side. Widen the forceps, and place the dam over the buccal side. Place the previously punched dam over the clamp bow, using the index fingers to stretch it over the clamp and anchor tooth. Pull the safety line to the outside. Fasten the dam to the last tooth at the opposite end with floss or cord. Place the dental napkin between the outer parts of the dam and the patient's mouth. Affix the dam frame over the oral cavity to hold the dam in place. Isolate the other teeth through the punched holes and push them into place by using dental floss or tape. Dry the teeth with the air syringe. Seal all edges by tucking or inverting them into the sulcus of the gum with a tucking instrument, before performing the desired procedure.

REMOVAL

The first step of rubber dam removal is to stretch the dam material outward with the middle or index finger. Cut each interseptal dam. Remove the dam clamp with the dam forceps by placing them into the forceps holes and compressing the handles to open the jaws of the clamp. Rotate the clamp toward each side for easy removal. Remove the holder, dam material, and napkin. Examine the dam to ensure no material is left interdentally. Floss the patient's teeth, if indicated. Knead the gum around the anchor tooth to improve circulation. Rinse the patient's mouth. Remove any remaining debris.

BITING FORCES AND THEIR IMPACT ON DENTAL MATERIAL SELECTION

Anything that exerts a push or pull on an object is a force. The object resists the force, causing stress. Significant stress causes a strain or alteration in the object. **Three forms of stress and strain** can occur from biting forces:

- **Tensile force**, or outward stretching and pulling, potentially causing elongation. Elastic bands used in orthodontics can cause tensile stress and strain.
- **Compressive force** or pushing together, which occurs during chewing or biting.
- **Shearing** or portions sliding across one another from side to side, such as when people grind their teeth (bruxism). It is important to select dental materials that can withstand tensile and compressive forces, properties known as ductility and malleability, respectively.

All of these types of stress and strain apply to dentistry; consider them when selecting dental materials, because biting forces are significant. People bite down on molars with forces in the range of 130-170 pounds, and about a quarter of that is on incisors.

Intraoral Procedures and Armamentarium

HAND CUTTING INSTRUMENTS

Prior to use of handpieces, hand cutting instruments were used to prepare cavities. Now, hand instruments are for fine detailing. They consist of a central shaft or handle connected to shanks on one or both ends, attached to a bevel and some type of working end, usually a blade and cutting edge. The hand instrument is described in terms of its shank angles (e.g., straight, slightly curved or Wedelstaedt, monangle, binangle, and triple angle) and the class of cutting edge. There are five common classes of cutting edge: Hatchet, chisel, hoe, margin trimmer, and angle former. Both hatchets and hoes plane cavity walls and floors. The dentist uses a pulling motion. Hatchets and angle formers hone angles. Chisels are used with a pulling motion to plane enamel margins and to trim margins on front teeth. Special gingival angle formers (gingival margin trimmers), which have curved working ends, shape the cervical cavosurface margin in amalgam and inlay restorations. Excavators have more rounded blades to extract decay and debris.

SLOW SPEED BURRS

A burr is a tool attached to the end of a handpiece to remove rough edges of tooth structure. They are composed of stainless steel, or carbide metal, or diamond chips. The shanks to which the head (working end) and neck are attached are either friction-grip (FG), latch-type (RA), or straight handpiece (HP) types. There are a variety of types of **slow-speed burrs**, including:

- **Acrylic burrs** are used for acrylic-based dentures or orthodontic appliances.
- **Straight HP finishing burrs** are principally utilized for finishing gold, amalgam or composite restorations.
- **Diamond stones** are used for crown preparation.
- **Green stones** are used for finishing gold, amalgam or composite restorations.
- **Acrylic stones** are, again, for acrylic dentures and orthodontic appliances.
- A **mandrel or shaft** can be connected to the handpiece and attached to sandpaper or abrasive discs with diamond or carborundum grit for finishing functions, or a bristle brush for tooth polishing.

HIGH SPEED BURRS

High-speed handpieces are principally used to remove undesired tooth structure swiftly, before finishing procedures. Therefore, burrs used with high-speed handpieces are made of carbon steel or diamond stones. Caries removal requires either round burrs or inverted cones.

- **Round burrs** open the pulp chamber for a root canal.
- **Inverted cones** are used for cavity preparation.
- **Fissure burrs** have flat ends and regularly spaced lines around the shaft. The straight fissure burrs, either plain cut or crosscut, make the initial opening into a tooth for smoothing the walls of a cavity or for axial retention grooves. The tapered versions are for inlay preparations or to open the pulp chamber for a root canal.
- **Finishing burrs** can be round, oval, pear or flame shaped. They are for finer aspects of amalgam or composite restorations.
- **Wheel burrs** form retentions.
- **End cutting burrs** form the shoulder for crowns.

Burrs are numbered to reflect their shape, size and differences.

BLACK'S FORMULAS FOR HAND CUTTING INSTRUMENTS

G. V. Black invented a formula to describe hand cutting instruments in terms of the size of the blade and its angle relative to the shaft. There are two different formulae, a 3-number and a 4-number.

- The **Black's Three Number Formula** describes chisels, hatchets, and hoes. It consists of the first number for the width of the blade in tenths of a millimeter, the second number for the blade's length in millimeters, and the third number for the angle between the blade and the long axis of the shaft in degrees centigrade (parts per hundred of a complete circle). Thus, a blade designated as (18 8 15) is 1.8 mm wide, 8 mm long, and at an angle of 15/100 of a circle to the handle.
- The **Black's Four Number Formula** describes angle formers and gingival margin trimmers. Its first, third, and fourth number correspond to the same descriptions as the first, second and third numbers in the Three Number Formula. The fourth number represents the angle of the cutting edge relative to the handle.

NON-CUTTING HAND INSTRUMENTS

Hand instruments not used for cutting fall into two classifications: Those used for basic examinations and those used to finish amalgam and composite restorative materials. Non-cutting instruments have configurations similar to cutting ones (handle, shank, and working end). Basic examination implements include mouth mirrors, explorers, cotton pliers, and periodontal probes. Categories of mouth mirrors include plane or regular with silver coatings on the glass back, front surface mirrors with rhodium on the front of the glass, and concave surface mirrors for magnification. The working end(s) of explorers are thin for probing; common configurations are the pigtail and shepherd's hook. Cotton pliers, which resemble large tweezers, transfer cotton rolls and other materials. Periodontal probes have round or blunt working ends and gauge the depth of the gingival sulcus.

NON-CUTTING HAND INSTRUMENTS FOR FINISHING RESTORATIVE MATERIALS

Non-cutting hand instruments that are used for finishing restorative materials include filling instruments, amalgam carriers, amalgam condensers, carvers, burnishers, files, and finishing knives. Most have the same basic configuration of handle, shank and working end. Filling instruments, which put restorative materials and cement bases into the cavity preparation, are thermoplastic or anodized aluminum. Hand amalgam condensers (pluggers) press amalgam into the cavity preparation; there are also mechanical vibrating versions. Carvers are designed with working ends that can get rid of excess restorative agents or carve tooth anatomy; they are generally used on crowns, inlays and onlays. Burnishers smooth coarse margins or shape matrix bands. Both files and finishing knives, which have sharper ends, trim excess filling materials. Amalgam carriers load and place the amalgam; there are amalgam guns for composites, glass ionomers and alloys.

ADDITIONAL MISCELLANEOUS HAND INSTRUMENTS FOR RESTORATIONS

Miscellaneous hand instruments for restorations include spatulas, articulating forceps, and scissors. The commonly used spatulas are stainless steel cement spatulas for mixing cements and other materials, plastic for mixing composite resins, and larger general laboratory spatulas for blending impression materials or plaster. Articulating forceps grasp articulation paper (special heavy paper showing marks if contact is made) for checking occlusion after adding the restorative material. The type of scissor used most often for restorations is the crown and collar scissors (also called the bridge scissors), which have short straight or curved cutting blades. Scissors cut retraction cords and trim matrix bands.

CROWN AND BRIDGE PREPARATION

CAST-GOLD CROWNS VS. CAST-GOLD INLAYS

Teeth for which cast-gold crowns are fabricated have more area removed than those receiving inlays. Prepare them with a high-speed handpiece and tapered fissure burrs or diamond stones. For full crowns, grind the complete occlusal surface to a clearance of three thicknesses of occlusal wax (28-gauge sheets of wax). Three-quarter crowns leave the facial aspect intact. The preparation appointment for cast-gold crowns includes the following procedures:

- Make a plaster model from an alginate impression.
- Make a plastic mold using a vacuum former with heating element (similar to making an acrylic resin custom tray).
- Fill the appropriate part of the mold with self-curing acrylics.
- Place this over the prepared tooth while the patient bites down during hardening.
- Remove the mold and separate it from the acrylic.
- Polish.
- Seat with temporary cement.

PREPARATION AND CEMENTATION FOR CROWNS AND BRIDGES

Crown and bridge preparation and cementation involved the following armamentarium:

- **Preparation**: Basic setup, anesthetic tray, periodontal probe, rubber dam setup, cords, bite block, temporary cement, crown and bridge bur block, viscostat, scissors, articulating paper, cord packer, cotton rolls, 2 x 2 gauze, triple tray X 3, impression material gun X 3, bite registration, light body, heavy body, bite registration tip, light body tip, heavy body tip, and tooth shade selector.
- **Cementation**: Basic setup, crown and bridge preparation kit with regular, fine, and superfine diamond points, etchant, silane coupling agent, acetone, try-in paste, bonding agent, brush, resin luting agent, polymerization light, porcelain polishing kit.

ARMAMENTARIUM FOR PLACEMENT OF A STAINLESS-STEEL CROWNS

Armamentarium required for the placement of stainless-steel crowns include:

- **Topical and local anesthetic**: Medications, a long needle, a short needle, and syringes should be available.
- **Mouth mirror:** For visualization or the oral cavity and to reflect light.
- **Periodontal probe:** Used to measure the depth of the gingival sulcus and to evaluate for any recession of the gingival tissue.
- **Crown-contouring pliers:** Used for enhancing contours and accurately design the contacts and gingival margins for placement of the crown.
- **Crown crimping pliers:** Used to crimp the gingival margins of the crown for accurate fit and placement.
- **College pliers:** Serrated pliers with angled tips to allow better visualization of the procedure field.
- **Large spoon excavator:** Used to tooth excavating and remove of glass ionomer material.
- **Heatless stone:** Made of silicone carbide abrasive and used to grinding and shaping.
- **Burlew wheel:** A knife-edged polishing wheel used for finishing.
- **Appropriate size burrs:** Used for reshaping and finishing.
- **Stainless steel crown:** The prefabricated crown form that is fit to fit an individual tooth and cemented into place.

CAVITY PREPARATION

Cavity preparation is the orderly cutting of tooth structure to remove any undesired portions, such decay, pits or fissures susceptible to caries, fractured tooth fragments, or enamel without underlying dentin support. The **four steps of cavity preparation** are:

1. Opening up the cavity with a burr.
2. Outlining.
3. Refining.
4. Finishing it with other instruments.

The dentist considers three and sometimes four factors when preparing a cavity. The first is the outline form or general shape of the preparation, which depends on the amount of decay, the material to be used, and how it can be retained. The resistance form is the internal contour of the cavity preparation. The dentist takes into account potential biting forces. The retention form is the internal profile of the cavity walls needed to keep the restoration in place, for example, using retention grooves or undercutting. There can also be a convenience form, which may be slightly larger than the outline form, to allow for use of instrumentation.

MEDICATING CAVITIES PRIOR TO RESTORATION

The dentist cleans the cavity and usually medicates it prior to inserting the restoration. **Medication** ensures maintenance of healthy pulp because it:

- Seals dentin tubules.
- Calms pulpal irritation.
- Stimulates pulp healing.
- Provides a barrier between dentin and the restoration material for thermal insulation or to discharge fluoride into the area.

Three substances are used for medication: Thin, creamy cavity liners, like calcium hydroxide or glass ionomer; cavity varnish; or cement bases, which include glass ionomer, zinc oxide and eugenol, and zinc phosphate. Suggested medication procedures depend on the restoration material and the depth of the cavity's preparation. For ideal depth cavity preparations, rinse the tooth and dry it with the air-water syringe.

PLACEMENT OF CAVITY LINERS, CAVITY VARNISH, AND CEMENT BASES

These procedures are executed by the dentist or the expanded-function dental assistant.

- **Cavity liners** include calcium hydroxide, glass ionomer or zinc oxide eugenol. Prepare as directed. Apply to the clean and dry cavity preparation. Place liner only into the deepest part of the preparation, using a ball attachment. Liners are either self-curing or light-cured for 10-20 seconds.
- **Cavity varnish seals dentin tubules**. Painted a thin layer over all exposed dentin with a cotton ball or pellet and sterile cotton pliers. Apply a second coat. Avoid contaminating the varnish.
- **Cement bases** are applied to the cleaned cavity preparation after a cavity liner and/or varnish. Mix the cement base materials as directed to a thick texture. Place onto the floor of the cavity preparation using a plastic filling instrument. Allow room for the restorative material.

MEDICATION PROCEDURES FOR AMALGAM OR COMPOSITE RESTORATIONS

Metal amalgam restorations require either two thin coats of cavity varnish or one of glass ionomer placed over the exposed dentin. Glass ionomer is recommended for composite or acrylic restorations. These are cavity liners. If the cavity preparation is of moderate depth, a cavity liner is also sufficient for amalgam restorations. Glass ionomer liners are suggested for composite restorations. Very deep cavity preparations require more extensive medication techniques. For amalgam restorations, usually the dentist applies calcium hydroxide to the deepest part then a cement base, and finally, two layers of cavity varnish. For composite restorations, an initial calcium hydroxide liner in the deepest portion should be followed by a glass ionomer base before the composite is added.

AMALGAM RESTORATIONS

TRANSPORTING AMALGAM AND AMALGAM RESTORATION PROCEDURE

Amalgam carriers hold the amalgam and its pistons push amalgam into the site. Amalgam condensers are hand instruments with flat working ends that push the amalgam against surfaces of the cavity preparation. There are also automatic versions. Matrix bans are strips of thin stainless steel, used to fashion an outline around a prepared tooth. They are only necessary for restorations where tooth structure is lacking (class II, III and VI). The dentist uses the matrix band in parts to support condensation (pressing the amalgam into place). The matrix band is removed at the end of the restoration. A matrix retainer holds the two ends of the matrix band in place. A contouring plier shapes the matrix band. Interproximal wedges are three-sided wooden or plastic sticks that fit between the teeth after matrix band placement. Wedges prevent amalgam leakage into the interproximal space and keep adjacent teeth slightly apart. One wedge is needed for class II and III restorations. Two wedges are necessary for class IV and larger.

PIN-RETAINED AMALGAM RESTORATIONS

Pin-retained amalgam restorations may be used for teeth with extensive damage. After the cavity has been prepared, the dentist makes starter holes where needed. The dentist drills further between the pulp and external part of the root, using a unique twist drill. The dentist screws threaded pins into the holes with an autoclutch handpiece or a tiny hand wrench. Then the matrix band and retainer are positioned. The amalgam is added and condensed around the retention pins. The band is removed after hardening. Carving and finishing are performed as usual. Retention pins can also be used to make a central amalgam core, over which a cast gold crown is placed.

PERFORMING A CLASS II AMALGAM RESTORATION

Class II amalgam restoration assumes an expanded role for the dental assistant, working in conjunction with the dentist. Dry the injection site. Apply topical anesthetic. Convey the mirror, explorer, gauze, and a syringe filled with local anesthetic. The dentist injects the anesthetic. The assistant rinses and evacuates. Help the dentist as needed with placement of a rubber dam. Transfer the high-speed handpiece with burr and the mouth mirror to the dentist for inserting the amalgam restoration. Retract the cheek and tongue. Keep the mirror clear with the air-water syringe. Evacuate as needed with the HVE. Transmit and receive instruments, as requested. After the preparation, clean the tooth with a cotton pellet (rinsed and dried). Prepare and transfer to the dentist on cue the cavity liner, the cavity varnish, and the base. If light curing is required, direct the light tip.

STEPS AFTER PREPARATION AND MEDICATION

After preparing the Class II amalgam restoration, assemble the matrix retainer and band apparatus. Hand it to the dentist in the correct orientation for placement. Transfer a wedge with cotton pliers or a hemostat. When the dentist indicates readiness, prepare the amalgam and activate it (twisting, squeezing, or putting in an activator). Mix in the amalgamator. Place the mixed amalgam into an amalgam well or Dappen dish. Load it into the amalgam carrier. Alternate placement of amalgam into the cavity preparation with packing with a condenser, until the cavity is filled. Amalgam may be placed by the dentist or assistant, but the condensing is a function of the dentist alone. When the filling is complete, the assistant transfers an explorer to the dentist for releasing amalgam from the matrix bind, cleans up amalgam fragments and puts them in a sealed container, and then hands carving, finishing, and band removal instruments as requested, while evacuating with the HVE. Remove the rubber dam. Dry the site. Use articulation paper to check occlusion before cleaning off the patient. Instruct the patient not to chew on the filled side for several hours.

VENEERS
PLACEMENT OF DIRECT COMPOSITE VENEERS

Veneers are thin layers of tooth-colored materials that are bonded to the enamel surface of teeth for aesthetic reasons, such as reshaping, concealing stains, or disguising diastema (large spaces between adjacent teeth). Before any type of veneering, the assistant polishes the teeth with pumice and water. There are both direct and indirect resin veneers. Direct veneers are made in one sitting. The dentist etches the teeth with phosphoric acid gel and applies two coats of bonding resin to the etched portions. Matrix strips are used if needed. Then the dentist applies composite resin in layers, followed by light curing and shaping. Opaquers and body shades may also be used before contouring and finishing is performed.

PLACEMENT OF INDIRECT COMPOSITE VENEERS

For indirect veneers, the dentist takes an impression at the first sitting. The laboratory fabricates the veneers, which are bonded at another appointment. The dentist applies a priming agent followed by a bonding agent (without light curing) to the tooth side of the veneer. The dentist places the veneer and checks for the shade of bond agent until the correct one is found, then temporarily removes it. The assistant installs matrix strips on either side of the tooth to be veneered. The dentist acid etches it, applies bonding agent to both the etched enamel and the tooth side of the veneer, and sets the veneer. Excess bonding agent is removed by the dentist. The assistant light cures the site for about a minute before the dentist finishes it. Indirect composite veneers are not as strong as porcelain veneers.

PLACEMENT OF ETCHED PORCELAIN VENEERS

Etched porcelain veneers are very strong, and desirable for aesthetic restorations of upper teeth. The dentist:

- Uses a diamond stone with a high-speed handpiece to take off some of the labial enamel (a retraction cord may be used).
- Takes a polysiloxane or polyether impression, makes a stone model, and sends it to the dental ceramist, who makes the veneers and etches them with a silane primer to encourages bonding.
- Installs temporary composite veneers, which are removed at the next appointment.
- Wets the veneers and tests them for fit prior to cementation.
- Instructs the assistant to place a matrix strip between the teeth.
- Etches the enamel.
- Spreads a resin bonding agent over both etched enamel and the tooth side of the veneer.
- Applies a fine layer of the appropriate shade of resin bonding substance on the tooth side of the veneer.
- Instructs the assistant to light cure the site for about a minute.
- Finishes the site with suitable burrs and stones.

CAST-GOLD RESTORATIONS

Cast-gold restorations include gold inlays, onlays, and bridges. All are made from gold alloys that have been melted and then cast and hardened into the needed shape. Gold alloys are readily melted, very strong to resist eating forces and edge fractures, non-corrosive, non-irritating, and non-allergenic. For gold inlays, the majority of the restoration is located within a tapered cavity in the tooth; these are appropriate for all cavity classes. Cast-gold onlays or crowns reach over the cusps of back teeth to ensure against fracture during mastication. Cast-gold crowns generally cover either three-quarters or the entire crown of the tooth. A three-quarter crown usually leaves the facial facet untouched for aesthetics. Cast-gold restorations always require two sittings: The first to prepare the tooth and take impressions before manufacture of the restoration in the laboratory (a temporary filling is inserted); and the second to fit and cement the restoration in place.

CAST-GOLD INLAY RESTORATION PROCEDURES

The dental assistant assists the dentist throughout with following procedural elements of cast-gold inlay restoration, and in some states is permitted to seat the retraction cord and make the final impression and/or a temporary filling. The dental team:

- Uses alginate to make an impression of the opposing teeth that will abut the finished inlay.
- Fits the bite registration onto an articulator, incorporating the opposing model impression, if possible.
- Applies topical anesthetic.
- Injects local anesthetic.
- Isolates the site with cotton rolls.
- Removes the rubber dam (if any).
- Retracts the gingiva.
- Prepares the cavity with smooth, slightly tapered walls for later insertion of the inlay.
- Uses hemostatic agents to stop bleeding.
- Removes the cord.
- Dries the cavity preparation.

- Takes an impression using agar hydrocolloid, polyether or polyvinylsiloxane.
- Temporizes the cavity preparation with a temporary filling of ZOE (zinc oxide and eugenol) or plastic.

CEMENTATION APPOINTMENT FOR CAST-GOLD INLAYS

Steps for the cementation appointment for cast-gold inlays are as follows:

- Apply anesthetics.
- Isolate the site with cotton rolls.
- Carefully remove the temporary filling with a spoon evacuator or burr, cotton pellets, and the air-water syringe.
- Seat the inlay with a wooden peg, orangewood stick, or other seating device.
- Check where the inlay contacts proximal surfaces of adjoining teeth and the cervical areas; make necessary adjustments.
- Tell the patient to bite down on articulating paper.
- Look for marks indicating hyperocclusion or too high an inlay; grind down, if any.
- Polish the final form with abrasives, externally on the tooth, and then on the dental lathe.
- Disinfect the form.
- Wash, dry, and isolate the tooth for cementation.
- Pretreat the preparation with cavity varnish if using zinc phosphate cement; non-irritating polycarboxylate and glass ionomer cements is preferable.
- Blend the cement and layer it onto the prepared tooth surfaces.
- Position the inlay and seat it with finger pressure.
- Place a bite device over the inlay and instruct the patient to bite down until cement is set.
- Check and finish margins.

ALL-CERAMIC RESTORATIONS

All-ceramic restorations are for occlusal and multiple-surface restorations. Usually, the laboratory makes them with porcelain or castable glass. They can be constructed chairside, using CEREC computerized design, which is expensive but only takes one sitting. The dentist prepares the cavity and makes a final impression, an opposing arch alginate impression, and a bite registration. The dental ceramist makes the restoration. The dentist installs a temporary acrylic filling. Prior to insertion at the next appointment (or same day for CEREC), the dentist etches the porcelain and applies silanating agent for bonding. The dentist removes the temporary filing. The assistant cleans the tooth and positions matrix strips and wedges between proximal surfaces. The dentist etches the tooth, applies a bonding substance to the preparation, then dual-cure composite cement to both the preparation and the tooth side of the restoration. The dentist inserts the restoration and the assistant light cures it for about a minute on each surface. The dentist finishes it, tests the occlusion, and adjusts the restoration.

COMPOSITE RESTORATIONS

CLASS II COMPOSITE RESTORATIONS

Assistant's tasks as they related to class II composite restorations are as follows:

- Rinses and dries the site.
- Applies topical anesthetic.
- Inserts a rubber dam to isolate the tooth.
- Keeps the area clear and evacuates it.
- Dries the preparation.
- Prepares the calcium hydroxide and/or glass ionomer base or liner for cavity medication and may light cure it.
- Rinses acid etchant.
- Mixes bonding agent, applies it, and light cures it.

- Holds the matrix tightly to maintain contours.
- Removes matrix strip, wedge, and rubber dam.
- Examines the site, dries, and rinses it.

Dentist's tasks as they related to class II composite restorations are as follows:

- Injects local anesthetic.
- Selects the shade of composite material that matches the patient's teeth.
- Prepares the cavity.
- Applies acid etchant.
- Positions celluloid matrix strips, plastic wedges, and sometimes a primer.
- Adds composite incrementally with a filling instrument, followed by light curing or chemical self-curing.
- Tests the restoration with an explorer.
- Finishes restoration with a low-speed handpiece and abrasive attachments.

CLASS IV AND V COMPOSITE RESTORATIONS

Composite restorations are called aesthetic because they are tooth-colored. Increasingly, composite restorations are being used for posterior teeth, even though they are grinding surfaces. Composites are appropriate for class III, IV, and V cavity preparations. **Class IV composite restorations differ from class III in these respects:**

- Pins are needed for retention in the cavity preparation.
- A cut-off portion of a celluloid crown form may be used to shape proximal and incisal portions.
- A celluloid crown form is used for composite insertion.

Class V preparations are usually easily filled with composite or glass ionomer, without matrix bands, and require minimal finishing. If the root surfaces are exposed, the tooth is conditioned with 10% polycyclic acid, the preparation is rinsed and dried, a calcium liner may be used, and then the composite or glass ionomer material is inserted.

COMPOSITE RESIN INLAYS

Composite resin inlays can be used for posterior restorations. Alternatives are gold or porcelain inlays. The dentist makes a replica or die of the tooth. The dental laboratory makes the inlay (which has high amounts of filler for strength). At the time of cementation, the dentist applies acid etchant to the prepared tooth, then bonding resin, followed by composite cement applied to the etched enamel and the interior of the inlay. The composite cement is a dual-cure bond agent because it has elements that need to be both light-cured and chemically-cured. The inlay is then placed into the cavity preparation, light cured, and attuned for margins and occlusion.

INSTRUMENTS AND SUPPLIES FOR COMPOSITE RESTORATIONS

When restorations use composite resins or glass ionomers, a filling instrument places the material in the cavity preparation. Long plastic or Teflon-tipped filling instruments are available, but usually a pistol grip composite syringe (with inserted cartridge) is used, so injection can be slowly controlled. Clear matrix strips and clamp-like strip holders retain the material. Usually, a surgical scalpel finishes composite restorations. A slow-speed handpiece may be used with various finishing stones and/or sandpaper finishing discs attached via a mandrel for polishing and contouring. These instruments need a water-soluble lubricant to reduce heat and clogging. There are special polishing strips for interproximal areas inaccessible to discs; use them like dental floss. Crown restorations require celluloid crown forms filled with composite or acrylic, positioned over the prepared tooth until hardened, which are then discarded.

TEMPORARY RESTORATIONS

Intermediate restorative material required for temporary restorations includes:

- **Zinc oxide eugenol-based materials:** This allows small amounts of eugenol to spread through the dentin to the pulp of the tooth. This may help with healing the pulp by delivering some anesthetic and anti-inflammatory effects. Its sedative effects also help the pulp to relax after a procedure, which further aides in healing. This is only used in small quantities because large quantities of eugenol can have damaging effects on the tissue.
- **Calcium sulfate-based materials:** Used as a temporary filling material. Cavit is soft and sets once it is permeated with water. Cavidentin will set after being immersed in water for 24 hours. Both materials are equally effective.
- **Glass ionomer materials:** This bonds to dentin to form an affective seal. This also has antibacterial qualities due to its release of fluoride, low pH, and the presence of strontium and zinc in the cement.
- **Biodentine:** Used as a dentine substitute. This can stimulate tissue regeneration, which produces an adequate response from the pulp.

SUTURES

TYPES OF SUTURES

Sutures are surgical seams for closing wounds. Sutures support healing, and reduce contamination with pathogens and food debris. The dental assistant helps the dentist insert sutures. Some states permit assistants to remove sutures. Here are the types of dental sutures, from most common to least common:

- **Simple suture,** which is threaded through two skin areas and tied with a surgeon's knot.
- **Continuous simple suture,** which is a chain of sutures tied at either end with surgeon's knots, used for multiple extractions.
- **Sling suture** for interproximal areas. It is threaded through the facial surface of the gum, enfolded around the lingual aspect of the tooth, put through the facial tissue on the other side of the tooth, wrapped back around the lingual side, and then the ends are tied.
- **Continuous sling variant** for a large opening, where the suture thread is wrapped onto the next tooth, instead of back around.
- **Mattress sutures** begin and end on the same aspect, e.g., the facial side, and the stitching is either horizontal or vertical.

PREPARING FOR SUTURE REMOVAL

Preparing for suture removal involves the following:

- Remove sutures when healing is indicated, usually between 5 and 7 days after insertion.
- Set up a standard cart.
- Review the patient's chart.
- Debride the site using air and warm water spray, a cotton-tip applicator with water or dilute hydrogen peroxide, or moist cotton gauze.
- Inspect the suture site for location and number of sutures, the suture types and patterns, and healing of tissues in the region.
- For large areas with multiple extractions, healed areas look slightly red, with evidence of granulation tissue.
- If there was no periodontal dressing, there should be no infection.
- If periodontal dressing was performed, then a milky film should be in its place.
- For smaller areas where there was no periodontal dressing, the region should look fairly healed, with dark pink granulation tissue and no evidence of inflammation.
- Any wounds that are red, tender or bleeding are either infected, irritated or insufficiently healed.
- Confer with the dentist before suture removal.

REMOVING SIMPLE AND CONTINUOUS SIMPLE SUTURES

Use aseptic technique for all suture removal. The dental assistant may only perform suture removal if the procedure is covered in their state under dental assistants' expanded functions. Otherwise, the dentist removes sutures. Do not disrupt the healing process; if you are unsure, consult the dentist before attempting removal. Control hemorrhaging by applying pressure with a gauze sponge. Do not cut knots. Do not pull exposed sutures and knots through the patient's tissue. For removal of simple or continuous simple sutures, gently lift the suture away from the tissues using a cotton plier. Cut the thread below the knot with a suture scissors near the tissue. Catch the knot in the pliers and pull it out. Place the suture on a gauze sponge for counting at the end of the procedure. Cut and remove each suture in a series of continuous simple sutures individually.

REMOVING HORIZONTAL AND VERTICAL MATTRESS SUTURES

As with all other types of suture removal, mattress suture removal is performed by the dentist or delegated to the expanded-function dental assistant if the state in which they practice permits it. Horizontal mattress sutures are placed by horizontal stitching through one surface, followed by the same on the other aspect, and tying. Vertical mattress sutures have vertical stitching on each surface. Nevertheless, suture removal is similar for both. Lift the knot with cotton pliers. Sever the suture below the knot near the tissue. Make another cut close to the tissue on the other surface. Remove the suture by holding the knot with the cotton pliers and pulling up. Place the spent suture on the gauze sponge for later counting.

REMOVAL OF SLINGS AND CONTINUOUS SLING SUTURES

As with all other types of suture removal, sling removal is performed by the dentist or delegated to the expanded-function dental assistant if the state in which they practice permits it. Using aseptic techniques, the sling suture is severed in two places and loosened on both sides of the tooth with cotton pliers. The knot is pulled up and cut close to the tissue. The thread on the other side of the tooth is lifted with the pliers and cut. Each thread is taken out with the cotton pliers by drawing it toward the wrapped side. For example, a sling suture entered from the facial side and wrapped around the lingual side is pulled toward the latter during removal. Sutures are placed on a gauze sponge for counting.

IMPRESSIONS

TYPES OF IMPRESSION TRAYS

Impression trays document tooth areas. They are for diagnosis, making temporary dental crowns, or developing an indirect casting. Commercially-available stock or preformed trays are used for preliminary and final impressions and temporary needs. They are sold in various sizes and materials, including metal, foam, and tough plastic. Impression trays can cover the full arch, a half arch (quadrant tray), or just the front teeth (section tray). Some are perforated, so the impression material bonds with the tray. Customized trays specially made for an individual are made of lightweight resins, either light-cured, acrylic or thermoplastic. They are used for final impressions, making temporary restorations, or vital bleaching (external surface teeth whitening).

PRELIMINARY IMPRESSIONS

An impression is a negative copy of teeth and adjacent structures. Preliminary impressions are diagnostic models for preparation of orthodontic and dental appliances, and provisional dental crowns. Impressions record tooth condition prior to and after treatment, especially for custom impressions. Preliminary impressions are created by the dentist or assistant (if legally allowed by the state) from alginate, a hydrocolloid comprised of potassium alginate and other compounds. Alginate is sold as a powder, to which the assistant adds an equal amount of water. The material first goes through a sol or solution phase that is liquid or semi-liquid. It proceeds to a gel or semisolid phase. Use 2 or 3 scoops of powder and equal measures of water for mandibular or maxillary impressions. Working time is 2 minutes for normal set and 1¼ minutes for fast set. Normal and fast sets have setting times of 4½ and 1-2 minutes, respectively.

ALGINATE IMPRESSIONS

Alginate has short working and setting times. To create an ideal alginate impression:

1. The dentist or assistant should be positioned so that insertion is quick and controlled.
2. The impression tray containing the alginate mixture is turned a bit initially, so the team can place a corner of it into the patient's mouth.
3. Retract the patient's cheek out of the way.
4. Slide the tray into the mouth.
5. Center it over the teeth.
6. Seat the back part of the tray before the front part, to prevent alginate flowing into the mouth and throat.
7. Push the tray into place very gently.
8. Pull the patient's lips out around the tray.
9. Hold securely in place until the alginate sets.

FINAL IMPRESSIONS

Final impressions provide more precise definition of the teeth and surrounding structures of interest than preliminary impressions. Occasionally, alginate is used for final impressions, but more often elastomeric impression materials are chosen. Two compounds are mixed together to create the final elastomeric material: a base and a catalyst. The various choices are defined by their viscosity or capacity to flow. Light, regular and heavy body materials are increasingly thick. Heavy body is the most commonly used. There are four types of final impression materials available: Polysulfide, polyether, condensation silicone, and addition silicone. In terms of stiffness and stability, the best choice is addition silicone, followed by polyether.

PREPARATION AND MATERIALS

Making final impressions is a two-person job. The assistant mixes. The dentist takes the impression. Mixing time is a minute or less for all final impression materials. Setting time averages 6 minutes for all, except polysulfide, which takes 10-20 minutes to set. If the base and catalyst come as two pastes, they are mixed either by swirling them together and smoothing them with a spatula, or by using an automix system. The automix system consists of extruder units with cartridges of the base and catalyst, which are mixed when a trigger is squeezed. Segregate the tooth for which the impression is taken by a retraction system. Rinse and dry. Insert a recently-mixed light-body impression material into the sulcus, around the tooth, and into adjacent areas. Mix the heavy-body material and place it into the impression tray. Load it in place over the light-body material. After setting, remove the impression. Examine and disinfect it. Placed it into a labeled precaution bag for transport to the laboratory.

GINGIVAL RETRACTION

Gingival retraction uses a cord to briefly push the gingival tissue away from a tooth and broaden the sulcus. Gingival retraction cords isolate a tooth for the final impression. When performing gingival retraction, first dry the tooth. Separate the quadrant with cotton rolls. Loop the retraction cord and slide it over the tooth. Push it into the sulcus in a clockwise motion with a cord-packing device. The end of the cord should end up on the facial side, where it remains sticking out; it may be placed into the sulcus. After several minutes, remove the retraction cord counterclockwise with cotton pliers. Dry the area and apply new cotton rolls. Procure the impression quickly. Sometimes, chemical retraction is used in conjunction with these procedures by initial use of a topical hemostatic solution, aluminum salt astringents, or epinephrine (an astringent and vasoconstrictor). Retraction can also be performed with a surgical knife or electric cauterizer.

OCCLUSAL REGISTRATIONS

Occlusal or bite registrations are impressions that document the centric relationship between a patient's maxillary and mandibular arches. The centric relationship is the position of optimally stable connection between occlusal surfaces of the two arches when the mouth is closed. Bite registrations are made of wax or paste, both of which do not flow easily. If wax is used, heat it for softening. Place wax directly onto the occlusal

92

surfaces. The patient bites down lightly into the wax until it cools. Remove the registration and store it Pastes set quickly, are odorless and tasteless, and conform easily to biting. Pastes have two cartridges or parts that are mixed. Spread paste right over the teeth or put in a gauze tray, then have the patient bite down for the impression.

<u>PROCEDURE</u>

Bite registrations are performed by the dental assistant under supervision, or by the dentist, aided by the assistant. Use either bite registration wax or polysiloxane. Sit the patient upright. Teach the patient how to bite in occlusion before the registration. If bite registration wax is used, determine the correct length, warm and soften it with water or a torch, and then place it on the mandibular occlusal edges. If polysiloxane is used, force the material through an extruder gun with a disposable tip, right onto the occlusal surfaces. The assistant watches to ensure the patient bites with proper occlusion, as previously directed. The patient holds the occlusion for a minute or two, while the wax cools, or until the polysiloxane hardens. Remove the bite material. Disinfect and label the impression. Store it for later use.

TOFFLEMIRE MATRIX ASSEMBLY

The universal Tofflemire matrix assembly is the most widely-used matrix retainer for amalgam restorations. The central frame is connected at one end to a clamp-like vise. The vise has a diagonal slot through it, to grip the ends of the matrix band. Guide slots orient the matrix band loop in the correct direction. A screw-like spindle is connected to the vise and fixes the bands in place. At the opposite end is the outer adjustment knob, which is used to tighten the spindle alongside the band. Internal to that is an inner knob, which slides, and can be used for adjustment. Tofflemire setups are viewed from a gingival or an occlusal aspect, meaning the diagonal and guide slots are or are not visible respectively.

PREPARATION FOR USE

When preparing the Tofflemire retainer and matrix band, hold the Tofflemire assembly in the left hand in a gingival aspect (slots toward the dental assistant or operator). Turn the outer knob clockwise until the spindle can be seen in the diagonal slot of the vise. Turn the inner knob until the vise is about 3/16 inch from the guide slots. Turn the outer knob counterclockwise, so the spindle is not visible in the diagonal slot. The dental assistant takes a matrix band, forming it first into a "smile" and then a loop. The occlusal edge makes the outer edge of the "smile." Insert the ends of the matrix band into the diagonal slot (occlusal edge on the bottom), while simultaneously threading the area closer to the loop into the guide slots. If the matrix band is for a tooth in the lower left or upper right quadrants, position the loop above the retainer. If the band is to a tooth in the lower right or upper left quadrant, face the loop downward. Secure the band by turning the outer knob clockwise. Adjust the loop size with the inner knob. The shape can be rounded by using the handle of a mouth mirror.

PLACEMENT AND REMOVAL

Place the Tofflemire matrix over the prepared tooth. The correct placement is with the smaller edge of the band toward the gums, the diagonal slot toward the gingiva, and the apparatus parallel to the buccal surface. Push the band loop through the interproximal surface. Center it on the buccal surface of the tooth. Tighten the using the inner knob of the Tofflemire apparatus. Check the margins between the matrix band and cavity preparation to ensure that the band is not too tight or loose; they should be approximately 1.0-1.5 mm at the gingival edge and a maximum of 2 mm at the occlusal edge. Use a ball burnisher to contour the band, so there is contact with contiguous teeth. Place interproximal wedges at the gingival margins. Check with an explorer to ensure there are no gaps. After the dentist performs the restoration, remove the wedge(s) with cotton pliers or a hemostat. Loosen the retainer with the outer knob. Lift it off. Remove the matrix band with cotton pliers.

ADDITIONAL MATRIX SYSTEMS

The main apparatuses other than the Tofflemire are the AutoMatrix, the plastic strip matrix, and sectional matrix systems.

- The **AutoMatrix** apparatus is convenient because it does not use a retainer. It comes with several sizes of conical bands that have tightening coils on the exterior for adjustment.
- **Plastic strip matrix systems** use thin, transparent strips, which are placed between the teeth, then around the preparation, and secured with a wedge. Secure the strip further after the restorative materials (not amalgam) are placed by pulling tightly and holding on or using a clip retainer. Plastic strips allow polymerizing light through. A variation is a crown matrix form, used for crowns on front teeth.
- **Sectional matrix systems** are comprised of relatively thick, contoured, oval matrix bands and rings to hold them. A discrete matrix band/ring pair is used for each tooth surface. Forceps are provided to open the rings. Wedges are put in between placement of the bands to position the rings. For pediatric patients, brass straight or curved T-bands or spot-welded matrix bands may be used.

TOPICAL AND LOCAL ANESTHETIC ADMINISTRATION

All anesthetics block nerve impulses, thus dulling pain sensations. The dentist or nurse spreads topical anesthetic directly over oral mucosa before injecting a local anesthetic. Topical preparations are usually ointments applied with a cotton swab, but they can be sprays, liquids, and patches. Local anesthetics are chemical amides and esters, and are injected in the proximity of the nerve associated with the tooth being treated. Local anesthetic agents have a particular timeframe after injection for induction of full numbing and later loss of numbing (duration). Local anesthetics are classified in terms of their duration as short-acting, intermediate-acting, or long-acting. Most procedures require the intermediate-acting duration of 2-4 hours. Most intermediate-acting and long-acting local anesthetic agents also contain small concentrations of vasoconstrictors, such as epinephrine, which decrease blood flow and bleeding to the region. These preparations are contraindicated in patients with hypertension, cardiovascular disease, liver or kidney disease, hyperthyroidism, or pregnancy.

ASSISTING WITH ADMINISTRATION

The assistant prepares local anesthetic. The dentist dries the injection site with a sterile gauze sponge and applies topical anesthetic with a cotton swab for one minute. The assistant transfers the syringe to the dentist, either beneath the patient's chin or behind the patient's head. Pass the syringe with the thumb ring toward the dentist, the bevel of the needle facing the alveolar bone, and the protective cap secure but loose enough to remove during the transfer. The dentist performs the injection. The assistant observes the patient for adverse reactions. The dentist replaces the needle guard by scooping or uses a mechanical recapping device. If the patient requires additional anesthesia, the assistant swaps in a new cartridge and transfers it, as above. Replace the recapped syringe on the tray. Rinse and evacuate the patient's mouth at the conclusion of the procedure. Remove the capped needle by unscrewing or cutting it off and discarding it in the sharps container. Remove the cartridge by retraction of the piston and deposit it in a medical waste container. Sterilize the syringe.

LOCAL INJECTION METHODS

Local anesthesia methods fall into 3 categories:

- **Local infiltration**: The dentist injects the agent into gingival tissues near the small terminal nerve branches, numbing the necessary tooth and/or gums. The anesthetic can also be injected using pressure right into the periodontal ligament.

- **Field block**: The dentist injects the agent at the larger terminal nerve limbs near the apex of the tooth. The advantages of field block technique are avoidance of messages to the central nervous system and swift onset of action.
- **Nerve block**: The dentist introduces the agent close to a main nerve trunk, which eliminates pain sensations to the brain, and over a relatively large local area.

ANESTHETIC SYRINGE

An anesthetic or aspirating syringe consists of the barrel, the disposable needle cannula, and the anesthetic cartridge. Both reusable stainless steel and disposable plastic syringes are available. The operator braces the thumb in a ring at one end and the index and middle fingers on grips. The barrel of the syringe is a long shaft, open on one side for cartridge insertion, with an observation window on the opposite side. Inside the barrel is a plunger or piston rod attached to a barbed-tipped harpoon at its end. There is a threaded tip at the end of the syringe, to which the sterile disposable needle (cannula) is attached. The cannula has a short cartridge end attached to needle hub, which is either pushed or screwed onto the threaded tip of the syringe. The slanted tip (bevel) on the other end penetrates tissue. The segment between is the shank; the solution travels through its internal, hollow lumen. Anesthetic cartridges containing the agent are made of glass. They have a rubber stopper end to attach to the harpoon of the syringe and an aluminum cap end for needle insertion.

PREPARATION OF THE ANESTHETIC SYRINGE

The dental assistant is responsible for preparation of the anesthetic syringe outside the viewing area of the patient. Take the sterile syringe out of its autoclave pouch. Hold the syringe in the left hand. Withdraw the piston rod by pulling back on the thumb ring. With the right hand, position the rubber stopper end of the cartridge into the barrel of the syringe. Connect the harpoon to the rubber stopper using medium pressure on the finger ring. Take off the cap of the syringe end of the disposable needle and screw or push it onto the threaded tip of the syringe. Remove the needle guard. Check for correct operation by forcing out a small amount of reagent, while holding the syringe upright.

CARE AND HANDLING

Sanitize the harpoon of a stainless-steel reusable aspirating syringe after each use and autoclave the entire syringe. From time to time, lubricate parts or the harpoon may require exchange. Discard plastic syringes in a biohazard container. Discard the cannula into a sharps container after normal use, if there is any evidence of a broken seal, or if tissue penetration occurs more than four times. Anesthetic cartridges come in sterilized, sealed blister packs and should be stored at room temperature in a dark area. Inspect the cartridge before use. Discard a cartridge that has expired or has large bubbles, rust, corrosion, or extruded stoppers. Dispose of a used cartridge in a tamper-proof container approved by the pharmacist. Be aware that addicts scavenge garbage for residual drugs.

CODING ANESTHETIC CARTRIDGES

Anesthetic cartridges labeled with the American Dental Association's seal of acceptance have standardized color codes on a band near the rubber stopper. Sometimes, the aluminum cap is also colored similarly, although it may be silver. There is unambiguous, black lettering on the cartridge, identifying the agent and concentration. Some other cartridges have colored writing on the side. The **ADA-approved color schemes** are as follows:

- Articaine 4% with epinephrine 1:100,000 or epinephrine 1:200,000 – silver or gold, respectively.
- Bupivacaine with epinephrine – blue.
- Lidocaine 2% either plain or with epinephrine 1:50,000 or 1:100,000 - light blue, green, or red, respectively.
- Mepivacaine 3% or 2% with levonordefrin 1:20,000 - tan or brown, respectively.
- Prilocaine 4% without or with epinephrine 1:200,000 – yellow or black, respectively.

95

Maxillary Local Anesthesia Injection Sites

Local infiltration or field block techniques desensitize individual maxillary teeth when injected near the apex of specific anterior teeth. A nasopalatine nerve block, in which the lingual tissue next to the incisive papilla is injected, numbs the front of the hard palate between the canines. The greater palatine nerve block uses injection near the second molar and in front of the greater palatine foramen to block sensations to the entire hard palate and soft tissues posterior to the canine. A maxillary nerve block is an anesthetic injection into the mucobuccal fold near the second molar, which blocks one entire oral quadrant, and the skin on that side of the nose, cheek, upper lip and lower eyelid. The anterior superior alveolar, middle superior alveolar, and posterior superior alveolar nerve blocks involve injection into the fold at the first premolar, fold at the second premolar, and near the apex of the second molar respectively; each affects two or three close teeth and tissues.

Mandibular Local Anesthesia Injection Sites

Local infiltration or field block techniques desensitize individual mandibular teeth by injecting near the apex of specific anterior teeth. Nerve blocks numb larger areas. Introduction of anesthetic into the mucobuccal fold in front of the mental foramen is an incisive nerve block, affecting teeth from the central incisors back to the premolars and the cheeks. Inferior alveolar nerve block or mandibular block dulls an entire quadrant, including teeth, mucous membranes, the front portion of the tongue, mouth floor, and soft tissues. It involves injection into the mandibular ramus, behind the retromolar pad. Lingual nerve block means the anesthetic is introduced lingually to the mandibular ramus and next to the maxillary tuberosity, affecting the mandibular teeth, the side of the tongue, and lingual tissues on one side. Buccal nerve block means the agent is injected into the mucous membrane behind the last available molar just to numb buccal tissue. Mental nerve block involves an injection between the apices of the premolars, to target the premolars, canines, and close facial tissues.

Alternative Methods of Administering Local Anesthetics

Alternative methods for the administration of local anesthetics include the following:

- One relatively painless and fast method is **intraosseous anesthesia**, in which the cortical plate of bone is first perforated using a solid needle connected to a slow handpiece. The anesthetic agent is then injected into the hole, using an 8 mm, 27-gauge needle.
- **Periodontal ligament injection** entails insertion into the gingival sulcus. A special injection syringe is used. It is gun-like, and the syringe is attached externally.
- Another technique is **intrapulpal injection** right into the pulp chamber or root canal, using a 25-gauge or 27-gauge needle.
- There are **computer-operated delivery systems** available for administration of local anesthesia, which offer the ability to control parameters, such as rate of delivery and pressure.
- There are also systems that deliver **electronic impulses**, instead of chemical preparations, in cases where chemicals are contraindicated.

Possible Complications of Topical and Local Anesthesia

Topical anesthetics can cause allergic and toxic reactions. Swelling, erythema, ulcerations, and difficulty swallowing or breathing up to a day or more after application indicate an allergic reaction, which should be treated with antihistamines. Toxic reactions are central nervous system (CNS) complications due to an overdose of topical anesthetic. The patient initially becomes talkative and anxious. His or her blood pressure and pulse rates increase, but later the patient becomes hypotensive and has a weak and thready pulse. Excessive administration of local anesthetic drugs can produce similar toxic reactions and paresthesia (numbness). Document reports of paresthesia because nerve damage can be permanent.

DRUG ADMINISTRATION ROUTES IN DENTISTRY

These are the routes of drug administration in the dental office:

- **Oral** as pills or liquids for prophylactic antibiotics.
- **Topical administration** for anesthesia (ointment or cream applied to the skin or oral mucosa).
- **Gas inhalation,** particularly nitrous oxide.
- **Injections**: Intravenous (into the vein for rapid response); intramuscular (into muscle); subcutaneous (underneath the skin) or intradermal (between skin layers).
- **Sublingual** (under the tongue, as with nitroglycerine and fentanyl).
- **Transdermal skin patch,** releasing medication at a steady rate, as with nitroglycerine cream or nicotine patch.
- **Rectal administration** of suppositories or enemas for patients at home before or after the procedure, e.g., Gravol for nausea or fentanyl for severe pain in cancer patients.

BLEACHING
IN-OFFICE VITAL TEETH BLEACHING AND AT HOME BLEACHING

Teeth can be bleached to remove both extrinsic stains from habits like coffee-drinking, and intrinsic stains from root canals, tetracycline use, damage, or fluorosis. Use sodium perborate, hydrogen peroxide, or carbamide peroxide. In-office bleaching of vital teeth is performed by the dentist with assistance. Smear protective gel on adjacent tissues. Isolate the area with a rubber dam and a ligature of waxed floss surrounding each tooth. Polish teeth crowns with pumice or prophy gel. Mix bleaching materials according to the manufacturer's directions until thick. Apply directly onto the facial and lingual facades of the teeth or in a tray. Some materials require use of heat or light, or reapplication of fresh gel every 10 minutes. After bleaching, rinse. Remove the dam and ligatures. Polish teeth with a resin polishing cup or prophy paste containing fluoride. Home bleaching involves taking an alginate impression, from which a cast and custom trays are made. The patient uses the trays at home with a bleaching kit, as directed.

NON-VITAL BLEACHING

Non-vital bleaching means lightening endodontically treated (usually root canal) or non-vital teeth. The dentist bleaches teeth with assistance. Apply protective gel to soft tissues. Place a rubber dam and a ligature of waxed dental floss around the indicated tooth or teeth. The dentist removes the crown restoration and debris and may scrub the open crown. The dentist applies a 2-3 mm layer of base cement, light-cured resin ionomer, or bonded composite to the top of the root canal to ensure bleach does not enter the root. There are two options for the actual non-vital bleaching:

- **Gel bleaching** in the office, which entails filling the chamber with bleaching gel for 30 minutes, with bleach changes every 10 minutes (and possibly heat application), followed by cotton roll isolation and placement of a temporary crown. Requires 3 appointments spaced 3-7 days apart.
- **Walking bleaching**, this is placement of a viscous paste of hydrogen peroxide and/or sodium perborate into the crown and covering it with temporary cement. Requires 3 appointments, spaced 2-5 days apart.

ARMAMENTARIUM FOR DENTAL PROCEDURES
TOOTH DESENSITIZATION, TOOTH EXTRACTION, AND TOOTH IMPACTION

Armamentarium refers to the supplies, equipment, and medicine used as part of medical/dental treatment. When utilizing the four-handed dentistry technique, the certified dental assistant should lay out the instruments and tools on the tray according to the order of use, which will vary depending on the type of treatment. The table with the instrument tray should be positioned so that the medical assistant can easily reach the instruments without changing position. Setups may vary according to preference.

Procedure	Armamentarium
Tooth desensitization	Desensitizing agent (fluoride gel, sealant, dentin bonding agents, potassium nitrate corticosteroid), application brush.
Tooth extraction	Basic setup (mouth, mirror, cotton pliers, explorer). Anesthetic tray (Syringe, needle with recapping device, anesthetic agent, cotton-tip applicator, local topical anesthesia). Extraction forceps or dental elevator, curette (for scraping socket), suture materials (if indicated) with needle holder and suture scissors, hemostat, gauze.
Tooth impaction	Basic setup, Anesthetic tray, periosteal elevators, curettes, forceps, sutures, needles, surgical HVE tip, blade holder and appropriate blades, suture scissors, hemostats, lip retractors

TOOTH IMPLANT, INCISION/DRAINAGE, DRESSING PLACEMENT/REMOVAL, AND DRY SOCKET

Procedure	Armamentarium
Tooth implant	Basic setup (mouth, mirror, cotton pliers, explorer). Anesthetic tray (Syringe, needle with recapping device, anesthetic agent, cotton-tip applicator, local topical anesthesia). IV solution, surgical HVE tip, sterile gauze and cotton pellets, irrigation syringe, sterile saline, low-speed handpiece, sterile template, sterile surgical drilling unit, scalpel, blades, periosteal elevator, rongeurs, surgical curette, tissue forceps, tissue scissors, cheek retractor, tongue retractor, hemostat, bite-block, oral rinse, Betadine, implant instrument kit, implant kit, suture setup.
Incision/ drainage	Armamentarium for performing an incision or drainage includes basic setup, anesthetic tray, and Bard Parker blade.
Periodontal surgical dressing placement/ removal	Placement: Basic setup, plastic instrument, gauze sponge, tongue depressors, mixing pad, periodontal dressing base/accelerator, cotton tip applicators, lubricant, saline, cold water, Gelfoam®. Removal: Basic setup, suture scissors, plastic instrument, floss, saline solution, HVE tips
Dry socket	The armamentarium needed for dry socket includes: basic setup, cotton balls, 2 x 2 gauze, topical anesthetic Eugenol, perioprobe, scissors.

NON-REMOVABLE DENTURE PLACEMENT

Armamentarium required for non-removable denture placement includes the following:

- **Chlorhexidine gluconate:** Used as a one-minute pre-rinse to disinfect.
- **Surgery setup pack**: Necessary PPE, drapes, and covers.
- **Paper products:** Gauze, cotton rolls, cotton-tipped applicators.
- **Suction tips:** Sterilized tips for saliva ejector and suction.
- **Sterile titanium box**: To hold the implant if it needs to be removed and reinserted.
- **Antibiotic ointment:** Applied to the abutment threads to aid in healing.
- **Blood pressure cuff:** To monitor blood pressure during the procedure.
- **Basic setup:** 2 dental mirrors, 2 cotton pliers, a periodontal probe, a hemostat, suction holder, surgical scissors, retractors, and scalpels.
- **Local anesthetic:** Medications and syringes should be available.
- **Surgical handpiece and motor:** With a sterile saline pump with tubing for irrigation.
- **Drill kits:** Arranged in order of the recommended drilling sequence based upon the implant diameter.
- **Digital caliper:** Used to measure drill stop lengths.
- **X-ray sensor holder:** With a sterilized cover.

- **Tissue punch kit:** Provides access to the implant site with minimal trauma.
- **Backup dental implants:** In case one is dropped.
- **Healing abutments:** Various diameters.
- **Provisional crowns:** Including composite, primers, condensers, bonding instruments, and a dental curing light.

OCCLUSAL EQUILIBRIUM/ADJUSTMENT

The purpose of occlusal equilibration is to equalize occlusal stress in order to create simultaneous occlusal contacts. The armamentarium required for this procedure are:

- **Chlorhexidine gluconate**: Used as a one-minute pre-rinse to disinfect.
- **Surgery setup pack**: Necessary PPE, drapes, and covers.
- **Paper products**: Gauze, cotton rolls, cotton-tipped applicators.
- **Suction tips**: Sterilized tips for saliva ejector and suction.
- **Basic setup**: 2 dental mirrors, 2 cotton pliers, a periodontal probe, a hemostat, suction holder, surgical scissors, retractors, and scalpels.
- **Blood pressure cuff**: To monitor blood pressure during the procedure.
- **Medications for sedation**: The procedure may be performed under sedation to make the patient more comfortable.
- **Small diamond wheel stone**: Used with a 12-sided football-shaped finishing burr for precise reshaping.
- **Marking ribbons**: Red and black marking ribbons are secured in Miller ribbon holders.
- **Topical fluoride**: May be administered to strengthen the enamel to better resist tooth decay and to decrease sensitivity.
- **Restorative dentistry materials**: Necessary if the patient will be receiving any onlays, fillings, or crowns following the procedure.

ROOT PLANING AND CURETTAGE

Armamentarium for root planing includes:

- **Topical and local anesthetic**: Medications, a long needle, a short needle, and syringes should be available.
- **Mouth mirror**: For visualization or the oral cavity and to reflect light.
- **Periodontal probe**: Used to measure the depth of the gingival sulcus and to evaluate for any recession of the gingival tissue.
- **Scalars and curettes**: Used to remove calculus from the surface of the teeth. Curettes can also be used below the gum line, but scalars are only used above the gingival tissue.
- **Cavitron tips**: Uses high frequency sound waves to clean tartar from the surface of the teeth.

Armamentarium for curettage includes:

- **Topical and local anesthetic**: Medications, a long needle, a short needle, and syringes should be available.
- **Mouth mirror**: For visualization or the oral cavity and to reflect light.
- **Periodontal probe**: Used to measure the depth of the gingival sulcus and to evaluate for any recession of the gingival tissue.
- **Gracey curettes**: Stainless steel instruments used to remove calculus. Designed with a cutting edge that can be used above and below the gingival tissue.

ARMAMENTARIUM FOR A GENERAL ORAL EXAM

The armamentarium required for the general oral exam include:

- **Setup pack:** Necessary PPE, drapes, and covers.
- **Paper products***: Gauze, cotton rolls, cotton-tipped applicators.
- **Mouth mirror:** For visualization or the oral cavity and to reflect light.
- **Explorer:** Used to examine tooth surfaces, evaluate root surfaces, remove cement, and to check fit margins.
- **Cotton pliers:** For placement and removal of small objects from the oral cavity.
- **Periodontal probe:** Used to measure the depth of the gingival sulcus and to evaluate for any recession of the gingival tissue.
- **Saliva ejector tip:** Uses low-volume evacuation to remove saliva to dry the procedure field.
- **Oral evacuator tip***: Uses high-volume evaluation to remove blood, saliva, and debris. This can help to remove microbes. May also be helpful with retraction to protect the tongue and cheek.
- **Light:** Used with a disposable mouthpiece to adequately illuminate the oral cavity, aspirate, protect the throat, and retrace the tongue and cheek all in one device.
- **Anesthetic syringe:** Aspiration is performed to check for blood drawn into the syringe before local anesthesia is delivered.
- **Intraligament syringe***: Used to inject anesthesia into the periodontal ligament space to supplement a nerve block.

ARMAMENTARIUM FOR ORAL SURGERY

Armamentarium required for **oral surgery** includes:

- **Chlorhexidine gluconate**: Used as a one-minute pre-rinse to disinfect.
- **Surgery setup pack**: Necessary PPE, drapes, and covers.
- **Paper products**: Gauze, cotton rolls, cotton-tipped applicators.
- **Suction tips**: Sterilized tips for saliva ejector and suction.
- **Blood pressure cuff**: To monitor blood pressure during the procedure.
- **Basic setup**: 2 dental mirrors, 2 cotton pliers, a periodontal probe, a hemostat, suction holder, surgical scissors, retractors, and scalpels.
- **Local anesthetic**: Medications and syringes should be available.
- **Retractors:** Retracts soft tissues (cheek and tongue) to better visualize the oral cavity.
- **Bite block**: Holds the mouth open wide comfortably.
- **Periosteal elevators**: Used to release the soft tissue surrounding the tooth.
- **Forceps**: There are several different styles, each used for grasping tissue.
- **Rongeur forceps**: Used to cut bone.
- **Chisel and mallet**: Used to remove bone.
- **Bone file**: Used for final smoothing.
- **Burr and hand piece**: Used in the final step of removing bone.
- **Curettes**: Used to remove small amounts of soft tissue.
- **Suturing materials**: Used for closing the surgical wound.

CONTROLLING BLEEDING AFTER ORAL/DENTAL SURGERY

Methods to control bleeding after surgery include:

- **Compression**: A wet piece of gauze, or paper towel if the patient does not have gauze at home, can be folded and placed over the surgical site. The patient should then bite down to apply pressure for at least 45 minutes.
- **Elevation**: The patient should keep his head elevated above the level of his heart. Due to gravity, bleeding will increase when laying down or having the head dependent.

- **Black tea bags**: Wetting a black tea bag and biting down on it over the surgical site can decrease bleeding. Black tea contains tannic acid, which works as an anticoagulant and can decrease bleeding.
- **Rest**: Resting can decrease complications from oral surgery. Being overly active or engaging in strenuous activities can increase the risk for bleeding.
- **Be careful with eating and drinking**: Do not use a straw to drink liquids for several days following oral surgery because this can dislodge the blood clot and increase bleeding. Smoking, drinking carbonated or hot beverages, and eating rough or crunchy foods can also dislodge the clot and increase bleeding.

COMMON POSTOPERATIVE COMPLICATIONS

The most common postoperative complications following oral surgery are dry socket and postoperative infection.

- **Dry socket**: A dry socket develops when the blood clot after a tooth extraction is dislodged or dissolves. Risk factors include smoking, using a straw, poor oral hygiene, and birth control pills. The patient will have significant pain at the site or a sore throat. On exam, the GCA will see a dry socket without a blood clot and white bone. This is treated by cleaning the socket and placing a gauze strip impregnated with clove oil in the socket. If there is an increased risk for infection, the dentist may prescribe antibiotics.
- **Postoperative infection:** Extensive oral surgery, poor oral hygiene, smoking, and diabetes are risk factors for post-op infection. There will be pain at the operative site and a bad taste in the mouth. On exam, the GCA will see redness and swelling at the surgical site, and there may be purulent drainage present. This often produces a bad odor. The dentist may prescribe antibiotics, or if severe, the wound may be opened and irrigated.

NITROUS OXIDE SEDATION FOR ORAL PROCEDURES

Analgesics are agents that relieve pain without loss of consciousness. Nitrous oxide (N_2O) is an analgesic dispensed simultaneously with oxygen (O_2) gas through a small nosepiece, connected via tubing to a tank. The inhaled gases migrate through the nasopharynx, the respiratory chambers, and eventually reach the alveoli in the lungs. The gasses are exchanged between the alveoli and the blood plasma and red cells. The circulatory system transports the gases by the blood to the brain, where the analgesic effect is initiated. Nitrous oxide and oxygen together have mild pharmacologic activity in the central nervous system. They create a state of calmness for the patient, called sedation. The setup generally includes an inside mask for inhalation of the gases, an outer mask attached to an external reservoir bag, and a vacuum to carry away exhaled and excess gas.

DISPENSATION AND MONITORING

Depending on the state, these functions may be done by the dental assistant under supervision of the dentist, or as a cooperative effort. The assistant is responsible for rechecking equipment, gas levels in the tanks, and preparing the patient. The dentist explains the procedure and hazards involved with the patient. Once the dentist has explained the procedure and potential hazards, ask the patient to sign an informed consent form. Tilt the patient back in the chair. Attach a sterile nitrous mask to the tubing. Connect it to the tanks and place the mask over the patient's nose. Tell the patient to breathe slowly through his or her nose. When indicated by the dentist, administer oxygen alone for one minute, at a rate of at least 5 L/min, to determine the normal tidal volume. Administer nitrous oxide in 500 mL to 1 L increments per minute, with equivalent reduction of oxygen flow. Observe patient response to determine the optimal mixture that provides sedation, without impeding cognition. The dentist gives local anesthetic a few minutes after nitrous oxide administration is initiated.

RECOVERY

Turn off the nitrous oxide under the dentist's direction. Allow the patient to receive only oxygen for about 5 minutes to stave off diffusion hypoxia, the inadequate supply of oxygen to bodily tissues. Remove the patient's mask and tilt the chair upright to avoid postural hypotension or fainting. Do not dismiss the patient until he or she feels clear-headed (usually a few minutes). Chart the nitrous oxide administration, including baseline levels of both gases, and the patient's reactions. A good method of judging the psychomotor ability of the patient is to give a Trieger test prior to administration and after recovery. The Trieger test involves connecting a pattern of dots. The patient completes the test in the upright position. Disinfect the connecting tubing after use. Depending on office procedures, the masks may be discarded, or given to the patient for later reuse.

SAFETY CONSIDERATIONS

The American Dental Association suggests that personnel in dental offices who administer nitrous oxide be monitored twice a year by dosimetry or infrared spectrophotometry. Nitrous oxide is associated with infertility problems.

Use nitrous oxide for:

- Apprehensive patients
- Patient with sensitive gag reflexes
- Heart patients, who benefit from supplemental oxygen and reduction of stress

DO NOT administer nitrous oxide to:

- Pregnant women in the first trimester
- Infertile individuals undergoing in-vitro fertilization procedures
- Neurology patients
- Drug abusers
- Psychiatric patients
- Immunocompromised patients in danger of bone marrow suppression
- Mouth breathers

TYPES OF PAIN IN DENTAL PATIENTS

The type and location of pain can help to determine the pain's underlying cause. The certified dental assistant should record the exact description of the pain and the degree of pain using the 1 to 10 scale and response to treatment and/or pain medication. Different types of pain include:

- **Acute pain:** The central part of the tooth, the pulp, contains nerve endings, and when the pulp becomes inflamed, because of a cavity or infection, the patient may experience severe pain. The pain may be localized to one tooth or to an area of the mouth.
- **Hot/Cold sensitivity (short-duration):** This may result from an exposed root or a small or loose cavity and may occur for a short period after recent dental work.
- **Sharp pain with pressure:** This may indicate tooth decay or a loose filling.
- **Persistent pain after contact with hot/cold foods:** This type of pain often indicates that the root is dying and a root canal is necessary.
- **Aching in sinus areas:** This may indicate a problem in an upper back tooth or in the sinuses.

DENTAL PROPHYLAXIS

ARMAMENTARIUM

Dental prophylaxis means preventing dental disease by identifying and removing plaque and debris from tooth surfaces. The armamentarium suggested for routine prophylaxis consists of various sickle scalers, a universal curette, an explorer, floss, a saliva ejector and HVE tip, a Dappen dish, disclosing solution, air and water syringe tips, cotton swabs, gauze sponges, prophy paste, and angle and ring holders. If root planing or smoothing is to be performed, include several Gracey curettes and a setup for local anesthesia, including the anesthetic.

GENERAL PROCEDURES

Routine dental prophylaxis consists of an assessment and a treatment phase. During the assessment phase, the assistant applies disclosing agent to the patient's teeth to identify plaque accumulation. The treatment phase has four parts:

- **Scaling or scraping** off undesirable substances on the surfaces of teeth, such as hard calculus and softer plaque with various scalers, and using the explorer to check subgingival portions. The dental assistant aids the dentist by using the oral evacuator or gauze sponges. Root planing may be performed now or scheduled separately.
- **Coronal polishing** is performed with a dental handpiece and prophy paste or an air-powder abrasive polisher, to remove further plaque and stains and leave a smooth surface. Again, the assistant aids with evacuation.
- **Flossing** is performed to guarantee plaque removal between teeth.
- **Fluoride treatment** is an elective procedure.

TYPES OF AVAILABLE SCALERS, CURETTES, AND EXPLORERS

Scalers are hand-held instruments that remove undesirable substances from tooth surfaces. Most scalers used for routine prophylaxis are either sickle or curette scalers.

- **Sickle scalers** have long tapered tips with pointed toes. They are suitable for scaling under interproximal contact areas in the front of the mouth. Common sickle scalers include single-ended and double-ended straight sickles and a curved straight sickle (usually two or more curved cutting edges).
- **Curette scalers** can scale all tooth surfaces and are especially useful for removing subgingival calculus and root planing. They have rounded tips and backs and cutting edges. A universal curette is often employed for routine prophylaxis. It is straight and the entire edge is used to cut. Gracey curettes are designed to scale specific tooth surfaces or for root planing. They are curved at the end and only one side and the tip are used to cut. Gracey curettes are designated by their angles at either end, ranging from 1 for anterior teeth to 16 for posterior teeth surfaces.

Dental explorers have very fine tips. They are used to check for calculus in subgingival regions during scaling.

ULTRASONIC SCALERS

Manual scalers have straight or curved sickles and pointed tips at each end; they are used most often to remove supragingival calculus. An alternative is the **ultrasonic scaler** (Cavitron), which removes heavy calculus and stain from tooth surfaces, cement, and bonding substances used in orthodontic work. An ultrasonic scaler uses high-frequency sound waves, which it translates into mechanical energy, in the form of high-speed vibrations at its tip. Water ejects at the tip to control heat buildup. The combination of vibrational energy and water facilitates thorough removal of debris. There are universal tips and narrower, slim line tips available. There are also sonic scalers, which are attached to the dental unit handpiece, and use air to remove calculus. Both have pen-like structures attached to their tips.

COMMONLY PRESCRIBED MEDICATIONS IN DENTISTRY

ANTIBIOTICS

Antibiotics treat bacterial infections. Broad-spectrum antibiotics kill many microorganisms, including helpful normal flora. Penicillin, and its derivatives amoxicillin and ampicillin, are broad-spectrum antibiotics. An antibiotic can only kill organisms that are sensitive to it; many organisms are now resistant due to overuse of antibiotics. Antibiotics can cause allergic skin or respiratory reactions, which are treated with antihistamines. Common antibiotic side-effects are nausea, diarrhea, and yeast infections due to disruption of normal flora. Prophylactic ampicillin taken 2 hours before teeth scaling prevent heart complications (for bacterial endocarditis) in patients who had rheumatic fever. The penicillin derivative oxacillin is for Staphylococcus aureus infections. Penicillin G is only for Gram-positive bacteria. People with penicillin allergies are generally given erythromycin, instead. Tetracyclines are antibiotics that discolor emerging teeth and precipitate kidney failure.

ANTICHOLINERGIC DRUGS, ANALGESICS, AND TRANQUILIZERS

Anticholinergic drugs block nerve impulses. They reduce lung secretions while the patient is under general anesthesia, treat bradycardia, and dilate the pupils of the eyes. Dentists give anticholinergics to inhibit the patient's salivation while an impression is made. The drugs of choice are atropine sulfate or propantheline bromide.

Any drug that relieves pain but does not cause unconsciousness is an **analgesic**. Non-narcotic analgesics include ibuprofen and acetaminophen; they are for mild to moderate pain. Narcotic analgesics produce stupor and sleep and are for moderate to severe pain. Dental narcotics include morphine sulphate and meperidine hydrochloride. Aspirin is avoided because it inhibits healing due to its blood-thinning and clot-suppressing qualities. It also irritates the stomach.

Tranquilizers, particularly diazepam (Valium), are often given prior to procedures to relax anxious patients.

TOPICAL FLUORIDE APPLICATION

Topical fluoride application in the dental office is usually done using 2% sodium fluoride, 8% stannous fluoride, or 1.23% acidulated phosphate fluoride (APF). Sodium fluoride preparations are stable, do not cause discoloration, and are gentle to tissues, but they must be applied weekly for four weeks each time. Stannous fluoride has many disadvantages, including instability, a caustic taste, and discoloration due to tin in the preparation. Thus, the APF preparations are used most often, as they are non-irritating, have a mild taste, do not cause discoloration, and need to be used only once or twice a year. Keep APF preparations in plastic containers to discourage acidification.

PROCEDURE

The dental assistant performs fluoride application after a rubber cup polish. Never apply fluoride before placement of orthodontic bands or sealants, as it deters adhesion.

1. Don personal protective equipment (PPE).
2. Select fluoride trays that encompass all erupted teeth but do not extend beyond them.
3. Fill each tray one-third full with the fluoride gel or foam.
4. Dry the patient's teeth with the air syringe.
5. Position the trays in the patient's mouth and shift them up and down to distribute the fluoride preparation.
6. Keep the saliva ejector in the patient's mouth throughout the procedure to remove saliva and moisture. Instruct the patient to keep his or her mouth closed for the recommended time.
7. Remove the ejector trays. Evacuate the patient's mouth.
8. Advise the patient not to eat, drink, or rinse for 30 minutes following the application.
9. Using overgloves, chart the application and any consequences.
10. An alternative to foam or gel application is the use of a fluoride rinse after tooth brushing or a rubber cup polish.

CORONAL POLISH

A coronal polish is a process by which soft deposits and extrinsic stains are removed from the clinical crown of teeth with abrasive material. The dental assistant will require a dental handpiece and a rubber cup for easiest application, but can substitute brushes, dental tape, or floss, if necessary. Perform coronal polishing after hard deposits are scaled away. The coronal polish is **performed for three main reasons**:

- It helps the patient maintain clean teeth and sustain good oral hygiene.
- The procedure enhances fluoride absorption and discourages buildup of new deposits.
- It prepares teeth for use of enamel sealant and for positioning of orthodontic brackets and bands.

In many states, the dental assistant or hygienist can legally perform a coronal polish. If the dentist delegates polishing to the dental assistant, the dental assistant should seat himself or herself in the appropriate operator's position.

ABRASIVE USE

Abrasives are rough, particulate materials that create friction to smooth out the tooth surface during coronal polishing. Abrasives come in powder or paste form, and usually contain water, a binder, and a humectant for water retention, coloring and flavoring. Available abrasive agents include fluoride pastes, flour of pumice, chalk, zirconium silicate, and tin oxide. The rate of abrasion for a particular type of abrasive is dependent upon the characteristics of the abrasive material, the speed of the handpiece, the pressure and amount applied, and the moisture level. Abrasion increases if the particles are sharp-edged, firmer, stronger, larger in size, or resist embedding in the tooth's surface.

MATERIALS REMOVED AND NOT REMOVED BY A CORONAL POLISH

A coronal polish can remove soft deposits and extrinsic stains. Calculus (hardened, calcified deposits) and intrinsic stains cannot be eliminated through coronal polishing. The dentist removes calculus prior to the polish via scaling. Intrinsic stains are within the tooth structure and are usually permanent. For example, dental fluorosis, metal poisoning, tetracycline exposure in childhood or pulp damage cannot be removed by polishing. There are **five types of soft deposits removed by coronal polishing:**

- **Materia alba**, a less structured precursor to plaque development, which contains microorganisms and leads to tooth decay, gingivitis and periodontal disease.
- **Plaque**, which contains microorganisms that damage teeth and gums.
- Food debris.
- **Pellicle**, a thin film containing saliva and sulcular fluid
- **Extrinsic stains** from endogenous sources can be removed by coronal polishing. For example, yellow or brown stains associated with poor dental hygiene and tobacco can be polished away.

PROCEDURES FOR PROPHY BRUSH USE

Prophy brushes are soft, supple brushes made of nylon or natural bristles. Perform prophy brushing after the rubber cup polish. Attach one brush to a low-speed dental handpiece. Only polish the enamel surfaces of teeth. Do not allow the brush to contact the gums. Spread prophy paste over the brush. Start polishing the most posterior tooth. For the back teeth, the major objective is to polish the occlusal surfaces. For each posterior tooth, direct the brush from the central fossa first, toward the mesial buccal cusp tip, and then toward the distal buccal cusp. For the anterior teeth, position the brush in the lingual pit above the cingulum, and then toward the incisal edge during polishing. All lingual surfaces with pits or grooves should be polished similarly. At the end, rinse the patient's mouth and clear it of debris.

PROCEDURES FOR RUBBERY PROPHY CUP USE

Procedures for coronal polishing using a rubber prophy cup are as follows:

1. Apply disclosing agent to teeth with a cotton applicator for easier plaque recognition.
2. Ask the patient if he/she is allergic to latex rubber; if yes, choose a synthetic rubber cup.
3. Attach a prophy cup to a low-speed dental handpiece at an angle.
4. Place abrasive agent into the cup; if more than one type is required, use an individual cup for each.
5. Hold the handpiece with cup in a modified pen grasp.
6. Apply foot pressure on the rheostat to regulate speed.
7. Polish one quadrant at a time. Position the cup near the sulcus of the gum on the mesial or distal surface of a tooth. Employ gentle pressure to bend the cup. Work toward the occlusal or incisal edge. Lift the cup a little. Duplicate the procedure on the other side of the tooth.
8. Frequently rinse and remove debris during the procedure.
9. Repeat on the adjacent tooth, until all teeth are polished.

10. Reapply disclosing agent to check work.
11. Rinse.

SUPPLEMENTAL EQUIPMENT

The dental assistant will also require a good dental light, cheek retractors, a mouth mirror, an air-water syringe, an evacuator, a saliva ejector, and wipes to polish teeth correctly. **Supplementary polishing aids** that might be useful during the final phase are dental tape and floss. One aid that is useful for patients with orthodontic work is a bridge threader, a plastic piece with a loop through which dental tape or floss is passed. A threader allows the assistant to work around orthodontic or other appliances. Various grit size abrasive polishing strips can be employed on enamel facades. Soft wood points can be used with abrasives. Small interproximal brushes can be utilized. The latter are especially useful for navigation around orthodontic appliances and other contact areas.

DISCLOSING AGENTS TO ASSESS EFFECTIVENESS OF CORONAL POLISHING

Disclosing agents are temporary coloring agents in chewable tablet and liquid forms, usually red. Disclosing agents adhere to plaque to help the assistant and patient identify it much more easily. The assistant uses agents to check coronal polishing technique. When the dental assistant or hygienist uses disclosing agent in the office, he or she should wear Personal Protective Equipment (PPEs). Spread petroleum jelly over the patient's lips and tooth-colored restorations. Decant agent into a Dappen dish. Paint the liquid agent onto the teeth with a cotton tip applicator or put it on the tongue to spread. Alternatively, ask the patient to chew a tablet and swirl it around in the mouth. Rinse and withdraw excess solution. Give the patient a hand mirror. The dental assistant may use a mouth mirror and air-water syringe. Chart the plaque present, using an overglove. Educate the patient about oral hygiene. Disclosing agents encourage the patient to use good oral hygiene at home.

POLISHING WITH DENTAL TAPE OR DENTAL FLOSS

After performing a coronal polish using a prophy cup and a prophy brush, polish them interproximally with dental tape and floss. Cut a 12- to 18-inch piece of dental tape. Apply abrasive to the interproximal contact places between teeth with the finger or a cotton tip applicator. Work on one quadrant at a time. Manipulate the dental tape between the middle fingers on each hand. Insert the tape obliquely into the contact area, using a back-and-forth motion and light pressure, and then wrap the tape around the tooth. Polish the proximal surfaces of each tooth with the tape, moving along adjacent teeth. Rinse and evacuate the patient's mouth. Remove any remaining residue with dental floss and subsequent rinsing. Use unwaxed floss if the dentist will follow with a fluoride application afterwards, because waxed floss coats the teeth and deters fluoride absorption.

SELECTING AND MANIPULATING DENTAL FINISHING AND POLISHING AGENTS

Finishing agents include abrasives with a range of particles, beginning with coarse hard particles that are used to remove surface irregularities and to contour teeth and graduating to finer particles following a standard abrasive sequence with each abrasive rinsed completely from the teeth before use of a finer abrasive. Finishing may be used to smooth a surface after restoration. Agents include silicon carbide, aluminum oxide disks, flint, and iron oxide. Finishing abrasives are usually impregnated in plastic or paper discs for air-abrasion units. Finishing is usually combined with polishing to ensure that the surface is smooth, making the surface easier to clean and more resistant to corrosion. Fine polishing agents (abrasives 1-2 Mohs units harder than surface) may be used in discs or mixed with glycerine or water to make a slurry. Polishing abrasives include calcite, Kieselguhr, pumice, rouge, silex, tin oxide, tripoli, zirconium silicate, and a number of prophylactic pastes. A slow speed should be used on the handpiece for polishing to minimize trauma.

SELECTING AND MANIPULATING DENTAL CLEANING AGENTS

Cleaning agents are used primarily to remove staining, biofilms, and soft deposits (after hard deposits are removed). Cleaning agents include abrasives and chemicals. Cleaning may include coronal polishing, which helps to eliminate biofilms and staining, with a rubber polishing cup and a fine abrasive. Plaque and stain may be removed by air-powder polishing, which uses water and sodium bicarbonate under pressure. The flow rate is adjusted according to the degree of stain. Another method to remove plaque and stain is rubber-cup polishing (the most common method), with the abrasive agent placed in a small rubber cup on a handpiece. The cup rotates against the teeth. Premixed abrasives or reconstituted powder abrasives may be used, but if mixing, it's important for the mixture to be wet but not runny. Bristle brushes may be used to reach into pits/fissures on the tooth surface but may damage the gingiva. Cleaning abrasives include silex (heavy stains), super-fine silex (light stains), pumice (persistent stains), zirconium (cleaning/polishing), and chalk (whitening).

ENAMEL SEALANTS

Enamel sealants are hard resins spread over occlusal surfaces of children's premolars or molars with no decay. Sealants bind to the pits and fissures on the occlusal surface to lock out possible decay for five to seven years. Both deciduous and permanent, including newly erupted teeth, can be sealed. Sealants are especially indicated for patients with many other occlusal caries or deep fissures. Fluoridate the teeth in conjunction with sealing. Enamel sealants are inappropriate for teeth that are:

- Decay-free for at least four years.
- Shallowly grooved, easy to clean, and decay-resistant.
- Well blended with pits and fissures.
- Already decayed.
- Restored.
- Resins enamel sealants are dilute concentrations of BIS-GMA dental composites or glass ionomers. They may be chemically cured two-paste systems or one-component light cured ones, and they may contain fluoride. Perform pre-etching and conditioning before application with phosphoric acid because the enamel binding is mechanical.

PLACING ENAMEL SEALANTS ON CARIES-FREE TEETH

Enamel sealing is performed by the dental assistant with expanded functions.

1. Polish the occlusal surface to be sealed with flour of pumice or prophy paste without fluoride.
2. Use a rubber cup. Rinse and dry the area. Isolate it with a rubber dam or cotton rolls.
3. Dab acid etchant/conditioner (phosphoric acid solution) over the occlusal surface into the pits and fissures to the upper two-thirds of the cusp, until the area looks chalky and white.
4. Rinse the tooth. Evacuate the mouth. Isolate tooth again with cotton rolls.
5. Prepare sealant according to the manufacturer's suggested procedure.
6. Place sealant into pits and fissures. Allow it to set (if self-curing) or light-cure it. Hold the curing light at the occlusal surface from 2 mm distance and expose it for up to one minute.
7. Test the hardness and smoothness of the sealant with an explorer.
8. Seal unsealed areas again, if necessary.
9. After setting, rinse or wipe the tooth surface.
10. Remove isolation materials. Check occlusion with articulating paper.
11. Gently finish. Apply fluoride.

DISMISSAL OF THE DENTAL PATIENT

After the operator has finished the dental procedure, the dental assistant is responsible for rinsing and evacuating the patient's mouth. The assistant pulls the dental light aside, positions the dental chair to upright, removes fragments on the patient's face, and takes off the bib. The assistant instructs the patient to stay seated for a minute, in case he or she is dizzy as a reaction to anesthetic. The assistant places the used bib, evacuator,

air-water syringe tips, and saliva ejector on the tray. The assistant either takes off the treatment gloves and washes his or her hands, or uses overgloves to immediately record procedures performed on the chart or electronically. The assistant collects the chart and radiographs. The assistant provides the patient with postoperative instructions and returns his or her personal items. The assistant leads the patient to the receptionist, who deals with later appointments and payments.

Chapter Quiz

Ready to see how well you retained what you just read? Scan the QR code to go directly to the chapter quiz interface for this study guide. If you're using a computer, simply visit the bonus page at **mometrix.com/bonus948/danbcda** and click the Chapter Quizzes link.

Dental Materials (GC)

Transform passive reading into active learning! After immersing yourself in this chapter, put your comprehension to the test by taking a quiz. The insights you gained will stay with you longer this way. Scan the QR code to go directly to the chapter quiz interface for this study guide. If you're using a computer, simply visit the bonus page at **mometrix.com/bonus948/danbcda** and click the Chapter Quizzes link.

Impression Materials

THERMAL PROPERTIES OF DENTAL MATERIALS

The important thermal properties of a potential dental material are its thermal conductivity and its thermal expansion. Thermal conductivity refers to the facility to convey heat. Materials with lower thermal conductivity are usually preferred, particularly if they are near the dental pulp. Thermal expansion refers to the rate of expansion and contraction when exposed to temperature variations. It is important to select a material that has thermal expansion rates similar to that of tooth structure. Thermal expansion can cause dimensional changes in the dental material, particularly during the setting process. This can result in a phenomenon called microleakage in which debris and saliva leak into the area between the tooth and restorative material. Later, tooth sensitivity or caries can result.

ACIDITY IN DENTAL MATERIALS

The parameter pH is a measurement of the relative acidity, neutrality or alkalinity of a solution or environment. It is quantified on a scale of 0-14. Low numbers indicate acidic environments. pH 7.0 is neutral. High numbers indicate alkalinity. Normally, the oral cavity is maintained at relative neutrality by saliva. However, sugary and acidic foods and bacteria cause ongoing fluctuations in pH. Select dental materials to withstand these fluctuations. Some dental materials themselves are acidic and potentially damaging to gum tissues or pulp. If used, acidic materials must be set up and inserted cautiously.

ADDITIONAL PROPERTIES OF DENTAL MATERIALS

Some important properties of dental materials to consider before selection include:

- **Adhesion**: The ability of dissimilar materials to stick together, either chemically or physically.
- **Elasticity**: The capacity to undergo distortion and return to the original conformation, such as rubber bands within their elastic limit.
- **Flow**: Gradual continual shape change under force, such as compression-associated amalgam changes.
- **Hardness**: Relative ability to resist scratching or denting.
- **Solubility**: Capacity to dissolve in fluid; extremely soluble materials are undesirable if in contact with saliva.
- **Viscosity**: Thickness or facility of a liquid to flow.
- **Wettability**: The capacity of a liquid (the dental material) to flow over and sink into another (the tooth).
- **Corrosiveness**: The ability to react with food or saliva causing pitting, coarseness or tarnishing, with metal-containing materials.
- **Galvanism**: Electric shock caused by reaction between dissimilar metals and carried by saliva.

RETENTION OF DENTAL MATERIALS

Retention is the act of keeping or holding something in place. In dentistry, retention is achieved by either mechanical or chemical means. Dental materials are held in place by mechanical retention by slanting the cavity walls inward, abrading the tooth surface with an etchant, or by furrowing the cavity walls. Chemical retention is achieved by some sort of chemical reaction between the dental material and the tooth surface. It is often used for insertion of gold inlays or crowns, which must be indirectly retained through use of cements or bonding agents.

ALGINATE IMPRESSION MATERIALS

Alginate is a general term for irreversible hydrocolloid impression materials. These materials make impressions for diagnostic casts and study models. Their main application in orthodontic work is as negative models for preparation of casts that can be used to formulate orthodontic appliances. Hydrocolloid impressions are also taken to make opposite models for prosthetics, temporary restorations, bleach trays, custom trays, and mouth guards. The main ingredient is marine-derived potassium alginate. It is soluble in water, forming a thick liquid or sol. When calcium sulfate is added, solidification (a gel) occurs. Hydrocolloid impression materials also contain trisodium phosphate, which slows down setting time, fillers like diatomaceous earth or zinc oxide for strength, and potassium titanium fluoride.

ADVANTAGES AND DISADVANTAGES

Alginate is used extensively because it is easy, cheap, and comfortable to use, it sets quickly, and little equipment is needed. Its elastic properties make it ideal for making impressions where there are recessed areas, and both tissue and teeth imprints can be taken. The major disadvantage is the possibility of some inaccuracy in the impression, due to changes in water content. Heat, dryness, or contact with air can result in syneresis or shrinkage of the material. Water gain can result in imbibition or an enlargement of the measurements of the impression. Tissue areas being imprinted may be distorted because of the thickness of the material. Other impression materials, such as elastomer, are more accurate.

BOWLS, SPATULAS, AND TRAYS

Dispensing units using premixed units require only dispensing tips. The mixture is distributed directly into the tray. When mixing the powder and water, use flexible rubber bowls and throwaway spatulas (generally two-sided for mixing of alginate or plaster). The bowl is sterilized or sanitized afterwards. There are also disposable spatulas and bowls with markings for water measurement. There are metal impression trays that must be sterilized after use and disposable plastic trays. Most have perforations to allow material through and keep it in place. There are also unperforated rim lock trays with rims to hold the impression material in place. Trays come in various sizes and should be selected so they fit the person's mouth, with room for 2 mm of the hydrocolloid. They should also reach several millimeters posterior to the molar area; if they do not, they can be extended using wax strips (beading).

PREPARATION

If legally allowed by the state, the dental assistant can take an alginate impression. The patient should be sitting up while the mouth is rinsed and evacuated. Test the impression trays for size. If the selected tray does not extend beyond the molars, add wax beading to the borders. Prepare the mandibular model first. Of note, be certain to utilize the provided powder scoop and water measuring cup that accompanies the specific alginate molding powder. Add two measurements (generally indicated by lines on the measuring cup) of room temperature water to one flexible mixing bowl. Next, fluff the powder by inverting the container of powder one or two times while the lid is on to ensure the proper consistency of the mold. Add two scoops of the powder to the water and mix with the spatula, first by stirring, and then by applying pressure with the smooth side of the spatula on the side of the basin. Mixing time should be about 30-45 seconds for fast set preparations, or 60 seconds for regular set preparations. A creamy, uniform consistency is desired. Put the preparation in the impression tray, starting from the lingual sides. The flat edge (and sometimes a moist, gloved hand) consolidates the material. Maxillary impressions, which have a greater tendency to cause choking, are prepared similarly later, except that 3 measurements of water and 3 scoops of powder are used.

CHARACTERISTICS OF AN ACCURATE ALGINATE IMPRESSION

Accurate alginate impressions are centered over the central incisors, include all essential areas, and illustrate well-defined anatomic detail of both teeth and tissues. The teeth should not pierce through to the tray, caused by pushing the tray up or down too far. The imprint should not have tears, bubbles or empty spaces. It should encompass the vestibule regions and have a good peripheral or marginal roll. Certain features should be evident. For the mandibular impression, these are the retromolar area, the lingual frenum, and the mylohyoid ridge region. For the maxillary impression, these are the tuberosities and the palate regions.

REMOVAL AND DISINFECTION OF THE ALGINATE IMPRESSION

Begin removal of the alginate impressions by using the fingers of one hand to break the seal between the tissues of the lips and the cheek and the tray. shield the opposite arch with the opposite hand. Abruptly remove the tray with a snapping motion, pulling up for the maxillary impression and down for the mandibular. Turn the tray a bit sideways for removal. Evacuate surplus alginate from the mouth. Tissue off surplus alginate from the face. Ask the patient to rinse and spit. Examine the impression for accuracy. Rinse it with tap water and spray it with an approved surface disinfectant, such as an iodophor. Alginate impressions that are not poured into casts immediately (within 20 minutes) should be enclosed in a labeled, covered container until use. If the impression is wrapped first in a moist towel, it leads to water intake and distortion over time.

POURING AN ALGINATE IMPRESSION FOR A STUDY MODEL

The dental assistant makes the study model. Mix the plaster and pour it into the alginate impression. Hold the alginate impression over a vibrator on low or medium speed while the plaster is added, starting at the back of one side of the arch. The plaster should stream down the back of the impression. Add more plaster until it flows toward the front teeth to the other arch and out the other end, thus permeating the anatomical part of the model. Take the impression off the vibrator and pack the rest of the impression with plaster. Briefly vibrate the impression again for amalgamation. This is the anatomic portion of the model. If an art portion is to be added, the surface should retain small drops of plaster.

PROCEDURE

The dental assistant is responsible for preparing the art portion of the study model. Pour the anatomical portion of the study model and set it for 5-10 minutes. Clean the flexible rubber or disposable bowl to prepare it for mixing more plaster. The ratio of water to powder for the art portion is 40 mL per 100 grams of powder (thicker than the 50 mL/100gm used for the anatomical portion). Use a spatula to put the mixture on a glass slab or paper towel, creating a base. Turn the anatomical part of the model over onto the base and position it so that the tray handle is parallel to the slab or paper. Scoop surplus plaster along the edges to fill gaps. This is the two-pour method. The art portion can also be poured right after the anatomical part is filled by a single-pour technique. The model is allowed to set for 40-60 minutes, plaster on the outside of the tray is cut off with a laboratory knife, and the model is separated from the impression by holding the tray and lifting upwards.

POURING AND ALGINATE IMPRESSION WITH PLASTER

When pouring an alginate impression with plaster, the dental assistant makes the impression. Measure 50 ml of room temperature water into a flexible mixing bowl. Weigh 100 grams of plaster into another flexible bowl. Transfer the powder into the bowl with the water and let it dissolve. This makes a Type II model or laboratory plaster. Blend the particles with a metal spatula for about a minute. Press and rotate the bowl on a vibrator platform for several minutes, set at low to medium speed. This process introduces air bubbles that form to the top of the mixture. The desired consistency is creamy and smooth, but thick enough to remain in position.

IRREVERSIBLE HYDROCOLLOID IMPRESSION MATERIALS
SETTING TIMES

The period between when the water is added to the powder and the total setting of the mixture is the gelatin time. This includes approximately one minute of working time for Type II regular-set alginate and less for fast-set Type I. Setting time occurs after that, in approximately 1-2 minutes for Type I or 2.0-4.5 minutes for Type

II, if the impression is taken at normal room temperature, about 70 °F. Both working and setting times are shortened at higher temperatures and lengthened at lower temperatures, for example, with use of cool water. In general, Type I is useful for children or people who tend to gag, whereas the slower setting Type II is convenient for more difficult insertions or in situations where there is only one operator.

STORAGE AND PREPARATION

Irreversible hydrocolloid impression materials or alginate may come packaged in:

- Hermetic plastic containers, with foil or plastic bags inside, containing the powder and measuring tools for water.
- Mixtures in sealed bags.
- Mixtures used with a dispensing unit.

Store irreversible hydrocolloid impression materials in areas where they will not be exposed to moisture or excessive heat. Shelf life is about one year. The method of mixing the powder and water is specified by the manufacturer. In general, the ratio between the two is 1:1, but two scoops of powder and two portions of water are used for mandibular impressions, while three of each is required for maxillary impressions. If too little water is added, the mixture will be too thick, and vice versa.

REVERSIBLE HYDROCOLLOID IMPRESSION MATERIAL

Reversible hydrocolloid impression material, also known as **agar-agar,** is similar in makeup to alginate. The difference is that hydrocolloid setting is achieved through a chemical reaction. The material is transformed from a gel to a solid state by boiling for 10 minutes in a hydrocolloid conditioner unit. It is maintained in a liquid state in a 150 °F water bath until about 5 minutes before use, at which time it is moved to a 110 °F water bath. Further cooling to convert the material back to a gel occurs in the mouth, using hoses connected to the dental unit. Reversible hydrocolloid materials are quite accurate, making them useful for final impressions and other applications requiring detail. The disadvantages of hydrocolloid include the expense of additional equipment, longer preparation and setting (10 minutes), and distortion over time if exposed to environmental changes.

PACKAGING AND EQUIPMENT

When packaging reversible hydrocolloid impression materials, use a three-compartment hydrocolloid conditioning unit. The separate sections all contain clean water maintained at different temperatures. Looking toward the unit, from the left the partitions are the boiling bath (150 °F, 66 °C), the storage bath (usually 110 °F, 45 °C), and the conditioning bath (water-cooled tray). The impression material is provided in collapsible plastic tubes or syringes, which are shuttled between the three compartments after the appropriate time. If tubes are used, they are positioned upside down, with tips tightly in place in each compartment. Syringes have special holding cases for the cartridge. Time must either be set digitally or watched by the dental assistant, particularly the boiling time (10 minutes) and conditioning bath (5 minutes). The tray must be cool enough for insertion to avoid burning the patient's mouth. Otherwise, taking the hydrocolloid impression is similar to use of alginate, except that the setting time is longer, about 10 minutes.

ELASTOMERIC IMPRESSION MATERIALS

Elastomeric impression materials are more flexible than other types. This means they are less prone to tearing and distortion upon removal. They are also relatively impervious to temperature changes. There are three general types of elastomeric impression materials: Polysulfide, silicone, and polyether. Each type is prepared by mixing a catalyst or accelerator and a base material, engendering a process called polymerization. During the polymerization process, the material converts from a paste into a rubber-like, elastic mass. Elastomeric impression materials are mixed using either a mixing pad and spatula, or an extruder gun, to which cartridges of base and catalyst and a mixing tip are attached externally.

POLYSULFIDE IMPRESSIONS

Polysulfide impressions are taken by the dentist, supported by one or two assistants. The patient should be sitting up. Rinse and evacuate the patient's mouth. Two different mixtures are prepared by separate individuals: one mixture for loading onto a syringe, and another for loading onto the impression tray. Parallel, non-touching lines of base and accelerator pastes are dispensed onto two paper pads. Each is mixed using a spatula, with the mixing of the syringe preparation initiated about a minute before that for the tray. Place the syringe preparation into an impression syringe that has an attached tip. Remove the cylinder by forcing it into the barrel, using the working end. Insert the plunger. Transfer the syringe to the dentist, who applies the material to the prepared tooth. Load the tray mixture into the impression tray with a spatula, smooth it out, and pass it to the dentist for insertion. Hold the tray in place to set for a minimum of 6 minutes. Clean the spatula by pulling the material off, followed by sterilization. Discard the paper sheet and disposables.

SILICONE IMPRESSIONS

To begin the two-step silicone impression, the dental assistant supports the dentist. The patient sits erect. The dental assistant must don vinyl gloves. Silicone impression materials come as two color-coded putties and scoops (base and catalyst), or a putty base and catalyst in liquid dropper form. Blend equal amounts and mold them into a homogenous patty. Load the patty into a stock tray with adhesive, within 30 seconds. Forge a dent where the affected teeth are to be placed. Place a plastic spacer sheet over the tray and place it in the patient's mouth. Remove the tray and spacer after about 3 minutes and allow the preliminary impression to set. Position a retraction cord over the desired tooth, in preparation for the final impression. Use an extruder gun because it mixes and dispenses a lighter body silicone preparation. Force some of the material through a mixing tip into the preliminary impression tray. Use an intraoral delivery tip to inject some material around the prepared tooth, after retraction cord removal. The dentist places and holds the tray in place a minimum of 3 minutes until set. Remove the impression and rinse, gently dry, and disinfect it.

POLYETHER IMPRESSIONS

When taking a polyether impression, first spread the two pastes, containing the base and catalyst, in parallel lines onto a paper pad. Quickly mix them for 30 seconds or less, using a spatula. Put the paste into the impression tray and hand it to the dentist for the preliminary impression. The dentist positions the tray and holds it for about 3 minutes in the patient's mouth before removal. About 2 minutes into this process, the tray is moved around. For the final impression, the base, catalyst, and sometimes a consistency modifier (for thinning) are mixed and forced into the open end of an injection syringe. This material is put into the preliminary impression, and the tray is reintroduced into the patient's mouth. Hold it in the mouth for about 4 minutes. Remove it abruptly with a snapping motion. Rinse, dry, and disinfect the impression for 10 minutes with 2% glutaraldehyde. Sometimes, only final polyether impressions are made.

PROS AND CONS OF ELASTOMERIC IMPRESSION MATERIALS

The pros and cons of elastomeric impression materials are as follows:

- **Polysulfide**: It comes as a two-paste system, with a base of thiokol polysulfide rubber and filler and a catalyst of lead peroxide. Material is stable after setting, very precise, and has a long shelf life. However, it has a sulfurous odor, stains, and has a long setting time (at least 10 minutes).
- **Silicone**: It comes as two color-coded putties, a base of polysiloxane or polyvinyl siloxanes, and a catalyst. The putties are mixed and dispensed using an extruder gun. Silicone impression materials are highly accurate, stable, odorless, tasteless, and do not shrink or change measurements. They are relatively expensive.
- **Polyether**: It comes as a color-coded two paste system. The pastes (base and catalyst) are spread in parallel on a paper pad and mixed with a spatula. Polyether systems are quite accurate and stable.

DENTAL WAXES

There are five categories of dental waxes:

- **Pattern wax** is composed of two hard waxes, inlay and baseplate. Inlay wax comes in dark sticks that are melted and placed on a die to create a pattern for a restoration, or heated to vaporization with the lost wax technique. Baseplate wax comes in sheets that are heated for use as denture bases.
- **Temporary processing waxes** include soft boxing wax, sticky wax, and utility wax. Soft boxing wax encloses impressions to keep gypsum in place. Sticky wax adheres to many types of surfaces when melted for temporary repair jobs. Utility wax has adhesive and malleable properties at room temperature, making it ideal for relieving patient discomfort. For example, place it over orthodontic brackets to making wearing more comfortable.
- **Impression or bite registration waxes** incorporate copper or aluminum particles.
- Hard blocks of study wax that can be whittled.
- **Undercut wax,** which is placed in undercuts before making impressions.

Operative Materials

AMALGAM

Amalgam is an alloy, a mixture of metals or metal and some nonmetallic material. Dental amalgam consists of silver, tin, copper and sometimes zinc which is then mixed with mercury. Unalloyed liquid mercury is a neurotoxin; treat it as a hazardous material. The way in which the dental alloy portion of the amalgam was prepared affects its properties, especially the relative concentration of components and the shape of copper particles. The major component (40% to 70%) of dental alloys is silver, which combines with the mercury to form a compound that eventually hardens. Tin, found in concentrations from about 22% to 37%, has a strong affinity for mercury and encourages the amalgamation. Copper increases the strength and hardness of the amalgam. Amalgams are usually defined as low copper (4% to 5%) or high copper (12% to 30 %), with the latter providing strength and corrosion resistance. Zinc may be added in small concentrations up to 1% to minimize the oxidation of the other metals.

SUPPLY OPTIONS AND MANIPULATIONS FOR USE

Amalgam is supplied in color-coded capsules containing premeasured amounts of silver alloy powder and mercury. The color indicates whether the amount of material is appropriate for small cavity preparations (a single spill), or for larger cavities (double or triple spills). A metal or plastic pestle is provided for mixing the two ingredients when the capsule is opened. An amalgamator is an instrument for mixing and initiating the amalgamation (chemical reaction) between alloy and mercury. The success of this mixing procedure, also called trituration, depends on mixing time, speed of mixing, and force applied. Larger amounts must be mixed longer. The dental assistant prepares the capsule (twist-off cap, squeezing, or using an activator), puts it into the amalgamator, mixes it as determined, and after removal empties it into a container (Dappen dish or amalgam well).

PRECAUTIONS RELATED TO MERCURY USE

Mercury, which is found in amalgam, is toxic to nerves. It is liquid at room temperature and can vaporize. Amalgam is regulated by the FDA for this reason, and has been deemed safe without any evidence of harm to individuals with amalgam restorations. Regardless, dental staff must take precautions at every step where exposure might occur. Follow the American Dental Association's guidelines for mercury use in the dental office. Wear disposable gloves, a face mask, and goggles when working with amalgam. Use premeasured capsules. Triturate in an amalgamator with a protective cover. Do not touch mercury with bare skin. If contact occurs, wash with soap and water and rinse well. Handle mercury only over impermeable surfaces and away from heat sources, like autoclaves. Do not eat or drink near mercury. Use a water spray, high-volume evacuation, and a mask when cutting or polishing amalgam. Store amalgam scraps and mercury in capped, unbreakable jars before disposal as hazardous waste. Properly ventilate the office. Carpet is not appropriate

flooring. Educate all staff about regular urinalyses and monitoring devices for mercury. A mercury spill kit must be available.

BONDING AGENTS

Bonding agents are materials that adhere restoration materials to either dentin or enamel. They are also referred to as adhesives or bonding resins. The main constituents of bonding agents are low-viscosity resins and sometimes fillers, enhancers, or fluoride. Most preparations are light-cured or dual-cured. In order for bonding to occur, surface alteration or scoring needs is performed before the bonding agent can penetrate the surface and form a mechanical bond. For enamel bonding, the first step is acid etching using phosphoric acid. Bonding to the more sensitive, organic and water-filled dentin is achieved by initially slashing the dentin with a burr, and then using an etchant to eliminate the resulting smear layer.

PLACEMENT

Bonding systems consist of the acid etchant, primer or conditioner, and the adhesive or bonding agent. The dental assistant is responsible for preparation and transfer of materials and maintenance of a dry and clean area. If the procedure is in close contact with the pulp, the first step is placement of lining cement, such as calcium hydroxide. The etchant is then applied to the enamel and then the dentin. Manufacturer's instructions indicate the correct application time. The tooth is rinsed. A brush or disposable applicator is used to apply a primer, which moistens the dentin, and seeps into the tubules. The bonding agent is then placed and solidified, using a curing light. Disposable tips or brushes are thrown away.

DENTAL CEMENTS

Dental cements are agents that bond other dental materials, like restorations to the teeth. Cements come in various forms that generally require mixing and preparation before use. The cements are hardened either by chemical self-curing or light curing with a special blue light. Cements are defined as temporary, intermediate, or permanent, depending on their expected duration. There are also thin liners that are used to seal and protect the pulp or wall and floor of the cavity. Bases are relatively strong dental cements that are thickly spread in a layer between the tooth and restoration for pulp protection. Besides restorations, cements are also utilized as luting or bonding agents to apply orthodontic bands, bridges, or inlays to the teeth.

TYPES

Most dental cements are permanent, including zinc phosphate, reinforced zinc oxide eugenol, polycarboxylate, glass ionomer, resin cement, resin-reinforced glass ionomer, and compomers. The cements that are used for permanent cementation of orthodontic bands and brackets are zinc phosphate, polycarboxylate, glass ionomer and resin cement, all of which are bases and used to cement crowns, inlays, onlays and bridges. Glass ionomer is also utilized to seal root canals and for restorations. Reinforced zinc oxide eugenol is not used for orthodontic work. Resin cement is employed for cementation of enzootic posts, ceramic or composite inlays and onlays, and resin-bonded bridges. Compomers are resins altered with polyacid. Resin-reinforced glass ionomer is used for metallic or porcelain-fused metallic restorations. Zinc oxide eugenol is used only for temporary cementation of crowns, inlays, onlays and bridges, as a root canal sealant, or as a periodontal dressing after surgery. Varnish and calcium hydroxide are examples of liners.

ZINC PHOSPHATE CEMENT

Zinc phosphate cement preparations are composed of two parts that are mixed together. The first is a powder made of zinc oxide, and a small quantity of magnesium oxide, and tints of white, yellow or gray. The second part is a buffered phosphoric acid solution. When the two are combined, a heat-liberating or exothermic reaction occurs, which must be dampened during preparation by using a cooled glass slab and spatula. The mixture hardens within about 5 minutes and is very strong. The mechanism of bonding is mechanical interlocking. The desired consistency depends on the use; it should be creamy in texture for luting and similar to thick putty for use as a base.

MIXING

The dental or orthodontic assistant mixes the zinc phosphate cement on a clean, cooled glass slab. The powder portion is spread, flattened, and divided with a stainless-steel cement spatula on one end of the slab. The liquid portion is dispensed with the dropper bottle onto the other end. The flat side of the spatula is used to integrate a portion of the powder into the liquid for about 15 seconds. The mixture is spread over a larger area of the slab and slowly more powder is mixed in with the spatula until the desired thickness is achieved. The mass is formed into a ball and transferred to the dentist on the slab under the person's chin. The assistant also transfers a plastic filling instrument to the dentist. The slab and spatula are wiped with moistened gauze, soaked in water or bicarbonate, and then sterilized or disinfected.

ZINC OXIDE EUGENOL CEMENTS

Zinc oxide eugenol (ZOE) cement comes in two types. The traditional type I preparation consists of a powder containing zinc oxide, zinc acetate, resin, and an accelerator, which are mixed with the liquid eugenol. ZOE is used only for temporary cementation or for post-surgical periodontal dressing because of its soothing properties. The variant type II preparation is reinforced with alumina and other resins in the powder and ethoxybenzoic acid in the eugenol, and it is useful for up to a year as an Intermediate Restorative Material (IRM). Zinc oxide eugenol is very soluble and of neutral pH. When reinforced, ZOE is also strong. ZOE is incompatible with acrylic or composite restorations. Mixing is done on either a paper pad or glass slab, using a stainless-steel cement spatula. Eugenol disintegrates rubber, so it should not meet the bulb. ZOE preparations are not used for orthodontic procedures.

MIXING THE POWDER/LIQUID FORM

For mixing powder or liquid zinc oxide eugenol (ZOE) the dental assistant dispenses the powder onto the mixing pad (paper or glass), followed by the liquid. The two should be placed near but not on top of each other. Mix the two with the cement spatula, using the flat part of the instrument and uniform pressure. Consolidate the mixture into a mass to check for consistency, which should be creamy for luting applications, and similar to putty if needed as an insulating base or intermediate restorative material. Transfer the material to the dentist under the individual's chin, using a plastic filling instrument. Wipe off both the spatula and plastic filling instrument after use. If a paper pad was used, remove the top paper. If a glass slab was used, clean it with alcohol or orange solvent.

MIXING THE TWO-PASTE SYSTEM

For mixing the two-paste system of zinc oxide eugenol cement, the dental assistant mixes and distributes pastes. If state law allows, the assistant can place pastes. If the law does not allow this extended responsibility, the assistant aids the dentist in placement of these preparations. Two-paste systems are used for temporary bonding. They consist of an accelerator and a base. Each paste is spread parallel to the other along a paper pad. A cement spatula is used to mix the two until they have a creamy texture, suitable for luting. This process is very fast (about 15 minutes), as is the setting time (5 minutes or less). The material is put in place with the plastic filling instrument. The cement spatula is wiped off with a gauze sponge.

POLYCARBOXYLATE CEMENT

Polycarboxylate cements are mainly used for permanent cementation of orthodontic bands and brackets. Polycarboxylate cements consist of two portions, which are mixed. The first is a powder, containing primarily zinc oxide, with smaller amounts of magnesium oxide and stannous fluoride. The second is a thick liquid made of polycyclic acid copolymer in water. Polycarboxylate cements adhere chemically to the teeth and mechanically to the restoration. They are relatively strong and non-irritating to the pulp. The chemical reaction does not release heat. These cements must be prepared and used quickly, as they have a mixing time of a minute or less and operational time of approximately three minutes, after which unutilized cement should be discarded when it appears dull or sinewy.

MIXING

When mixing polycarboxylate cements, the dental assistant mixes cement. Place powder on one side of a paper pad or glass slab and drops of the liquid on the other. Manufacturer's directions should indicate the ratio of drops to scoops of powder. The relative amount of water is less if a base consistency is desired, or if the preparation is to be used for bonding. The powder is quickly incorporated into the liquid with some pressure for wetting. The mixture should have a glossy texture. For luting purposes, it should adhere to the spatula somewhat if raised an inch. It should be stickier for use as a base. The mixture should be applied within about 3 minutes, before it develops a dull and/or sinewy appearance. The spatula is wiped off with wet gauze, or bathed in 10% NaOH, if the cement has dried. Dispose of the paper pad.

GLASS IONOMER CEMENTS

There are five types of glass ionomer cements:

- **Type I** is conventional, viscous, or condensable. It has fine grains and chemically binds to the tooth. Use it for orthodontic bonding and closing fissures and pits.
- **Type II** is conventional modified with resin by the addition of HEMA. It is coarser and is for restorations.
- **Type III** is dual-cured hybrid for luting.
- **Type IV** is tri-cured glass for opaque structures. It releases less fluoride than conventional glass ionomers.
- **Type V** is any metal reinforced admixture containing glass ionomers. It is used with silver or amalgam restorations for crown or core buildups.

Unless reinforced, these cements come as a silicate glass powder containing calcium, fluoride and aluminum, and an aqueous suspension of polycyclic acid. Glass ionomer cements are quite strong. They bond both chemically and mechanically to the teeth, discharge fluoride, and are relatively non-irritating. While the setting and working times are short, about 1 and 2 minutes respectively, these cements do not set completely for about a day. Resin-reinforced glass ionomer cements are stronger, less water-soluble, and more adherent.

MIXING

When mixing the glass ionomer cement, the dental assistant first rinses and evacuates the patient's mouth. Dispense the powder and then the liquid portions onto a paper pad or cool glass stab. Immediately recap the liquid to avoid evaporation. Work quickly and move a portion of the powder into the liquid with a flexible stainless-steel spatula. Mix and incorporate the remaining powder until the proper consistency is achieved. If the cement is for luting orthodontic work, the texture should be creamy and glossy. If it is a base, then the consistency should be stickier. Transfer the mixture to the dentist under the patient's chin along with the plastic filling instrument. Cleanup involves wiping off the instruments with a moistened gauze and disposal of the top paper. If glass ionomer capsules are used instead, the seal between the powder and liquid sides is broken in an activator and the tablets are mixed for about 10 seconds on an amalgamator. Place the capsule in a dispenser and transfer it to the dentist for application. Discard the remainder and disinfect the equipment.

CALCIUM HYDROXIDE CEMENTS

Calcium hydroxide cements are placed in thin layers to protect the pulp by gently chafing the pulp enough to encourage secondary dentin formation. They are also used as liners under restorations. Calcium hydroxide cements are not very strong. Their formulations contain other chemicals, in addition to the calcium hydroxide, and may be either self-curing or light-curing. The most common system consists of two pastes, one of which is the base, and the other the catalyst for the reaction. With a two-paste system, equivalent small quantities of base and catalyst are dispensed onto a paper pad. The two are blended quickly (up to 15 seconds), using a small ball-ended instrument or explorer and a circular motion, until a consistent color is achieved. The assistant transfers the combined pastes on the pad to the dentist under the patient's chin. The duration before setting can be from 2-7 minutes, depending on the preparation. The assistant wipes the instrument between applications and afterwards discards the paper pad.

RESIN CEMENTS

Resin cements are made up of bisphenol A-glycidyl methacrylate (BIS-GMA) or dimethacrylate resins, in combination with low-viscosity monomers, and sometimes fluoride. The cements do not bond directly to metal or ceramics. Instead, an etchant must first be applied to the tooth surface, or a silane coupling agent must be used to achieve mechanical or chemical bonding, respectively. Resin cements have a variety of applications. The curing method is related to the application. Self-curing or chemical-cured cements, which have an initiator and activator that are mixed, are used with metal restoration materials or endodontic posts. Orthodontic brackets and porcelain/resin restorations or veneers indicate use of light cured materials, which are supplied in syringes. There are also dual-cured materials that come in two parts, which are mixed, applied, and light-cured. There are polyacid-modified compomer cements with similar properties.

PLACING ETCHANT AND RESIN CEMENT USING A DUAL CURING TECHNIQUE

When placing etchant and resin cement using a dual-curing technique, clean the tooth surface beforehand. Segregate the site with cotton rolls. The dental assistant prepares the etchant applicator and holds it on the tooth surface, per manufacturer's specifications, up to 30 seconds. The etchant may be transferred to and applied by the dentist. With the dual-curing method of resin cement placement, the tooth is then dried and the adhesive applied. The assistant quickly mixes resin components, initiator, and activator on a paper pad with a stainless-steel spatula to a uniform, creamy consistency. The assistant transfers the pad near to the patient, along with the plastic filling instrument. The placement is performed by the dentist. The assistant sets up the curing light. Actual curing or hardening may be done by the dentist or assistant, using the curing light and a protective shield or glasses when the light is on. Gauze sponges are used for cleanup and disposables are thrown out.

CAVITY VARNISH

Cavity varnishes close up dentin tubules before an amalgam restoration. They are applied in a thin layer to the dentin. All preparations contain some type of resin. Place universal varnishes under any restoration materials. Varnishes that include organic solvents are called copal varnishes, which are only appropriate under metal fillings. Varnishes are one of the weakest types of restorative materials, but they are impenetrable to oral fluids and are useful against microleakage or infiltration of cement acids into the dentin. The dental assistant prepares cavity varnishes. One's state may allow the dental assistant to apply varnish, or may stipulate that the dentist does. The patient's mouth should be clean and dry. Apply two coats of varnish using two small cotton pellets and two cotton pliers. While holding it in the pliers, moisten the first pellet with the varnish. Recap the varnish to avoid evaporation. Dab away extra varnish with gauze. Coat the desired surface using the cotton pellet. After drying, repeat the procedure with the second pellet and pliers. Discard pellets. Wash the pliers with solvent.

DENTAL BASES

Dental bases are intermediate restorative materials that are placed between the restoration and the dentine to protect the pulp. This is usually applied in a fairly thick layer to provide adequate protection. The dental base provides thermal insulation at the floor of the cavity and absorbs occlusal forces. There are several different types of compounds used in creating dental bases:

- **Zinc oxide eugenol:** This may help with healing the pulp by delivering some anesthetic and anti-inflammatory effects. Its sedative effects also help the pulp to relax after a procedure, which further aides in healing.
- **Zinc phosphate:** May be used to serve as a cement base for metallic restorations.
- **Glass ionomer:** Bonds to dentin to form an affective seal. This also has antibacterial qualities due to its release of fluoride, low pH, and the presence of strontium and zinc in the cement.
- **Polycarboxylate:** Primarily used for porcelain restorations, but can be used as a base for metallic restorations.
- **Flowable resin:** The dentin canals should be adequately sealed before using this to prevent irritation of the pulp.

DENTAL LINERS

Dental liners are usually used over exposed dentine within the base of a cavity. While bases are generally applied in a thick layer, dental liners are usually applied in a thin layer. The liner effectively seals the dentine for protection, provides thermal insulation, and can help to stimulate the formation of irregular secondary dentine to aid in healing. These actions help to promote healing and prevent infection. There are two different types of compounds used in creating dental liners:

- **Glass ionomer:** Usually used in a paste-liquid form, this forms a strong bond to dentin to form an affective seal, which can prevent micro-leakages. This also has antibacterial qualities due to its release of fluoride, low pH, and the presence of strontium and zinc in the cement.
- **Calcium hydroxide:** This aides in producing an irregular secondary dentine to promote healing and can prevent infection. Because of its poor strength properties, it cannot be applied in a thick enough layer to provide thermal for the pulp.

PREPARING, DELIVERING, MIXING, AND STORING DENTAL MATERIALS

BLEACHING AGENTS, BONDING AGENTS, AND PIT/FISSURE SEALANTS

Bleaching agents, bonding agents, and sealants all have specific preparation, delivery, mixing and storage protocols:

- **Bleaching agents**: Carbamide peroxide or hydrogen peroxide in various concentrations (usually 15-38% for office and 3-15% for home). Typical preparations are in premixed gel form in tubes or prefilled applicators and must be stored at room temperature.
- **Bonding agents**: Resins used to adhere dental composite materials. Many different bonding agents (with or without etchants) are available. Some are universal but others are specific to the type of material to which it will bond. Some are light-cured, and some vary in strength of bonding depending on the substrate. Some require more than one layer, some have strong odor, and some require longer curing time. Dry storage at room temperature.
- **Pit/Fissure sealants**: Plastic coating to fill in grooves, pits, and fissures in chewing surfaces of back teeth to decrease the risk of bacterial buildup. A variety of sealants include resin-modified glass ionomer cements, glass ionomer cements, fluoride-releasing composites, and adhesives. They may last for up to 10 years and should be in dry storage.

ENDODONTIC MATERIALS AND ETCHANTS

- **Endodontic materials:** Endodontic materials include irrigants (sodium hypochlorite 1-10%, chlorhexidine gluconate, saline), refrigerant spray (for pulp testing), lubricants, intra-canal medications (paramonochlorophenol, polyantimicrobial paste), fill material (silver bulk fill, dental amalgam, medicated pastes, polyester resin), and sealants. These materials should be in dry storage. Refrigerant spray must be stored in a well-ventilated, locked space as it may explode if overheated and may cause suffocation if inhaled.
- **Etchants:** 37% phosphoric acid is used to etch a tooth before applying bonding. Many products are now self-etching and do not require separate etching. Instead, they are rubbed on the tooth for 15 seconds and then air-dried. Some self-etching bonding agents come in two bottles with a drop or two placed on the tooth from each bottle or solutions mixed together prior to application. They should be kept in dry storage.

DRESSINGS

- **Cellulose dressings** (Surgicel, Benacel, SureStop) are absorbable cellulose hemostatic agents in sheets or plugs that are applied to the socket and create a gelatinous pseudo-clot. Cellulose dressings require dry storage and are packaged in individual sterile packets or blister packs.
- **Light-activated surgical dressing gel** (Barricade) supplied in a disposable syringe for easy application. Dry storage.

- **Absorbable collagen** (OraTape, OraMem, OraCote): Packaged in plugs and sheets in sterile packages. Sheets can be cut to size and sutured into place and absorb over 10-14 days. Dry storage.
- **Sedative dressing** is a mixture of clove oil and zinc oxide that is used as a temporary filling when restoration cannot be completed in one setting or when the decay is at or near the nerve to allow the tooth time to begin healing. Zinc oxide powder is mixed with a few drops of clove oil to make a very thick paste that is malleable but not sticky. Commercial products are also available. Ingredients are stored at room temperature.

Laboratory Materials

GYPSUM MATERIALS

Gypsum materials are used to make impressions for dental models. All gypsum products are made from mined hard rock, heated to remove water in a process known as calcinations, which changes the ratio of calcium sulfate to water from 1:2 to 2:1 (from calcium sulfate dihydrate to hemihydrates). The resultant material is pulverized and colored; the particle size and color are indicative of the type of gypsum product. Finely ground gypsum materials are denser, stronger, and require less water for wetting and setting. When water is added to the particles, they convert back to the dihydrate form, discharging heat in an exothermic reaction. Setting is virtually complete when the model is cool to the touch, although complete setting may take a day. The setting time is conversely related to the water temperature. The water-to-powder ratio is crucial, as it determines strength and fluidity, and cannot be changed once setting has begun.

TYPES OF GYPSUM PRODUCTS

There are five types of gypsum dental products. Proceeding from Type I to Type V, the particles are finer, denser, stronger, and require less water for optimal setting.

Type	Main Use	Water per 100 g of powder
Type I	Impression plaster for impressions	60 mL
Type II	Model or laboratory plaster for casts/models	50 mL
Type III	Laboratory stone	30 mL
Type IV	Die stone for strong or dyed models	24 mL
Type V	High-strength, high-expansion die stone	18-22 mL

Orthodontic stone is a combination of Type II laboratory plaster and Type III laboratory stone. Plaster is calcinated by an open kettle technique, making the particles very irregular and permeable. Die stone is processed by autoclaving with calcium chloride, making it denser and more uniform. Stone is alpha-hemihydrate. Plaster is beta-hemihydrate.

DENTAL LABORATORY PRESCRIPTION FORMS

The dental laboratory prescription form is used to communicate to the dental laboratory exactly what restorative prosthetic is needed. A generic order or a specific form supplied by the dental laboratory should be used for accurate ordering. The order should be very specific in order for the finished product to be accurate. The dentist and the office staff should be familiar with the components necessary for creation of an accurate prosthesis and a positive outcome for the patient. Components to include on the dental laboratory prescription form are:

- Patient information: Name, age, gender, occupation, and lifestyle.
- Date of the request.
- Detailed description of the prosthetic needed.

- Specific materials and composition to be used – Acrylic, metal, ceramic, etc.
- Shade using a number and specific guide for instruction.
- Desired occlusion: Include accurate casts and the occlusal record. Dental photos may be included for accurate visualization of what type of prosthesis will be necessary.
- Desired turnaround time: An estimate should be given to the patient based on experience with the dental laboratory and their normal turnaround time for different types of prostheses.

Chapter Quiz

Ready to see how well you retained what you just read? Scan the QR code to go directly to the chapter quiz interface for this study guide. If you're using a computer, simply visit the bonus page at **mometrix.com/bonus948/danbcda** and click the Chapter Quizzes link.

Purpose and Technique (RHS)

Transform passive reading into active learning! After immersing yourself in this chapter, put your comprehension to the test by taking a quiz. The insights you gained will stay with you longer this way. Scan the QR code to go directly to the chapter quiz interface for this study guide. If you're using a computer, simply visit the bonus page at **mometrix.com/bonus948/danbcda** and click the Chapter Quizzes link.

Purposes of Radiographic Images

INTRAORAL RADIOGRAPHS

There are three types of intraoral radiographs:

- In a **periapical radiograph,** the goal is to display the location, outlines, and distance from the central jaw arch of the teeth into the surrounding tissue area. The entire tooth and root, including minimally 2 mm of the periapical bone, should be recorded.
- **Bitewing radiographs** are held in place with tabs or holding apparatuses during exposure, and they are designed to show the scope of the crown or visible part of the tooth covered by enamel as well as a portion of the bone and roots in the jaw. Bitewing x-rays are useful for observation of calcium deposits, configuration of the pulp area, decay, periodontal issues, and the like. Their advantage is proximity to the teeth and the favored perpendicular beam orientation. Combinations of periapical and bitewing radiographs are used to take a complete-mouth (CMX) or full-mouth (FMX) x-ray survey.
- There are also **occlusal radiographs** that look at the cutting-edge surfaces of the teeth and the planes in the mouth; these are useful for observation of obvious abnormalities in the oral cavity.

SIZES AND AREAS OF FOCUS

Intraoral x-ray films can be described in terms of type or area of documentation. The three types come in various sizes for various purposes.

- The first, the periapical film, is used to record the apical or top area of the tooth, nearby bone structures, and crown. This type of film comes in a single child size (No. 0) and two adult sizes (No. 1 for the front and No. 2 for the back and bitewings as well).
- Bitewing films are used to simultaneously document the crown area and the interproximal alveolar bone crests. This can be accomplished by adding a tab to the No. 2 film above, using some type of holder, or by using two films.
- Occlusal films (size 3) are much bigger and are designed for use in larger areas like the floor of the mouth.

Other numbering systems have child (#0), narrow frontal (#1), adult (#2), preformed bitewing (#3) and occlusal (#4) sizes available.

CLASSIFICATIONS BASED ON SIZE AND SPEED

The American Dental Association has classified intraoral films by a number that combines both the type and size of the film. Periapical film classifications are generically represented by 1.X where X is the size of the film. Similarly, bitewing films are defined as 2.X, with X again being the size. There is one type of standard occlusal film, the 3.4. Radiographic film speed is really a reflection of the sensitivity of the film. High-speed x-ray films generate radiographic images with relatively short exposure times. Currently there are three speeds of film available, the fastest is group F, followed by group E and then group D. In theory the slowest film speed would be classified as group A. The fastest speed films have been achieved in recent years by the Eastman Kodak

Company by the incorporation of tabular shaped (instead of round) grains into the emulsion, thus increasing effective surface area.

OCCLUSAL RADIOGRAPHS

MAXILLARY TOPOGRAPHIC PROJECTION

A maxillary topographic projection is a type of occlusal radiograph designed to document a large portion of the upper jaw. Higher speed, large occlusal film packets, and longer 16-inch positioning devices are generally utilized. The smaller potential difference of 65 kVp and 15 mA current are the usual exposure factors. The film is positioned far back in the mouth with the rough surface against the maxillary teeth, and the patient holds it in place by biting down. The ala-tragus line should be parallel to the ground, and the midsagittal plane should be at right angles to the ground. The theory of bisecting angles is used to take the x-ray, which means that the central portion of the x-ray beam is directed perpendicular to the bisecting line between the planes of the film and the upper incisors. In order to achieve this angulation, the positioning device is usually placed about +65° to the film plane near to the nose but not touching it.

MAXILLARY MANDIBULAR CROSS-SECTIONAL PROJECTION

A mandibular cross-sectional projection is a type of occlusal radiograph used to document the presence of bodies like stones or calcified areas in glands in the lower jaw area. Settings are similar to those used for mandibular symphysis projections, but the head is tilted much further back until the plane of the maxillary teeth is actually upright and perpendicular to the floor. The film is positioned with the rough surface against the mandibular teeth and centered along the midline. Its back edge should be placed against the front of the rami or branching parts of the cavity. The middle part of the x-ray beam is directed at right angles to the occlusal film by positioning the BID (beam indicating device) close to the lower chin but not touching it.

MANDIBULAR SYMPHYSIS PROJECTION

A mandibular symphysis projection is a type of occlusal radiograph designed to document a large area of the incisor region of the lower jaw. The film is placed with the rough side facing the occlusal surfaces of the mandible. In this procedure, the patient's head is inclined backward to form a 45° angle between the floor and the biting surface plane. The midline plane should be perpendicular to the ground. The bisecting angle technique is employed to center the x-ray beam. This translates to an angle between the film and x-ray of about 55° and a vertical angulation of about -20°. The beam indicating device is usually placed against the chin.

POSTERIOR OCCLUSAL PROJECTIONS

Posterior occlusal topographic projections can be taken for both the upper and lower jaws. For the maxillary jaw, this type of film is useful for visualization of the sinus and other structural areas in the posterior or back. In this case, the film is placed lengthwise along the midline on one side of the face, the patient bites down on it, and the positioning device directs the x-ray beam at about a 55° angle through the profile near the premolar region. For the mandible, separate projections for each side of the mouth are usually unnecessary, but if they are required the film can again be placed on one side with the long edge positioned anteroposteriorly along the center. Here the film packet should touch the ramus of the lower jaw, and the beam still needs to be directed perpendicular to the film.

PANORAMIC RADIOGRAPHS

ADVANTAGES

The area covered in a panoramic radiograph, also called a **pantomogram**, is much larger than combined intraoral techniques. Even in the full-mouth survey, intraoral radiographs basically cover the teeth, alveolar ridges, and some of the associated bone. Panoramic tomography extends the observed area far beyond these structures; the jaw, nasal cavities, and temporomandibular joint regions are now included, increasing the diagnostic value. One newer diagnostic use is identification of calcifications in the carotid arteries, which if utilized in conjunction with other tests can help recognize stroke or other cerebrovascular risk. Panoramic techniques are generally easier and less time consuming than intraoral procedures, and therefore tend to

cooperate more and have a lower incidence of retakes. Radiation doses delivered during panoramic techniques are usually less than during other procedures, with the highest dose near the center of rotation.

DISADVANTAGES

Pantomograms generated during panoramic tomography tend to have a poorer image quality than intraoral radiographs. Use of intensifying screens or fast films with large grains further decreases this definition. In particular, the definition is decreased rendering panoramic radiography relatively unsuitable for certain diagnoses. Periodontal disease, tooth decay, and pathological conditions in the periapical region are not picked up well on pantomograms, which means that bitewings and some periapical x-rays used in conjunction may be necessary. Only areas lying within the focal trough or image layer are distinct on panoramic radiographs, and machines with adjustable areas are expensive. In fact, any panoramic apparatus is generally costly. Lack of clarity can occur due to overlapping of images particularly in the premolar area, superimposition or obscuring of areas especially by the spinal column, and various sources of distortion. The panoramic machine should never be used in cases where only single or limited intraoral radiographs will suffice.

POSTEROANTERIOR PROJECTIONS

A posteroanterior projection is an extraoral exposure of the skull taken by directing the x-ray beam from about 3 feet behind the patient. The central ray is aimed at the occipital protuberance in the ear, and the film is in front of the individual, normally with the forehead and nose positioned against the cassette. This technique is useful for identification of fractures, malignancies, and widespread disease states in the skull area. A variation in which the patient opens their mouth and places their chin and nose against the cassette is called the Waters' view. This change enables visualization of the middle of the face, particularly the maxillary sinus region.

CEPHALOMETRIC RADIOGRAPHS

Cephalometric radiography is a specialized technique that quantifies parameters of the skull in order to predict growth patterns. The method is used primarily by orthodontists or dentists that see mostly children. Cephalometric radiography requires a unique machine that employs an apparatus called a **cephalostat** to hold the individual's head in place with rods and ear posts. All measurements are made relative to the midsagittal or midline plane that divides the face in half, and the Frankfort line is used as the relative horizontal marker. The most popular stance is a lateral exposure with the cassette, located extraorally, against the left side of the face and the radiation beam projected a long distance (about 5 feet) from the other side. The film must be placed in equidistant alignment to the midline. The radiograph is interpreted by looking at facial relationships and angles in an attempt to predict later growth patterns. Lateral oblique projections, where the beam is at a slight upward angle, are also captured.

CT SCANS

CT or **computed tomography scans** are images produced by directing an x-ray beam at an individual and then digitally transmitting information about the degree of penetration to electronic sensors. The number of pixels in an area is directly related to the density of the tissue, and they are represented as CT numbers or Hounsfield units. Tissue types have characteristic units. For example, water has 0 Hounsfield units, while bone has +1000 units, and air has -1000 units. No film is utilized as they are in other forms of tomography. The beam is projected through the patient while rotating through a plane. This plane can be axial, coronal, or sagittal, meaning it is either parallel to the ground, through the imaginary line dividing the front and back of the head, or through the midline separating right and left. Some CT scanners, in particular those used for the head and neck region, project a beam that is either round or cone-shaped onto a two-dimensional detector. In this case, radiation exposure is minimized.

ADVANTAGES AND DISADVANTAGES

Computed tomography is great at distinguishing between slight differences in tissue density, and in addition contrast and density can be manipulated to look at different areas. CT can be done in a variety of planes while eliminating superimposition of unnecessary images outside the focal plane. Pictures can be reformatted relative to other planes. The technique is easy and accurate. However, the patient is generally exposed to more radiation with CT than with ordinary film techniques, although dosage can be reduced through the use of cone beam machines or software that localizes the imaging. The latter is often used for dental implant preparation. Considerably more radiation is delivered during CT scanning of the head than an ordinary skull film, but this negative aspect is obliterated by the high incidence of repeats in skull filming. CT scans are more costly to the patient than films. Metals in the field produce CT scan artifacts just as they do on films.

CONE-BEAM COMPUTER TOMOGRAPHY (CBCT)

Cone-beam computer tomography takes three-dimensional images through a cone-shaped x-ray beam that moves about the patient's head and face with 360° rotation for 10–40 seconds. While exposing the patient to less x-ray than a standard CT, the dental cone-beam CT still has increased exposure over standard radiography but produces superior images, especially of bony structures and soft tissue, including muscles, lymph nodes, vessels, and nerves. Cone-beam CTs are used primarily in orthodontia. Patients must remove all metal objects on the head and neck as well as removable intraoral prostheses, hearing aids, and underwire bras because the metal may affect the image.

DUAL FILM PACKAGES

A dual film packet contains two pieces of film between black lining paper. The second sheet of film provides a duplicate or the original without the need of additional exposure, so an originating dentist and a specialist can each have an original film. However, the dual film packet requires slightly increased radiation exposure and is expensive.

SNAP-A-RAY PLASTIC FILM HOLDERS

Snap-A-Ray plastic film holders by Dentsply Rinn are unbacked. Thus, they provide less irritation and are generally better tolerated. This makes this type of film holder particularly useful in pediatric patients, individuals susceptible to gag reflexes, and situations where distortion is not a great issue. The latter situations include evaluations of toothless individuals or dental pulp (endodontic) disease. Teeth further back in the mouth are often appraised using these types of holders because it is easier to arrange the film parallel to the teeth. Thus, premolars and molars in the lower jaw or mandible as well as third molar projections of either jaw are often looked at using devices like the Snap-A-Ray film holders.

Surveys Used for Specific Conditions and Landmarks

ASSESSING ORAL CAVITY VARIATIONS

A number of anatomical variations or **sensitivities** that may be present in the oral cavity can affect the use of radiography. Film positioning is difficult for shots of the lower jaw in individuals with large tongues, for example. If the roof of the mouth is shallow, it may be difficult to maintain a parallel relationship between the film and the long axes of the teeth in the upper jaw. Vertical angulation may need to be increased, which increases the probability of a foreshortened image. There are several types of common bony outgrowths or exostoses that can create problems. About one-fifth of the population has this type of growth in the middle of their hard palate (torus palatinus) and a smaller proportion of people have similar growths on the lower jaw (torus mandibularis). In both cases, the film should not be placed over the bony growth. Some people have very sensitive mucous membranes or high muscle attachments in the area around the premolars of the lower jaw, and film placement may need to be adjusted accordingly. Sensitivity in the mandibular incisor area is also common. Lastly, some patients will be fully or partially edentulous, and exposure times for these individuals can be minimal.

ASSESSING IMPLANT THERAPY

When sites for possible dental implants are selected, it is necessary to know the amount of bone present and the position of certain anatomical structures. Numerous images of the area are needed. Tomography should be used to assess and obtain a three-dimensional view of various sites. Two different cuts, cross-sectional and sagittal, may be traced with linear tomography. Alternatively, computed tomography or a CT scan can be utilized. CT has some disadvantages including high cost, augmented radiation exposure, obscuration by artifacts, or general lack of image detail. In reality, many dental practices do not use tomography for assessment of implant therapy, substituting a combination of other types of radiographs. These substitutions are not recommended because they do not give accurate three-dimensional views.

IMPROVING EXPOSURE OF THIRD MOLARS

It is difficult to get good exposures of third molars, and often extraoral or panoramic views must be taken. The major problem with normal intraoral exposures of the upper jaw is excitation of the gag reflex. A hemostat is generally used to keep the film away from the palate and vertical angulation is increased to minimize spatial errors. In the mandible, it is very hard to place the film far enough back in the mouth, so techniques to relax the muscle on the floor of the mouth, move the tongue to the side, and/or direct the beam from the distal side are usually employed.

ASSESSING PATIENTS WITH ENDODONTIC PROBLEMS

Individuals undergoing management of endodontic or pulp problems usually have rubber dams in the oral cavity. The best way to take a radiograph is to remove the frame of the dam and arrange the film packet by using a hemostat or Snap-a-Ray holder. The patient holds the film-holder in an orientation parallel to the tooth. The shot should be taken very quickly. Several types of radiopaque products that aid visualization may be used in conjunction with the radiograph. These include intraoral grids placed on the film packet or injection of radiopaque media into certain areas.

ASSESSING PATIENTS WITH TRISMUS

Patients with infections or some type of injury may be unable to open their mouth to some extent due to a condition called trismus. Diagnostic radiographs are usually indicated in these individuals. If possible, intraoral exposures can be taken by inserting the film with a hemostat, orienting it correctly after insertion, and instructing the patient to hold the hemostat. If intraoral films cannot be successfully attempted, then panoramic or extraoral techniques can be employed. Good operator chairside technique is crucial for problems like these.

ASSESSING EDENTULOUS PATIENTS

Edentulous patients have partial or complete areas in their mouth where there are no teeth. A large proportion of these individuals have pathological abnormalities like infected areas, cysts, remnants of roots, or unerupted or extra teeth. If possible, a panoramic survey should be performed on edentulous individuals. Otherwise, a series of 10 to14 different No. 2 periapical films is usually taken by directing the x-ray beam into the center of each film. Film-holders and the paralleling technique can be used in some of these patients without significant resorption. The bisecting angle method is also often used.

ASSESSING THE TEMPOROMANDIBULAR JOINT

The TMJ or temporomandibular joint connects the mandible to the temporal bone on the side of the head. Visualization of this region is diagnostic for a number of problems. The radiographic techniques are very specialized and generally are performed outside the normal dental practice. In a normal dental office, the only types of TMJ analysis usually available are either transcranial lateral projections or specialized adaptations of panoramic projections. A transcranial lateral view obliquely angles the center of the x-ray beam from above toward the condyle on the opposing side; the image is usually quite distorted and does not pick up some vital diagnostic areas. Specialized panoramic projections can be used to pick up obvious changes, but the beam can only be directed obliquely to the axis of the condyle which limits the utility of this technique as well. Sometimes submentovertex projections, where the beam is directed from below the chin, are used to observe TMJ.

TMJ TOMOGRAPHY

The TMJ region is usually documented in specialized facilities that have machines to perform analysis beyond the usual projections. One of the techniques used for TMJ is TMJ tomography. The principle involved is similar to panoramic radiography in that an x-ray tube and film cassette are rotating in opposite directions around a central fixed point in this case. The focal plane is primarily visualized, and the rest is blurry. The thickness of the focal plane is controlled by the angle between shots, and its position is influenced by the position of the central fulcrum. The relationship between the tube and film can be linear or in some other trajectory like circular, elliptical, or cloverleaf. CT scanning is a type of tomography that uses digital imagery; the method is more expensive but can provide finer details.

USE OF MRI

Magnetic resonance imaging or MRI can be employed to visualize the TMJ or other areas without the use of ionizing radiation. It is the only technique that can document all areas related to TMJ functional abnormalities, including the discs and rear attachments of the temporomandibular joints, the condyle, and the fossae or groove of the lower jaw. In MRI, the individual is subjected to a magnetic field. Atoms of hydrogen in the body are realigned by the electromagnetic forces generated. After the area being documented is subsequently bombarded with radio frequency waves, the protons release the energy absorbed. A sensor picks up this information and sends it to a computer which provides an image. The technique is especially useful for visualization of soft tissues.

DEVELOPMENTAL ABNORMALITIES THAT AFFECT FILM PLACEMENT

If an individual has a **narrow dental arch**, it may be necessary to use smaller #0 or #1 films for exposures of the front of the mouth. If the patient has a **shallow palatial vault**, it may be difficult to place the film in the correct position using the paralleling method; solutions include use of a smaller film size or the bisecting technique. Some people have **stiff lingual tongue attachments**, which make it difficult to place a film packet on the floor of the mouth; here the bisecting-angle technique is generally used. If a patient has a **bony ridge or torus in the mandible**, the film packet must be put over it, and the vertical angulation must be augmented to balance the larger angle between the film and the long axis of the tooth. Presence of an **oversized palatial cusp** at the first premolar of the maxilla is a widespread abnormality. In these cases, the canine will appear to be overlapped unless the direction of the x-ray beam is more distal.

RADIOGRAPHIC SURVEYS FOR PEDIATRIC PATIENTS

Childhood is the time to diagnose and develop treatment plans for dental and other pathological problems. Dental cysts and tumors as well as other pediatric malignancies tend to occur during the period during childhood when teeth are developing. Children with genetic predisposition or other risk factors for caries should have posterior bitewings taken as soon as possible after the spaces between the teeth in these areas are closed up. If there is no decay, bitewings are generally done every year to 1 ½ years until permanent teeth come when the interval can be lengthened to 2 years.

GUIDELINES

The **best technique to use in children** is a panoramic radiographic, if appropriate machinery is available, because it exposes them to less radiation. Posterior bitewings can be used supplementally. If a panoramic machine is unavailable, then the types of radiographs taken should depend on the child's age or dentition. Surveys for young children in the early eruptive stage (usually up to 5 years of age) generally consist of occlusal films of both jaws and back apical and bitewing projections. Because their mouths are small, smaller No. 1 and No. 0 films are substituted instead of adult parameters. Between about 6 and 9 years of age, pediatric patients tend to have mixed dentition with both temporary and permanent teeth. In this age range, the radiographic documentation generally resembles a regular full-mouth survey except that smaller No. 1 films are usually used, with an occasional No. 2 film for posterior bitewings. Subjects in the older preadolescent group, about 10-12 years old, usually have a complete set of periapical films done.

Patient History

INDICATIONS FOR RADIOGRAPHIC EVALUATION IN NEW AND RETURNING PATIENTS

If dental history includes any periodontal or endodontic (pulp) treatment, soreness, or evidence of trauma, radiographs may be needed. X-rays are usually taken when there is familial history of dental problems or there is a need to check demineralization. There are numerous clinical signs that can indicate use of radiographs. In addition to evidence of various types of dental disease, unexplained symptoms in the area like bleeding, sensitivity, discoloration, or eruptions warrant radiographs. Sinus problems, neurological abnormalities or asymmetry in the facial region, and temporomandibular joint (TMJ) problems are just a few other clinical symptoms that dictate probable use of diagnostic radiography.

UNIQUE SITUATIONS REQUIRING RADIOGRAPHS

Occasionally dental radiographs are taken simply to monitor the growth and development of the oral and maxillofacial region of a child or adolescent. Clinical judgment is necessary in these instances since repeated radiation exposure is involved. Periapical or panoramic films are often taken in adolescents to gauge the development of the third molars. Radiographs can also be done to look at dental implants (or potential sites), assess pathological changes, measure periodontal treatment progress, diagnose dental pulp diseases, locate areas that need restoration, or find minerals in decayed areas.

PATIENT PREPARATION FOR RADIOGRAPHIC EXPOSURE

Patient preparation for radiographic exposure includes:

- **Intraoral radiography**: The patient's head and neck must be examined. The patient must be asked to remove glasses and any removable intraoral prosthesis as well as jewelry that lies in the beam path, such as nose and tongue rings/studs. Patient protection includes the thyroid lead collar and lead apron that covers the chest and abdomen.
- **Panoramic radiography**: The patient must remove glasses, removable intraoral prostheses, and hearing aids as well as all head and neck jewelry and metal items, such as earrings, barrettes, and nose and tongue rings/studs. Patient protection includes the panoramic shield apron that covers front and back but is higher in the front than the back because the beam is directed from the back of the head to the front in a superior direction. The thyroid collar is not used because it may interfere with midline imaging. If the apron is longer on one side than the other, the long side should be placed against the patient's back.

ENSURING PROPER COVERAGE FOR X-RAYS

An x-ray should generally include visualization of five tissue types, the tooth enamel, its underlying dentin or hard calcium-containing portion, the sensitive central pulp with nerves and blood vessels, the alveolar or jaw bone, and the surrounding soft tissue. For a periapical film, several millimeters of bone should be seen. All areas needed for diagnostic purposes should be included, if possible, with the initial film or visualized on supplemental images such as occlusal films. There are also guidelines for inclusion of other areas like the periodontal membrane space and superimposition of certain cusp tips. Proper coverage can be attained by a combination of the accurate alignment of film and radiation beam, use of the correct film type, and amplification if necessary.

Intraoral and Extraoral Techniques

EXTRAORAL VS. INTRAORAL DENTAL X-RAY FILMS

Extraoral x-ray films (screen films) are indirectly exposed by changing the x-ray photons to light energy by use of screens on either side of the film. In the process, the signal is also amplified facilitating a smaller dosage of radiation. This technique is useful for documenting larger areas. Light sensitive films are used.

Intraoral films directly expose the radiation to the film. These types of films are used only for small areas inside the oral cavity. They come as separately enclosed double-emulsion films protected by a lead backing which provides stiffness, protects against further scattering, and catches excess radiation. Current films of this type always identify the side to be placed against the x-ray tube with a raised dot.

PARALLELING TECHNIQUES FOR PERIAPICAL RADIOGRAPHS

DECREASING DISTORTION USING FILM DISTANCE

Of the two periapical radiographic techniques, the paralleling technique is generally preferred over the bisecting angle technique because there is less distortion with paralleling. This decrease in distortion is accomplished by holding the film parallel to the long axes of the teeth and directing the beam perpendicular to both. In order to achieve this parallel orientation, the distance between the film and the teeth usually needs to be increased, which could theoretically decrease the image clarity. Therefore, sharpness and magnification are usually restored by increasing the distance between the x-ray beam source and the film. For this reason, longer 16-inch positioning devices are often utilized.

QUANTIFICATION OF THE ANGULATION OF THE X-RAY BEAM

The tubehead of the x-ray machine is oriented both vertically and horizontally relative to various planes during periapical radiography. The occlusal plane along the top ridge of the teeth should be placed parallel to the floor, and the tubehead height is changed to accommodate this. This **vertical angulation** is calculated in degrees and is positive if it angles downward or negative if it angles upward. The angle of the beam is also quantified in terms of its angle from the sagittal plane. In other words, beams directed at back teeth have greater horizontal angles than in the front. This **horizontal angulation** is determined by the location of the targeted teeth. If feasible, the horizontal angle of the beam should also be parallel to the floor and the flat plane of the film. The beam should be aimed at the desired area or point of entry, and it should cover the entire location of the x-ray film.

FILM HOLDER DESIGNS

Rectangular collimation is preferable for the **paralleling** technique because it directs the x-ray beam in a rectangle, which is the same shape of the film. It limits unnecessary radiation exposure by restricting the area of the beam in contact with the patient. Some x-ray machines have built-in rectangular collimators or positioning devices with rectangular outlets. Several commercial film-holders achieve rectangular collimation by attachments that either fit on the end of the beam indicating device or are integral parts of the film. Masel manufactures Precision Film Holders of the second variety. Dentsply Rinn makes both types as well as a disposable polystyrene holder that has markings enabling the operator to position it at different places depending on the desired film. The same manufacturer also produces plastic film holders (proprietary name Snap-A-Ray) that are unbacked and fit directly into the mouth; the disadvantages of these holders are possible breakage, image distortion, and difficulty obtaining the correct angles without an alignment device.

CRITERIA FOR GOOD FILM PLACEMENT AND BEAM INDICATING DEVICE POSITIONING

In the paralleling technique, there are six rules for superior technique; the first three involve placement of the film and the last three cover the positioning of the beam indicating device.

- Film placement
  - The film should include all teeth in the area to be covered.

- o The juxtaposition of the tooth's long axis and the film's vertical axis should be parallel. Since the apical or top edge of the tooth must be included, this rule dictates that the expected distance between the tooth and film must often be increased. This increased distance should be used for visualization of teeth in the back of the upper jaw. The front incisors in both jaws tend to tilt outwards, and films of these regions need to be positioned relatively far back in the oral cavity.
  - o The horizontal plane of the film should be at the same angle as the mean tangent for the region. The tangent is a flat plane connecting the two end points in the small area being x-rayed.
- Beam indicating device positioning
  - o The device should be angled vertically with its flat open end parallel to the film container in order to avoid distortion.
  - o The positioning tube should also be angled horizontally to the plane of the area to be covered, thus aiming the x-rays perpendicular to the film.
  - o The center of the cone of x-rays must be localized over the middle of the film in order to avoid partial images or an incomplete pattern known as cone-cutting.

X-Rays of Pre-Molar and Molar Regions of the Upper Jaw

For the pre-molar and molar regions of the upper maxillary jaw, the plastic posterior periapical bite block is generally used with a No. 2 film. In these maxillary areas, the holder is placed horizontally to either center the second premolar (premolar region) or to have the second premolar at the front edge of the film (molar region). Part of the canine should be included for the second premolar shot. Sometimes the molar projection is moved further back to visualize third molars that have not erupted yet. The film should be aligned parallel to the tangent of the region horizontally and to the long axis of the desired teeth vertically. The bite block is held in place by positioning it against the biting surface of the teeth, inserting a cotton roll below it in the mandible, and instructing the patient to bite down to keep it in place. The aiming ring if present is pulled down to touch the patient's skin, and the positioning device is aligned horizontally and vertically before exposure.

X-Rays of the Anterior Region of the Upper Jaw

X-rays of the front or anterior regions of the upper maxillary jaw are typically performed using a plastic anterior bite block that holds the film package attached to a stainless-steel rod that lines up the positioning device and the film. In order to avoid cone-cutting, there is usually a ring that can also be attached to the rod to center the BID and the film. A No. 1 film is usually inserted vertically into the bite block with the plain face outwards. The desired exposure parameters are set on the x-ray machine. The film is centered over a particular tooth depending on the region being radiographed, the maxillary midline for central incisors, the lateral incisor for that region, or the canine for that area. The long axis of the targeted tooth should be parallel to the film. A cotton roll is placed between the bite block and the teeth in the lower jaw. The aiming ring on the indicator rod is slid down to touch the patient's skin, and vertical as well as horizontal angulation is established before the exposure is taken.

Procedures for the Lower Jaw vs. the Upper Jaw

The same plastic bite blocks and film numbers are used for similar regions in the maxillary and mandibular jaws. The position of the film holder needs to be inverted. For the incisors in the mandible, the film packet is placed relatively far back near the premolars in order to align the long axis of the teeth in parallel to it. The holder is centered in much the same manner as for the equivalent area of the maxilla. In the mandibular molar region, the third molar should be covered and the film should be put in the groove between the teeth and the tongue. The cotton roll is placed between the bite block and the corresponding maxillary teeth. As in the radiographs for the upper jaw, the aiming ring is placed next to the skin, the positioning device is aligned horizontally and vertically, and the exposure is taken.

BISECTING ANGLE RADIOGRAPH TECHNIQUES
CORRECT PLACEMENT AND PROCEDURES

First, the head must be correctly positioned for a bisecting angle radiograph. For shots of the maxillary teeth, the plane of the teeth being documented should be parallel and the dividing plane of the head should be perpendicular to the floor. Radiographs of the mandible are taken with the mouth open necessitating inclination of the head backward to keep the plane of the head parallel to the floor. The centers of the film and area to be documented should be superimposed. The middle of the x-ray beam should be angled vertically in the center of the field perpendicular to the bisecting line. The horizontal angulation is determined by directing the beam at right angles to the tangent in the area being documented. The point of entry should be the middle of the desired area.

RULE OF ISOMETRY

The rule of isometry asserts that two triangles are equivalent when they have a shared side and two equal angles. Extrapolation of the rule of isometry in the bisecting angle technique results in the assumption that the central portion of the x-ray can therefore be aimed perpendicular to the line that bisects the angle between the film and the long axis of the tooth (the shared side of the two triangles). In reality, distortion is still quite likely when applying this rule because teeth are not flat planes. Therefore, the bisecting angle must be strictly observed. If the perpendicular orientation of the BID is close to the angle of the tooth, the image will appear elongated. If the perpendicular orientation of the positioning device is close to the film instead, a phenomenon called foreshortening can occur.

VERTICAL ANGULATION OF THE POSITIONING DEVICE

The vertical angulation is the angle between the positioning or beam indicating device and the occlusal plane of the teeth. For the bisecting technique, this angle is always positive for examination of maxillary teeth and usually negative for shots of mandibular teeth. The appropriate angle for short 8-inch positioning devices can vary but starting points ranging from +30° for molars up to +55° for incisors are generally used. The angles are slightly less for longer 16-inch BIDs. When documenting mandibular teeth with this method, the vertical angulation usually ranges from 0° for molars to about -20° for incisors for the short BID and slightly less for the longer devices. Dentsply Rinn manufactures anterior and posterior holders called BAI for the bisecting angle technique that facilitate the determination of angulation, and their Stabe holders can be used for this technique as well.

DISTORTIONS IN PARALLELING AND BISECTING TECHNIQUES
DECREASING GEOMETRIC UNSHARPNESS AND DISTORTION

Geometric unsharpness or the amount of penumbra on the image is best controlled by the use of an x-ray machine with a small focal spot on the anode target. This is an inherent property of the equipment and cannot be changed. As the distance between the focal spot and the film is increased, the sharpness increases. Conversely, as the distance between the object being documented and the film is increased, the sharpness decreases and more of the film is blurry. These distances primarily affect the magnification of certain areas and their relative distortion. The relationship between true object size and these parameters is as follows:

$$\text{Object size} = \frac{(\text{distance between source and object}) \times (\text{length of image})}{\text{distance between x-ray source and film}}$$

IMPACT OF POSITIONING DEVICES ON MINIMIZING DISTORTION

The length of beam indicating (BID) or positioning device should be selected based on the technique employed to minimize distortion. The bisecting technique can only be performed with the shorter 8-inch BID generally; it allows the film to be positioned close to the teeth to be x-rayed. Any length device can be used for the paralleling technique since it is placed perpendicular to both the teeth and film. The longer tubes (16 inches generally) are better because the distance between focal space and object is increased and sharpness is subsequently augmented.

MINIMIZING DISTORTION CAUSED BY SHAPES AND DIMENSIONS OF OBJECTS

Distortion caused by differences in shape and size can be minimized by two techniques, paralleling and bisecting.

- **Paralleling** refers to the placement of the long axis of the object in parallel to the film.
- **Bisecting** means positioning the radiation beam perpendicular to the midpoint of the angle between the film and the long axes of the teeth.

Less distortion and greater anatomical accuracy are generally seen with the paralleling technique. In the bisecting technique, the depth dimension differs for various teeth and this can foreshorten or elongate the image.

BITEWING TECHNIQUES

PROCEDURES FOR THE PREMOLAR AND MOLAR BITEWING RADIOGRAPHS

Number 2 films are typically used for bitewing radiographs of the posterior regions of the oral cavity. They are placed horizontally in the bitewing holder. Exposure parameters are selected. The film holder is held in place by placing it on the hard occlusal surfaces of the bottom teeth and biting down. The premolar bitewing radiograph is centered in the areas that would be covered by both upper and lower premolar periapical films. The molar bitewing is held similarly and is placed far enough back to cover all three molars. The aiming ring is slid into place near the patient's skin, the positioning device is aligned both horizontally and vertically, and the exposure is taken.

GUIDELINES FOR VERTICAL AND HORIZONTAL ANGULATION

Most positioning devices for bitewings are round. If the BID device is short with an 8-inch distance between the x-ray source and the film, it is generally aimed at approximately +10° to the tab. This is because the film tends to angle slightly back from the upper teeth that tilt back, and this vertical angulation establishes a perpendicular relationship between the x-ray and film. For a long BID with a source to film distance of around 16 inches, the angle can be reduced to 8° for a molar bitewing and 6° for a pre-molar bitewing. The flat surface of the positioning device should be parallel to the film. As always, the central portion of the x-ray beam should be aimed at the middle of the film packet.

FILM HOLDERS DESIGNED FOR BITEWING RADIOGRAPHS

Instruments designed for bitewing radiographs typically have a tab or wing connected to the rough grainy side of the film packet. This tab is used to bite down on and hold the film in place. The tab is positioned on the hard surface of either the molars or premolars (depending on the desired shot) of the lower jaw with the film between the teeth and tongue. In order to accomplish this, the technician must initially insert the apparatus by keeping part of the tab against the front of the tooth with one index finger while keeping the film portion vertical with the other one. The patient then closes their teeth down on this wing while the operator keeps the tab portion in place. Separate bitewings for the premolar and molar regions using standard size bitewing films (No. 2 usually) are generally performed, with the front edges positioned at either the canine or second premolar respectively.

PERIAPICAL RADIOGRAPH TECHNIQUES

ORIENTATION OF THE PATIENT'S HEAD

Generally, a patient is seated erect during periapical radiography. This position places the plane of the teeth parallel to ground, and the sagittal or right/left midline plane of the head perpendicular to the ground. All points along the ala-tragus line (also known as the maxillary orientation line) should be equidistant from the floor plane for maxillary bone radiographs. The patient's head should be inclined slightly backward during the mandibular shots to rectify the angle changes that occur when the mouth is opened. If muscles on the floor of the mouth become taut, the patient should be instructed to swallow to relax them. Chair height adjustments are often necessary to ensure proper positioning and operator comfort.

PROCEDURAL PARAMETERS FOR PEDIATRIC PATIENTS

The most important consideration when performing radiography on a pediatric patient is the reduction of radiation exposure. This reduction can be optimized by using a longer length positioning device, a higher potential difference range, the fastest film speed possible, a rectangular-shaped collimator, and a film holder that directs the beam. In addition, the child's body should be protected by lead shielding using both an apron for the torso region and a cervical collar for the thyroid area. Child seats for positioning are also available.

PANORAMIC RADIOGRAPH TECHNIQUES

ROTATIONAL PANORAMIC RADIOGRAPHY

Rotational panoramic radiography exposes the patient to much less radiation than intraoral procedures; for example, a panoramic view utilizes only about 1/10 the dose of a typical full-mouth survey. It also covers a larger area of the dental arches and surrounding tissues. The images generated by panoramic radiography are comparatively free of distortion and there is little overlay of different structures. Since the film is not placed in the mouth, the possibility of infection is greatly reduced. Diagnostically, panoramic radiography offers many advantages, including the decrease in the detection window for decay, periodontal disease, and pulp abnormalities.

ROTATION OF THE X-RAY

In rotational panoramic radiography, the x-ray beam is rotated in the horizontal plane through a narrow slit around an imperceptible rotational axis in the mouth. The effective focal spot for this plane is essentially the same area targeted on a normal intraoral projection because the moving positions of the ray cross at that position (also identified as the center of rotation). The vertical plane is not influenced by this rotation so its focal spot corresponds to that generated by the x-ray tube. Typically, the vertical plane is angled slightly negative, about -4° to -7°, to direct that aspect through the base of the skull. The film is also rotated in the opposite direction through a horizontal axis in order to equilibrate the horizontal and vertical magnifications. Otherwise, the horizontal aspect would be exaggerated relative to the vertical.

TOMOGRAPHY

Tomography is a radiographic procedure that records images in one plane while obscuring or getting rid of images in the other plane. The concept is actually utilized for a number of techniques, including panoramic radiography, computed tomography (CT), and magnetic resonance imaging (MRI). For rotational panoramic radiography, as the x-ray source and film are rotated around the stationary patient, a tomogram or pantomogram is generated. The unblurred plane is called the focal trough or image layer, and only objects in the center of the intersecting projections will be clear. Therefore, patient positioning is crucial in order to target the desired focal trough.

SEQUENCE OF OPERATION

While there may be some variations with different machines, in general there are five steps involved in patient positioning and subsequent exposure with panoramic radiography:

1. Generally, the first step is to have the patient bite into the groove of the bite block. If the individual is edentulous, a chin rest can be used instead. This step basically centers the patient and their front teeth.
2. Next, guides located on the side of the apparatus are locked in place to steady the patient's head and centralize their rear teeth.
3. The chin is then lowered onto the chin rest, which usually has a slight negative incline equivalent to the upward tilt of the x-ray beam.
4. The cervical spine in the neck is then aligned either by having the individual stand erectly or using any means including pillows to achieve straightening in a sit-down type of machine.
5. The patient is then directed to close their lips and place their tongue against the hard palate and remain still while the technician takes the exposure, which typically lasts up to 22 seconds.

SIX ZONES AND HALLMARKS OF GOOD IMAGES

There are six zones on a panoramic radiograph:

- The largest zone examined on a panoramic radiograph is the **central dentition or array of teeth**. In a good image, each tooth is distinct, the array spreads upward toward the back resembling a smile, the sizes and relative overlap of teeth on both sides are similar, the tops of teeth are not cut off, and front teeth should be clear.
- Above this area is the second zone, or the **nose and sinus region**. Here the lower bones or turbinates of the nasal passage and corresponding air spaces should all appear to be within the nasal cavity, and the hard palate should be observed in this area with the tongue against it. Nasal cartilage should not be visible.
- Below the central dentition is the **mandibular body area**. Not much besides the lower border of the mandible should be observed in this third zone.
- The four corners of the radiograph comprise two different zones. The **upper corners**, Zone 4, should have centered rounded condyles in the temporomandibular joint area. The **lower corners**, Zone 6, should primarily be occupied by the hyoid bone.
- The **areas on the sides** of the center are Zone 5, should show each ramus or branching part of the lower jaw and possibly some of the spine.

POSITIONING LIGHTS

Most panoramic radiographic machines have several positioning lights that are activated before an exposure is taken to ensure correct placement of the patient. Usually there are two vertical lights, one that should be positioned at the corner of the mouth, and another that is focused along the midsagittal plane which should be perpendicular to the floor. There is also a horizontal light that is usually centered along the Frankfort plane, which is the imaginary projection between the floor of the eye socket or orbit and the ear's auditory meatus. In theory, this line should be parallel to the ground. Some panoramic machines have positioning lights that are supposed to run along the ala-tragus instead.

TYPES OF LEAD APRONS

In panoramic radiography, a leaded apron that looks like a poncho covering both the front and the back is used. This is required to block rays to both the front and back during the rotational pattern of the x-ray beam. However, unlike most other types of exposure, a thyroid collar should not be worn, and the apron should not extend into the thyroid area. The beam in panoramic procedure is angled slightly upward and would be projected into shields in the thyroid region resulting in clear, non-exposed parts on the radiograph. Radiation exposure is not a significant problem, however, because the total dosage used in the panoramic technique is considerably less than with a complete intraoral series.

CONTROLLING THE IMAGE LAYER

There is a direct relationship between the width of the image layer and the effective projection radius. The latter term refers to the distance between the beam's rotational center and the central plane of the image. The relatively unblurred image layer will be increased as this radius increases. The width of the slit beam affects the size of the image layer inversely, so narrow slits augment the size of the focal trough. The speed at which the film is moving also influences the focal trough by modifying the relationship between the rotational center and the focal spot; faster speeds increase the width of the image layer. The x-ray beam is generally moved in a pattern that shifts the effective rotational center along a desired path depending on the area being documented. This requires keeping the central part of the x-ray beam perpendicular to the tangent of the area at each moving point on the curved path.

APPEARANCE OF SOFT TISSUES AND AIR SPACES

It is generally easier to observe soft tissues on panoramic radiographs than with other types of x-rays. This is due to the fact that these types of tissues like cartilage (or fluid) absorb the radiation and thus can appear as light shadows on the x-ray. Nevertheless, poor technique has occurred if structures like the tongue or nose are

135

visible on the image. On the other hand, air spaces do not absorb the radiation and therefore should be black on the radiograph. These characteristic air spaces are known, such as in the nasopharynx, and the presence of other black areas indicates poor methodology as well.

TYPES OF DISTORTIONS

During panoramic radiography, the x-ray beam is always projected slightly downward with some negative angulation. Therefore, teeth or other entities that are near to the beam relative to the film will appear somewhat wider and those that are comparatively nearer to the film will seem thinner. Additionally, objects toward the back of the oral cavity may appear slightly larger relative to those in the front. Patient positioning can augment these distortions greatly by shifting the focal layer. Only objects in the central plane appear relatively undistorted.

DOUBLE IMAGES

When an anatomical structure or other object is located along the midline, a single image is generated if the entity is between the film and the rotational center of the radiation beam. However, there is a central diamond-shaped area emanating from the midline where the beam can pick up structures twice as it rotates. Objects in this area can appear on the radiograph as double images. One representation is the mirror image of the other, but both are real. Anatomical structures that often appear as double images include the hard palate and hyoid bone.

GHOST IMAGES

Objects that are situated between the center of rotation and the x-ray source can appear as ghost images on panoramic radiographs. These phantom images are not mirror images. Instead, they show up on the opposing side of the radiograph, relatively blurry, and positioned higher than their real location. The vertical plane of these ghosts is particularly fuzzy because it is magnified more than the horizontal component. Ghost images can often be observed when the object is located relatively posterior to the mandible, either internally like the horn of the hyoid bone or the back of the hard palate, or externally like earrings or other jewelry. Real single, real double, and ghost images can all appear on the same panoramic x-ray.

REMOVAL OF INTRAORAL AND EXTRAORAL ITEMS PRIOR TO PANORAMIC RADIOGRAPHY

If they are not removed, most intra- and extraoral items in the facial regions will show up on the panoramic image as both real and ghost images. Acrylic dentures in the front part of the mouth are the only type of intraoral item that might be left, in order to maintain proper interrelationships in that area and steady the patient. Any extra oral item has the potential to disrupt the image, and most should be taken off. Artificial hairpieces, hearing aids, or eye prosthesis are occasionally left in place.

FLATTENING OF STRUCTURES

A panoramic image is generated on a **flat plane**. The film cassette has a protective lead front with a slit, and as the x-ray tube rotates, the film moves across the slit as well. The facial area being documented is curved, but the film is flat. Therefore, the midsagittal plane is in the middle of the image but the teeth and other structures on either side are somewhat flattened and spread-out. Even structures near to this midline can appear flattened if the patient positioning is incorrect; this is an undesirable condition that may disguise other objects as well.

ADDITIONAL EXTRAORAL RADIOGRAPH TECHNIQUES

INTENSIFYING SCREENS

Extraoral radiography is performed by resting a cassette along the side of the face or head and directing x-rays externally from the opposite side. Large screen films that are dual-coated with emulsion are inserted into the cassette, which has intensifying screens on either side to form a sandwich. The intensifying screens serve to take in the radiation energy and convert it to light energy for latent image formation on the film. The intensifying screens have several layers for backing, support, and protection, but the most important layer is the phosphor layer. The phosphor layer contains a substance that will fluoresce or emit visible or other light

when the x-ray strikes it. The film utilized should coordinate with the screen in terms of the spectral sensitivity or color range given off by the phosphor. The main purpose of intensifying screens is the amplification of the image which in turn reduces the necessary radiation dose.

RARE EARTH SCREEN

A rare earth screen is an intensifying screen that incorporates elements as phosphors whose extraction from the earth is complex and costly. The spectral emission pattern of these elements, primarily lanthanum (La) and gadolinium (Gd) encompasses over half of the green wavelength area. Therefore, these types of screens are used in conjunction with films that have been developed to be sensitive to this green light spectrum area. One of the most widely used green-sensitive films is T-Mat film. T-Mat employs flat grains to increase the cross-sectional area, and it comes in several forms depending on the desired contrast.

EXTRAORAL CASSETTE CONSTRUCTION

Extraoral cassettes are designed to enhance the penetration of the x-ray beam on the incoming side and stop the beam and its scatter on the far side. Therefore, the side placed against the patient is relatively thin and made of materials with small atomic numbers such as cardboard or plastic. The back is generally faced with a heavy metal like lead or aluminum. The film is layered between the two attached intensifying screens and held in place by spring clips or metal bars that applies pressure. There are usually external holding devices as well. Panoramic machines sometimes use a type of extraoral cassette that envelops a rotating drum apparatus; here the entire cassette must be more flexible and is generally made of plastic. Identification of the side of the patient and their name by some means is essential. Most of these cassettes have attachable lead pieces that say "R" or "L" for right or left.

Digital Imaging Techniques

DIGITIZATION

Digitization is the transformation of pieces of an analog image into relative intensities and the reassembly of these intensities into a visible analog image on a computer screen. An ordinary radiograph is an analog image because the finished product is a direct representation of what has been documented on film. Digital procedures take the analog image and initially convert it to numbers on a grid that represent relative levels of brightness. The number within each grid measures the number of pixels in that area. No film or processing is required with digital imaging, the radiation dose is low, and the cost is minimal. The computer-generated images can be viewed right away, manipulated, or transmitted electronically. Use of digital imaging is controversial, however, because it does not produce a hard copy and it may not be recognized legally or by insurance companies. Initial cost outlay is considerable and the quality of the image is generally inferior to film techniques.

SELECTION OF IMAGE RECEPTOR SIZE FOR RADIOGRAPHIC VS. DIGITAL IMAGING

Radiographic image receptors, which change x-rays into images, are commonly used for radiographic film. They are classified according to sensitivity (direct action for intraoral, non-direct action for extraoral), use (intraoral, extraoral, duplicating), speed (slow, fast, super-fast), packaging (single, double) and type of emulsion (single or double coated). The size selection depends on the area to be filmed and the mouth size. Sizes include:

- Periapicals or bitewings:
    - Size 0: 22 mm X 35 mm (used for children)
    - Size 1: 24 mm X 40 mm (used for anterior teeth)
    - Size 2: 31 mm X 41 mm (used for adults for posterior bitewings)
    - Size 3: 27 mm X 54 mm (used for adults to view all posterior teeth in a single film)
- Occlusals:
    - Size 4: 57 mm X 76 mm (used for large maxillary, mandibular areas)

Digital image receptors, which decrease radiation exposure, include the charge-coupled device (CCD), which may be wired or wireless, but the sensor is bulkier than those for radiographic film and inflexible. The other type is the photostimulable phosphor plate (PSP), which is flexible and similar to film but is reusable. Sizes are generally comparable to radiographic image receptors, sizes 0, 1, 2, and 3.

SELECTION OF COMPUTER AND OTHER COMPONENTS OF DIGITAL IMAGING

When selecting a computer to perform digital imaging, either a laptop or desktop model can be used. The processor speed determines the rapidity of image processing. Sufficient RAM should be chosen to enable data retention and processing during the exposure without having to temporarily store the information on the hard drive. After processing, the image probably will be kept on the hard drive so its memory should be large. Various types of printers, each with its own pros and cons, can be selected. A number of dental imaging software packages are available; it is preferable to buy one that conforms to standards established by Digital Imaging and Communications in Medicine (DICOM).

DIGITAL IMAGING DEVICES
CHARGE COUPLED DEVICE

A charge coupled device or CCD is one type of sensor that can detect x-rays and transform them into electronic data for computer interpretation and visualization. CCDs consist of transistor grids that change x-ray photons striking them into electrons. CCDs can be used with visible light. For x-ray exposures, the beam passes through a scintillation screen and a fiber-optic faceplate before reaching the CCD sensor. The scintillation screen serves to convert the x-ray picture into fluorescing visible light. The fiber-optic plate focuses the light and reduces passage of the x-rays by use of leaded glass. The CCD receives the light as pixels on the grid, which are then

138

interpreted in terms of brightness and position to form a digital image. CCDs are used in direct digital imaging or indirectly in conjunction with a scanner.

CMOS/APS

CMOS/APS is the abbreviation for a Complementary Metal Oxide Semiconductor with an Active Pixel Sensor. It is another device used to directly produce digital images from x-ray exposure. It is similar to a CCD in that it employs a scintillation screen to convert the x-rays to visible light and an integrated circuit board to convert the light to digital images for computer interpretation. The main difference between CMOS/APS devices and CCDs is that the CMOS/APS includes amplifying transistors on each of the pixels. Advantages of CMOS/APS sensors include the ability to put circuitry directly onto the chip, use of less power, and reduction of pixel size. These devices can also be linked to a computer via a simple USB port.

DIGITAL IMAGING WITH CMOS OR CCD SENSORS

Detectors used for CMOS or CCD digital imaging are thicker than normal film. This difference means that either film-holders must be converted to accommodate the sensors or proprietary holders must be utilized. After positioning, the software in the computer regulates the sensor and clarifies the appropriate time to snap the exposure. Since no development is necessary for either of these techniques, the image is available within seconds, and the viewpoint or characteristics of the picture can be modified with the software.

HOW DIRECT DIGITAL IMAGE SENSORS INTERFACE WITH THE COMPUTER

CCDs currently interface with the computer for digital imaging via a Universal Serial Bus (USB) or Firewall connector. Older CCD sensor systems utilize computers with special circuit boards incorporated into them, but newer models can process the picture through external packs or processing boards. CMOS/APS sensors generally interface with the computer through a simple USB port. Both CCD and CMOS sensors produce images on the computer within seconds. PSP plates do not directly connect to the computer; instead, the laser scanner (which fluoresces the latent image on the plate) is directly attached to the computer. The time between exposure and reading for PSP imaging is much longer than that required with the other sensors.

RESOLUTION OF DIGITAL IMAGES
GRAY-LEVEL RESOLUTION ON DIGITAL IMAGES

Gray-level resolution is the total number of shades of gray that a particular digital image is capable of displaying. Every pixel in the image has an assigned number, which is related to the computer storage capacity. Each bit of computer storage capacity exponentially increases the gray scale resolution according to the formula 2^x where x is number of bits of storage capacity. While current computers may have up to 12 bits or more of storage space, 8 bits are shown on the monitor generally. Since 8 bits represents 2^8 or 256 shades of gray, considerably more than can be distinguished by the human eye, this is sufficient. The numbering is represented as 0 for pure black up to 255 for pure white.

SPATIAL RESOLUTION ON DIGITAL IMAGES

The spatial resolution of a digital image refers to the number of pixels used to create the image. An image with high spatial resolution has more pixels per a specified dimension than an image that has less pixels per the same dimension (low spatial resolution). Resultingly, an image with high spatial resolution is clearer/more detailed than one with low spatial resolution. Spatial resolution as it applies to dental imagery is important in declaring the image's ability to show the required level of detail for abnormalities to be identified and diagnosed.

ACQUIRING DIGITAL IMAGES INDIRECTLY

Regular radiographic films can be converted to digital images, a process known as the indirect method of obtaining a digital image. In this technique, some type of camera or scanner is used. In the first case, a digital or video camera takes a picture of an extant radiograph. If a video camera is used, a computer transforms the image into a digital one. If a digital camera is utilized, the digitization occurs internally, and the picture is later

downloaded onto a computer. Indirect acquisition can also be done with a scanner with an attached transparency adaptor that delivers light through the x-ray. This light is then transmitted to a CCD, which assembles a digital image.

ACQUIRING DIGITAL IMAGES DIRECTLY WITH PSP IMAGING

Photostimulable phosphor (PSP) imaging is one method of converting x-ray exposures directly into digital images. Rare earth phosphors, typically barium europium fluorohalide, are coated onto imaging plates. When x-rays strike these plates, the radiation energy is amassed on the plate as a type of latent image until processing. PSP plates are later processed by scanning them with a laser to produce fluorescence. The signals are interpreted by a photodiode which transfers the digital image to a computer. PSP imaging uses plates that are similar in size to regular dental films. Other advantages of this system include less radiation to the patient, an expanded and linear range of exposures that can produce a good image, and the ability to take the film without being hooked up to a computer.

STEPS INVOLVED IN PSP DIGITAL IMAGING

For digital imaging that utilizes photostimulable phosphors, the first step is the erasure of images on the plates from previous exposures. This step is very easy. Basically, the phosphor-coated side of the plate is set on top of a lighted viewbox for several minutes to obliterate the prior image. Then the plates are enclosed in tight barrier envelopes or the panoramic cassette. The x-ray exposure is taken. Then the covering is removed, and the PSPs are loaded onto a drum. This drum is placed into the scanner, and the exposures are scanned with a laser. The images are transmitted directly to a computer.

ADAPTING DIGITAL IMAGING FOR PANORAMIC OR CEPHALOMETRIC MACHINERY

CCDs and PSP systems are both currently used with many panoramic or cephalometric systems. For PSP systems, the major adaptations are larger plates and scanners to accommodate the cassette. Resolution in terms of line pairs per millimeter is generally reduced for PSP relative to regular films when panoramic views are taken in order to reduce scan time and film size. On the other hand, CCD sensors can be used at resolutions comparable to regular film for panoramic or cephalometric views. These types of machines use multiple CCDs stacked into a grid-like linear array. The array travels around or scans the individual gathering a series of single vertical lines to form the image. Most new CCD panoramic systems do only digital imaging, but there are kits available that convert film-based machines for digital use.

TYPES OF MODIFICATIONS IN DIGITAL IMAGING

Various software and other tools incorporated into digital imaging processing equipment can be used to modify the image for better visualization or diagnostic purposes. One of the most common software packages can turn over the generated picture to give the mirror image; this is used to orient the views like a conventional film array. There are various controls that can change the brightness, manipulate the contrast into a suitable gray scale range, or zoom for magnification of specific areas. There is usually a mechanism to exchange black and white areas or reverse the gray scale in order to see certain objects better, and another that colorizes or designates a color to the gray ratio. The computer usually has incorporated filters to reduce noise and sharpen the picture. Software may also permit measurement of certain areas on the film.

SUBTRACTION RADIOGRAPHY

Subtraction radiography is a technique employed with digital image processing. The technique digitally merges two different images and then subtracts the common areas from the radiographic representation. Therefore, only the variations between the original images are seen. This practice is useful for visualization of sequential changes in decay development or bone loss as well as for observation after surgical procedures such as implants or periodontia. At present, the legal implications of permanent storage of this type of manipulation of the images as well as other modifications are somewhat unresolved. Usually, the manipulated image can only be earmarked as a copy, not an original.

Storing Digital Radiographic Images

Original or manipulated images can be stored on the computer with software that typically compresses or reduces the size of the file. Files can be compressed with either no loss of computer data or with some ("lossy") deficit of original data. Both methods permanently change the image, but studies have found that diagnostic utility is not compromised with compression up to 1/12 of the original. Digital image formats include TIFF, which does not discard any data, and JPEG, which does reduce the image as much as 100 times and is therefore a lossy compression. Thus, the JPEG format can initiate image degradation. Typically, the images are also backed up on DVDs or other storage media. They can also be transmitted via networking to other individuals.

Purpose and Maintenance of Radiographic Equipment

FILMS

HANDLING DENTAL X-RAY FILMS

Closed boxes of dental x-ray film need to be kept in a refrigerator or another cool area. After opening, the unused film should either be stowed in lead containers, away from the screening area (intraoral), or near the area but in containers that block light (screen film). This is because the emulsions are responsive to a number of situations including excessive heat, light exposure, other radiation, touching, and gas fumes. Films designed for use at high speeds are more finely tuned and thus even more susceptible to these factors.

PARTS OF RADIOGRAPHIC FILM PACKETS AND ORDER OF REMOVAL

Plastic film envelopes, if present, are removed and wiped of saliva (preferably with disinfectant) before transportation to the darkroom and are not part of the actual film packet. Typical radiographic film packets all have four components. The radiographic film is surrounded by black light-proof paper and backed by a sheet of lead foil. The whole package is enclosed with a moisture and light-proof barrier packet which has a color-coded end. In the darkroom, the film is removed by holding that part of the packet and pulling back the black tab to remove the film with its black-paper covering. The film is shaken out of the black paper over a paper towel before development.

DENTAL FILM STORAGE

Film storage areas must ensure films are properly maintained. Dental film can be damaged by high temperatures, exposure to chemicals, or radiation, so film must be protected from these elements. Film should be stored at temperatures of 50-70 °F. In many practices, film is stored in refrigerators to avoid overheating. Humidity should be 30-50%. Film should not be stored near chemical fumes, x-ray machines, or radioactive materials as radiation may result in damage or fogging. Packages of films should be stored vertically and not in horizontal piles as the weight may cause damage. The expiration dates on films should be checked at least weekly and the oldest film placed for first use so that film is rotated properly. A log should be maintained with a checklist and signatures to ensure correct storage.

MANUAL PROCESSING

Manual processing of x-rays involves the following process. First, lock the darkroom. Label processing hangers. Agitate developer and fixing solutions with individual stirrers and chemicals; refill if necessary. Check temperature of the water bath and adjust, if necessary, by means that will not dilute the solution. All white light should be eliminated; activate safelight. Using gloves, open the film packet. Remove gloves and insert films into their hangers. Adjust interval timer to the development time (usually 5 minutes for a 70 °F bath). Lower film into the developer solution and begin timing. Initially, rapid agitation up and down is suggested to get rid of air bubbles and saturate the film surfaces. At the end of the development period, the film is transferred to the rinsing tank (water bath) and swirled for about a half minute to remove developer. The film is put into the fixer solution for approximately twice the development time, typically 10 minutes. After fixation, normal lighting can be turned on and the safelight turned off. The film is washed in the bath for 15-20 minutes, dried on a rack, and then mounted.

TEMPERATURE CONTROL

The effective temperature range for the manual processing of x-rays is 60-75 °F, and the suggested temperature is 70 °F. Above this temperature range fogging can occur due to excessively rapid development, and below this range both development and fixation proceed too slowly. At 70 °F, film density and contrast are fairly ideal, and the processing time is convenient. This temperature can be sustained easily in the master water bath or rinsing tank by a mixing valve that combines the hot water and cold water coming in. Typically, 2 different insert tanks for either developing or fixing chemicals are put into this tank. A thermometer should be clipped to the tank to ensure maintenance of the proper temperature, and a timer should be used to control development and fixation intervals.

WET READING OF MANUALLY PROCESSED RADIOGRAPHS

In emergencies, a manually processed radiograph can be wet read. This means that the radiograph is removed from the fixer early and observed near the safelight. Actual clearing of the solution means that the cloudy appearance of the film has disappeared, and the silver halide crystals have been converted. This reaction takes about 2 minutes, which means that a wet reading can be taken shortly thereafter (3 or 4 minutes of fixation) if necessary. For permanent documentation, however, recommended fixation times should be employed. A short fixation time (such as termination after wet reading) means that the emulsion is not hardened enough, drying will be prolonged, and the image may be lost with aging. Alternatively, too long of a fixation time can result in irreversible binding of the fixer to the gel and subsequent brown discoloration of the radiograph.

MANUAL FIXER SOLUTIONS

The purpose of fixation is to remove unexposed silver halide crystals and terminate the development process. The fixing or clearing agents that remove the unexposed silver bromide crystals from the emulsion gel are typically thiosulfates coupled to either ammonium or sodium. The acidic medium that actually terminates the development by neutralization is usually either acetic or sulfuric acid. A preservative like sodium sulfite is included as well to prevent the breakdown of the fixing agent. In addition, a chemical that shrinks and hardens the gelatin is added; examples of hardeners are aluminum chloride, aluminum sulfide, and potassium aluminum sulfate. All of the chemicals are dissolved in water.

COMPONENTS OF MANUAL DEVELOPER SOLUTION

The primary purpose of the developer solution is to reduce the silver halide crystals generated during the radiation into black metallic silver. Usually, the reducing agents employed are metol, which acts rapidly to induce gray tones, and hydroquinone, which acts more gradually but generates better contrast. Developer solutions also contain an activator like sodium carbonate, which provides an alkaline pH and also softens the emulsion. The solutions include an agent called a restrainer that prevents the non-exposed silver bromide crystals from developing and producing unwanted fog; typically, potassium bromide is used. Lastly, developers contain a preservative such as sodium sulfite to stop the solution from oxidizing. All of the chemicals are dissolved in water.

AUTOMATIC PROCESSOR

FEEDING FILM PACKETS

If the automatic processor has a daylight loader, film packets are opened and fed into the machine inside this loader. Therefore, provisions for keeping light out are unnecessary. If the machine does not have a loader, packets are opened with gloves in a locked darkroom with a safelight. In either case, films are inserted into the processor with bare hands in a very controlled, deliberate manner in order to avoid jamming the machine. This is particularly essential for panoramic films which are fed lengthwise. For a bent film, the straight side should be introduced first. The time interval between insertions of different films should be at least 5 seconds. Films must be dry when inserted to avoid roller contamination and lines on later films.

MAINTENANCE

Some procedures should be performed daily in order to properly maintain automatic processors. These include replenishment of the solutions as needed depending on the daily development load, maintenance of the suggested temperature, and evaluation of the transport rollers for proper alignment. About twice as much developer relative to fixer is used and needs to be replenished; some machines have infrared sensors that automatically determine the needed replenisher. The automatic processing solutions should be completely changed at intervals appropriate to the workload, which can be as often as weekly in a busy office. When the machine is not being used, the lid should be left slightly ajar to permit fumes to escape and reduce subsequent film fogging. The processor should be cleaned about once a week, and lubricant should be applied to gears, bearings and the like about once a month.

TIMING FOR MANUAL VS. AUTOMATIC PROCESSING OF RADIOGRAPHS

When an automatic processor is used, the total processing time is greatly reduced over manual methods. The total time involved can be as little as one and half to 5 minutes. This time reduction is achieved through use of rollers that guide the film through the processor and wring out excess solutions as well as by increasing the temperature and the concentrations of reagents. Some chemical substitutions and additions are made as well. The reducing agent in the developer is changed to phenidone instead of metol because the former works faster in conjunction with the hydroquinone. Glutaraldehyde is typically added to the developer to harden the gel, and sulphates are included as well to prevent swelling. The goal is the prevention of sticking to the rollers in the machine. Instead of approximately 70 °F, processing temperature is around 83 °F. Solutions are replenished often by injection into the floor of the tank. Drying is performed in the machine with streams of heated air, and the finished radiograph is automatically dropped onto a platform.

SAFELIGHTS

A safelight is a weak light used with filters in a darkroom to enable the technician to process radiographs without excessive fogging. The wattage of the bulb is very low, typically between 7.5 and 15 watts if it directly illuminates the area and up to 25 watts if the lighting is indirect. The light source should be at least 4 feet from the processing area, and processing time should be kept to 8 minutes or less. Filters are placed between the light source and the processing area to screen out portions of the light spectrum. Amber or red filters are most often utilized because the yellow and red region is complementary to the most sensitive colors for x-ray film, blue and green light. Currently, the most commonly used filter is the red Kodak GBX-2, which is suggested for higher E and F speed films of the oral cavity as well as extraoral films that contain rare-earth substances that emit light when irradiated.

QUALITY ASSURANCE

Quality assurance is the summation of administrative and technical steps required to maintain reliable and reproducible results in any type of work setting. In the context of a dental radiological setup, quality assurance efforts translate to practices that will assure consistent, comprehensible radiographs with minimal radiation exposure. There are usually two components to quality assurance. The first component is quality administration, which is the administrative aspect of coordinating efforts to ensure high-quality work. The other part to quality assurance is quality control, which encompasses the actual test procedures and technical practices required to maintain consistent, first-rate results.

RECOMMENDED QUALITY CONTROL PRACTICES

Auxiliary equipment such as leaded aprons and thyroid jackets, panoramic cassettes, and viewboxes need to be checked at regular intervals. Documentation should include a retake log book, which includes explanations of errors for reference and a general quality assurance register that records all procedures, outcomes, and remedial actions taken. Settings for exposure parameters and film speed under all possible scenarios should be clearly displayed in the work area. Charts illustrating time versus temperature for processing and darkroom maintenance procedures and schedules should also be posted. All equipment measurements and manuals should be readily available. Film expiration dates should be monitored.

CHECKING X-RAY MACHINE'S POTENTIAL DIFFERENCE AND ACCURACY

The potential difference or kVp, the precision of its setting, and the size of the focal spot all influence the quality of the x-ray beam emitted from the machine. These parameters should be checked once a year. The test generally used to evaluate the potential difference or penetrating power of the beam is the half-value layer test. Sheets of aluminum of various thicknesses are placed between the positioning device and a pocket dosimeter. With the x-ray equipment at highest voltage or potential difference, the beam is directed through the aluminum and the output in mR is measured by the dosimeter. Half of the maximal output should pass through a particular disc as outlined by federal guidelines; failure to do so indicates needed repair.

Accuracy of the voltage setting is typically checked with commercially available meters. These meters quantify the wavelength and frequency of a beam directed at a target; since potential difference determines these two parameters, its accuracy is ascertained.

USE OF POCKET DOSIMETER IN QUALITY CONTROL

A pocket dosimeter is a small rod-shaped ionization chamber used to quantify the radiation being emitted from the x-ray machine. It basically consists of an air-filled chamber, a quartz fiber, a lens, and a switch that is charged prior to use. The dosimeter is used to compare radiation produced through a series of exposure settings relative to the same settings at baseline. The number of milliroentgens generated or the relative gray scale on a wedge should be equivalent to the baseline values. If the current readings do not match the reference value, then the timer and the mA circuit must be checked as well. There are commercially available meters to check timers, but this can also be done manually by directing the central x-ray beam perpendicularly to a spinning top apparatus attached to a film and counting the number of dots shown on the film. After checking the timer, the filament or mA circuit can be evaluated in one of two ways. If more than one current setting is available, output in milliroentgens can be measured at the same theoretical mAs product for each; if readings do not match, repair is indicated. With only one mA setting available, outside servicing is required. These procedures should be performed yearly.

EVALUATING COLLIMATOR EFFICACY

Collimator efficacy should be checked every year. A collimator is a device that limits the shape and size of the x-ray beam. There are several ways to perform a collimation test. One method is to direct the end of the positioning device onto either a panoramic cartridge or a rare earth fluorescent screen and expose the screen briefly; the technician then either records the area of fluorescence by looking through the leaded window or develops the panoramic packet. The area of exposure should not exceed the BID's diameter. Alternatively, smaller films can be arranged around the tip of the BID with the device covering about half of each packet, each is exposed simultaneously. After processing, the arrangement is reestablished to see whether total exposure area is within the established guidelines. If examination indicates that the radiation beam is not centered, generally the collimator position can be readjusted or a new one purchased.

CHECKING AND EVALUATING THE FOCAL SPOT SIZE

The focal spot size is the surface area covered by the x-ray beam. Typically, the spot size deteriorates and becomes larger over time due to constant bombardment with electrons. If the spot size is enlarged, the resolution or ability to differentiate adjoining structures in the image is decreased. Spot size is checked with a simple plastic tube, usually 6 inches in length. The tube has a leaded closed end with slots that the BID is placed against, and an open end that is positioned over a large occlusal film. Exposure is performed, and the resolution on the test film is evaluated by counting the number of line pairs per millimeter that can be resolved. Generally, if the resolution is less than or equal to 7 pairs per millimeter, resolution is inadequate. In this case, either a new machine should be bought, or the tubehead can be reconstructed.

MONITORING RADIOGRAPHIC PROCESSING SOLUTIONS

The amount and temperature of processing solutions can affect the density of radiographs. Therefore, related quality control procedures should be performed every day. The best way to accomplish these processing solution checks is to keep a cadre of refrigerated reference films that are opened and run through the processing procedure daily. The reference films have gradated levels of exposure produced placing the film under a step-wedge. Aluminum step-wedges are commercially available, but a similar device can be made using lead foil strips. After the processor is brought to the correct temperature for its type, a reference film is processed and then compared to a baseline film that was developed when solutions were fresh. The films are viewed on an illuminator, and if the daily contrast and density has degraded relative to the baseline film, solutions should be replenished. Developer and sometimes fixer may need to be added every day if processing volumes are large or contamination occurs. Consequently, in larger Stage III facilities, sensitometers and densitometers are utilized together to generate reproducible images and check them for contrast and density respectively.

DETECTING AND CONTROLLING FOG IN THE DARKROOM

Every month, a **fog check** for undesired density and its causes should be performed. The fog or excess density is due to exposure of silver halide crystals as a result of white or undesired wavelengths of light. The basic check is done by turning off every source of light in the closed darkroom. After the technician acclimates to the darkness, they observe and subsequently block off any area where white light seeps into the room. The safelight should also be tested because there is a finite amount of time, generally up to 8 minutes, during which even this light can be on during processing. One procedure called the coin test involves processing a series of pre-exposed films at various time intervals by placing a coin on each film after opening the packets and observing how long it takes before the coin is outlined on the film. The maximum time a safelight can be used corresponds to the time when the coin's ridges are visible on the processed film. Safelight timing for cephalometric or panoramic films can be determined by pulling them out of a box at one-inch intervals per minute, and then checking when a line of density begins to emerge on one of the films (in other words, the maximum time for safelight use).

Patient Management

MANAGING PAIN AND ANXIETY

Some patients are anxious or tend to experience discomfort during radiography. If all desired areas can be visualized on a panoramic radiograph, its substitution for intraoral procedures can alleviate anxiety and discomfort. Sometimes films used for intraoral radiography can be bent if the inflection does not mask the teeth being documented. There are ways to relax the muscles in the area being x-rayed. These include placing the film closer to the tongue or using commercially available tissue pads attached to the top edge of the film. Anesthetics can be applied topically to the region, but they should be rinsed out after the dental procedures. Occasionally, patients are given prescription tranquilizers like diazepam to reduce their apprehension.

MANAGING PATIENTS WITH SPECIAL NEEDS

A good chairside manner is paramount in dealing with any patient. The major physical disability that might pose a problem in dental radiology is a patient's **inability to control movement** as in certain spastic disorders; here a friend wearing protective gear should assist and steady the patient, not the dental professional. Individuals with **developmental disabilities** are usually harder to manage, and use of sedatives or anesthesia may be necessary. Most types of radiographs can be done without moving an immobile patient out of a wheelchair, and if they are confined to their beds or home, there are mobile x-ray units available. Alternative methods of communication need to be used with individuals who have **hearing or vision impairment**.

MANAGING PEDIATRIC PATIENTS

Pediatric patients may be unfamiliar with the process of having x-rays taken, so any attempt to explain or show them what will occur during the exposure is helpful. One of the major management issues is getting the pediatric patient to understand that they must remain perfectly still when the shot is being taken. In addition, some children cannot endure certain types of film placements. Since their mouth is smaller than that of an adult, more latitude can be allowed in the technique or placement of the film. For example, an acceptable exposure can be taken by having the child bite down on a periapical film while the operator increases the vertical angulation. Reverse bitewings are often done on pediatric patients because they tend to dislodge regular bitewings; in the reverse technique the bitewing is positioned near the cheek and the exposure is taken as a lateral oblique view from the opposite side. Occasionally, extraoral films are done instead.

GAG REFLEX

The gag reflex is the tendency to choke or vomit. A portion of dental patients will experience this tendency during dental procedures such as radiography. The reflex is initiated when its receptors, which are located on the back third of the tongue as well as the rear of the throat, are irritated. Nerves located in these regions send messages to the gag center in the medulla oblongata portion of the brain. Nerves from the brain transmit signals to muscle fibers associated with the gag reflex. Initially, the patient cannot breathe, and later muscles in the upper part of the abdominal cavity and the upper portion of the throat contract. This choking reaction may be accompanied by regurgitation of undigested food as well.

INTERVENTIONS FOR PATIENTS WITH A SEVERE GAG REFLEX

Interventions for severe gag reflex include the following:

- Have the patient breathe through the nose.
- Have the patient breathe slowly and concentrate of breathing.
- Spray the back of the patient's throat with an anesthetic mouth spray, such as Chloraseptic.
- Have the patient make a tight fist with the left hand and concentrate on it.
- Rinse the patient's mouth with salt water before examination.

- Talk to and distract the patient.
- Ask the patient to lean forward when taking impressions so material doesn't ooze toward the back of the throat.

RESULTS OF POOR PATIENT PREPARATION

Patient preparation errors with regard to unacceptable radiographic images generally fall into two categories.

- The first category is the additional **overlapping of radiopaque artifacts**. These artifacts result from failure to remove primarily metallic hardware from the body or oral cavity. Examples include dental hardware, many types of jewelry, glasses, and artificial hairpieces.
- Any type of movement from the patient including touching the equipment can result in **unsharpness or blurring** of the image by increasing the peripheral penumbra area of the focal spot.

Good chairside technique from the technician should eliminate these errors.

Mounting

PROCEDURE FOR MOUNTING RADIOGRAPHS

The recommended procedure for mounting radiographs is to place them in a relationship as though the viewer is looking straight at the patient. This orientation requires that mounting be done with all the raised dots of the film facing the observer and is sometimes termed **labial mounting**. Sometimes older readings were done in the opposite orientation (**lingual mounting**), but that procedure is no longer suggested. A viewbox is used for observation. Radiographs are arranged on it with all raised dots upward and segregated according to anatomical location. They are touched only on the periphery with either clean, dry hands or cotton gloves. Identification of anatomical sites can be aided by the knowledge of various landmarks.

MOUNTING IMAGES USING THE FACIAL VIEW

Mount dental images according to position in the mouth from the anterior views, which are labial (facing lips) to posterior views, which are buccal (facing cheeks). Steps include:

1. Lay film on viewer with identification dot facing upward and on incisal edge for anteriors and periapicals.
2. Separate film into 3 groups: anterior (6), bitewing (4) and posterior (8).
3. Place anteriors (which are vertical). The central anteriors are longest, and the maxillary anteriors are larger than the mandibular. The canines are placed on the right and left. Note when placing right and left to place according to the direction of the roots. The sinus line indicates maxillary position.
4. Place bitewings according to the curve of Spee (smile line) beginning with premolars (bicuspids) toward the inside and molars toward the outside. Any unusual findings in the x-rays, such as chipped teeth or metal rods, can help to identify placement.
5. Place periapicals checking sinus line to identify maxillary teeth. Additionally, maxillary molars typically have 3 roots and mandibular molars 2 roots.

MOUNTING A FULL MOUTH SURVEY

Typically, in a full mouth survey, the back teeth of the upper jaw are arranged first with their crowns facing toward the bottom of the viewbox, using landmarks of the dental arch to distinguish pre-molars from molars. Then maxillary teeth toward the front are arranged with their edges facing downward. The incisors are placed in the center with laterals and canines to the appropriate side as identified by landmarks. Similarly, mandibular radiographs are arranged with the crowns or incisal surfaces facing upwards. Bitewing radiographs are then mounted in the middle on the sides with the planes between the two biting edges oriented upward toward the back of the cavity. A useful landmark for these radiographs is the root pattern, as molars in the lower jaw have two roots while those in the upper jaw have three.

TYPICAL ANGULAR CONFIGURATION OF TEETH

In the upper jaw or maxilla, most teeth are angled outward from the jaw. This configuration is known a buccal or facial tilt. In the lower jaw or mandible, the angle between the teeth and the jaw typically changes from a buccal tilt in the front six teeth to an almost upright orientation at the premolars to a small inward or lingual tilt at the back. The real axis of the root of a tooth is the line between the tip of the root, which is not visible to the eye, and the end of the visible part of the tooth. Assumptions about the location of the tip or apical area of the root in the maxilla can be made by envisioning a line between the tragus, the bulge anterior to the ear opening, and the ala or wing of the nose and extrapolating to identifying facial features. The line for similar extrapolation to the mandible is about a half centimeter below the jaw.

Anatomical Structures and Dental Materials Observed on Images

DIFFERENTIAL ABSORPTION OF X-RAYS

Tissues and other materials found in the jaw area are subject to differential absorption of x-rays. Metals used in restorations tend to have high atomic numbers and thus absorb a greater proportion of x-rays. Therefore, restorations and to a lesser extent enamel and cortical bone usually are observed on x-ray films as radiopaque areas. This means that those areas are very bright and transparent because they have already absorbed the x-ray energy and it does not strike the film. At the other end of the spectrum, dark or radiolucent portions of the radiograph result from areas that are easily penetrated by the x-ray. These include the softer tissues. Scattering can produce similar dark spots. Teeth and bones are comprised of a considerable amount of calcium and phosphorus, which both have mid-range atomic numbers (20 and 15), but the rate of absorption can be affected by age and presence of decay or other disease in these structures.

INTERPRETING STRUCTURES ON RADIOGRAPHS

Teeth and other structures or areas on a radiograph are generally interpreted in terms of how radiolucent or radiopaque they are. Radiolucent areas allow a great deal of radiation to penetrate them and thus appear dark or black on the radiograph. Radiopaque areas block the passage of x-rays and thus emerge as relatively light or white on the radiographic image. These terms are used not only for film-based radiographs, but also to describe the relative densities generated using other techniques such as computed tomography. Radiopaque sections are described as being denser than radiolucent portions. These known density differences are used to interpret the structures and processes observed on the radiograph or a computer-generated image.

AREAS OF MOUTH THAT ARE RADIOLUCENT

There is a cavity enclosed by the dentin and enamel of the tooth called the pulp space. This cavity is radiolucent or dark on a radiograph generally. The portion protruding down into the apex of the root of the tooth is termed the root canal space, and it should appear radiolucent on the image as well. The pulp areas can become inflamed secondary to microbial infections from injury or diseases of the teeth or surrounding areas. Typically, there is also a dark or radiolucent border between the lamina dura and the root section of the teeth representing the periodontal ligament space (PDLS). This space appears wider in a number of metastatic diseases or if the teeth have been shifted (primarily through orthodontia).

AREAS OF MOUTH THAT ARE RADIOPAQUE

The enamel of the teeth, the dentin underneath, and another part called the lamina dura all appear as white or somewhat light areas (radiopaque) on a radiograph. These structures all absorb the x-rays to some extent. The enamel or hard calcium-containing layer on the outside of the tooth is very white on a radiograph, while the underlying dentin is slightly less dense and appears lighter on the image. Tooth decay or caries can be visualized in both these areas. There is also a very delicate layer of alveolar bone surrounding the tooth socket called the lamina dura which also should be radiopaque on the radiograph. This bone becomes thicker at the top when a new tooth is emerging, and it can shrivel or disappear in certain disease states. The other portions of the alveolar bone surround the teeth and are relatively radiopaque as well. Thinning of this bone suggests a disease state such as periodontal disease or even osteoporosis.

STRUCTURES IN MAXILLA THAT APPEAR RADIOLUCENT

The anatomical structures of the maxilla or upper jaw that appear radiolucent on a radiograph are those that are some type of natural opening or groove. One of these structures is the median maxillary or palatal suture. This structure is a fixed joint in the roof of the mouth beginning at the center of the incisors and extending posterior along the midline. There is also a dark cavity to either side of the front of this line called the nasopalatine or incisive foramen, whose major function is to receive nerve responses and blood vessels. Occasionally, four cavities are observed instead of two. If the area has a white border, cyst formation is suggested. Any hollows containing air are dark-appearing nasal fossae, including small indentations in the

alveolar bone of either jaw called incisive lateral fossae. These areas do not indicate disease processes. Parts of the maxillary sinus appear radiolucent as well.

STRUCTURES IN THE MAXILLA THAT APPEAR RADIOPAQUE

There are several characteristic anatomical structures in the maxilla that appear radiopaque or relatively white on a radiograph. Typically, a white section that looks like an inverted Y is seen in the canine area. This inverted Y represents the junction between the front border of the maxillary sinus and the floor of the nasal fossa. This area is used as a landmark even in toothless individuals, and pathological conditions can change its appearance. Tuberosities are rounded protuberances found in the back of the jaw; they also are relatively radiopaque. Just behind the tuberosity is another light area that resembles a hook, called the hamular process. One of the cheek bones in the upper jaw is termed the zygomatic or malar bone, and it is generally visualized as a radiopaque U-shaped area or arch above the teeth.

STRUCTURES IN THE MANDIBLE THAT APPEAR RADIOLUCENT

In the front of the mandible, there are two radiolucent areas. The first is the mental foramen, which is a round-shaped section just below both sets of pre-molars; its serves as a tributary for nerve impulses and blood vessels. There is a genial tubercle along the midline in the front of mandible, which appears as a dark spot in the middle for passage of blood vessels surrounded by a lighter area where muscles are attached. There is also a dark passage called the mandibular or inferior alveolar canal that runs down the side of the lower jaw between the mandibular foramen and the mental foramen. A major artery traces the canal area and relatively light areas are seen to either side.

STRUCTURES IN THE MANDIBLE THAT APPEAR RADIOPAQUE

The coronoid process is the forward-sloping triangular shaped portion of the mandible or lower jaw. It projects from the sigmoid notch of the mandible and connects to a muscle called the temporalis. This process appears relatively radiopaque on a radiograph, and it is often seen on images of the maxilla because of its proximity. Other radiopaque areas in the front of the mandible include the mental ridges or bones on the front of the lower jaw, parts of the genial tubercles below and along the midline, and the lower cortex of the jaw. White lines are also seen extending from the mental tubercle back to the anterior portion of the branching ramus (the external oblique ridge) and lingually from the pre-molar to molar regions (mylohyoid line). The softer tissues are sometimes seen as relatively radiopaque areas on the image if pressure from biting the film packet forces them into the area being x-rayed.

APPEARANCE OF MAXILLARY SINUS ON RADIOGRAPH

The maxillary sinus or antrum is a hollow space within the alveolar bone that contains air. It is one of the sinuses surrounding the nose. Typically, only the bottom half of this cavity is observed on a periapical projection as a radiolucent shadow surrounded by a delicate jagged radiopaque edge. Occasionally, this sinus cavity will expand into the area between the roots of the back teeth and form what looks like a depression. This condition is referred to as pneumatization, and it can be observed with chronic sinus diseases, aging, or early extraction of molars in the maxillary jaw.

READING PANORAMIC RADIOGRAPHS

Individuals who read panoramic radiographs must be familiar with a variety of common anatomical landmarks in the maxillofacial region and other areas of the face in addition to the teeth. These landmarks include bones, arch structures, ridge formations, palates, typical air spaces, and the like. They must also be aware of what types of structures can obscure others on the image and conditions that affect the relative radiolucency of objects. A much larger area is covered on a panoramic radiograph than any other type of x-ray. The interplay between the teeth and other structures can be visualized to a large extent, which means pathological conditions can be more easily diagnosed.

RADIOLUCENCIES AND RADIOPACITIES IN PANORAMIC RADIOLOGY

Any object in the path of the x-ray beam can produce single, double, or ghost images depending on its orientation. These objects include not only anatomical or other entities located on the patient, but also parts of the machinery. All of these images are superimposed on the radiograph, but certain types of tissues and materials block out others to an extent. **Radiopaque objects** absorb x-rays and **radiolucent entities** do not in general. Therefore, black air spaces can make it difficult to see hard tissues. Soft and hard tissues are both relatively radiopaque, but hard tissues absorb the radiation to a greater extent and can obscure soft ones. Soft tissues can mask air spaces, and ghost images can be visible over everything else. These concepts can be used to diagnose pathological conditions because changes in an area generally make that region more radiolucent.

LOCALIZING UNERUPTED TEETH AND FOREIGN OBJECTS ON RADIOGRAPH

In general, there are two ways to localize entities like unerupted teeth, foreign bodies, or other irregularities on a radiograph. The first technique is the **tube-shift method of localization** in which a series of periapical radiographs is taken with the tubehead positioned differently horizontally for each. If the object in question shifts in harmony with the tubehead, it is located on the lingual or tongue side. If the entity appears to move in opposition to the tubehead, then it is located on the facial or buccal side. Another principle that can be applied to localization of objects is the **buccal-object rule**. Again, two radiographs of a region are necessary; vertically aligned images are discriminated through changes in horizontal angulation of the x-ray beam while horizontal aligned images are discerned through changes in vertical angulation. Here hidden or unidentified entities that are buccal known objects move in the same direction as the x-ray beam or positioning device, and lingual objects shift in opposition to beam movement.

LANDMARKS ON RADIOGRAPHS THAT HELP DETERMINE BONE HEIGHT

The level of bone on the facial side can be estimated by using the lamina dura. The lamina dura is the portion of the bone seen as a radiopaque line on the radiograph. The point at which it starts to become less opaque or solid is a good approximation of where the interseptal bone begins. The level of bone on the lingual or tongue side is usually determined by finding the faint line that undulates across the center of the teeth. This line distinguishes between the areas of the root that are covered by bone and those that are not and represents the level of the alveolar crest. From the alveolar crest to the apex is the bone height for the lingual aspect.

FURCATION INVOLVEMENT

Teeth further back in the jaw can be bifurcated or trifurcated. In other words, they can have roots that branch or divide into two parts or three parts because the periodontal pocket has enlarged. If there is a pocket in the gum tissue around the root, there is furcation involvement. A radiograph that shows widening of the periodontal ligament space or significant bone loss suggests furcation. Usually, the dentist investigates this condition by inserting a probe into the top of the area (possibly in conjunction with warm condensed air). Furcation involvement can be found near many teeth, but it is observed most often initially in the first molar area.

INDICATIONS FOR FURTHER UNCONVENTIONAL RADIOGRAPHIC METHODS

There are four methods of defining the relationship between different structures in the oral cavity. In the first method, two objects are localized by definition on a normal radiograph. In other words, the more defined object is considered to be located lingually on the tongue side because that is the position of the film. The tube shift approach compares two radiographs whose only difference is a slight shift of the x-ray tube's horizontal angulation. Here a principle called the buccal-object rule is employed; according to this rule, buccal objects appear to move in the opposite direction. These techniques are also employed to localize foreign objects or unerupted teeth. A similar type of relationship can be found when observing some older pantomographic exposures. Periapical films used in conjunction with occlusal films taken at right angles can provide information about structural relationships as well.

APPEARANCE OF DENTAL DEVICES ON RADIOGRAPHS

ENDODONTIC OR OTHER RESTORATIVE MATERIALS

Various types of foreign restorative materials are inserted into the dental cavity for treatment of endodontic or pulp diseases. These materials can contain silver, gold, a pliable latex substance called gutta percha, or various amalgams (typically mercury, silver, and tin). During the actual endodontic process, other objects like rubber clamps or files might be inserted into the region as well. On a radiograph, all of these materials are observed as intensely radiopaque, even relative to the tooth enamel. Other restorative materials that appear radiopaque can include newer tooth-colored composites and various types of cements. On the other hand, many modern restorations utilize acrylic or composites made with it, and the acrylic is radiolucent. Older porcelain crowns also appear relatively dark on the image.

ORTHODONTIC DEVICES, PEDIATRIC RESTORATIONS, OR PROSTHODONTIC MATERIALS

Most orthodontic devices are bands, wires, brackets, spacers, or retainers containing stainless steel, so they are seen as intensely radiopaque areas on radiographs. Unfortunately, some of these devices obscure evidence of underlying tooth decay. There are also newer clear plastic aligners available, but these would normally be removed before the shot.

Prosthodontic materials like dentures or bridges should also be taken out before radiographs are taken. Again, these devices mask other disease processes if left in; the metallic portions would appear extremely white and the porcelain or acrylic sections would prevent absorption of the radiation and seem darker. Infrequently, materials inserted for hygienic or periodontal purposes may also show up as radiopaque areas on an image.

FOREIGN MATERIALS INSERTED DURING ORAL SURGERY

There are a variety of wires, bars, crowns, bridges, and screws that might be permanently or temporarily inserted into the jaw area during oral surgery. Usually, these insertions are done after some sort of traumatic incident like an automobile accident or explosion. Most of the foreign materials utilized contain a metal, either stainless steel or some type of amalgam, which means that they appear as very white, radiopaque areas on the radiograph. Bone should surround the implant. White fragments visualized on an image can also be clues to a patient's history, because these pieces can remain imbedded.

OTHER TYPES OF FOREIGN MATERIALS SEEN ON RADIOGRAPH

Sometimes devices used during the exposure of a radiograph might appear on the image. For example, bite blocks are often seen as either white regions (if metallic) or relatively dark areas (if plastic). Other devices used to position the film can be seen as radiopaque areas, and there are varieties of previously described artifacts with characteristic appearances. External jewelry, eyeglasses or other materials are generally observed as white areas. In addition, occasionally radiopaque materials are injected into various passages to visualize structures or make them denser; these areas will be light on the radiograph as well.

PERIODONTAL DISEASE

Periodontal disease is a blanket term for processes that change the gums or tissues that envelop and support the teeth. The majority of these diseases are caused by microbial infections resulting from plaque buildup, other pathogenic exposure, restorative work, or tartar. The disease is distinguished by inflamed gums, development of pockets in the area, and damage to the associated ligaments and alveolar bone. Progression of bone loss is diagnostic for periodontitis. Periodontal pockets are grooves of soft tissue that can be identified only by use of probing instruments. If left untreated, periodontal disease can result in tooth loss.

STAGING AND GRADING

Periodontal disease is diagnosed by a combination of methods. The staging phase, as outlined by 2018 AAP guidelines, involves measuring interdental calculus, radiographic bone loss, tooth loss, probing the gums, and assessing bone loss and furcation involvement. Assessing these elements involves a variety of techniques:

- Pockets are generally identified by **probing** with an instrument or by **inserting radiopaque substances** in the area and taking an exposure.
- Visualization of bone requires sequential radiography and digital subtraction techniques.
- Radiographs alone cannot determine the characteristics of the bone deformity. There is also an instrument called the **Nabors probe** that can be used to detect furcation or separation of the tooth from the underlying bone; sometimes this can be seen radiographically as a dark area.
- **Dental calculus or mineralization** can sometimes be picked up as white lines or spurs on exposures.
- **Progression toward tooth loosening** can be diagnosed if the periodontal ligament space gets wider, but this is rarely observable on a radiograph because other structures obscure the changes.

SEQUENTIAL RADIOGRAPHS

Radiographs cannot show depth, and thus bones and teeth are generally visually laid over each other in the image. This means that a single radiograph might pick up bone loss and indicate periodontal disease, but it is not useful in determining the extent or rate of progression of the condition. Small amounts of bone loss are difficult to see on an individual image. On the other hand, if **sequential radiographs** at different time intervals are taken, changes can be visualized using computerized digital subtraction. The two images are digitally merged, the common areas are subtracted out, and the resultant picture shows only the differences. Tiny changes can be measured by this technique. The paralleling method with high voltage and a long positioning device should be used.

INITIAL CHANGES ASSOCIATED WITH PERIODONTAL DISEASE

An early radiographic indication of periodontal disease is the blurring or discontinuity of the lamina dura or bone surrounding the periodontal ligament. These are known as irregularities of the alveolar bone crest. Another early indication is the widening of the periodontal ligament space which can sometimes be seen as a darker triangular or funnel-like area. Radiographs can sometimes pick up early interseptal bone changes as dark protrusions into the alveolar bone region. The mechanism involved is the expansion of blood vessels in the bone as a result of increased inflammation of the gum. The concentration of minerals in the tissues is decreased as well. Eventually, the teeth may appear to be completely detached from the underlying bone. Calculus deposits may be seen between the surfaces of the teeth.

COMMON FUNCTIONAL PROBLEMS CONTRIBUTING TO PERIODONTAL DISEASE

The two most common functional issues that contribute to periodontal disease development are occlusal traumatism and a high crown-to-root ratio. The occlusal surfaces of the teeth can become traumatized primarily through undesirable oral practices such as grinding of the teeth (known as bruxism) or firmly holding and clenching the teeth. These practices tend to collapse the underlying ligaments, cause bone to reabsorb, enlarge the periodontal ligament space, and eventually lead to loosening of the teeth. Radiographs can aid with clinical diagnosis of occlusal traumatism. In addition, when individuals have teeth with long crowns relative to the root, or a high crown-to-root ratio, the load applied to the gum is high. This condition can be clearly seen on a radiograph, and it is prevalent in the Latin American population.

RISK FACTORS FOR PERIODONTAL DISEASE

Periodontal disease is primarily an inflammatory disease of the gum area caused by buildup of bacterial plaque. There are a number of factors that can predispose an individual toward development of this buildup. A radiograph can only detect these factors; it cannot determine the exact role they may play in development of periodontal disease. The first element is deposition of calculus or tartar, which is the concretion of bacteria and other organic materials on the surface of the tooth. Calculus is often described in terms of where it is found and the source of the other organic materials. Supragingival and subgingival calculus have contributions from

saliva and serum respectively. Restorations or implants that are done incorrectly are other significant causes of periodontal disease (now categorized as peri-implant disease) because they can leave overhangs or gaps where bacteria can grow and attach. Similarly, areas that allow food to become impacted or stuck can predispose a person to periodontal disease. Examples of these types of areas include sections that have worn away on the tooth surface or are decayed.

USE OF RADIOGRAPHS TO DETERMINE RATE OF PERIODONTAL DAMAGE

Periodontal damage can be an active or relatively static process, and radiographs are useful for determination of the **rate of destruction of the gum area**. The appearance of the crests of the interseptal alveolar bone is generally used to assess the activity level. If this crest is uneven and less defined, the periodontal destruction is probably active. If on the other hand, the crest is smooth, distinct, and relatively radiopaque, the gingival breakdown is not active at that time. Usually, diagnosis is made by comparing sequential radiographs. The prognosis or final outcome can only be estimated by assimilation of all available data, which should include radiographs and clinical evaluation.

BONE LOSS
DETERMINING BONE LOSS WITH RADIOGRAPHS

Bone loss is actually evaluated by comparing the amount of enduring bone to the expected amount of bone. The most common site for initial evaluation is the interproximal septal bone. The cementoenamel junction (CEJ) is the part of the tooth where the enamel ends and the dentin starts. The distance from that point towards the apex of the tooth is normally 1.0-1.5 millimeters; therefore, bone loss is measured as the difference between the observed height and the expected height. Bone loss can be generalized (evident consistently on the majority of teeth), or it can be localized to only certain teeth. In either case, inflammatory processes resulting from periodontitis usually occur concurrently, and thus loss of contact between the dentition is also observed on the radiograph.

DIRECTION OF BONE LOSS

Bone loss can occur in different planes. If the deficiency is generally found in the plane equidistant from the CEJ of adjoining teeth, the loss is considered horizontal. If the **pattern of bone loss** is more angular and inconsistent between adjacent teeth, the loss is defined as vertical or angular. The latter configuration may also show enlargement of the periodontal ligament space or pockets below the bone. Both types of bone loss probably involve local inflammatory responses, but a vertical pattern may indicate systemic involvement as well. Evidence of vertical bone loss without accompanying plaque buildup or gingivitis in teenagers is called localized juvenile periodontitis (LJP). LJP often occurs in the premolar-molar region and the rate of bone loss can be very high. The etiology of LJP is unclear, but it is probably infectious or immunologic in nature.

INFRABONY POCKETS

Infrabony pockets are regions created through crestal bone loss and observed on radiographs as dark areas protruding into the bone area between the teeth. These pockets or defects extend below the level of the adjacent alveolar crest and typically have one, two, or three bone walls. A one-wall or hemiseptum defect occurs when only one wall of the interseptal bone is damaged leaving the other intact. Two-wall infrabony pockets are the most common type, in particular a variant called an osseous crater, which constitutes over half of all defects in the lower jaw. An osseous crater appears on the radiograph as a concave indentation in the bone between two teeth. A three-wall pocket is bounded by three bony walls and the root, and a four-wall defect entirely encompasses the root area. Usually, these defects are confirmed by probing with an instrument.

DENTAL CARIES

Dental caries or tooth decay is the breakdown of hard dentin tissue in a tooth. Caries development is dependent on three aspects. All must be present for tooth decay to occur.

- First, the host must have a propensity towards caries development.
- Then, specific bacteria or microflora must be present.

- Lastly, dietary sugars that can ferment or be broken down into acids and other substances must be available. The acids are the substances that actually demineralize or decalcify and break down the hard enamel of the tooth. As the breakdown proceeds over time, eventually tooth decay or caries can be detected.

Typically, radiographic visualization occurs when about half the calcium and phosphorus is broken down.

INTERPROXIMAL ENAMEL CARIES

Interproximal enamel caries is the tooth decay that occurs between two abutting tooth surfaces. Initially, interproximal enamel caries starts just underneath the point of contact. At this point, the lesion looks white and chalky, and a small dark notch is visible on a radiograph. As the destruction proceeds, the shape of the lesion usually becomes an elongated triangle. The longer tip of the triangle is directed downward toward the dentinoenamel junction (DEJ). Caries visualization on a radiograph is influenced by the spatial parameters of the adjoining tooth, in particular the area of the contact point which can obscure the extent of the decay.

TYPES

There are several types of interproximal enamel caries that do not have the characteristic triangular appearance running along the edge of the tooth.

- One is **incipient caries**, which is decay that has not completely penetrated the enamel. On a radiograph, incipient caries usually looks like a small, dark funnel-shaped area.
- Another type is **lamellar caries**, which appears as a dark line that progresses into the dentin region.
- There can also be decay primarily within the dentin called **dentinal caries**. This type of decay looks restricted to areas under the enamel on a radiograph, and it can destroy tubules in the dentin.

ACUTE VS. CHRONIC CARIES

The terms acute and chronic as applied to dental caries differentiate between the rates of penetration of the lesion, in other words fast versus slow. In addition, acute caries tends to arise from a relatively tiny surface point compared to chronic cases. Tooth decay in younger people tends to proceed more rapidly than in older individuals. For example, a condition called rampant caries, in which the decay has an abrupt onset and extremely rapid progression, commonly occurs only in children and adolescents. Rampant caries is rarely found in adults, except in some cases of xerostomia or dry mouth. Acute caries is prevalent from adolescence to about age 25, and chronic tooth decay is usually the type found above that age range.

RADIOGRAPHIC CLASSIFICATION SYSTEM FOR DENTAL CARIES

The extent of dental caries is currently classified into 4 groups depending on the penetration of the destruction as visualized on a radiograph. The decision to treat caries should be based upon the combination of this radiographic classification and clinical evaluation.

- **Incipient**: Enamel is penetrated by a lesion less than halfway.
- **Moderate**: Enamel is penetrated by a lesion more than halfway.
- **Advanced**: Enamel is fully penetrated at least to the DEJ, but not more than halfway to the pulp.
- **Severe**: Lesion extends through enamel, dentin, and more than halfway to the pulp.

RADIOGRAPHIC APPEARANCE OF CARIES ON FACIAL OR LINGUAL SIDES OF TOOTH

Tooth decay can occur on the facial or lingual sides of the tooth as well as the neck or cervical region of the crown. The point of entrance of the caries is usually relatively large compared to other decay types. These types of lesions are visualized as very well-defined radiolucent circular areas on the radiograph generally, although they might also appear as dark oval or arc shapes. Caries on these surfaces is hard to detect until it has progressed to a certain point. These smooth surface types of caries are usually identified by using a mirror and some type of exploratory probe.

OCCLUSAL CARIES

Caries that begins on the occlusal surface of a tooth is extremely common in younger patients, particularly in the molar and pre-molar regions. The occlusal surfaces of teeth in these areas are very uneven and layered deeply with enamel. Poor dental hygiene in the back of the mouth increases the possibility of caries in this area. Occlusal tooth decay is usually not detected on a radiograph until it has broken through the dentinoenamel junction (DEJ), at which point it appears as a dark line or region just below the DEJ. Actually, the caries spreads up into the enamel as well. Therefore, mirrors and certain probes are usually used to identify cases of occlusal caries.

ROOT CARIES

Tooth decay can occur in the root area of the tooth without enamel involvement. This type of root or cemental caries usually begins in the cementoenamel junction or CEJ region as a result of plaque retention along receding gums. The caries usually radiates outward from the point of origin, eventually merging into a circular area. Radiographically the decay appears to engulf and blur the entire root area, and clinically it erodes the cementum located at the CEJ. The enamel is not directly affected, but cemental caries can broaden into regions very close to it. Root caries is prevalent in the elderly population.

PULPAL CARIES

A radiograph is of limited value in the diagnostic evaluation of pulpal caries. Pulpal caries is decay that has extended into the central tooth pulp, which contains nerve endings and blood vessels. Since radiographs cannot show depth, it is very difficult to angle the beam to pick up pulp involvement without creating other distortions. In particular, the exposure may obscure the extent or absence of pulp involvement because the radiolucent decay area is shown over the pulp. This distortion is exaggerated further if the picture is overexposed.

RADIATION CARIES

Radiation caries is the progressive decay of teeth or bones in the maxillofacial region after high dose radiation treatment of head or neck cancer. When doses of about 6000 rad are used to kill cancerous cells in the region, the softer tissues like the salivary glands are often affected as well. The amount of saliva produced is depleted and it becomes thicker. Friction in the mouth and the predilection towards development of caries are both increased. Another condition called osteoradionecrosis, or destruction of bone tissue, may also develop.

HALTED CARIES

Various types of caries can be halted or arrested if the environmental milieu changes into one that does not promote decay. Incipient caries, in which the decay has not penetrated much of the enamel, is common, and typically the enamel is as hard as that in a healthy tooth. The mechanism in this case is probably remineralization of the enamel. This type of arrested caries is often seen adjacent to another tooth that has been removed. Sometimes tooth decay on occlusal surfaces stops because the dentin has become so hard upon repeated buffing that bacteria are sloughed off. In this case, there is a characteristic radiographic appearance including a missing crown with a ragged, radiolucent space in its place.

SECONDARY CARIES

Secondary caries is tooth decay that emerges after restorations for various types of previous caries. It is usually visualized on a radiograph as a dark radiolucent spot near the restoration. The secondary or recurrent caries can have two different types of causes. In some cases, dentitional caries in the hard part of the tooth under the enamel was not entirely eradicated before the restoration was done. New caries can also develop if tin or zinc leaks out from the filling or cement. In the latter case, the current theory is that the metal ions combine with demineralized dentin to initiate fresh areas of decay.

157

CERVICAL BURNOUT

Cervical burnout is an artifact that appears to be caries on an exposure. The cervical neck of the tooth is tapered. Therefore, it attracts fewer energy photons and appears darker on a radiograph than the crown above or root below it. Thus, a radiolucent band or collar may be observed on a radiograph, but there is actually no decay. In the posterior teeth, the radiographic appearance of cervical burnout can be more pie-shaped. Similar contrast artifacts may be observed at the cementoenamel junction, with certain root arrangements, or if the beam is directed incorrectly horizontally. Correct horizontal angulation usually eliminates cervical burnout.

REASONS THAT THE EXTENT OF CARIES CAN BE OVERLOOKED

The relative thickness of the tooth and its area of decay can influence interpretation of the extent of caries on a radiograph. X-ray beams are impeded and absorbed by interaction with the enamel. In areas where the carious lesion is narrowing, such as where it may be entering the dentin, the large enamel area can obscure the much smaller radiolucent decay area. In addition, at least half the calcium and phosphorus must be destroyed before a lesion can be visualized on a radiograph, a trait that leads to inherent underestimation of caries involvement.

CONDITIONS OF THE TOOTH ENAMEL THAT LOOK LIKE CARIES ON A RADIOGRAPH

Areas of the tooth can be mechanically worn down and look like caries on a radiograph. One type of corrosion is called attrition, in which occlusal or incisal edges are worn down. If the attrition is severe enough to include dentin involvement, a hollow space that appears to be caries can develop. The other type of corrosion that mimics decay is called abrasion, and it is usually observed in the root area with receding gums. In addition, there is a condition called enamel hypoplasia in which incomplete development results in fissures in the enamel. These fissures may stain and appear to be decay. Enamel hypoplasia can be distinguished from caries by using an exploratory probe; the probe detaches easily in hypoplasia but does not with true caries.

RESTORATIVE DENTAL MATERIALS THAT MAY RESEMBLE CARIES

Restorative dental materials made from substances that are also radiolucent like decay can resemble caries formation on a radiograph. In general, this situation only occurs when the restoration is relatively old and materials like certain plastics, silicates, or calcium hydroxide were used. The cements used to affix these materials generally contain metals, however; the adjacent cement appears as a white area on the exposure and aids in differentiation between these materials and true decay. Newer restorations generally are comprised of high molecular weight metals, either gold or amalgam mixtures, rendering them radiopaque. Thus, newer dental work is rarely confused with caries.

PULPITIS

The pulp chamber and its canal are areas in the middle of the crown and root of the tooth. Generally, they do not contain calcified materials like bones do, and therefore they appear as radiolucent areas on a radiograph. The configuration of the pulp area is reduced with aging, in a few developmental abnormalities, or if the area is irritated. Dentin is deposited on the walls of the area as well during these processes. If there is irritation from decay or other trauma, the result is a condition called pulpitis. Pulpitis cannot generally be identified on a radiograph. Occasionally, there may be small areas with calcification in the pulp chamber that show up as radiopaque regions, but in general they have no clinical significance.

PERIAPICAL DISEASE

Periapical disease is any disruption of the lamina dura at the apex of a tooth. The lamina dura is the cortical bone surrounding the periodontal ligament. Healthy individuals have dense lamina dura that appears radiographically as a narrow, white line running near the apex of the tooth. When the line loses its continuous appearance due to resorption of the lamina dura and alveolar bone, some sort of periapical disease exists. The classification of the type of periapical disease generally requires additional clinical investigation. Some periapical diseases are acutely symptomatic with pain and edema, but others persist chronically without significant clinical signs. Many of these conditions are actually periodontal disease as well.

ACUTE APICAL PERIODONTITIS

Acute apical (or periapical) periodontitis, also known as AAP, is inflammation in the region of the periodontal ligament near the apex of the tooth. Clinically, the area is extremely painful, especially if tapped. Often, there is no change seen on a radiograph in the lamina dura or periodontal ligament spaces, although the latter may be wider than usual. There can be a variety of reasons for this inflammation. The most common causes are either some sort of irritation derived from pulpitis traveling via the root canal or response to some injury or foreign material (including restorations). If pulpitis is the causative agent, the damage is irreparable, the pulp tissue may be dead, and the pulp may need to be removed and a root canal procedure performed.

ACUTE APICAL ABSCESS

If acute apical periodontitis caused by a dead tooth pulp is left untreated, an acute apical abscess (AAA) can develop. The infection is evidenced by pus accumulated at the apex of the root, generalized pain and edema in the area, and pain and tenderness on percussion. Eventually, the tooth can come out of its socket and move around. The purulent exudate must be drained immediately to alleviate symptoms. On a radiograph, an early AAA may be difficult to pinpoint. Changes to look for include an expansion of the periodontal ligament space. Advanced cases can show dark areas where the alveolar bone has been damaged.

CHRONIC APICAL ABSCESS

A chronic apical abscess (CAA) is the end-result of a persistent acute apical abscess. It is often identified because a tooth is loose, or gum tissues are tender or swollen. As with the AAA, the pulp is dead, and an infection is present in the apical area. A glaucomatous sac surrounds the purulent materials. There are two ways that chronic apical abscesses present themselves, and they are differentiated by the route for pus drainage. Most CAAs form canals or fistulas from the abscessed area through the alveolar bone to the outside of the gum where a boil or parulis is formed. Drainage of the CAA is generally then performed through this boil to alleviate the swelling and pain. On a radiograph, the fistula looks like a dark channel. Sometimes the chronic apical abscess does not form a fistula and the purulent material drains internally into the circulatory or lymphatic systems. For this type of CAA, the radiolucent sac has very indistinct borders indicating dispersion into other areas. In either type of CAA, a root canal procedure is indicated.

APICAL GRANULOMA

When apical periodontitis becomes chronic, an apical granuloma may form as a mechanism to confine the irritants from the dead pulp and root canal. Essentially, a fibrous pouch forms along the periodontal ligament around the chronically inflamed tissue in the apical area. Clinically, this sac formation relieves some of the pain and may arrest pustule formation, but generally root canal procedures are still necessary to prevent tooth loss. On a radiograph, an apical granuloma looks like a small dark rounded or oval area protruding from the apical area of the tooth. In the molar area of the upper jaw, this condition may cause the mucosal membranes of the sinus to become inflamed as well; this is known as antral mucositis.

APICAL CYST

When an apical granuloma expands in size, an apical cyst can form within the granuloma. The apical cyst consists of layers of squamous or scale-shaped epithelial cells that form a sac filled with liquid. Pressure builds up within the cyst, and bone near the apex is resorbed. Clinically, the area may not hurt unless it has become infected. Nevertheless, all irritating substances in the dead pulp are generally eradicated, and the root canal is closed up. Cysts are relatively easy to recognize on a radiograph because they appear as large radiolucent areas attached to the apex of the tooth and rimmed by a radiopaque outline of the bone.

APICAL CONDENSING OSTEITIS

Apical condensing osteitis (ACO) is dense bone formation in the apical tooth area that occurs in response to low-grade bacterial infection of the pulp. The alveolar bone is not actually destroyed in ACO. The condition is often asymptomatic but probing, and other types of stimuli indicate that the pulp tissue is necrosed. On a radiograph, radiopaque areas are observed near the tooth apex. Condensing osteitis is prevalent in the premolar and molar regions of the mandible. As with other apical conditions, root canal treatment is generally performed in these patients.

BENIGN CONDITIONS IN THE APICAL REGION

Apical cementoma, also called periapical cementoma or cemental dysphasia, is a disorder in which connective tissues overgrow and destroy the lamina dura. The lesions themselves emanate from the periapical area and appear dark on a radiograph with possible radiopaque infill containing cementum or bone during more advanced stages. Since pulp is not destroyed in this condition, the teeth are alive, and no root canal or other type of management is necessary. Another benign condition of the apical area is hypercementosis, in which excessive amounts of cementum deposit along the root of the tooth. On a radiograph, hypercementosis presents as either generalized enlargement of the root area or a nodule on the tip of the root.

ABNORMAL DENTITION NUMBERS

There are a number of developmental aberrations in which the normal distribution or appearance of teeth is not seen. If the normal number of teeth is not observed, there are three possible conditions.

- **Anodontia** is a genetic disorder in which no teeth ever develop. People with anodontia are said to be edentulous.
- **Hypodontia** is a genetic condition in which one or more teeth are missing. If many teeth are missing, the condition is sometimes referred to as oligodontia.
- **Hyperdontia** is a genetic condition in which additional teeth are present. The extra teeth are also termed supernumerary.

DIVISION OR FUSION ERRORS RESULTING IN ABNORMAL DENTITION NUMBER

There are several conditions where division or fusion errors give the appearance of an abnormal dentition number. Two of these alterations are primarily observed in the front incisors.

- **Gemination** occurs when an individual tooth bud tries to split, but the division only occurs near the top. This gives the appearance of two teeth near the crown, but there is a common root canal.
- When two adjoining teeth join at the dentin and/or enamel areas, a process called **fusion** occurs. This condition reduces the total number of teeth observed, but a radiograph shows that there are actually two separate root canals.

ABNORMAL TEETH SIZE

Teeth can be larger or smaller than expected.

- Relatively large dentition, termed **macrodontia**, is not very common. Pituitary giants experience generalized macrodontia, but other people may have individual teeth that are enlarged. Individuals with diminutive jaws appear to have macrodontia.
- Some people have **microdontia** in which all or some of the teeth are abnormally small relative to jaw size. The most common examples are small lateral incisors in the maxilla, a condition that tends to segregate in families, or small third molars. Microdontia is seen in pituitary dwarfs.

TAURODONTISM AND SUPERNUMERARY ROOTS

Both taurodontism and supernumerary roots are conditions in which the shape of root area of the tooth has developed abnormally. In **taurodontism**, the root is abbreviated and the pulp compartment is enlarged, giving a squared-off appearance to the apical area. **Supernumerary roots** are additional roots on a tooth giving a branching appearance on a radiograph. Sometimes there are separate relatively small root canals in each branch as well. The number of branches is typically two or three. The periodontal ligament spaces can shift with supernumerary roots. This condition is most common in the canine and pre-molar regions of the lower jaw.

IMPACT OF TOOTH SHAPE CHANGES ON EXTRACTION AND ORTHODONTIC PROBLEMS

Adjacent teeth can join in the cementum region during root growth or eruption (occasionally later), and this phenomenon is known as **concrescence**. The most common sites for concrescence are various molars, particularly in the maxilla. The lack of separation and distorted relationship makes tooth extraction and corrective procedures very problematic in these teeth. Teeth can also be bent, particularly in the root area but sometimes in the crown. These curved shape changes are called dilacerations, and they can have a myriad of causes that are usually traumatic in nature. If a tooth is bent, the teeth in the area can be positioned incorrectly which again interferes with orthodontia or extraction.

DENS INVAGINATUS AND DENS EVAGINATUS

Dens invaginatus and dens evaginatus are both abnormalities in the pattern of the folding of the enamel at the occlusal surface. In dens invaginatus (also called dens in dente), the enamel on the crown folds inward, leaving a hollow. This anomaly is relatively common. Since this invagination makes the pulp more vulnerable to exposure and the tooth more prone to decay, the crater is often closed up during youth. In dens evaginatus (also known as Leong's premolar), the enamel on the crown folds outward, creating a bump. During dental probing, teeth with this type of elevation can be subjected to mechanical and inflammatory stresses, so decay and pulp problems can occur here as well.

ENAMEL PEARLS

Enamel pearls are tiny spherical or oval pieces of enamel that adhere to the outside of the tooth. They are usually found in the molar region on the cervical neck of the tooth or in areas where branching has occurred. Since these pearls or enamelomas are made of enamel, they appear as opaque dots on a radiograph when observed in certain orientations that do not obscure them. Enamel pearls originating at branching points predispose an individual to periodontal disease if they are not removed because a pocket can form at the furcation. Enamel pearls can be confused radiographically with calcified areas in the pulp because both are radiopaque. The two can be distinguished by the fact that pulpal calcifications will be seen in various orientations whereas enamelomas will not.

AMELOGENESIS IMPERFECTA

If defective enamel formation or enamel hypoplasia is **inherited**, it is called amelogenesis imperfecta. Tooth decay is rare in individuals with this hereditary alteration. There are three types of amelogenesis imperfecta.

- In the first **hypoplastic variation**, the enamel's structure is unaltered, but the width of its layer is very narrow.
- In the **hypomineralized deviation**, the concentration of minerals in the enamel is low, which renders the tooth susceptible to pitting or splintering.
- The third variant is the **hypomaturation type** in which the grinding surface of the tooth has a white or pitted tip.

DENTINOGENESIS IMPERFECTA

Dentinogenesis imperfecta is an inherited abnormality that involves the dentin and its connection with the enamel. The teeth have a shimmery appearance and they tend to crack. There are three classifications of dentinogenesis imperfecta differentiated primarily in terms of the association or lack thereof between generalized bone disease and changes in the tooth structure.

- **Type 1** occurs in individuals who also have generalized bone disease or osteogenesis imperfecta. In the other manifestations, this disorder only affects the teeth.
- **Type 2** can be seen in the general population without other inherited disorders.
- The more severe **Type 3** occurs only in restricted populations in the eastern United States. On a radiograph, the pulp area looks destroyed, and the roots are shortened and narrow with no evidence of a root canal.

ENAMEL HYPOPLASIA

Any condition in which the milieu of the enamel has been altered is called enamel hypoplasia. There are a number of possible manifestations of flawed enamel formation. If the alteration is localized to a single tooth as a pitted appearance, the causative agent was probably external trauma or infection. In baby teeth, this anomaly is often referred to as Turner's tooth. If a child is malnourished or contracts certain infections that produce a high fever, they can develop pitting or enamel hypoplasia on all or the majority of their teeth. This condition can develop in both primary incisors as well as permanent incisors if the deficiency or infection occurs during the first two years of life. Excessive exposure to fluorine can also produce another form of enamel hyperplasia in which the tooth surface appears mottled or discolored.

DENTAL DYSPLASIAS

A dysplasia is some type of unusual growth or absence of a part. Two types of dysplasias are found in dentition.

- One is **dentinal dysplasia** in which the enamel appears normal but underneath the pulp and root areas are either defective or destroyed. Root development is minimal with this abnormality.
- In another type of dysphasia called **regional odontodysplasia**, both the dentin and enamel do not develop properly, and the delineation between them disappears. Thus, on a radiograph, the tooth is less radiopaque and has a ghost-like appearance. The pulp cavity also looks relatively large.

Both of these conditions are uncommon.

ABNORMALITIES DURING TOOTH ERUPTION

Tooth eruption is the time period when the tooth emerges through the gum. If the tooth migrates or moves in a strange pattern prior to eruption, it will remain buried within the jawbone. If the tooth moves after it has erupted, contact between normally adjacent teeth may be lost and this is referred to as **drift**. Teeth can also exchange normal positions upon eruption, a condition known as **translocation**. Translocation is usually not a major issue because no crowding or dental arch changes occur. On the other hand, sometimes a tooth can break out into an abnormal position. This situation, known as **ectopic eruption**, can create space problems and change the shape of the arch. Another condition, especially prevalent in the third molar region, is **tooth impaction**. Here, some spatial impedance such as another tooth changes the orientation of the imbedded tooth making eruption impossible; these teeth are usually extracted.

ACQUIRED TOOTH DEFECTS

Tooth defects can be initiated through various types of **mechanical or chemical wear and tear**.

- **Attrition** and **abrasion** can look like tooth decay on a radiograph. Attrition is the wearing away of teeth by normal occlusal forces, whereas abrasion is wearing away by a mechanical device that has been introduced into the area. These mechanical devices include things like workplace items (for example, a hairdresser puts hairpins in her mouth), toothbrushes used incorrectly, ritual insertions into the oral cavity, and cocaine use. The abrasive pattern depends on the item used, but in all cases a radiolucent area is observed on a radiograph.
- **Erosion** or the chemical breakdown of the tooth's surface can also occur, possibly revealing the dentin underneath. Many of the causes involve exposure to acids from medications or soda. Disorders of the digestive tract like bulimia or vomiting often lead to tooth erosion. On a radiograph, the crowns may look darker if erosion has occurred.

CLEFT PALATE

A cleft is a narrow surface indentation that occurs because certain embryonic processes failed to fuse during development. In the context of dentistry, clefts can be found in the roof of the mouth, in either the bony front hard palate, the soft muscular palate located further back, or possibly in both. On a radiograph, the cleft area is radiolucent. Other developmental abnormalities can be found in conjunction with a cleft palate because the bones are shifted. Malpositioning is common as well as changes in the number of teeth ranging from complete anodontia to extra supernumerary dentition.

Fissural and Dentigerous Cysts

A cyst is any type of bone cavity lined with epithelial cells. Fissural cysts are sacs that emerge along embryonic junctures. There are three types of typical **fissural cysts**, each with a characteristic position. All look like radiolucent sacs on a radiograph.

- The **nasopalatine cyst** is typically located along the midline adjacent to the apices of incisors in the upper jaw.
- Further back along the midline, a **median palatine cyst** can occur.
- A **globulomaxillary cyst** is more elongated and is found between the lateral incisor and canine in the maxilla.

A **dentigerous cyst** has a completely different origin; it occurs (usually in the third molar) when a tooth bud degenerates to form a cyst or sac. Again, a dark sac is observed on a radiograph.

Fractures and Embedded Structures

Fractures to any part of the tooth appear as dark lines on a radiograph. If they occur in the crown area, they are easily recognizable. Cracks in the root area are more difficult to visualize because the alveolar bone is also in the area. Identification of fractures is important, because pulp damage can lead to other undesirable pathology. Most foreign bodies like implants contain metal and are readily identifiable because they are very radiopaque. Root tips can sometimes be embedded within the jaw and should be removed; they can be found by looking for their canal or their funnel-like shape.

Classifying Unknown Lesions

Areas that appear abnormal on a radiograph, but are not easily identified, can be tumors or cysts. A **benign tumor** is not cancerous, does not grow rapidly, and is usually not life-threatening. On a radiograph, a benign tumor presents as a dark, well-defined area. Other structures may be moved around on the radiograph, but they are not destroyed. Conversely, a **malignant tumor** is cancerous and fast-growing, and it does participate in the destruction of other processes. Thus, on a radiograph, a malignant tumor is relatively radiolucent but generally more diffuse and the borders between the malignancy and other structures are less distinct. Tumors can also be radiopaque on the exposure if the density of the tumor tissue is higher than that in the type of cells it is infiltrating, such as bone or cartilage.

Salivary Stones

Calcifications, or salivary stones, can occur in the soft tissues of the salivary glands and associated ducts. They can predispose an individual to infection, edema, and obstruction. Thus, even though they do not directly affect the teeth, salivary stones do have diagnostic significance. The stones are easily visualized on radiographs as intensely radiopaque spots. Because of their position, salivary stones are usually identified on occlusal or panoramic films, although they can sometimes be seen on periapical exposures. Salivary stones can also be visualized by injecting radiopaque media into the salivary ducts and glands, a technique called sialography.

Diagnostically Acceptable Images

Determining Diagnostic Quality of a Dental Radiograph

The diagnostic or radiographic quality of a dental radiograph is the exactitude of the representation of anatomical structures and their clarity on the film. This clarity is comprised of the sharpness or definition of the various structures on the film plus the detail or micro-architecture of these structures. Quality radiographs should demonstrate the proper density and contrast, they should be anatomically correct, they should include all areas of interest, and they need to be sharp. Sharpness or definition can be improved by minimizing distortion and various inherent impediments as well as by controlling magnification.

Criteria for Judging Radiographic Image Quality

Radiographic image quality is judged by a number of interrelated characteristics. The radiograph should have enough **detail** to differentiate between various components on the film as well as sufficient **definition** to show structural characteristics and clear demarcation between the components. In general, the latter characteristic, definition, is adequate when surrounding spaces are distinct from the teeth being documented. While detail is primarily controlled by the potential difference applied, and to an extent the development procedures, definition is more a function of factors that can be controlled by the operator such as film speed, movement, or length of the positioning device. The darkness of the film in general is the density, which should be in a range where surrounding tissues can be faintly observed; it is affected by a number of parameters. A related characteristic is contrast, which is the differentiation in densities between adjoining areas. This factor is primarily determined by the voltage applied. Suitable contrast is important for observation of smaller details and tooth decay. In addition, there should be no significant handling or development errors visible.

Criteria for Judging Radiographic Structures and Distortion

In a full mouth survey, the tip of every tooth and its adjoining bone should be observed on at least one of the x-rays. For documentation of particular regions, all spaces between, surrounding and/or retromolar to the teeth desired should be visible on the film. Partial images as a result of cone cutting are unacceptable. The cutting edge of the tooth should be oriented toward the raised bump on the film. Distortion of the comparative size and shape of structures should be kept to a minimum. For bitewing radiographs, interproximal connections should be distinct, the visible parts of the teeth in both jaws should be in the center, the peak of the alveolar bone should be visible and differentiated from the teeth, and the biting surface of the teeth should be horizontal. On the other hand, the molar ridges or cusps should be somewhat overlapping.

Radiographic Errors

OVERLAPPING MISTAKES

Overlapping on radiographic images can occur as a result of two types of errors. The first type can occur when the flat surface of the film packet is not placed parallel to the mean tangent of the area being documented. As a result, the contacts and openings between the teeth appear to slide over one another or overlap. Incorrect horizontal angulation of the positioning device also can be visualized on a radiograph as overlapping. The most common horizontal angulation error is direction of the beam obliquely, not perpendicularly, to the plane of the film. As a result, definition and density are both diminished. Both types of overlapping errors can be corrected by observing the principle of directing the x-ray cone perpendicular to the mean tangent of the area and keeping the film in the same orientation as the tangent.

FILM PLACEMENT ERRORS

A common film placement error is the positioning of the packet too shallow to record the entire tooth while leaving quite a bit of blank area near the crown visible. This error usually occurs because the patient experiences discomfort and does not bite down enough. Sometimes the entire region desired is not documented, which is a situation that should not occur if landmark guidelines are followed. If the film has been positioned backwards with the lead foil surface exposed to the x-ray beam, an image will be recorded, but there will be a tracking pattern from the foil superimposed on the radiograph, and its orientation will be inverted. If the radiolucent raised dot on the film packet is inadvertently placed toward the apices of the teeth, it may be superimposed on the radiograph. Double images will be recorded if a film packet is used twice by mistake. If the tongue or a finger is in the path of the x-ray beam, it will appear as an artifact on the radiograph. All of these errors warrant repetition of the procedure.

BLANK RADIOGRAPHS AND DENSITY ISSUES

If a radiograph is blank, no radiation was delivered. Most often this is due to failure to turn on the machine, use the correct tubehead, or activate the exposure button. This situation can also occur if the positioning device was severely malpositioned or the film indicated was not used. If the film has been overfixed or inadvertently left in the water bath for a day or two, it may also be blank or clear because emulsion has been washed off. If the film has clearly been exposed, but is very light, the amount of radiation delivered was insufficient or the film was not completely developed. A number of factors can influence the quantity of radiation given, but underdevelopment is usually due to depletion of developer in the processor. If the developer evaporates and is low in the tank, a partial image may be seen only where the development occurred. High-density, very dark films are generally a result of overexposure.

DISTORTION ERRORS

Distortion of shapes on radiographs results from either improper vertical angulation or incorrect placement of the film. Elongation or apparent extension of the tooth image occurs when the vertical angulation used is too small, and the less frequent phenomenon of foreshadowing or apparent reduction of tooth size can happen if the vertical angle used is too large. Distortion sometimes occurs if the film package protrudes in the center due to either excessive biting down by the patient or full or partial removal of the film backing. The relative dimensions of parts of an image can also be distorted when the bisecting angle method is utilized, especially when this technique is applied to documentation of maxillary molars. In this case, the roots are not in the bisecting angle plane and therefore the paralleling method is preferable here.

PROBLEMS UNIQUE TO AUTOMATIC FILM PROCESSING

When a film is inserted into an automatic processor, the machine can jam and stop transporting the film along the processor. There are many reasons for this occurrence, ranging from inadequately hardened gelatin to dirty components to improper feeding. If films are fed into the machine too rapidly, they can stick together producing dark dense spots in those areas. Marks can appear on the surface of the radiograph if the rollers are encrusted or have irregularities or if the film has been improperly handled prior to insertion. Rinse water that is dirty or too low or contaminated clearing solution can generate films that appear chalky. Films should be dry when they exit from the automatic processor, but if they are wet or sticky a number of parameters related to the dryer and temperature controls should be checked. Brown discoloration observed with manual processing can occur with automatic machines, but films can also come out greenish yellow in color if inadequate fixation occurred or processing was too rapid.

ARTIFACTS

If the exterior of the film is contaminated before development is performed, black artifacts can be found on the final x-ray. Sources of contamination include developer chemicals and other liquids including saliva, stannous fluoride, seepage of light into the film package, or later adherence of films together during fixation. Many black artifacts are due to fingers with developer on them. Artifacts that appear white on the image are also the result of contamination, in this case generally drops of clearing solution, air bubbles, or fingers dipped in fixer solution. A variety of apparent timesavers as well as dirty rollers in the automatic machines can result in black streaks on the radiograph. Chemicals from the processing solutions or present on film hangers can precipitate out of solution and appear as deposits on the radiograph. Depleted reagents during processing or inadequate rinsing can result in staining of the finished radiograph. This phenomenon most commonly occurs when the fixer is not sufficiently removed during the final wash. Here, a brown stain occurs over time because silver sulfide is formed from the reaction between hyposulfite and metallic silver. Shrinking or reticulation of the film is possible if it has been exposed to rapid temperature changes.

ERRORS IN FILM HANDLING

Pressure marks can be found on incorrectly handled films; these marks can be either black teeth marks or white marks formed by writing on the front of the film packet. Black lines appearing on radiographs are the result of intentional bending of the film to alleviate patient anxiety. If saliva is not removed from the film packet, the black protective paper on the film can stick to the emulsion producing black marks on the radiograph. Black streaks or marks can also be generated on films if static electricity contacts the film; therefore, humidity levels need to be maintained in the darkroom especially during the winter. Careless handling of films can result in tearing, scratching, or artifacts resulting from contact with powder or other contaminants. The biggest problem that occurs, however, is the undesired density of film fogging. Film fog can result from many types of errors, including light leakage, incorrect use of safelights, unsuitable storage conditions, overdevelopment, and film deterioration.

ERRORS IN PANORAMIC IMAGES
INCORRECT POSITIONING

During panoramic imaging, if the patient bites too far forward into or up against the front of the bite block, the width of the entire image is shrunk. Thus, the most common potential errors are narrowing or missing the crowns of the front teeth or the visible overlap of the cervical spine in the ramus or condyle areas. Sometimes this forward positioning is done intentionally to diagnose sinus disorders because it also shows the structures in the nasal cavity better. If the patient bites too far back into the groove, the image is widened, which means that all the zones other than the bottom corners are significantly affected. Undesirable visualization of soft tissues can occur, the front teeth are widened, the condyles may be eliminated from view, and ghost images may appear in several areas.

INCORRECT CHIN ANGLE

When the chin is angled downward too much or tipped up too high, the relative curving smile-like configuration of the dentition is changed. An excessive downward chin tilt exaggerates this configuration, while tilting the chin upwards too much destroys this relationship and flattens out the dentition on the image. Consequently, the front teeth of the upper jaw are either quite prominent or their tops are not seen. Front teeth in the lower jaw either have their apices obscured or they are very clear. Sometimes these errors are deliberately exploited to improve the image quality in those areas. In addition, when the chin is tipped too low, the mandible tends to be drawn out vertically in the front and shows images of the hyoid bone, and the condyles may be cut off. If the chin is angled too high, the nasal-sinus cavity can be seen as a large primarily radiopaque area and the condyles may again be eliminated from the image.

ERRORS IF PATIENT'S HEAD IS TILTED IN THE MACHINE

The purpose of closing the side guides on a panoramic machine is to ensure that the individual's head will be upright and not tilted. However, if the patient's head is inclined to the side, this will be very obvious on the radiograph. The back teeth are generally wider and the rows further apart on one side. The mandible looks larger on that side as well, and its lower edge tilts upwards. The condyle on the same aspect also appears to be bigger and higher than the one on the other side. In addition, it is difficult to discern bony details in the upper zones of the image because they tend to be either shadowy or streaked.

ERRORS IF PATIENT IS INCORRECTLY POSITIONED UPRIGHT

The cervical spine in the patient's neck should be straightened before exposing a panoramic radiograph. Sometimes the patient's chin ends up not being against the chin rest. This does not affect the documentation on the central dentition area of the radiograph, but structures normally on the top third of the x-ray are cut off, and little is seen on the bottom third. If the individual is slumped over and the spine is not straight, a ghost image of the spine tends to obscure other structures, primarily the front teeth in the central dentition zone as well as parts of the lower jaw.

ERRORS IN THE EXPOSURE STEP

During the exposure step of panoramic radiography, there are generally three kinds of errors that might occur.

- If the patient does not close their lips and place their tongue against the palate as directed, air between the lips masks the crowns of the front teeth and another air space in the palatoglossal region between the tongue and palates obscures the apices and bone in the maxillary jaw.
- If the patient moves during the exposure, the main radiographic errors observed are waves or other distortions in the mandible.
- Mistakes in the actual exposure process can also be made. Typical examples include double exposure, density errors due to incorrect potential difference applied, and labeling mistakes.

PROCEDURAL ERRORS

One common procedural error in panoramic radiography is beginning at the wrong place during exposure. This results in loss of part of the anatomic region desired, which shows up on the radiograph as a blank area. Another procedural mistake is failure to remove thick clothing, to place the lead apron correctly, or to adjust for individuals with short necks or broad shoulders. In this case, as the cassette rotates around it may find resistance when it touches the individual. When this disengagement occurs, a vertical band of the film will be overexposed and dark. Some dental offices take out the bite block or other parts (a practice that is discouraged), which can cause a number of radiographic errors including lack of clear separation between rows of teeth and malpositioning of the patient.

ADDITIONAL PROCEDURAL ERRORS

Light leaks in the darkroom can cause fogging or overexposure of a portion of the radiograph. Precautions against leakage are similar to those for other types of x-rays, but the integrity of the film cassette should be checked as well. If the films are **either under- or overexposed**, the voltage and/or the current needs to be either increased or decreased respectively. **Low developer solutions** could cause underexposure as well. It is mandated that panoramic machines have markers distinguishing right from left on the image (typically "R" and "L"); if these are not visible on the radiograph, it should be thrown out. Patient identification should be done with a film imprinter or special tape or pen on the edge of the film after exposure and before processing, not incorporated before exposure. Double exposures should be discarded.

IMPACT OF DAMAGED FILMS, SCREENS, OR CASSETTES

Panoramic film will crimp if it has been removed in a rough manner from either the box or the cassette. In this case, a small area of the emulsion is destroyed which shows up on the radiograph as a black, curved mark. Certain types of softer, more flexible cassettes have screens that are pulled out and folded back for film placement. Here, the potential for damage and eventual fissures in the screen is great. Scratches or foreign objects like lint or paper can occur on screens that have not been inspected as well. White lines or spots will appear on the x-ray in all of these types of screen damage because fluorescence during exposure will be prevented in these areas. Cassette damage generally results in light leaks that show up on the film as overexposed, black regions. The more bendable types of cassettes made of vinyl are most prone to damage, but rigid ones can also eventually develop leaks.

IMPACT OF STATIC ELECTRICITY

Rooms can be very dry, particularly in cold weather. If dry air conditions exist, and a film is pulled out quickly from the box or the cassette, friction usually occurs. This combination of friction and dry air produces static electricity. On the film, this static electricity appears as black electrostatic artifacts that look like lightening streaks, dots, starbursts, or other shapes. These artifacts are more common on extraoral than on intraoral films. Therefore, darkrooms should be humidified during these periods and care should be taken in film handling throughout the entire process. The potential for development of static electricity exists any time until processing has begun.

PROBLEMS ASSOCIATED WITH ENDODONTIC RADIOGRAPHY

Endodontic radiography is primarily used to look for dental pulp diseases. In this situation, the film is held in place by special film-holders, and no bite block is used. A rubber barrier dam, hemostat, or other endodontic instruments are usually present in the oral cavity to facilitate visualization of the teeth and general area on the radiograph. These instruments will be visualized on the x-ray. Usually, several different views are necessary to get a three-dimensional perspective. There are a number of commercially available endodontic film-holders. A hemostat also works quite well to hold the film in place using the paralleling technique, especially in the molar and pre-molar regions of the lower jaw. A number of views are usually documented, including from the top, from the back, and from the side.

CORRECTION OF ERRORS IN ACQUIRED IMAGES

The following errors in acquiring images can be corrected by:

- **Distortion**: Switch from the bisecting angle to a parallel angle for intraoral images as this increases clarity and reduces distortion.
- **Contact surface overlap**: Correct horizontal angulation or film-holder placement. Correction should be made if the overlap includes more than 50% of the enamel width.
- **Shortened images**: Result from excessive vertical angulation. Decrease angulation by 10° or more.
- **Lengthened images**: Results from insufficient vertical angulation. Increase angulation by 10° or more.
- **Off-centering of occlusal plane with bitewings**: Correct placement of film by centering tab and first seating distal part before moving medially.
- **Crowns of anterior teeth missing**: Results from excessive vertical angulation for bisecting angle or incorrect film position for parallel angle. For bisecting, decrease PID angulation. For parallel, reposition film holder.
- **Apices missing**: Increase vertical angulation. Switching from bisecting to parallel view may alleviate problem.
- **Cone-cutting**: Results from incomplete coverage of the film by the PID. Redirect PID.
- **Blurred image**: Results from movement of some type. Remind patient to hold very still.

Preparing Images for Legal Requirements, Viewing, Duplication, and Transfer

HIPAA REGULATIONS

The HIPAA or the Health Insurance Portability and Accountability Act of 1996 has three sections: (1) privacy standards, (2) patients' rights, and (3) administrative requirements. The Act requires electronic standardization of patient health care data. The privacy standards section deals primarily with protected health information or PHI. It requires the professional to obtain authorization from the patient before health information can be disclosed for treatment, payment, or healthcare related procedures. This can be in the form of written consent, or they can sign an Acknowledgment of Receipt Notice of Privacy Practices. There are only a few exceptions to these requirements such possible child abuse. Non-adherence can result in civil penalties, fines, or criminal punishments.

ADMINISTRATIVE REQUIREMENTS

The administrative requirements section of the HIPAA mandates that dental offices have a written privacy policy, which can be distributed to the patient. It also requires the dentist to train and familiarize the other personnel in details of the privacy policy and means of documentation. This section also compels the dentist to appoint an office privacy officer to monitor these policies, and another individual to handle complaints. A Notice of Privacy Practices must be in place. If third parties are to have access to patient information, they must be clearly acknowledged as well.

PATIENTS' RIGHTS

The patients' rights section of the HIPAA deals with the entitlements of patients or their representative to obtain their health information. The essence of patients' rights is that they can look at their records, copy them, question violations of rules, and request non-electronic forms of transmission. For minors, these rights generally apply to their parents unless there has been another legal edict. In addition, if the healthcare or dental professional wants to release any information for reason besides treatment, payment, or operations, they must inform the patient.

PREPARING IMAGES FOR LEGAL REQUIREMENTS, DUPLICATION, AND TRANSFER

Dental images may be transferred to other dental practitioners upon written request by the patient, but the dental films and dental records remain the property of the originating dentist, who should retain them indefinitely. Patients may ask for copies of records and films but may need to pay a fee, especially if an entire record is involved. If dual film was utilized, the second original image may be transferred; otherwise, a duplicate or a digital image must be made and transferred. The patient should not be required to undergo additional imaging to produce new originals. Duplicated film should be mounted and labeled as appropriate. The film and dental records should generally be transferred directly to other dental practitioners through carrier, mail, or internet and not given to the patient to carry, although patients do have that right if they insist.

DUPLICATING FILMS

Duplicating films are used to copy previously taken radiographs. These films have undergone a process called solarization, which overexposes the film to the point where maximum density is reversed. This is achieved through chemical treatment of the film or bombardment with light. One side of the duplicating film consists of the solarized emulsion on polyester base; it is identified by its purple color. The other side is protected with a layer of dye that absorbs reflected light (halation) to eliminate unsharpness in the copied image; this antihalation layer is typically glossy in appearance. Because the film is a type of direct-reversal film, exposure times affect the density in reverse order to a normal film.

PROCEDURES

Radiographs can be copied in the darkroom with safelight illumination. Duplicator machines are commercially available. An ultraviolet light source is directed through the original radiograph onto the purple solarized emulsion surface of the duplicating film. The original and duplicating films must be in intimate contact to avoid blurring of the duplicated image. The initial radiograph is put on the surface of the duplicator or illuminator, and the solarized side of the duplicating film is placed directly on top of it. The cover is closed, and the filmed is exposed for the time interval suggested by the manufacturer. After exposure, the film needs to be developed as usual.

LEGAL IMPLICATIONS OF BILLING AND PATIENT'S RIGHTS TO OBTAIN X-RAYS

There is legal precedence of the opinion that x-rays are owned by the dental facility generating them, not the patient. By themselves, x-rays are of little value to the patient who is not adept at interpreting them. Therefore, **billing for radiographs** should always be bundled with the cost of dental diagnosis and treatment to avoid the issue of ownership of the x-rays. Negligence claims or malpractice suits can occur if x-rays are delivered to the patient or if they are not applied diagnostically. A radiograph can be submitted as factual evidence in certain legal situations and should therefore always be high-quality. On the other hand, while a dentist is not legally compelled to send completed x-rays to other dentists upon request, they may transmit duplicates via certified or registered mail upon written solicitation by the second practice.

Chapter Quiz

Ready to see how well you retained what you just read? Scan the QR code to go directly to the chapter quiz interface for this study guide. If you're using a computer, simply visit the bonus page at **mometrix.com/bonus948/danbcda** and click the Chapter Quizzes link.

Radiation Safety (RHS)

Transform passive reading into active learning! After immersing yourself in this chapter, put your comprehension to the test by taking a quiz. The insights you gained will stay with you longer this way. Scan the QR code to go directly to the chapter quiz interface for this study guide. If you're using a computer, simply visit the bonus page at **mometrix.com/bonus948/danbcda** and click the Chapter Quizzes link.

Factors Affecting X-Ray Production and X-Radiation Characteristics

COMPOSITION OF TYPICAL RADIOGRAPHIC FILM

Typical radiographic film is double-sided or double-emulsion film. In the center of the film, there is a transparent, blue-colored plastic sheet or base. An emulsion is attached to either side of the base with some type of adhesive. The emulsion is a mixture of silver halide or silver iodobromide crystals, which interact with x-ray photons to produce what is known as a latent or invisible image, and clear gelatin. The silver compounds usually employed are 90% or greater silver bromide (chemical formula $AgBr$) and silver iodide (AgI) as the remainder. The outer layer on both sides of the radiographic film is a protective coating.

LATENT IMAGE

Before the addition of developer, an invisible or latent image is produced in the radiographic emulsion. The silver, bromine, and iodine atoms that are typically present in an emulsion will form crystals that are bound by the electrovalence forces of ionic bonding. When x-rays bombard these crystals, they eject energetic photoelectrons, and a chain reaction is set up. When these released electrons encounter deliberately manufactured imperfections or specks of silver sulfide, the electrons are trapped in that position. A cascade of positively charged silver ions is then attracted to the trapped electrons, and silver atoms are produced to form what is known as a latent or invisible image. When development chemicals are added, the silver catalyzes the reaction that makes these images visible.

BENSON LINE FOCUS PRINCIPLE

The path of x-rays can be deflected, and this property is exploited in the design of dental x-ray tubes to sharpen images. The Benson line focus principle reduces the effective dimensions of the focal spot. This is accomplished by an anode design with an angled face to the electron path, typically at 15-20° relative to the cathode. When the electrons strike the focal spot, they are therefore deflected through an x-ray window below the diverted path to the photographic film. The resultant "effective" focal spot is considerably smaller than the spot on the anode and image quality is improved. In addition, the anode can absorb more heat because it is spread over a larger area of that electrode.

SETUP OF A SIMPLE X-RAY TUBE

A simple x-ray tube consists of a tightly closed housing made of leaded glass (usually Pyrex), a negative terminal or cathode comprised of a tungsten filament wire surrounded by a molybdenum cup, and a positively charged copper anode with a central area made of tungsten. The tungsten filament of the cathode serves as a source of electrons when heated. These electrons are set in motion by the application of an extremely high voltage or electrical potential difference between the cathode and anode. The central area of the anode is called the **focal spot**. At the focal spot, about 1% of the energy generated is changed into x-rays with the remainder dissipated as heat production or infrared radiation in the outer portions of the anode. The anode serves as means of suddenly stopping or decelerating the electrons. Tungsten filaments are used because they have very high melting points and are destroyed.

FUNCTION OF THE CATHODE FOCUSING CUP AND REGULATING ELECTRON FLOW

The focusing cup is a receptacle that surrounds the tungsten filament of the x-ray tube cathode. It is usually made of molybdenum. The main purpose of the focusing cup is to direct the flow of electrons to the anode so that they strike a smaller, more focused area of the anode. Otherwise, the electron beam would spread out more, electrons would strike a larger portion of the anode, and the image would not be very distinct. The speed of electron flow is controlled by the amount of potential difference or voltage between the two electrodes. While there is a maximum voltage or peak (kVp or kilovoltage peak) that can be applied, the actual voltage of individual electrons is variable and usually less that the maximum. A greater gap potential difference will produce a faster electron flow or current, and subsequently x-ray photons with higher frequencies and energies are generated. Higher energy x-rays can penetrate further than those with lower energies.

GENERATION OF ELECTRONS

Electrons are generated in the **tungsten filament of the cathode** of the x-ray tube. When the filament is heated, thermal energy is transmitted to the tungsten and the electrons in its outer orbital shells are stripped off to form a cluster of electrons. This phenomenon is known as thermionic emission. Tungsten does not melt until it reaches 3420 °C, and the filament is typically heated to about two-thirds of that melting point. The rate of electron flow or electrical current measured in milliamperes (mA) is directly related to the applied temperature and the number of electrons pulled off. A typical dental x-ray apparatus generates 7-15 mA.

RESULT WHEN ELECTRONS HIT ANODE AND ITS TARGET IN THE X-RAY TUBE

Electrons streaming from the cathode to the anode in an x-ray tube have what is termed **kinetic or motion-related energy**. When these electrons reach the anode, they are stopped or decelerated. A portion of these electrons hit the tungsten target where the electrons in the shell orbits of the tungsten become excited. This means that these latter electrons temporarily possess higher energy levels, but as they revert to their initial states energy is given off in the form of either infrared radiation (heat) or as x-rays. The small proportion of x-rays generated (less than 1% usually) are redirected in many directions in the tube, and the x-rays that manage to pass through the x-ray window represent the useful beam for imaging and other purposes.

TYPES OF RADIATION

BREMSSTRAHLUNG RADIATION

In an x-ray tube, two types of radiation are produced, Bremsstrahlung and characteristic radiation. Bremsstrahlung (also called Brems or general radiation) is the dominant type of x-ray elicited by dental x-ray equipment. This general radiation represents photons of energy emitted as a result of a deceleration of the high-speed electrons at the tungsten anode target. This occurs in one of two ways. Usually, high-speed electrons streaming from the cathode are attracted to the positively charged nucleus of the tungsten in the anode target. If opposing nuclear forces are stronger, the fast electron is deflected and slowed down near the nucleus, and x-ray photons are emitted. This pattern of attraction followed by deflection, deceleration, and photon emission continues until the electron's energy is depleted. On the other hand, if the high-speed electron actually collides with and penetrates the nucleus, only one discrete photon of x-ray energy is produced.

CHARACTERISTIC RADIATION

Characteristic radiation is a type of x-ray that is generated when a high-energy electron from the cathode ionizes or removes an electron from an inner orbit of the target. A typical x-ray tube has a tungsten target at the anode. If the cathode electrons hit the target with enough energy, an electron in the innermost K shell of the tungsten is initially ejected. Subsequently, an electron from the next L shell moves to occupy the space in the K shell where the electron was pulled off, and a photon of so-called "characteristic radiation" is released. Characteristic radiation represents the disparity between the binding energies in the two orbital shells, and it is always the same for a particular element (tungsten in this case). In an x-ray tube, a photon of characteristic radiation is 59 keV, or the difference between the binding energy of the K shell of tungsten, 70 keV, and the L shell, 11 keV. This type of radiation is only emitted if the potential difference in the tube equals or exceeds the 70 keV binding energy of the K shell.

HETEROGENEOUS VS. HOMOGENEOUS RADIATION

Most Brems radiation emitted from a typical dental x-ray tube controlled by alternating current (AC) is **heterogeneous**. This means that the radiation is released in a range of energies and wavelengths. This variety occurs for two reasons. First, the electrons coming from the cathode possess a continuum of speeds due to the AC, and second, most of the electrons gradually lose energy by a series of interactions with different nuclei. Longer wavelength photons either bounce around inside the tube or are filtered out. If the apparatus is designed to convert the AC to direct current (DC), then a more **homogeneous** radiation is effectively emitted, greater penetration of the soft tissues is achieved, and image quality is improved. This is because all the cathode-derived electrons achieve the same voltage difference near the peak applied, and the subsequent radiation emitted is more uniform as well. This also allows for somewhat lower doses of radiation because there are no relatively useless longer wavelength species.

X-RAY GENERATORS

COMPONENTS

A typical x-ray generator used for dental x-rays is comprised of two distinct parts. The first is the **control panel**, which contains all of the controls for parameters such as the exposure time, current selection (mA or milliamperes), potential difference (kVp or kilovoltage peak), and the like plus the actual x-ray emission light. The other part is the **tubehead assembly**, which consists of the x-ray tube and transformers. All of the tubehead assembly is submerged in oil to shield the apparatus and thwart sparks between different components.

SELF-RECTIFICATION OF CURRENT

Most x-ray generators provide electrical energy to the dental x-ray tube in the form of alternating current (AC), typically as 110 or 220 volts in cycles of 60 Hertz (Hz or cycles per second). This means that the electrons generated flow first in one direction from the cathode to the anode by attraction, and then in the other direction. A wavelike pattern is produced in which the current reaches a peak, returns to baseline, and then goes through a trough and returns to baseline when the current is reversed. During this latter trough, current does not stream through the x-ray tube because the anode is already negatively charged. The result is **self-rectification** or effective conversion of the alternating current to unidirectional direct current (DC). In addition, while direction of the AC is changed every 1/120 of a second, the number of useful cycles per second is halved (in other words, 60 Hz).

TRANSFORMERS

Transformers are electromagnetic pieces of equipment that step the voltage potential difference up or down in an efficient manner. They usually consist of an iron core surrounded by two different loops of wire at either end. As the current passes through the core and the first or primary circuit wire, a magnetic field is generated. This in turn sets up a secondary current in the second loop of wire if the magnitude of the magnetic field is shifting, such as when alternating current is applied. The number of times each wire is coiled around the end relative to the other wire determines whether the transformers can step-up or step-down the voltage. The voltage generated in the secondary coil is directly related to the number of coils it possesses relative to the primary wire loop. Some dental x-ray machines have variable autotransformers in which there is only one large coil encircling the iron core. In this case, there are multiple areas where the insulation of the wire has been removed; a metal conductor can be moved to different exposed areas to generate and control the magnitude of the secondary circuit.

CHANGES FACILITATED BY TRANSFORMERS

In a dental x-ray machine, a filament circuit is activated when the exposure switch is closed. When a step-down transformer is used, the voltage is decreased from the applied 110 or 220 volts in the primary loop to a much lower voltage of about 8-12 volts in the secondary wire. This generates a large current of about 3-6 amperes to heat the cathode filament, which in turn produces more electrons at that location. If a step-up transformer is utilized instead, the applied current is increased in the secondary coil to a very high voltage of about 60-100 kVp. In this case, this extreme potential difference accelerates the movement of the cathode electrons to the anode, while also decreasing the current to about 10-15 milliamperes. Autotransformers are typically used as step-up transformers that can vary the voltage.

IMPACT OF CURRENT ON X-RAY EMISSION SPECTRUM

The current applied using a dental x-ray apparatus is directly related to the number of electrons produced at the cathode filament and the subsequent number of electrons flowing to the electrode. For each heterogeneous x-ray beam, there is a spectrum of emission of x-rays of various wavelengths or photons of different energies. This can be represented in a distribution curve. The setup of a particular machine can shift the proportion of types of x-rays emitted, but in general the beam intensity can be proportionately affected by changes in the current (mA) applied and the electron flow.

RELATIONSHIP BETWEEN EXPOSURE TIME AND CURRENT

More photons of x-ray energy are generated by increasing the exposure time. Often the maximum potential difference (kVp) and current (mA) are preset when doing dental x-rays, and the only variable is the exposure time. In this case, increasing exposure time augments the total energy or intensity. Exposure time can be expressed as either fractions or whole multiples of a second or as the number of impulses of electrical energy applied in a second. Either expression of exposure time can be multiplied by the current applied to give values known as mAs or mAi respectively. In general, the goal is to maintain either mAs or mAi as constant, which can be achieved by changing the current and exposure time in opposition. In other words, if the current is increased the exposure time is decreased and vice versa.

IMPACT OF KILOVOLTAGE ON X-RAY PRODUCTION

Kilovoltage (kVp) is the maximum voltage that occurs across an x-ray tube from the cathode to the anode (although the voltage is not constant). The voltage setting determines the gray scale contrast and quality of the image. X-ray machines may have a fixed setting of between 65 and 75 or may have adjustable settings between 50 and 100. If the kVp is adjusted higher, the velocity of electrons increases and better penetrates, but this decreases contrast in the image, which is then grayer. If the kVp is adjusted lower, the velocity slows and the image has higher contrast, but lacks shades of gray. In both cases, the image suffers, so the ideal settings are usually somewhere in the range of 65-75. The radiation exposure to the patient varies little between 60 and 80. However, settings below 60 increase exposure to the patient, so they are usually avoided.

IMPACT OF KILOVOLTAGE ON WAVELENGTH, FREQUENCY, AND ENERGY

The kilovoltage or potential difference applied influences the number and degree of penetration of the x-rays emitted. Potential differences of between 60 and 65 kVp generate x-rays that do not penetrate much and are termed "soft." These x-rays have relatively long wavelengths and low frequencies and energies. Larger potential differences of usually 85-100 kVp produce x-rays that penetrate either much more or completely and are termed "hard." Here the associated x-ray wavelengths are relatively short, and the energies and frequencies are higher. These differences can be exploited when performing dental x-rays by using larger voltages in areas that are thick or dense.

X-RAY BEAM INTENSITY

The intensity of an x-ray beam is its total energy emitted per unit area and time. Total energy is the product of two key components, the quantity or number of photons in the beam, and the quality or energy of the specific photons. Area is defined in terms of the cross-sectional space at the point of measurement on the film; this is proportional to the distance from the source which can be controlled. The exposure rate or time can also be regulated by the technician as can the voltage and current applied. Thus, the beam intensity can be calculated as:

$$\text{Intensity} = \frac{(\text{quantity of photons}) \times (\text{quality})}{(\text{cross sectional area}) \times (\text{exposure time})}$$

RADIOGRAPHIC DENSITY

Radiographic films are interpreted by observing them facing an illuminator or view-box. Radiographic density is a measurement of the amount of light that passes through a radiographic film relative to the intensity of the light striking it from behind the illuminator. The density is a reading of the relative darkness, blackness, or radiolucency of areas of the film. The parameter is a reflection of the composition of the film, variables employed during the radiation procedure, and the size of the resultant silver aggregates. Density is defined by a logarithmic relationship as the $\log_{10}$ of the proportion between the intensity of incident light (I) and the percent of light transmitted through the film (T). This translates to a density of 1.0 if 10% of the light passes through and a density of 2.0 if 1% is transmitted, which are radiographic densities usually considered acceptable versus very dark. Technicians sometimes use densities as light as 0.3.

CHARACTERISTIC CURVE

A characteristic curve is an xy-plot of film density (y) versus the logarithm of the exposure time (x). Each type of film has its own characteristic curve. The plot looks like an elongated S with a bottom or toe part, a long relatively straight-line portion in the middle, and a shoulder at the top. The middle straight-line part of the curve can be defined by its slope, or the change in the density relative to log of relative exposure time (y/x). The straight-line portion is also the zone of correct exposure. Films with steeper slopes provide more contrast than those with shallower slopes.

IMPACT OF ACCEPTABLE EXPOSURE TIMES

The range of acceptable exposure times can also be extrapolated from the characteristic curve by drawing lines from the y density axis in the desired range (for example, about 0.5-2.5); only exposure times falling in that range are diagnostically useful. There is a degree of tolerance or exposure error, termed latitude, inherent in the film that is inversely proportional to its slope and corresponding contrast. In other words, there is little latitude or room for error with high contrast films and vice versa. Kilovoltage applied affects the amount of latitude in the acceptable range of exposure times directly because of its inverse relationship to contrast.

INFLUENCING VARIABLES

Aspects of the actual radiographic exposure are the most important variables that control radiographic density, particularly the product mAs. Milliampere seconds, or mAs, is the multiplication product between the current in milliamperes times the exposure time in seconds. This is important because it directly affects the number of x-rays hitting the film and the amount of silver that aggregates. The kilovoltage difference in the x-ray tube is also significant because it controls the wavelength and frequency of the x-rays, and the most penetrating x-rays occur with high voltage and resultant short wavelengths. Density is also inversely related to the square of the distance between the x-ray beam and the film. There are other less important factors that contribute to the control of radiographic density including film speed, use of grid devices to filter out scattering, and utilization of screens that change x-ray into light energy. During the development process, it is also possible to under develop the film if chemicals are depleted.

VOLTAGE CHANGES, EXPOSURE TIMES, AND THE ABILITY TO CONTROL DENSITY

When voltage is increased, the intensity of the emitted x-ray increases as well. However, this relationship is more than linear; the factor the voltage is stepped up by must be squared to calculate the intensity. In addition, voltage increases are related to the current produced and ideal exposure time. A particular density or darkness of the film is usually desired. Two schemes are generally followed to achieve this density. One states that the current in milliamperes should be cut in half for every 15% augmentation in voltage. Alternatively, the exposure time must be divided in two for every voltage rise of 15 kVp or doubled for each similar reduction of potential difference.

INVERSE SQUARE LAW IN RELATION TO DEVICE POSITIONING

X-rays generated at the target on the anode are filtered through a collimating device upon leaving the tubehead. Then these rays are usually directed to the patient through the use of a beam- or position-indicating device. The intensity of the x-ray beam at the film in the patient's mouth is related to the distance of the film

from the target source by a relationship called the **inverse square law**. This law states that the intensity of the radiation at the level of the film is inversely related to the square of the distance between the source and the film. For example, doubling the length of the positioning device cuts down the radiation intensity on the film by a factor of 4 (in other words, $2^2 = 4$). This can be compensated for by increasing the exposure time by the same factor of 4.

CONTRAST

LONG-SCALE VS SHORT-SCALE RADIOGRAPHIC CONTRAST

Radiographic contrast is the difference between the densities of extremely dark and light portions of a radiograph. The most important factor controlling contrast is the kilovoltage potential difference in the x-ray tube. Generally, at lower kilovoltages of 60-65 kV, **short-scale contrast** is observed; at these voltages, the x-rays emitted have long wavelengths but lower energy. Since relatively few silver aggregates are formed on the film, there are not many gradations between light and dark in the image. On the other hand, if higher voltages of 80-90 kV are used, **long-scale contrast** is usually observed. Here the x-rays have shorter wavelengths and greater penetrability, and more silver bundles develop resulting in more gradations of gray. An aluminum step wedge device, also called a penetrometer, can be used to measure these changes.

RELATIONSHIP BETWEEN CONTRAST, DENSITY, AND EXPOSURE TIME

Contrast is theoretically controlled by the kilovoltage applied. The density or darkness of a film is affected by a number of factors. The most important variable is milliampere seconds, but kilovoltage also increases the density. When either exposure time or the mAs product is altered, film density is changed, but contrast is not, unless the kVp potential difference is also changed. In practice, lower mAs (and exposure times) are usually utilized with the higher voltages producing low or long-scale contrast, and higher values of these parameters are generally used with lower voltages and high or short-scale contrast.

INDICATIONS

Use of long-scale radiographic contrast conditions is generally preferred for radiographs of the periapical areas and bony changes like periodontal or periapical disease. Conditions favoring short-scale radiographic contrast are usually recommended for bitewing images and the illustration of caries or tooth decay. Ideal densities and contrasts are subjective, however. Low voltage, short-scale films, may not show early pathologic alterations. Long-scale films with their gradations can identify early changes better, and some clinicians prefer these for caries. The downside of long-scale films is that they are not as crisp and visually pleasing.

SPATIAL CHARACTERISTICS THAT INFLUENCE THE DETAIL AND DEFINITION OF IMAGES

The central sharp area of a radiographic image is called the **umbra**, and it is surrounded by a blurrier area called the **penumbra**. The less sharp penumbra area can be reduced by decreasing the target area on the anode and the effective focal area. Images are also distorted on radiographs because materials furthest from the film will be magnified more than those closer. This distortion can influence the perceived shape of the tooth or other objects as well. These distortions are related to the attempt to visualize three-dimensional objects on the flat plane of a film. Detail or definition is also influenced by the distances between the film and either the focal point or the object. Movement of the patient or any equipment or the use of intensifying screens can decrease definition and produce blurriness. Definition is directly related to contrast.

X-Radiation Physics

BASIC STRUCTURE OF AN ATOM

An atom is the smallest portion into which an element can be divided and still retain its inherent properties. Elements are the simplest units of matter and they cannot be broken down into other substances by chemical reactions. The number of identified elements has changed over time; 118 is the current number. The atom is comprised of a central nucleus containing a set number of positively charged protons and neutral neutrons, which is surrounded by rings or orbits of negatively charged electrons. These electrons stay in orbit because of their electrostatic attraction to the protons. The atomic or Z number is an expression of the number of protons in the atom.

IONIZATION

Ionization is the conversion of an atom from a neutral to either a positive or negative charge. The charge represents the discrepancy between the number of protons in the nucleus and the number of electrons after ionization, and the charged atom is called an ion. If outer orbital shells are unfilled, the atom has a tendency to acquire electrons, and it becomes a negatively charged anion. If electrons are lost, the result is a positively charged atom or cation. X-ray bombardment of an atom conveys energy to the orbital electron; the electron is ejected but forms a loose attraction to the atom termed an ion pair.

FORCES OF ATTRACTION AND BINDING ENERGY FOR ORBITAL ELECTRONS

Electrons circle around the nucleus in up to 7 different paths or shells, which are sequentially lettered from K to Q. Shell K is closest to the nucleus, and shell Q is the theoretical furthest path. Normally, there is equilibrium between the centrifugal and electrostatic forces that enables each electron to stay in orbit. However, electrons in the outer orbital shells are more easily removed from the atom since less work or energy is required to strip the electrons from outer orbital shells than the inner paths. Electrons occupying the external shell are called valence electrons because they are easily removed and can thus establish the atom's chemical properties, including its optical spectrum. Binding energy is the amount of energy needed to extract an electron from its orbit; this parameter is distinctive for each element and each orbital shell.

ELECTRON VOLT AND BINDING ENERGY

An electron volt is a measurement of kinetic or motion-related energy. It is defined as the amount of energy generated by moving an electron through an electrical potential difference of 1 volt. It is often expressed as kiloelectron (keV) or megaelectron (MeV) volts, which are 1000 or 1 million times a single volt. Each shell of an atom has a defined binding energy which is generally expressed in keV. Electrons can be removed from the shell if that binding energy is achieved through bombardment with x-rays or other rays or particles. While loosely held electrons in the outermost paths can be removed by low energy visible light or UV rays, electrons in the closer shells can only be pulled off with higher energy x-rays, gamma rays, or certain particles.

PARTICULATE RADIATIONS

Particulate radiations are small masses that travel linearly at rapid speed and can penetrate matter. Only one type of particulate radiation is neutral in charge, the neutron. All of the other types are electrically charged, and the degree of penetration is generally inversely related to the particle mass. One variety is the alpha particle, a helium nucleus without the associated electrons, which is 2 protons plus 2 neutrons. These particles are emitted from heavy metals and are heavy and highly charged; thus, alpha particles lose energy quickly and do not penetrate matter as well as other types of particulate radiation. The much smaller electrons penetrate tissue and air much more effectively. Electrons are emitted as particulate radiations as either beta particles (negatrons) from radioactive nuclei or as cathode rays (electrons). Cathode rays are actually flows of orbital electrons that are generated from the filament of an x-ray tube and travel from the cathode to the anode. The nuclei of the hydrogen atom can be sped up and emitted as another form of particulate radiation, a proton, but the mass of these protons is large, and they do not penetrate very effectively.

ELECTROMAGNETIC RADIATION AND DIAGNOSTIC RADIOLOGY

Electromagnetic radiation is energy traveling in space while generating electric and magnetic force fields. There are two types of electromagnetic radiation, **gamma rays** discharged from disintegrating radioactive nuclei, and **x-rays** emitted outside the nucleus without mass or electrical charge. X-rays can travel through tissues further than other forms of radiation without focal localization, making them important for forms of diagnostic radiology including dental radiographs. Particulate radiation like alpha and beta particles or the electromagnetic gamma rays are more useful in nuclear medicine treatments.

PARTICLE CONCEPTS OF ELECTROMAGNETIC RADIATION

In addition to spreading in a wave-like pattern, x-rays and other narrow wavelength, high frequency electromagnetic radiations can act like particles. Distinct parcels of energy called quanta or photons are disseminated by these types of radiations. These energy bundles do not have mass. If the frequency of the wavelength is increased (in other words, the wavelength is shortened), the energy of the photon is increased proportionately. If the energy level reaches or exceeds 15 electron volts, orbital electrons of atoms can be pulled off. This is known as ionization, and the associated types of rays are considered to be ionizing radiation. Examples of this type of radiation include not only x-rays but gamma rays and certain types of ultraviolet rays.

WAVE PROPAGATION

Electromagnetic radiations, including x-rays, disseminate energy in **wave-like patterns**. The speed of dissemination of these rays is equivalent to the speed of light, which is defined as either 186,000 miles per second or 3×10^8 miles per second. Electromagnetic waves are distinguished by the fact that they do not require a medium to pass through; instead, they can spread in a vacuum. X-rays and other waves are characterized by the interrelated constant speed of light (often shown as the letter c) and the variables of wavelength and frequency. Wavelength is the length between the same phase in adjoining waves, and it is usually expressed in meters or the Greek letter lambda (λ). Frequency is the number of wave cycles occurring per second, it is measured in hertz, and it can be represented by the Greek letter nu (ν). The relationship between these can be expressed as $c = \lambda \nu$.

ELECTROMAGNETIC SPECTRUM

The electromagnetic spectrum is the entire range of electromagnetic types of radiation. It is defined by the classification of the type of radiation and its associated wavelength range. The wavelength differences represented in the spectrum are quite large. The **long wavelength**, **low frequency** forms include alternating current, radio waves, television, and radar. These wave cycles range from about 10^{12} meters down to several meters. Infrared, visible, and ultraviolet light have **mid-range wavelengths**. Ionizing radiations such as gamma rays and x-rays have extremely **short wavelengths** and are thus often represented in nanometers (nm), or 10^{-9} meters. The effective wavelengths for medical or dental x-rays are about 0.01–0.05 nanometers. Another unit of measurement is the angstrom unit (A) which is equivalent to a tenth of a nanometer.

CHARACTERISTIC X-RAYS AND THEIR USE IN DENTISTRY AND MEDICINE

X-rays are extremely short wavelength electromagnetic radiations that travel at the speed of light. They have no mass. They disseminate in wave-like patterns in a straight line, but they can be redirected into other linear paths. X-ray beams spread out with increasing distance from the source. X-rays can go through materials that are impenetrable by longer wavelength sources. Certain materials such as photographic film can selectively absorb x-rays. X-rays can trigger fluorescence, or the emission of longer wavelength radiation, in some substances, and this property is often exploited to amplify the response. X-rays can ionize substances including gases; this property is utilized in ionization chambers. X-rays can also induce changes in biological materials such as human tissues, and this is the basis for their utility in therapeutic radiology.

PRIMARY VS. SECONDARY RADIATION

Primary radiation is the central x-ray beam that leaves the tubehead and is sometimes referred to as the useful x-ray beam because it is responsible for production of the radiographic image. This type of radiation is the most penetrating.

Secondary radiation occurs when the primary radiation interacts with the tissue. When x-rays deflect as they interact with tissue, this form of secondary radiation is referred to as **scatter radiation**. Scatter radiation can go in all directions and poses a risk to both the patient and the operator who may be exposed, so the operator must be at least 6 feet from the patient or behind adequate shielding. Types of scatter radiation include:

- **Compton**: Collision with an electron causes the photon to lose energy and change path, and ionization occurs. Compton scatter is responsible for about 62% of scatter radiation.
- **Photoelectric**: When an x-ray photon is absorbed, an inner shell electron is ejected, and then another electron releases a characteristic photon to fill that void. The photoelectric scatter is responsible for about 30% of scatter radiation.
- **Coherent**: Also called Thompson or unmodified scattering, this collision alters the photon path, but no ionization occurs. Coherent scatter is responsible for about 8% of scatter radiation.

THE PHOTOELECTRIC EFFECT

X-rays can be taken into matter and tissues when the two interact, a process called **photoelectric absorption**. This generally happens when the energy level of the photon is slightly greater than the binding energy of the material's K or innermost orbital shell. The x-ray is absorbed into and transfers its energy to the orbital electron, which is expelled and taken in by another atom. Atoms with higher atomic numbers tend to absorb x-rays more readily. Photoelectric absorption is more prevalent with high frequency, low wavelength x-rays or when the interacting material is thick or dense. This phenomenon has also been classified as **characteristic radiation**; the energies to expel the K shell electron and replace it with an L shell electron are both predetermined. The energy difference defines the energy of the resultant x-ray. A small portion of x-rays go right through the tissues without contact, but remnants from this type of interaction can still be seen as dark film spots after processing.

FILM FOG

Film fog or undesired darkness occurs when radiation that has been scattered touches the film. There are two ways in which these changes of direction can occur.

- A small portion of the radiation can undergo **Thompson scattering**, also known as unmodified or coherent scattering. In this case, lower energy photons change direction when they encounter matter but little else occurs.
- Another phenomenon called Compton or **incoherent** is more prevalent, and it is a potentially greater problem for x-ray interpretation. Here higher energy x-rays expel outermost orbital electrons upon interaction with matter; this results in a positively charged atom loosely coupled to a negatively charged Compton or recoil electron. The origin photon changes direction and undergoes subsequent similar interactions and directional changes. If the angle of change is small, most of the intensity of the photon remains, and it can easily arrive at the film as fog.

The majority of dental x-ray photons experience this type of scattering, so manipulations are usually necessary to reduce it. These manipulations can include use of rectangular collimators and changing other parameters to shorten exposure time.

X-Radiation Biology

EFFECTS OF X-RADIATION ON ATOMS AND MOLECULES

When an x-ray photon comes in contact with an atom or molecule, the molecular structure is changed. In some cases, the energy from the photon causes orbital electrons in the atom to vibrate or become excited. The result is either release of light and heat or the actual disruption of molecular bonds. If the energy of the x-ray is enough to expel the orbital electron from the atom, a second phenomenon called **ionization** occurs. In this case, an electron can be ejected or loosely bound to form an ion pair with the now positively charged atom. If molecular bonds are broken, molecules act differently and cell function can be disrupted.

RADIOLYSIS

Radiolysis is the breakdown of chemicals into smaller components by x-rays or other radiation. The term usually refers to the interface of this radiation with water molecules because water makes up about 80% of the body. Subsequently, an ion pair of the positively charged water and a free electron or radical is created. The term free radical can describe any molecule containing an unpaired electron, though, and all of these are very chemically reactive and able to destroy life components like deoxyribonucleic acid, DNA, and adenosine triphosphate, ATP. For example, two hydroxyl (*OH) radicals can combine to form a harmful substance called hydrogen peroxide (H_2O_2).

THEORY OF ACCUMULATIVE EFFECT OF RADIATION

It has been theorized that the biological effects of radiation are cumulative. That means that the untoward effects of radiation exposure accumulate in increments with each contact. The consensus opinion is also that low-dose ionizing radiation (like that used in dentistry) has a non-threshold, linear type of dose-response curve. The concept of accumulative effect is premised upon the idea that repair after radiation exposure is never complete. This cumulative effect eventually can lead to malignancies, birth defects, aging, and other diseases. Damaging effects are not evident until a certain amount of time, called the latent period, has elapsed between exposure and documented consequences. The potential effects of the radiation are dependent on a number of host factors and radiation parameters.

TYPES OF EFFECTS THAT RADIATION HAS ON BIOLOGICAL MATERIALS

Radiation can affect biological materials either directly or indirectly. When radiation interacts directly with biologically active materials, the destruction is a direct effect. The most significant direct effect is the breakdown of DNA in the nucleus of the cell, which prevents further cell processes including replication resulting in cell death. Radiation can have a direct destructive effect on other important molecules like proteins and ribonucleic acid (RNA) as well. Ionizing radiation can also act indirectly by producing free radicals that later either react with life-sustaining molecules or form intermediate toxic substances that affect biological materials. The effects of radiation can be cell damage or in rare instances malignant changes.

RESPONSES OF SOMATIC AND GENETIC TISSUES TO RADIATION DOSES

When somatic tissues are exposed to radiation, changes do not occur until a particular threshold radiation dose is reached. The relationship between the radiation dose and subsequent tissue damage is not linear but looks like a curve on a two-dimensional plot. These effects do not affect the genetic makeup of the individual. Rather they include effects like sunburn or other skin reddening, hair loss, development of cataracts on the eye, or sterility.

On the other hand, genetic changes such as those occurring in reproductive tissues involve mutations in the DNA that can be passed on to the next generation or cause malignancies. In these tissues, the relationship between the amount of radiation exposure and number of mutations is linear. These genetic tissues do not need a threshold dose of radiation before mutations occur (termed non-threshold). There are other cellular mechanisms that can moderate the effects of radiation such as repair of DNA and other structures, destruction of the cell by other cells called phagocytes, and stimulation of the immune system.

REASON FOR INCREASED SUSCEPTIBILITY TO THE EFFECTS OF RADIATION

Most mammals, including humans, are more susceptible to the effects of radiation than other species. It is difficult to pinpoint why certain individual human beings are more sensitive to radiation damage than others. However, it has been demonstrated that certain human organs and tissues are more radiosensitive than others. The most sensitive cell types are those that divide very rapidly, in particular tissues involved with blood formation (like bone marrow) or reproduction (such as the ovary) or those cells that are already malignant; cells in these categories are killed relatively easily by exposure to radiation. The least sensitive cell types, termed radioresistant cells, are those that do not divide often, such as muscle and nerve cells.

GREATEST BIOLOGICAL RISKS FROM DENTAL RADIATION EXPOSURE

The greatest biological risks from dental radiation exposure are the possible development of two types of **malignancies**: leukemia and thyroid cancer. Dental x-rays augment the natural probability that an individual may develop these cancers by increased exposure. Leukemia is cancer of the bone marrow, which is involved in blood cell production. Since about 10% of the body's bone marrow is in the skull region, and about a tenth of that is located in the actual mandible, dental radiography does slightly increase the probability of leukemia. The thyroid gland, the endocrine gland at the base of the neck, is close enough to the region typically irradiated during dental x-rays to be subject to scatter radiation. There are thyroid collars that can be worn by the patient to eliminate about half of the already low dose of scatter radiation.

AREAS OF BODY TO AVOID DURING DENTAL RADIOGRAPHY

Genetic abnormalities and malignancies can result from radiation exposure. For dental radiography, the gonads and reproductive systems of patients should always be shielded to prevent these abnormalities or fetal congenital defects. Exposure to the bone marrow, thyroid gland, or unnecessary areas of skin should be avoided as well because of the possibility of development of leukemia or other malignancies. In addition, cataract development has been associated with exposure of the lens of the eye to radiation so that area should be avoided as well.

TRANSMISSION OF RADIATION EFFECTS TO THE NEXT GENERATION

In general, the changes induced by radiation exposure are only transmitted to the next generation when these effects occur in genetic or reproductive tissues. In these types of tissues, the radiation actually causes changes in the genetic material, and these changes are then passed on to the next generation. On the other hand, all other cell types are termed somatic; they include skin, connective tissues, nerves and a wide variety of other tissues and organs. When somatic tissues are changed by radiation exposure, these changes are not transmitted to the progeny.

WHY DENTAL RADIOGRAPHY IS CONSIDERED RELATIVELY BENIGN

There are various types of radiation. The radiation from dental x-rays is sparsely ionizing. This means that the energy they transfer is dispersed and these x-rays are said to have a low linear energy transfer (LET). Other types of radiation, in particular alpha particles, have a higher LET, deposit the energy in more discrete bundles, and have a considerably higher potential for biological damage. In addition, very small quantities of radiation are used for dental radiographs, most of the x-rays do not reach internal tissues because they are absorbed by outer layers of the skin, and only small areas of the head and neck are generally exposed. Short but intense acute exposure to radiation is generally more damaging than prolonged but smaller chronic exposure. Dental radiography might be considered chronic exposure because of its low level, repetitive nature.

MINIMIZING BIOLOGICAL RISKS

Most dental offices utilize leaded torso aprons for their patients while taking dental x-rays, thus virtually eliminating whole body and specifically reproductive organ exposure. These aprons are especially important as preventive measures for pregnant females to reduce the possibility of fetal congenital defects. There are few documented studies about the effects of radiation on genetic changes in reproductive organs and subsequent transmission to children. Even without aprons, the uterus and fetus receive only minor secondary radiation.

Other possible risks like cataract development require a threshold dose of radiation before untoward effects are observed. At the exposure levels of typical dental x-rays, the risk is very small because the values are far below the threshold.

MEASUREMENT SYSTEMS FOR RADIATION DOSE

The traditional **units of measurement** for radiation dose were the **roentgen or R, rad**, and **rem**. All of these terms are equivalent, and measurements of dosage can be expressed with the smaller units of milliroentgens (mR), millirads (mrad), or millirems (mrem). While these units are still often used, there is also a newer **SI classification system**. In the SI system, units are expressed in gray (Gy) or sievert (Sv) units as well as centigray or cGy and milligray or mGy. The relationship between the two systems is 1 gray per 100 rads. These are all units of dose, or the amount of energy from the x-ray that is taken in per mass unit of tissue. For example, the gray unit represents the number of Joules of energy absorbed per kilogram of tissue. Dose absorbed is a more important parameter than exposure because it corresponds to potential biological destruction.

RADIATION EXPOSURE VS. RADIATION DOSE

Radiation exposure represents the number of photons producing a particular electrical charge in a volume of air. Originally, exposure was measured by converting the number of roentgen units, which quantified the number of ion pairs per cubic centimeter of air, into the electrical charge produced, which was expressed in coulombs or C. Today, exposure is expressed in exposure units, which are defined as one coulomb per kilogram of air. Exposure does not necessarily reflect the actual radiation dose delivered to tissues, and this dosage is highly dependent on a number of factors like tissue density and host response. The modern dose unit is the SI unit or gray. Dose was previously (and still is sometimes) expressed in rad; 1 rad is equivalent to 100 erg (a measurement of energy as well) absorbed per gram of tissue.

DOSE EQUIVALENTS
MODELS OF DOSE EQUIVALENTS

Different types of radiation can produce varying amounts of biological damage with the same dose. X-rays, beta particles, and gamma rays all possess the least potential for destruction. They have been assigned a quality factor (QF) of 1. Other more damaging types of radiation have been assigned higher QFs, which represent their relative destructive power. The concept of dose equivalents (H) expresses the relative destructive effects of different radiation types in Sieverts or mSv by multiplying the dose (D) in Gy by the assigned quality factor (QF). All types of radiation (including x-rays) with a QF of 1 have equal doses and dose equivalents so the number of Gy and Sv are the same. For more destructive types of radiation like neutrons or alpha particles, the number of dose equivalents (Sv) is larger than the dose absorbed by a factor, the QF.

EFFECTIVE DOSE EQUIVALENTS

The risk of development of genetic defects or cancer from radiation exposure is dependent on the location and breadth of exposure in addition to the number of dose equivalents absorbed. The reason is that certain tissues are more susceptible to damaging biological effects and malignancy, in particular reproductive and blood-forming tissues and certain organs like the breast. Therefore, the concept of effective dose equivalents defines the relative destructive power based on area of exposure. In dentistry for example, a bitewing or panoramic radiograph exposes the patient to very low effective dose equivalents, while a full-mouth intraoral set using multiple exposures and films multiplies this effective dose. Use of faster films lessens the effective dose. X-rays used in other settings such as nuclear medicine expose the patient to beams in much larger areas of the body including potential genetic targets and deliver much higher effective doses. They are often termed whole body exposures.

Patient/Operator Exposure to Radiation and Radiation Safety

IMPACT OF FILTRATION, SHIELDING, COLLIMATION AND PID LENGTH

Factors influencing radiation safety include the following:

Filtration	Aluminum filter placed at cone base covers the opening through which the x-ray beam travels to absorb low-energy photons and allow-high energy photons to pass through, reducing exposure. Filters range from a minimum of 1.5 mm for machines with kVp below 70, to 2.5 mm for machines with kVp above 70.
Shielding	Lead and lead-equivalent shielding devices, such as thyroid collars and aprons, reduce exposure.
Collimation	Lead diaphragm restricts x-ray beam to conform to the size and shape of the image receptor in order to decrease scatter radiation and patient exposure. The lead collimator with a round or rectangular opening limits the beam size to ≤2.75 inches.
PID [cone] length	The length of the position indicating device (PID) or cone, which is lead lined, affects the focal-film distance. While cylindrical and rectangular PIDS do not spread scatter radiation, the cone-shaped PIDs do. A short cone (8 inch) requires less radiation but results in more scatter radiation. A long cone requires 4 times more radiation.

REGULATING BODIES FOR RADIATION HEALTH AND SAFETY

NATIONAL ORGANIZATIONS

There are a number of bodies in the United States and internationally that make recommendations on, or actually govern, radiation health and safety. In the United States, a subsidiary of the Food and Drug Administration (FDA), the Center for Devices and Radiological Health (CDRH) controls the manufacture of x-ray machines and other devices emitting radiation. Occupational exposure guidelines are established by the Nuclear Regulatory Commission (NRC), the Occupational Safety and Health Administration (OSHA), or indirectly by the Environmental Protection Agency (EPA) as well. There are also several nationally-based organizations that make recommendations related to radiation health and safety including the Biological Effects of Ionizing Radiation Committee (BEIR) operating under the National Academy of Sciences and the National Council on Radiological Protection and Measurement (NCRP). Every state has a Bureau of Radiation Safety that regulates radiation procedures locally.

INTERNATIONAL ORGANIZATIONS

Several international organizations keep abreast of radiation biology research and make recommendations based on current information. These bodies include the United Nations Scientific Committee on the Effects of Atomic Radiation (UNSCEAR) and the International Commission of Radiological Protection (ICRP). There is also an official worldwide group that proposes standards for radiological units of measurement called the International Commission on Radiation Units and Measurements (ICRU).

OSHA HAZARD COMMUNICATION STANDARDS FOR CHEMICAL AGENTS

According to the OSHA Hazard Communication Standards (HCS) regarding chemical agents, employees must have access to hazard information associated with their workplace. OSHA's minimum requirements include:

- **Hazard communication program**: A document that outlines the employer's responsibilities, including a list of hazardous chemical and notation of where the list and material safety data sheets (MSDSs) will be maintained. It should include warning labeling requirements, a description of training courses, and methods of informing contractors of hazards
- List of any hazardous chemicals used in the workplace.
- **Copies of manufacturers' MSDSs** for every chemical used in the workplace.

- **Employee training**: This should include summary of OSHA HCS, detection methods, health hazards, signs/symptoms of exposure, good practices, need for personal protective equipment, emergency procedures for spills or exposures, first aid measures for exposures, locations of chemical lists and MSDSs, explanation of MSDSs, labeling system utilized, and where to obtain additional information.

REGULATIONS GOVERNING DENTAL EQUIPMENT AND LICENSURE REQUIREMENTS

Use of various types of dental equipment must meet official federal performance standards. Radiation standards are generally also established locally by the city, county, and state. In particular, radiation inspections are usually required 2 or 3 times a year. In terms of professional licensure for radiation use, states generally set their own guidelines. A dental hygienist is a licensed specialist, but additional certification in radiography may or may not be obligatory. A dental assistant may be expected to take an examination related to radiology if they take radiographs. For both types of professionals, some states only require general supervision by or presence of a dentist.

AMERICAN DENTAL ASSOCIATION (ADA) GUIDELINES
NEW PATIENTS

Exposure to radiation through use of dental radiographs is a clinical judgment call, and it is not always necessary every dental visit. All radiographic exams should be individualized for new patients. Children who do not have permanent teeth yet may not require x-rays, but if the dentist cannot inspect certain areas of the mouth, some periapical, occlusal, or posterior bitewing views might be taken. After their permanent teeth begin to erupt, these types of radiographs plus panoramic views are usually taken. For adolescents or adults with complete or at least partial dentition, posterior bitewings plus panoramic and/or some periapical views are typically done. If history or evidence of dental disease is present, a full mouth radiograph is usually taken. The diagnostic plan for edentulous or toothless adults should be very individualized based on clinical criteria.

RETURNING PATIENTS

The dentist should exercise clinical judgment before radiographs are done on returning patients. If the patient had previous caries or appears to be at risk for development of decay, then posterior bitewing radiographs are usually indicated at 6- to 12-month intervals for children and adolescents and up to 18-month intervals for adults. If caries development or predilection was not previously observed, the period between bitewing x-rays can be increased up to 2 years for children and 3 years for adolescents and adults. If periodontal disease is observed, the dentist should decide what radiographs need to be taken, but typically they include selected bitewing or periapical views. Generally toothless adults do not need to have radiographs done.

PATIENT PROTECTION FROM UNNECESSARY X-RAY EXPOSURE

Unnecessary x-ray exposure may result from:

- Improper positioning of the patient and/or equipment
- An x-ray beam that is larger than necessary, exposing additional tissue
- Use of a cylindrical collimator with rectangular image receptor, allowing increased scatter radiation
- Use of long cone rather than short increases radiation exposure
- Inadequate use and/or placement of body shielding
- Multiple unnecessary exposures, such as with retakes and duplicate views rather than using dual film
- Too frequent dental x-ray screening
- Inadequate training of operator in proper techniques
- Use of standard radiography rather than digital, which has less radiation exposure
- Use of slow film rather than fast, requiring longer duration of exposure
- Use of bisecting method for the x-ray beam rather than parallel, increasing exposure to the eye and thyroid gland
- Short focal-film distance (8 inches) with parallel method increases tissue exposed to radiation

MAXIMUM PERMISSIBLE DOSE

MPD is the abbreviation for maximum permissible dose of radiation a person is permitted to receive from artificial causes of radiation. The MPD is generally a recommendation of the NCRP, which acquires legal status through local or federal legislation. The MPD is generally higher for groups that are occupationally exposed like dentists and their assistants than for staff members or the general public, who are said to be non-occupationally exposed. A radiation worker who is pregnant is allowed to receive approximately the same lower level of dosage permitted for those non-occupationally exposed. These limits are not imposed for dental or medical procedures that may utilize radiation for patient benefit.

CURRENT RECOMMENDATIONS

At present, the annual effective MPD dose for radiation workers is a whole-body dose of 50 mSv, with higher amounts to certain body parts up to 750 mSv on the hands. Workers falling into this category are permitted to receive a cumulative lifetime exposure of 10 times their age in years (for example, 500 mSv for an individual 50 years of age). The public or anyone non-occupationally exposed should receive only 1-5 mSv, depending on whether their exposure is continuous (as in several dental x-rays) or infrequent. Doses to specific areas like the lens of the eye can approach 150 mSv. Anyone training in the dental profession who is younger than 18 years old is subject to these limits as well. A pregnant woman should never receive more than 0.5 mSv a month up to a maximum of 5 mSv during the time she carries the child. In practice, the recommendation is to permit "as low as reasonably achievable" (ALARA) radiation, which is ideally lower than imposed MPD.

SAFE DISPOSAL OF RADIOGRAPHIC WASTE

When an x-ray is taken and developed, several types of waste are created. The first is **solid waste** including the radiograph itself. Though the discarding of radiographs is not regulated by the government, silver can be extracted from them by heating them above the melting point of silver. The lead foil inserts from the film package should be returned to the manufacturer for proper disposal. Another type of waste is the discarded **fixer solution**, which contains silver as well, and whose disposal may be regulated locally. The silver in these solutions can be precipitated out by chemical means or electrolysis. In addition, any waste that may have **been contaminated by blood or saliva** is considered medical waste and should be sent in marked containers to proper disposal facilities.

SOURCES OF BACKGROUND RADIATION

The environment exposes individuals to background radiation. In the United States, this background level is about 3 mSv with the major type of exposure being from radon gas. In some other countries, the background radiation levels have been documented to be up to 13 times higher than in the United States without demonstrable changes in the population rate of malignancies or birth defects. Areas of high altitude have a slightly higher background level of radiation. Typically, the effective dose of ionizing radiation that an individual in the U. S. receives from dental x-rays is only about 0.1 percent of their total radiation received. Medical diagnostic procedures on average account for much greater doses experienced than dental x-rays. Nevertheless, background radiation undoubtedly supplies the greatest dosage, more than 80% of the total in the US. Total dosage in the U. S. is projected to be about 4.4 mSv per person.

LOWERING RADIATION DOSAGE EXPOSURE DURING DENTAL RADIOGRAPHY
MANAGING X-RAY MACHINE PARAMETERS

Lowering radiation exposure through x-ray machine adjustment can be achieved by using the higher potential difference in the tube (though no greater than 90 kVp) and/or filtering out the longer wavelength x-rays. The filtration is commonly accomplished by insertion of an aluminum filter. Legislation also dictates that the cross-sectional area of the beam can be no greater than 7 centimeters in diameter if round. Therefore, x-ray machines usually have diaphragms or collimators that restrict the beam area. Rectangular is superior to round collimation because it lessens the exposed area, reduces scatter-induced fogging, and thus produces a better image as well. Selection of a longer 16-inch beam indicating device that is lined with lead restricts radiation dosage most effectively. Use of machines with integrated electronic timers provides more precision. In

185

addition, some newer machines have generators that can convert AC to DC and thus produce a constant wavelength beam.

GOOD DARKROOM AND VIEWING TECHNIQUES

Utilization of a variety of practices to ensure the proper development of radiographs eliminates the need for repeat x-rays and exposure to the patient. The potential for film fog should be reduced by careful measures to eliminate light leaks into the darkroom. Low 15-watt bulbs with appropriate safelight filters placed at least 4 feet from the development area should be used. Manual development should not be assessed visually; it should always continue for at least 5 minutes at 70 °F. Quality control measures regarding the processing solutions should be in place. These measures should include periodic stirring and changing of the solution, especially if contamination has occurred. The chemical tray should be covered to avoid oxidation during periods of non-use and regularly cleaned. Elevated temperatures should be avoided as well. The radiographs should be viewed in a lowly lit room through an opaque view box.

REDUCING DOSAGE TO THE PATIENT OUTSIDE OF THE X-RAY MACHINE

Potential whole-body and thyroid irradiation can be drastically reduced through the use of leaded torso aprons and thyroid shields. Film selection is important because faster films allow for lower exposure times and less potential radiation dosage; the fastest is speed F. Gadgets that hold the film in place should be used for many reasons including elimination of finger exposure and more precise placement of the film relative to the teeth and the positioning device. For panoramic or extra oral films, special films that incorporate rare earth intensifying screens are available that augment film speed further.

OPERATOR X-RADIATION EXPOSURE

SOURCES OF X-RADIATION TO OPERATORS AND OTHER STAFF

Sources of x-radiation to operators/other staff while exposing image receptors include:

- **Secondary radiation** from standing too close to source of radiation or not being properly shielded. Operator should be at least 6 feet from source or behind shielding.
- Exposure to **primary radiation** if standing in the direct path of the beam or outside of the safe zone (90–135° to the primary beam).
- Size of x-ray field exceeds that of the image receptor, allowing increased scatter radiation.
- Malfunctioning or improperly maintained equipment.
- **Holding the receptor in place in the patient's mouth** or the PID, especially without a film holding device.

MONITORING OPERATOR X-RADIATION EXPOSURE

Techniques for monitoring individual x-radiation exposure include:

- Keeping accurate record of radiographic imaging, including frequency and number of images. Patient dosage information should be included in their dental health record when available.
- Avoiding unnecessary or too frequent imaging.
- Wearing a radiation dosimeter (operators): Dosimeter badges contain film, powder, or a lithium fluoride crystal that is sensitive to radiation. The body badges should be placed on the body (attached to clothing) between the neck and waist. Ring badges are also available and used on the hand most likely to come in closest contact to radiation and under gloves. These badges are for occupational use only and should not be worn when receiving x-rays.
- Utilizing an area radiation dosimeter if there are concerns about x-radiation exposure.

REDUCING OCCUPATIONAL RADIATION EXPOSURE

The dental technician or other personnel operating a dental x-ray machine must stand in a position that shields them from the useful x-ray beam as well as potential radiation leakage from the tubehead or scatter from interaction with the patient. In general, this means that dental professionals need to position themselves at least 6 feet away from the patient and at an angle of 90–135° relative to the x-ray beam. If this is impossible, then the operator must wear a leaded protective barrier or stand behind a wall that is dense and deep enough (such as drywall) to absorb the radiation. Other office personnel should be located outside the wall. Radiation exposure to occupationally as well as non-occupationally exposed employees is usually monitored with a film badge. Individuals wear this film badge, which consists of a lithium fluoride crystal, and periodically a film badge dosimetry monitoring service uses the badge to quantify the person's radiation exposure. The badge should be worn in the neck, chest, or hip area.

DETERMINING PROTECTIVE BARRIERS FOR RADIATION PROTECTION

A guide number for protective barriers or walls can be calculated as the product of the workload (W) times the use factor (U) times the occupancy factor (T). Workload is expressed in milliampere minutes per week the machine is used, the use factor is determined by the type of surface (wall versus floor or ceiling) and its orientation to the main x-ray beam, and the occupancy factor reflects the percentage of time the individual remains behind the barrier. Thus, the U for walls is $\frac{1}{4}$, much greater than the U for walls or ceilings which is $\frac{1}{16}$. Similarly, the occupancy for regular office personnel right behind the barrier is 1 while the T for individuals in other areas is much less. Concrete, cinder block, and thick drywall are generally acceptable construction materials.

Protocols for Informed Consent and X-Ray Machine Malfunction

INFORMED CONSENT

Dental and medical professionals must obtain informed consent from the patient or their representative (such as the parent or guardian) before initiating procedures. Informed consent involves a complete explanation or full disclosure of the process including its rationale, its benefits, and the possible negative consequences. In the dental office, informed consent should be obtained before performing radiography. If informed consent is denied, the radiograph cannot be taken and an essential part of the diagnostic process is lost.

RESPONDEAT SUPERIOR

The concept of *respondeat superior* is a legal doctrine placing professional and legal liability with the supervising professional. In other words, in a dental practice, the dentist accepts responsibility for the actions of other professionals like dental hygienists or assistants. A hygienist or an assistant under the employ of the dentist is not ultimately responsible, but they could be expected to accept some of the financial burden if found negligent. Therefore, liability insurance is still necessary. An independent contractor can be found responsible and can be sued. In addition, negative input in the office setting can be used as legal evidence of negligence.

DENTAL RECORDS AND OWNERSHIP/RETENTION PARAMETERS

Dental records including radiographs are legal documents. Therefore, dates, number and types of radiographic procedures must be immediately entered. The radiographs themselves must also be tagged, dated, and securely fastened to the chart. All parts of the record are confidential and are considered to be owned by the dentist. The latter means that the dentist is not allowed to give the radiographs to the patient or insurance company, although rules pertaining to distribution of duplicates vary by locality. The minimum period for record retention is 6 or 7 years (depending on local legislation) after the individual stops their association with the dental office.

PROTOCOLS FOR SUSPECTED X-RAY MACHINE MALFUNCTION

Various protocols exist for suspected digital and standard x-ray equipment malfunction:

- **Digital x-ray equipment**: Begin by checking the guides for both hardware and software for troubleshooting advice. Items that can be easily assessed before calling for technical support include:
  - USB ports: Try connecting other devices to see if the port is functioning.
  - USB cables: Try switching cables.
  - Interface box: Switch interfaces boxes with one from another room if available to determine if the first is malfunctioning.
- **Standard x-ray equipment**: Begin by checking the manufacturer's guide for troubleshooting advice. Protective covers on equipment should only be removed by certified technicians, so troubleshooting involves checking various aspects of the system, depending on the problem:
  - Poor image quality: Verify kVp and tube current. Adjust exposure time, kVp, or tube current.
  - X-ray does not function: Check that power cord is connected and power switch in ON position.
  - Pre-termination error (underexposed image): Results from premature release of exposure switch.

If the problem cannot be easily identified and remedied, the machine must be removed from service until it can be repaired.

Chapter Quiz

Ready to see how well you retained what you just read? Scan the QR code to go directly to the chapter quiz interface for this study guide. If you're using a computer, simply visit the bonus page at **mometrix.com/bonus948/danbcda** and click the Chapter Quizzes link.

Infection Prevention and Control (RHS)

Transform passive reading into active learning! After immersing yourself in this chapter, put your comprehension to the test by taking a quiz. The insights you gained will stay with you longer this way. Scan the QR code to go directly to the chapter quiz interface for this study guide. If you're using a computer, simply visit the bonus page at **mometrix.com/bonus948/danbcda** and click the Chapter Quizzes link.

Standard Precautions for Equipment and Supplies

DEFINING SURFACES BASED ON LEVEL OF REQUIRED DECONTAMINATION

A classification system originally developed by E. H. Spaulding breaks down the level of decontamination required for infected objects. In dental radiology, theoretically none of the apparatus or equipment used falls into the highest **critical category**. This classification includes contact with blood products or breaching of tissue, and equipment must either be sterilized or disposed of. Most equipment used in oral and maxillofacial radiology falls into the **semicritical category** because it is in contact with mucous membranes but does not penetrate the tissues. While sterilization procedures are preferred for semicritical items, high-level disinfection measures or barriers can be used. Equipment employed in panoramic or extraoral radiography often falls into the **noncritical category** because while it may come into contact with intact skin, it generally does not touch mucous membranes or saliva, nor does it breach the surrounding tissue. Noncritical items as well as environmental surfaces that the patient does not touch should be sanitized, disinfected with mid-range level products, or protected by barriers.

SOURCES OF CONTAMINATION OF DENTAL PROCESSING SOLUTIONS

The radiographic developer and fixer solution can sustain microbial growth if present for up to 2 weeks. Therefore, intraoral film should be handled aseptically prior to processing to avoid bacterial load. Panoramic films can become contaminated by contact with the bite block. If the bite block is wrapped with a plastic barrier, then the wrapping should be properly discarded after use. The bite block should be placed in a container and decontaminated after each use. Apparatus involved with panoramic and extraoral filming should be periodically disinfected as well.

Standard Precautions for Patients and Operators

UNIVERSAL PRECAUTIONS

Universal precautions are a set of safety measures employed in any setting where personnel or patients might be exposed to pathogens that can be transmitted via the blood or saliva. Viruses such as various types of hepatitis (particularly types B and C) and human immunodeficiency virus (HIV) as well as many infectious bacteria are conveyed by blood or saliva. Dental professionals rarely deal with the patient's blood, but they do regularly come into contact with saliva. OSHA has developed the Bloodborne Pathogen (BBP) Rule, and this federal agency can fine medical or dental facilities that do not adhere to the rules. Most states have a State Board of Dental Examiners (BDE) that also enforces guidelines set up by OSHA and other agencies like the American Dental Association (ADA) and the Centers for Disease Control (CDC). The dental healthcare worker must abide by these rules, but responsibility rests with the employer.

PERSONAL PROTECTIVE EQUIPMENT

Personal protective equipment includes impermeable gowns, masks, disposable gloves, and protective eyewear. All of these are usually worn by healthcare workers in many medical settings and in dentistry if the patient is possibly infectious. Examples of the latter include presence of any respiratory infection like a cold or evidence of coughing and possible discharge of fluid aerosols. Since the outbreak of the COVID-19 pandemic, dental radiology personnel are recommended to wear a surgical mask in addition to gloves during all patient contact.

ANTIBIOTIC USE IN SPECIFIC PATIENTS AND DENTAL PERSONNEL IMMUNIZATION

In dentistry, there is a small risk of exposure to blood products. Any invasive treatment could theoretically cause bleeding in the patient. While dental radiography is usually not invasive, the patient typically undergoes other oral probing by the dentist at the same visit. Therefore, a patient may be pre-medicated with **antibiotics** prior to an oral procedure, particularly if they have a history of certain cardiac diseases or artificial joint replacement.

Dental personnel should be **immunized** against tetanus, influenza, varicella, and hepatitis B virus (HBV) because of their potential exposure to infectious blood products.

INFECTION CONTROL PROCEDURES

PANORAMIC RADIOGRAPHY

Panoramic radiography is not invasive. The technician can perform the technique with clean, ungloved hands and theoretically does not need any personal protective equipment during the procedure. The patient should wear a leaded apron, however. The bite guide should either be disposable or can be covered with a plastic bag. Patient cooperation is required because they should use an antibacterial mouthwash and perform the actual placement and removal of the bite block or its covering. After the radiography is performed, equipment that was touched by the patient such as rests or guides should be cleaned.

INTRAORAL RADIOGRAPHY

There are three acceptable methods of handling film from intraoral radiography to reduce the possibility of infection.

- The least desirable procedure is the **overglove method**, in which a plastic overglove is aseptically put over the contaminated powder-free latex glove only during transport to the darkroom, films are placed into the processor with clean, bare hands, and another pair of gloves is donned before darkroom cleaning is performed.

- A better procedure is the **three-glove method**. Here contaminated films are placed in a cup, the initial contaminated gloves are removed in the x-ray apparatus room, films are taken to the darkroom or loader ungloved after washing, another pair of gloves is put on to unwrap the films there, and equipment cleaning procedures are performed using a third set of gloves.
- There are also films available that come in **plastic barrier pouches** that shield the actual film from contact with saliva, or these types of envelopes can be purchased. After the radiograph is taken, the pouches are opened into a cup or onto a paper towel, and then they are taken to the darkroom with washed, bare hands.

HAND SANITIZATION FOR THREE-GLOVE OR BARRIER ENVELOPE METHODS OF EXPOSURE

The x-ray operator needs to disinfect their hands at several stages during the three-glove or barrier envelope methods of exposure. In practice, the operator disinfects their hands by soap washing; simple hand soaps can be used but soaps containing 4% chlorhexidine gluconate or 3% parachlorometaxylenol are recommended. Before the procedure, it is preferable to have the patient take off dental hardware and eyewear and rinse their oral cavity with an antimicrobial rinse including chlorhexidine gluconate, some type of phenol, or the herb sanguinarine. The technician dons the initial pair of gloves and then briefly examines the patient's oral cavity, sets the machine parameters, opens the sterile film holder and attaches the film, and sets up the positioning device. Parts of the machine that are touched should be covered with plastic. The exposure should be activated with a foot switch or a plastic-covered button. Films are dropped into separate paper cups (after barrier removal if present), the initial glove is removed, and the technician washes their hands and transports the cup to the darkroom or loader.

DIGITAL IMAGING

None of the detectors used with digital processes can be sterilized using heat, and cold chemical methods of sterilization are impractical as well. Infection control procedures for digital imaging with charge coupled devices or CMOS sensors are similar. For both, two layers of plastic barriers are used, a sleeve and an additional finger wrapper. For phosphor (PSP) apparatuses, the primary infection control procedure is the placement of the plate in some type of commercially-available barrier envelope before exposure. The plate is kept bagged until before it is placed in the scanner.

DARKROOM

Using the preferred three-glove method in the darkroom, exposed films are dropped from the paper cups used for transportation onto a paper towel. The technician then puts a new pair of powder-free gloves over clean hands and removes the film. The film itself is never touched, and it is dropped onto a second paper towel. The technician discards the gloves, rewashes their hands, and processes the film with bare hands being careful to touch only the edges. Handwashing after the processing is also recommended. If a daylight loader is used instead of a manual or automatic processor, the main difference is that the operator works through sleeves that go into the daylight loader and films are usually dropped into cups before loading. Disinfecting and infection control procedures and film removal techniques are similar except those wrappings are initially discarded in the chamber instead of the waste bin as is done in the darkroom. A third pair of gloves must be donned during cleanup.

AFTER TAKING AND DEVELOPING X-RAYS

For dental radiation procedures, all of the contaminated disposables like gloves, paper towels, and film packets are not defined as infectious materials and can therefore be thrown out in the regular waste. Most other exposed equipment does need to be cleaned or in some cases sterilized. In particular, contaminated film holders must initially be put into temporary solutions and later be subjected to other procedures that decontaminate and sterilize them. For sterilization, the holders can be put in bags with other contaminated dental equipment and then the bags are autoclaved (steam sterilized) or put in a dry-heat oven. Plastic wrap covering switches or other parts of the x-ray machine can be replaced or sprayed or swabbed with a disinfectant, and lead aprons and collars should be disinfected as well. A third pair of gloves should be worn

during these procedures. Gowns or protective eyewear, if worn, should be regularly laundered or disinfected respectively.

Chapter Quiz

Ready to see how well you retained what you just read? Scan the QR code to go directly to the chapter quiz interface for this study guide. If you're using a computer, simply visit the bonus page at **mometrix.com/bonus948/danbcda** and click the Chapter Quizzes link.

Standard Precautions and Prevention of Disease Transmission (ICE)

Transform passive reading into active learning! After immersing yourself in this chapter, put your comprehension to the test by taking a quiz. The insights you gained will stay with you longer this way. Scan the QR code to go directly to the chapter quiz interface for this study guide. If you're using a computer, simply visit the bonus page at **mometrix.com/bonus948/danbcda** and click the Chapter Quizzes link.

Diseases and Modes of Transmission

REASONING BEHIND PRACTICING INFECTION CONTROL

Infection control should be practiced **in the dental setting** to deter transmission and disease development at any point and in any direction. Infectious agents can be spread from the patient to members of the dental team and vice versa, between patients, from the dental office into the community, and from the outside community to the patients. The main pathway of cross-contamination from patient to members of the dental team is from the patient's mouth, either through direct contact via skin breaks, droplet infection (through inhalation, skin breaks, or mucosal contact), or indirect contact via cuts or punctures. Similarly, the main patient-to-patient or office-to-community means of transmission are via the mouth through indirect contact. The dental team can transmit infections to the patient's mouth directly through hand lesions or bleeding or indirectly on instruments. They can also contaminate the patient by droplet infection through inhalation or contact with oral mucosa. The main way dental workers transmit infections to their family is through intimate contact with bodily fluids, and the primary community to patient mode is direct contact with contaminated municipal water.

MAIN GOAL OF INFECTION CONTROL

Whether or not exposure to an infectious agent results in contracting the disease or not is dependent on three interrelated factors in a relationship defined as follows:

$$\text{Presence of disease} = \frac{(\text{virulence of the infectious agent}) \times (\text{its dose})}{\text{resistance of the host}}$$

In other words, if the infectious agent is of low virulence and low exposure dose, and the individual has good defense mechanisms and high resistance, health is favored over disease. Conversely, a highly virulent microorganism administered at high dose to a person with low resistance will most likely result in disease. **Virulence** is an inherent property of each species of microorganism and host resistance is hard to control, so the factor that can be regulated is exposure dose. Infection control is focused on the dosage part of the equation. The **main goal of infection control** is to decrease the dose of microorganisms that may be transmitted between people or between individuals and surfaces, thus reducing the likelihood of contracting a disease.

INFECTION CONTROL DURING OFFICE REMODELING OR CONSTRUCTION

One of the biggest concerns during office remodeling or construction is the potential environmental dissemination of microorganisms resulting in nosocomial infections. **Nosocomial infections** are those acquired while in a hospital or another medical facility, such as a dental office. Construction activity creates additional moisture and water in the area, which creates a favorable environment for certain microorganisms. Some of the most common construction-related infectious outbreaks involve fungi like *Aspergillus* or bacteria

such as *Pseudomonas* or Group A *Streptococcus.* It is crucial to keep construction activity as isolated from patient care areas as possible, and provisional barriers may need to be constructed between the two. Contractors are responsible for cleaning their working zones, but non-construction areas will need to be cleaned more often and more comprehensively. Extra precautions for both employees and patients are generally needed, and certain types of patients may need to be rescheduled until after completion of the construction work (for example those with respiratory problems).

INFECTIOUS DISEASE

DEVELOPMENT

There are basically 6 steps in the development of an infectious disease. The first two involve the source of the microorganism and the subsequent escape of it from the source. Escape routes include coughing, talking, and removal of anything that has been in the mouth (instruments, x-ray film, etc.). An infectious disease can also escape in droplets or aerosols generated through equipment use. The next step is the transmission of the agent to a new individual through direct contact such as at the mouth, indirect contact with anything that has been contaminated (for example surfaces, hands or sharps), contact with large droplets that are sprayed or splattered, or inhalation of smaller airborne droplets or aerosol particles. Further development of the infectious disease includes entry of the agent into the new person (through inhalation, ingestion, contact with mucous membranes, or through breaks in the skin), the infection phase in which the microorganism endures and multiplies in or on the body, and lastly, causation of some type of harmful bodily damage.

STAGES

Infectious diseases have four stages:

1. The first is the **incubation stage**, which is the time from when the infectious agent entered the body until symptoms of disease are evident. The length of this stage is extremely variable depending on the disease, ranging, for example, from several days for influenza to a decade or more for HIV.
2. After the incubation period is a **prodromal stage**, which is when initial symptoms such as malaise or headache present.
3. As symptoms progress and the person becomes visibly sick, he or she enters the **acute stage**. This is the period with the most potential for transmission of the agent, and when dental visits should be avoided if possible.
4. The last stage is generally the **convalescent or recovery stage** in which the microbe levels are decreased and detrimental microbial products are being deactivated by the body. Transmission is still possible, however, as the infectious agent has not been entirely eradicated.

Again, the length of convalescence is quite variable depending on the agent, and some diseases are chronic. During any stage, some people appear asymptomatic but are still carriers.

INFECTION CONTROL PROCEDURES FOR MODES OF TRANSMISSION

Briefly, the means of controlling the possibility of disease transmission are as follows:

- **Patient to dental team**: Overall measures used by the dental team consist of hand washing, gloves, other personal protective equipment, rubber dams (for droplet infection protection), and immunization. In addition, indirect contact can be prevented with recommended needle safety and cleanup procedures.
- **Dental team to patient**: Transmission can be avoided by the use of hand washing, gloves, immunization, instrument sterilization, surface disinfection, and masks and face shields (for droplet infection protection) by the dental team.
- **Patient to patient**: As this type of transmission is mainly through indirect contact, infection control procedures include things like sterilization of instruments, disinfection of surfaces, flushing of dental unit water lines, changing of personal protective equipment when needed, and use of disposables.

- **Office to community**: Preventing spread of disease from the office to the community requires measures such as proper handling of waste and contaminated laundry.
- **Dental team to family:** The dental team can protect family members by immunization.
- **Community to patient**: Preventing the spread of disease from community to patient requires good water control procedures.

BLOODBORNE DISEASES

Bloodborne diseases are any diseases that can be transmitted via the blood or other bodily fluids, such as semen, mother's milk, or saliva. Saliva is deemed potentially infectious because bleeding can release bloodborne pathogens into the fluid. The bloodborne diseases of particular interest to the dental worker are **viral hepatitis** (particularly the form transmitted by hepatitis B virus (HBV), which is extremely virulent) and **human immunodeficiency virus (HIV),** which can develop into acquired immunodeficiency syndrome (AIDS). AIDS is currently manageable but not eradicable. Other bacterial and viral diseases can also be spread via the blood or bodily fluids.

BIOCHEMICAL COMPONENTS OF MICROBES

Categories of microbes include bacteria, viruses, fungi and protozoa. Each has a different structure, but these microbes share many of the same biochemical macromolecules. All microorganisms carry their genetic information through their DNA (deoxyribonucleic acid) and/or RNA (ribonucleic acid) as do humans and other organisms. They contain protein composed of amino acids utilized as structural components (cell walls, cytoplasm membranes, flagella in bacteria; capsids and envelope proteins in viruses) or enzymes acting as biochemical catalysts. Microorganisms also contain polysaccharides and lipids. Polysaccharides are made up of monosaccharides or sugars such as glucose and fructose and are found in structures such as capsules or storage granules. They can be complexed to proteins as glycoproteins, which are found in things such as surface projections on bacteria called fimbriae or as components of viral envelopes. Lipids are made up of fatty acids and glycerol and are found in structures like bacterial cytoplasm membranes and viral envelopes. They are associated with proteins as lipoproteins in cell walls and with polysaccharides as lipopolysaccharides, such as endotoxins, in some bacteria.

BACTERIA

TYPES

Bacteria are designated by their genus and species within that genus. They are tiny (micrometer range), single cell organisms. Each type of bacterium has a characteristic size and shape visible microscopically (known as cell morphology), a typical staining pattern, distinctive colony growth on agar media, certain metabolic properties, distinguishing antibodies on their surface that elicit immunological responses, and species-specific genetic potential expressed on their DNA and RNA. All bacteria are either spherical, rod-shaped, or spiral, termed cocci, bacilli, or spirilla respectively; cocci and bacilli may exist in clusters or chains. The most common staining method used is called a Gram stain, which differentiates all bacteria as either gram-positive (blue or purple) or gram-negative (red).

BASIC STRUCTURE AND FUNCTIONS OF COMPONENTS

Bacteria have a nucleus or nucleoid structure composed of **DNA**, which controls cellular activities; there may also be small plasmids containing DNA. Bacteria have a larger **cytoplasm** surrounding the nucleoid enclosed within a cytoplasmic membrane. The cytoplasm is relatively viscous and also contains essential macromolecules, water, oxygen, waste products, and storage granules. The surrounding cytoplasm membrane is made up of **lipids** and **proteins** and serves to regulate the transport of nutrients, metabolic functions, waste expulsion, cell wall synthesis, and DNA synthesis during cell division. Some, primarily gram-positive, bacteria have infoldings from the cytoplasm membrane into the cytoplasm containing **hydrolytic enzymes**. External to the cytoplasmic membrane is a rigid **cell wall** composed of peptidoglycan, polymers, peptides, and polysaccharides, which function to retain cell shape and protect the cell from mechanical injury.

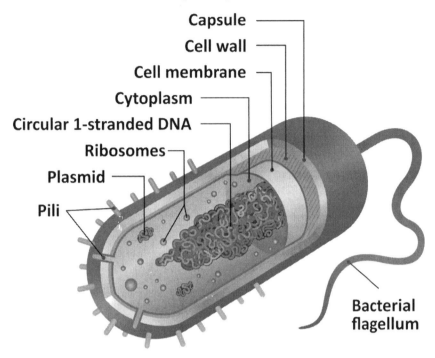

Unique Structures

In gram-negative bacteria, there is an outer membrane containing **endotoxin** surrounding the cell wall. Endotoxin, which is a lip polysaccharide-protein complex, can be discharged after cell death and cause various untoward reactions in the host. Some bacteria have **capsules** outside the cell wall (gram-positive) or outer membrane (gram-negative). Capsules, which contain polysaccharides (possibly in conjunction with proteins) and water, are generated by the cytoplasmic membrane and aid in functions such as surface attachment, defense against phagocytosis by the host, and protection against drying. Certain bacteria have **proteinaceous threads** projecting outward called flagella, which aid in locomotion. Many bacteria have **fimbriae** (also known as pili), which are short projections that make it easier for the bacterium to attach to surfaces and transport DNA between cells. Bacteria with pili tend to be more virulent because they can attach more easily to their host. Another means of increased virulence found in some bacteria is endospore or spore production. **Spores** are found within the cell. They have thick walls and can remain dormant and then be released, and they are quite resistant to infection control procedures.

Oxygen Requirements

Different types of bacteria have varying oxygen requirements. They fall into 4 categories. In 3 of these categories, the bacteria possess enzymes called **superoxide dismutase (SOD)** and **catalase**. SOD breaks down toxic superoxides into molecular oxygen and hydrogen peroxide and catalase converts the hydrogen peroxide into water and molecular oxygen. Thus, all three of these groups can thrive to a certain extent in the presence of oxygen. They are **obligate aerobes**, which can only grow in the presence of about 20% oxygen, **microaerophiles**, which can endure only lower concentrations of oxygen of about 4%, and **facultative anaerobes**, which can tolerate oxygen but do not require it. The last category, **obligate anaerobes**, do not have SOD or catalase and cannot proliferate in the presence of oxygen.

Basic Growth Pattern

Bacterial cells **divide** by binary fission producing two daughter cells. Under the right conditions this fission process occurs very rapidly (minutes) through successive generations. Bacterial growth is influenced by the temperature of the environment, its acidity, the available nutrients, whether or not its oxygen requirements are met, and the presence of water. Each bacterium has an optimal temperature range. Some are thermophiles, which thrive at 56 °C (range 45–70 °C). Most bacteria that endure in the human body fall into the second category of mesophiles, which survive at 22-45 °C (optimally 37 °C), and there are some bacteria that are psychrophiles, which thrive best at 1-22 °C (best 7 °C). Bacteria usually grow best in the human body at neutral pH 7 or in the slightly acidic to slightly alkaline range of pH 5.5 to 8.5. However, some can endure lower pHs and are known as aciduric while others generate acids during growth (acidogenic), contributing to dental decay. Bacteria have varying needs in terms of nutrients and metabolism as the presence or absence of oxygen (both discussed further on other cards).

REGULATING BACTERIAL GROWTH

Bacterial growth can be prevented, and bacteria can be killed. Agents or states that can thwart bacterial growth but not actually kill bacteria are referred to as bacteriostatic. **Bacteriostatic** measures include freezing to shatter the cell membrane, refrigeration (unless the bacteria thrive at that temperature), regulating oxygen levels (depending on the type of suspected bacteria), or use of extreme pH. Situations that kill bacteria are termed **bactericidal**. The most effective bactericidal measure is exposure to extremely high temperatures through steam, dry heat, or chemical vapor sterilizers, which can break down bacterial proteins, nucleic acids, and structures. There are chemicals that can kill bacteria on inert objects (such as surfaces) and are therefore bactericidal. Similar destruction of viruses or fungi is termed **virucidal** or **fungicidal** respectively. In the body, bacteria can be inhibited or in some cases killed by use of antibiotics.

REQUIRED NUTRIENTS AND METABOLIC ACTIVITIES OF BACTERIAL CELLS

Metabolism in living organisms is the totality of chemical reactions within them. **Nutrients** must be brought into the organism and converted into the macromolecules required for sustenance. Metabolism consists of both catabolism, the breakdown of nutrients into utilizable forms, and anabolism, the synthesis of new molecules. In bacteria, nutrients enter the cell through the cytoplasmic membrane and are catabolized to generate the building blocks and energy needed for anabolism. Catabolism can occur through fermentation or respiration. Fermentation is the anaerobic splitting of sugars, ultimately producing lactic acid that contributes to caries formation. Respiration occurs aerobically. Here sugars are broken down into pyruvic acid, which undergoes a course called the electron transport chain and generates ATP. ATP, adenosine triphosphate, is an energy source for synthesis during anabolism. Both respiration and fermentation generate waste products. Metabolic processes require enzymes or protein catalysts and sometimes metallic cofactors or organic coenzymes. Anabolic processes generate needed proteins, nucleic acids, lipids, polysaccharides, and vitamins within the bacterial cell.

WAYS BACTERIA ARE CULTURED IN LABORATORIES

In the laboratory, bacteria are **cultured** either in a liquid broth or on a semi-solid agar medium made up of a polysaccharide derived from seaweed. Both are sterilized by boiling and are then cooled before use, and particular nutrients are added. Using sterile technique, potential bacterial cultures are inoculated into broth cultures to observe for turbidity or opaqueness indicating growth. Likewise, they are streaked onto plates containing the agar medium, which separates them into cells or groups thereof called colony-forming units (CFUs). Subsequent plates can be streaked further with individual CFUs to obtain pure clones or colonies. Specific bacteria have characteristic growth media (containing set nutrients or incubated under certain conditions) in which they thrive and proliferate, thus, aiding in identification.

PROPERTIES OF PATHOGENIC MICROORGANISMS

Depending on the specific microorganism, a microorganism may have properties that **enhance infection, interfere with host defenses, or directly damage cells or tissues**. Infection enhancement properties include means of attachment to host cells (for example fimbriae or surface polymers on certain bacteria and through the capsid or envelope on viruses) and ability to multiply at a body site by utilizing nutrients. One additional dental application is the resistance of *Lactobacillus acidophilus* to acids. There are many ways in which microorganisms interfere with host defenses. These include things such as destruction of phagocytes, inhibition of their attraction by certain extracellular products, ways to evade engulfment or digestion by

phagocytes, or mechanisms that suppress or circumvent the immune system. The latter is particularly true for viruses such as HIV, herpes simplex, and influenza. The last category of properties includes microorganisms that damage cells or tissues. There are numerous microorganisms in this category. Certain bacteria produce histolytic enzymes, serotoxins, cytotoxic waste products, and endotoxins or persist in chronic forms that eventually damage the immune system. The latter is also true for certain viruses.

NORMAL ORAL MICROBIOTA

Newborns acquire microorganisms during passage through the mother's birth canal, but most of these do not remain as **normal oral microbiota**. During childhood, kids are exposed to environmental organisms that become part of their oral microbiota if they affix to oral surfaces and multiply. When new teeth erupt, microorganisms can also enter the oral cavity through bleeding. By the early teens, the normal oral flora is generally established as a mixture of as many as 40 types of bacteria genera and often the yeast *Candida albicans.* Saliva and plaque contain millions of bacteria.

MICROBIOLOGY OF DENTAL CARIES

Dental caries or decay starts when acidogenic or acid-producing bacteria on the teeth are present in an environment of a susceptible host and sugars in the diet. The dietary sugars are metabolized producing acids, which accumulate at the tooth surface to create a low pH acidic environment leading to demineralization or loss of tooth structure. After demineralization (indicated by white spots on the teeth) dental caries or tooth decay will result. Decay development only occurs if there is a susceptible host, presence of caries-causing bacteria in the form of dental plaque or impactions, the correct substrate (sucrose or other sugars), and time for development. Plaque is actually a biofilm of bacteria entrenched in an intercellular matrix of other molecules, particularly glycoproteins from saliva, that coat the tooth surface with a thin layer called the pellicle.

PLAQUE-ASSOCIATED PERIODONTAL DISEASES

Periodontal diseases at the neck or root of a tooth develop because plaque-associated bacteria and their harmful products accrue in these areas causing tissue damage, inflammation, and immune interactions. When plaque is allowed to accumulate, the bacteria in it produce potentially harmful products, such as endotoxins and serotoxins, noxious metabolites, histolytic enzymes, and substances with immune effects, such as antigens, immunosuppressants, and antiphagocytic factors. These cause damage to the periodontal tissues and elicit immune responses. The result can be simple gingivitis, which is inflammation and possibly bleeding that can be reversed with plaque removal. It can also be necrotizing ulcerative gingivitis or trench mouth, which is also reversible. If, however, there are inaccessible bacteria-filled periodontal pockets, periodontitis is the diagnosis. If untreated, this can lead to progression of the periodontitis into higher stages (severe periodontitis, Stage III or IV) in which bone is slowly and progressively destroyed. In people with weak body defenses, other forms of periodontitis may arise. Many gram-negative bacteria are found in subgingival plaque as opposed to the most prevalent caries-causing bacteria, which are gram-positive.

BACTERIA MOST LIKELY TO CAUSE CARIES

The bacteria present that are most likely to cause caries are **mutans streptococci** (*Streptococcus mutans or Streptococcus sobrinus),* which are acidogenic, aciduric, and tend to build up on the teeth. Mutans streptococci have enzymes called glucosyltransferases that break down sucrose into polysaccharide glucans and bind to cells encouraging further plaque formation and fructose which is ultimately processed into lactic acid. ***Lactobacillus* species** are also conducive to caries formation as they are acidogenic and acid uric, but they do not have good ways to attach to tooth surfaces by themselves. ***Actinomyces naeslundii*** if present are conducive to plaque formation and development of root caries in particular.

ACUTE DENTAL AND OTHER TYPES OF ORAL INFECTIONS

Pulpitis, which is inflammation of the pulp of the tooth, is caused when caries spreads into the pulp region. Pulpitis can spread further to the apex or periapical region and in some cases to the adjacent facial tissues as cellulitis or inflammation of subcutaneous tissues. Pulpitis is generally treated endodontically by a root canal

procedure, which is the removal of dead pulp tissue, killing and pulling out bacteria in the root canal and adding inert materials to the canals. Antibiotics may also be given.

Transient bacteremia, in which normal oral microbiota get into the bloodstream because of oral bleeding, can be a problem. Individuals with heart valve damage, for example, can experience further injury or subacute bacterial endocarditis (inflammation of the heart). Rarely, *Actinomyces* species can cause jaw, neck, or lung infections.

BACTERIAL DISEASES TRANSMITTED BY RESPIRATORY AND ORAL FLUIDS

Various species of streptococcus cause **respiratory** diseases. Pharyngitis and scarlet fever are spread via droplets containing *Streptococcus pyogenes* (discussed further on another card). Pneumonia, inflammation of the lung, can be caused by a number of bacteria or viruses, including *Streptococcus pneumoniae. S. pneumoniae* is transmitted via respiratory/oral droplets and is prevalent asymptomatically in a large number of children and adults. The bacterium can also cause middle ear infections, meningitis, and sinusitis. Pneumonia can also be caused by other agents, such as *Staphylococcus aureus* and *Haemophilus influenzae.* The latter can produce meningitis, sinusitis, conjunctivitis, and bronchitis. Other bacterial respiratory diseases of interest are diphtheria with *Corynebacterium diphtheriae* as the causative agent and meningitis caused by *Neisseria meningitides. C. diphtheriae* is generally not a problem as it, along with agents for pertussis (whopping cough) and tetanus (lockjaw, causative agent *Clostridium tetani*), is included in the DPT vaccine given to children.

SYSTEMIC DISEASES THAT HAVE ORAL LESIONS

Syphilis, caused by the spirochete *Treponema pallidum,* can initially show up as an open ulcer on the tongue or lip. However, it is a systemic disease, and if left untreated, can result in secondary patches on the mucous membranes of the oral cavity about 2-10 weeks after the initial lesion.

The two main systemic viral diseases that can result in oral lesions are **chickenpox** and **infectious mononucleosis**. The causative agent of chicken pox (as well as shingles in older individuals) is human herpesvirus type 3, also known as vermicelli zoster virus. It is transmitted by droplet infection to the respiratory tract, the bloodstream, and eventually to the skin and other organs, possibly manifesting orally as vesicles. Another herpes virus, HHV-4 or Epstein-Barr virus, is the causative agent of infectious mononucleosis, which is transmitted by contact with saliva or sometimes through blood transfusions. The infected individual generally has a fever and fatigue and may have a number of oral manifestations, such as sore throat, oral ulcers, red areas in the palate called petechiae, whitish tongue lesions called hairy leukoplakia, and a number of cancers.

TUBERCULOSIS

One of the biggest concerns globally is the possibility of contraction of **tuberculosis**, a respiratory infection caused by *Mycobacterium tuberculosis.* Persons at greatest risk for contraction of tuberculosis are those in intimate and prolonged contact with an active carrier or individuals who have a compromised immune system. The symptoms of tuberculosis are a lengthy productive cough, blood in the sputum, headache, fever and night sweats, loss of weight, and a general fatigue. Since tuberculosis is transmitted by prolonged exposure to concentrated amounts of the bacteria in airborne droplets, the risk of spread in a dental office is low but possible. Generally, dental work should not be done on individuals with active tuberculosis. Active disease is characterized by pneumonia or another exudative lung condition, formation of tubercles or fusion of granulomatous tissues if more advanced, and eventually lung tissue destruction. There may also be complications in other organs where the bacteria have traveled via macrophages. Drugs used to treat tuberculosis include rifampin, isoniazid, and ethambutol, but many strains are resistant to one or more agents.

TUBERCULIN SKIN TEST

INTERPRETATION

The tuberculin skin test, also known as the **Mantoux test** or **purified protein derivative (PPD) test**, is a screening check for exposure to *Mycobacterium tuberculosis.* A small quantity of PPD is injected intradermally

on the underside of the forearm. The test must be read 48 to 72 hours later. The amount of induration or hardening of the injected is noted, keeping in mind various factors. In general, anyone with an induration of at least 15 mm is considered positive. Smaller indurations of at least 5 mm are deemed positive in individuals with HIV or risk factors for the disease, those who have been in recent contact with people with active tuberculosis, or those who have fibrotic chest radiographs consistent with healed disease. The cutoff is at least 10 mm for the following high-risk groups: HIV-negative IV drug users; those with medical conditions that could be complicated by active TB, such as bypass, renal failure, diabetes, or hematologic disease patients; young children; other high-prevalence groups, such as people born outside the United States and Europe; those in low-income groups; and people in long-term care facilities.

INDURATION

Individuals with positive skin tests are considered recent converters if the size of **induration** becomes more intense over a two-year period. The cutoffs are increases of at least 10 mm if the person is younger than 35 and at least 15 mm if they are 35 years of age or older. Dental and other healthcare workers should be subject to the same recommendations for interpretation of the skin test as others (described elsewhere). Healthcare workers should be considered recently exposed to tuberculosis if the two-year increase in induration is greater than or equal to 10 mm, although the 15 mm cutoff is sometimes used.

CDC GUIDELINES FOR PREVENTING TUBERCULOSIS IN DENTAL SETTINGS

The **CDC (Centers for Disease Control)** recommends that infection control in a dental setting be based on regular risk assessment for *Mycobacterium tuberculosis* exposure, usually using PPD skin testing. Infection control should include evaluation of tuberculosis in the community and in the dental office. There is minimal risk of exposure if none were reported in either setting or very low risk if none were seen in the office. There is low probability if fewer than 6 patients with active disease were seen the previous year and no dental workers seroconverted. If more patients had active tuberculosis or dental workers seroconvert, the risk is intermediate or high respectively. Routine practices should also include documentation of tuberculosis in the patient's history, referral for assessment of those patients with potential tuberculosis (based on history or signs), provision of surgical masks to these patients, delay of elective procedures until full evaluation, isolation of patients requiring critical care if tuberculosis is suspected, evaluation and temporary removal of dental workers presenting with tuberculosis-type symptoms (such as persistent cough for at least 3 weeks), and provision of state of the art engineering if tuberculosis patients are treated.

MAJOR ORAL DISEASES OF BACTERIAL OR FUNGAL ORIGIN

Pharyngitis, inflammation of the pharynx, can be caused by two main types of bacteria: *Neisseria gonorrhoeae* and Streptococcus *pyogenes. N. gonorrhoeae* is primarily sexually transmitted but can be found orally after engaging in certain practices. *Streptococcus pyogenes,* technically a respiratory disease, causes strep throat or scarlet fever as well as skin infections and is carried by up to 20% of children. *Streptococcus mutans* is another species linked to dental caries and endocarditis. The other bacterial disease with oral manifestations is **syphilis**, caused by the spirochete *Treponema pallidum.* Normally syphilis is a systemic disease but oral lesions or chancres containing the spirochete can be found in up to 10% of instances.

The main **fungus causing oral manifestations** is the opportunistic yeast *Candida albicans*. It proliferates under certain opportune conditions such as depression of the immune system with HIV or leukemia, lengthy use of broad-spectrum antibiotics, mouth trauma usually from poorly fitting dentures, or transmission during birth. The possible oral manifestations are candidiasis or thrush, which are whitish lesions, and denture stomatitis, which appears as reddish regions.

VIRUSES

Viruses are very small (0.3 microns or less) microorganisms consisting of a central nucleic acid core (either DNA or RNA) and a protein coat called the capsid. Certain viruses also have an external envelope made of proteins, polysaccharides, and lipids. Viruses cannot replicate unless they exist within a susceptible host such as the human body. Their life cycle is initiated by adsorption or attachment to the host cell. This is followed by penetration of the host cell, uncoating of the capsid (which discharges the viral nucleic acid), replication (which is use of the host cell to generate new viral nucleic acid and capsid), assembly of a new viral particle, and release of it upon lysis of the host cell (enabling the virus to infect other cells). If the viral nucleic acid remains integrated into the host DNA, it continues to be replicated, lying latent or dormant until some later event reactivates the virus. Viruses can also cause chronic or slow persistent infections. Certain viruses transform host cells but do not lyse them, often resulting in tumors. Viruses can be killed on surfaces with measures used for bacteria, but they cannot be killed inside the body.

ORAL DISEASES OF VIRAL ORIGIN

Oral diseases of viral origin are primarily caused by some type of human herpesvirus or coxsackievirus. There are 8 types of DNA-containing human herpes viruses (HHV-1 to -8). Oral lesions known as cold sores or aphthous ulcers are primarily caused by HHV-1, occasionally by the predominantly genital type HHV-2 (also known as herpes simplex types 1 and 2), and as infectious mononucleosis or hairy leukoplakia of the tongue by HHV-4 (Epstein-Barr virus). Herpesviruses trigger recurrent episodes because they are retained on nerve ganglia and can be reactivated. Direct contact with anyone having active lesions such as fever blisters or herpes labialis can result in transmission. In the dental setting, a healthcare worker touching a lesion directly can get herpetic whitlow on his or her hands. There is also some possibility of contracting the virus even if the patient is asymptomatic. Coxsackievirus can cause herpangina, vesicles generally found in the back of the mouth, or hand-foot-and-mouth disease in which there are vesicles on many oral areas such as the cheek and tongue.

VIRAL DISEASES TRANSMITTED VIA RESPIRATORY/ORAL FLUIDS

Some forms of pneumonia are viral in origin, including influenza virus, adenovirus, and respiratory syncytial virus. The common cold is caused by any number of possible rhinoviruses plus other viral agents. There are a number of influenza viruses that can bring about influenza (fever, sore throat, headache, dry cough, muscle pain, etc.), bronchitis, and pneumonia. Several human herpesviruses can have respiratory manifestations. Chickenpox (HHV-3) can be spread by airborne droplets, and herpesviruses types 5, 6, and 7 have all been demonstrated in saliva, possibly causing CMV, cytomegalovirus disease, and roseola respectively. The herpesviruses may also have unknown consequences. HHV-4 or Epstein Barr virus is the causative agent of infectious mononucleosis as well. Measles (rubeola), rubella, and mumps can all be transmitted by inhaled respiratory/oral droplets; the MMR vaccine given to children provides protection against all three. Measles is characterized by rash and fever, rubella by rash on the face and often elsewhere, and mumps by swelling of the salivary glands.

HEPATITIS B VIRUS

Hepatitis B virus (HBV) is one form of viral hepatitis, which is inflammation of the liver. HBV is a double-stranded DNA hepadnavirus. It is a bloodborne disease, meaning it is transmitted via blood or bodily fluids; it has been found to be spread parenterally, sexually, through skin or mucous membrane contact, perinatally, through sharing of contaminated needles by intravenous drug users, and through other fluid contact. HBV is rarely spread through transfusions these days because of the excellent blood screening tests now available. After an incubation period of about 45-180 days after exposure, hepatitis symptoms usually show up gradually. About two-thirds of those exposed are asymptomatic or have mild symptoms; less than 1% have fulminant or severe hepatitis, and the rest become symptomatic (jaundice, dark urine, joint pain, fever, etc.). Most people exposed to HBV recover, but about 5 to 10% become carriers (hepatitis B surface antigen positive). About half of these individuals clear the infection within 5 years but the other half become chronic carriers of the virus, predisposing them to hepatocellular carcinoma and cirrhosis, progressive liver disease.

RISK OF TRANSMISSION IN DENTAL SETTING

Dental workers who are not vaccinated against HBV are at least twice as likely as the general public to contract hepatitis B virus. Over the last few decades, this risk has been cut down tremendously because several vaccines that provide protection against HBV have been developed. OSHA, the Occupational and Safety and Health Administration, now requires all health care professions, including dental offices, to offer **HBV vaccines free**

of charge to anyone with potential bloodborne exposure. Those who take the vaccines and show seroconversion are protected against the virus. The biggest occupational threats for infection with HBV are punctures with contaminated sharps, exposure to blood or saliva through skin cuts or cracks, or spraying of these fluids into lacerations or mucous membranes. Since dentists and other dental personnel are usually vaccinated, the risk of dental worker to patient transmission is minimal. There is possibility of patient-to-patient spread of the virus. HBV can be viable for a month or more at room temperature, but general office sterilization and disinfection procedures should kill the virus.

ANTIGENS AND ANTIBODIES

The most important antigen is **HBsAg**, hepatitis B surface antigen. HBsAg is a soluble antigen detectable in serum during periods of active infection or in the carrier state for hepatitis B. Antibody to HBsAg, **anti-HBs**, is indicative, when found in the serum, of past HBV infection and development of immunity through exposure, vaccination, or passive administration of HBIG (hepatitis B immune globulin). The other important HBV antigens are the hepatitis B core antigen (HBcAg) and hepatitis B e antigen (HBeAg) proteins. HBeAg, which is closely related to HBcAg, is soluble and correlates with evidence of HBV replication; thus, it is indicative of current HBV infection when found in serum. Appearance of its antibody, anti-HBe, implies a lowering of viral titer. There are also tests for antibodies to the core protein, anti-HBc and IgM anti-HBc, which, if present, point to prior or recent infection with HBV respectively. Presence of antibodies to both surface and core antigens signify immunity. The actual HBV virus or Dane particle can also be looked for, although this is not routinely done.

HEPATITIS C VIRUS INFECTION

Hepatitis B, C, and D viruses are bloodborne. **Hepatitis C virus** (HCV) is an enveloped single-stranded RNA flavivirus. Its incubation period is from one to five months, and its onset is usually insidious. The routes of transmission are similar to those for HBV except that about half of cases have been found to be related to intravenous drug abuse. Unlike HBV, most (up to 85%) of HCV-infected individuals go on to be chronic carriers of the virus and about 1/5 of them contract chronic liver disease, including hepatocellular carcinoma and cirrhosis. There is no current vaccine. There is a risk of contracting the virus in the dental setting, although it is less than for HBV transmission because the virus is less virulent. There are good available screening tests for anti-HCV, antibody to HCV. Presence of anti-HCV indicates current or previous HCV infection, although it does not pinpoint the acute, chronic, or resolved state.

HEPATITIS D INFECTION

Hepatitis D virus (HDV) is a bloodborne, non-enveloped, single-stranded RNA virus. It only exists as a satellite or defective virus; in other words, it is only capable of infection in the presence of hepatitis B virus. It is spread like other bloodborne pathogens. The incubation period is from 21 to 90 days and symptoms are generally acute. The primary antigen of HDV is Delta antigen or Hdag. It is demonstrable in early acute delta infection, and its antibody, anti-HDV, indicates current or past infection. HDV can exist chronically in carrier states and cause hepatocellular carcinoma and cirrhosis. Acute infection with HDV, which can only occur in conjunction with HBV coinfection, can result in death in up to 30% of cases. If antibody to hepatitis B surface antigen (anti-HBsAg) is detectable in the serum, an individual is immune to HDV as well. Because the virus is bloodborne, it presents an occupational hazard in the dental setting.

HEPATITIS VIRUSES SPREAD VIA FECAL-ORAL ROUTES

The two main hepatitis viruses that spread via fecal or oral routes are hepatitis A virus and hepatitis E virus. Since neither has been demonstrated to be transmitted via blood or bodily fluids, they do not present particular risks for dental workers. Neither exists chronically in carrier states or has any possible sequelae. Both have acute onsets starting about 15 days to several months after exposure.

- **Hepatitis A virus (HAV)** is a non-enveloped single-stranded RNA picornavirus. Acute infections almost never result in death. There is an available vaccine for HAV (usually suggested for those traveling to countries with inadequate sanitation) as well as antibody screening tests. The latter include anti-HAV, antibody to HAV, which can be found at onset of symptoms and endures throughout life, and IgM anti-HAV, which detects the IgM class of antibodies only present after recent infection.
- **Hepatitis E virus (HEV)** is a non-enveloped, single-stranded RNA calicivirus. There are no vaccines for protection against HEV and no available tests to detect anti-HEV, antibody to HEV, which theoretically would indicate exposure. Contraction of HEV during pregnancy can prove fatal.

HIV

TRANSMISSION

Human immunodeficiency virus, HIV, is a bloodborne disease. It is **transmitted** through exposure to HIV-positive blood, through sexual contact, or perinatally from mother to child. Excellent screening tests for anti-HIV and other characteristic proteins such as p24 now make the likelihood of exposure through blood transfusions practically nonexistent. However, other high-risk practices, such as sharing of injection needles by intravenous drug users, account for about a quarter of cases. HIV has been identified in other bodily fluids, including saliva. The largest source of HIV infection is transmission through unprotected sexual practices with an HIV-positive individual. HIV can also be passed across the placenta perinatally from mother to child or occasionally via breast milk. This transmission can be dramatically diminished through drug therapy during pregnancy.

COURSE OF INFECTION

Human immunodeficiency viruses 1 and 2 (HIV-1 and HIV-2) are single-stranded RNA retroviruses. HIV-1 is more common, particularly in the United States. A retrovirus replicates within a host cell, in this case primarily helper T4 or CD4 lymphocytes, by using its RNA as a template to make viral DNA copies, which are integrated into the chromosomes of the host's lymphocytes. This leads to formation of viral particles within and destruction and depletion of T4 lymphocytes. Within about a month after infection with HIV, a person may exhibit mild symptoms such as fever, enlarged glands, or fatigue. These symptoms comprise acute retroviral syndrome. The individual will develop anti-HIV antibodies and seroconvert within the next few weeks to months, but these antibodies are not protective, and replication and T4 lymphocyte killing continues. The individual usually appears relatively asymptomatic until his or her immune system has become undermined enough to generate the symptoms of AIDS (acquired immunodeficiency syndrome). These symptoms include susceptibility to opportunistic infections such as fungal pneumonia from *Pneumocystis jiroveci* or malignancies, including rare ones such as Kaposi's sarcoma.

DENTAL MANIFESTATIONS AND RISK OF TRANSMISSION

Once an individual reaches the early stages of acquired immunodeficiency syndrome (AIDS), many of the first indications are oral, including **candidiasis or thrush, histoplasmosis, warts, periodontitis or gingivitis from bacterial infections, Kaposi's sarcoma, and others**. The documented and potential transmission to dental workers is much lower than for some other types of healthcare workers, such as nurses or laboratory personnel. Nevertheless, any healthcare worker who incurs some type of puncture or cut and is exposed to HIV-positive blood has the greatest chance of contracting the virus. To date, there has only been one dentist implicated in transmission of HIV to patients. Common dental practices using personal protective equipment, disinfection, and sterilization virtually eliminate patient exposure to the virus. For example, HIV is readily deactivated with heat or gas sterilization and by most liquid sterilizers and surface disinfectants. In addition, contaminated sharps must be dealt with carefully and disposed of properly to reduce potential exposure.

RICKETTSIAE INFECTIONS

Rickettsiae are tiny parasitic microorganisms that live in and multiply in a variety of hosts. These microorganisms are transmitted by the host to humans. The transporter is usually a flea or tick, which in some cases, is carried by a rodent. In terms of dentistry, the rickettsiae of greatest interest are those spread by head lice to school age children, causing pediculosis. Head lice are small, bloodsucking, wingless parasites that produce eggs that can be visualized on hair shafts. Measures such as medicinal shampoos, combing, and hot water washing of all clothing and bedding are needed to rid the child of these microorganisms. Most other rickettsial diseases are rare, including Rocky Mountain Spotted Fever, which causes flulike symptoms and pick spotting, and typhus, which rapidly causes high fever, headache, pain in the back and extremities, confusion, a rash, and weakening of the heartbeat.

PROTOZOA INFECTIONS

Protozoa, or **amoebas**, are single-celled microorganisms. They are often found in contaminated water and can survive in bodily fluids such as blood or in the fluid found in the oral cavity or intestinal tract. They are larger than bacteria (about 100 microns) and reproduce by binary fission. They entrap food in a unique manner by altering their shape to surround and ingest food and incorporate it into an internal food vacuole. These shape changes also help with mobility as do the flagella possessed by many of these organisms. Protozoa are important in dentistry for several reasons. They usually contribute to periodontal disease along with bacteria by their presence in periodontal pockets. One important protozoal disease is amebic dysentery, which is caused by *Entamoeba histolytica* and is characterized by serious diarrhea and occasionally liver abscesses. Protozoa are also responsible for malaria and sleeping sickness spread via mosquito and tsetse fly bites respectively in tropical countries.

INFECTIONS CAUSED BY FUNGI

Fungi are generally spore-producing microorganisms that reproduce by budding. They may be single- or multicellular. They lack chlorophyll, making them nonphotosynthetic, and they are eukaryotic with visible nuclei and organelles. Molds and yeast are forms of fungi causing infections. Mushrooms also are considered fungi. The fungus of greatest interest is *Candida albicans,* which causes candidiasis (also known as thrush or moniliasis). *C. albicans* is a constituent of many individual's normal flora, but it is an opportunistic infection that can take over when a person's immune defenses are lowered such as in presence of AIDS or with the overuse of antibiotics. Thrush is characterized by raised white or cream-colored patches in the oral cavity. It can be painful and should be treated with antifungal drugs. Tinea is a group of fungal infections. Variants are tinea pedis or athlete's foot, tinea corporis or ringworm, and tinea unguium, which are white patches on nails. Oral and/or topical fungal medications are indicated.

ENDOGENOUS AND EXOGENOUS INFECTIOUS DISEASES

Infectious diseases are illnesses caused by multiplication of harmful microorganisms or pathogens in the body and subsequent tissue damage. They can be classified as endogenous or exogenous depending on the source of the infection:

- **Endogenous** infectious diseases are produced by microorganisms generally present on or in the body without untoward effect. These microorganisms can be opportunistic, however, and if certain events occur, they can take over or penetrate areas and become harmful. In the dental setting, normal oral flora can cause endogenous diseases such as decay, periodontal disease, and pulpitis.
- **Exogenous** infectious diseases are ones that are caused by microorganisms not generally present invading the body. Most infectious diseases fall into this category. These external exogenous microbes can act directly by penetrating the body and multiplying or they can produce toxins or poisons with untoward effects (known as toxigenic diseases).

EMERGING DISEASES

Emerging diseases are previously unrecognized new infectious diseases. Many of these emerging diseases evolve through close contact with animal (zoonotic) contacts or insect vectors. Rodents are common animal vectors and mosquitoes and ticks are frequent insect vectors. Over the last few decades, an average of one emerging disease per year has been identified with the majority being viral. Changing demographics, such as movement into cities, overcrowding, and the increase in international travel and business dealings, account for some of these discoveries. Technological advances such as global food distribution methods or water-handling devices, while beneficial, can encourage transmission of infectious agents to new areas. Many microorganisms can mutate into slightly-modified new forms. The best examples are the constantly changing influenza virus and antibiotic-resistant forms of various bacteria.

NATURAL HOST DEFENSE BARRIERS TO INFECTION

There are four types of natural or innate host defense barriers to infection.

- There are **physical barriers** such as intact skin and mucous membranes at various sites (mouth, eyes, respiratory tree, etc.).
- There are also **mechanical barriers** to infection that cleanse the system of the microorganisms. These include oral saliva and mucus, a cilia escalator that traps and moves inhaled particles back out the mouth, the regular shedding of skin and mucous membrane cells, nasal hair, and expulsion through coughing or sneezing.
- The body produces a number of **chemicals** with antimicrobial properties, such as hydrochloric acid in the stomach, organic acids on the skin and vaginal area, lysozyme in the saliva and other secretions, a whole complex of components called the complement system, and the mainly antiviral substance called interferon.
- Lastly, the white blood cells **neutrophils and macrophages** act as phagocytes to surround and destroy microorganisms.

RANGE OF PROTECTIVE ACTIONS OF ANTIBODIES

Antibodies bind to foreign antigens, such as those on microorganisms, present in the body. Through their binding properties, they can augment phagocytic destruction of microorganisms either directly or through activation of the complement system. Antibodies can deter attachment of the agent to host cells; they might inactivate toxins or histolytic enzymes by binding to certain destructive molecules; they can lyse gram-negative bacteria or enveloped viruses through activation of the complement system, and they can also lyse virus-infected cells by binding to both those cells and macrophages. The main goal of vaccination or immunization is the injection of antigens that have been modified enough so that they won't cause harmful effects but will generate protective antibodies. It is hoped that vaccination or immunization will create long-term, artificially-created immunity. Protective antibodies are of the IgG class, or early in infection, the IgM class.

ACQUIRED DEFENSES THAT FIGHT INFECTIONS

When a microorganism invades the human body, **immune responses** are activated to prevent harmful damage and impart protection against further assault with the same agent. The immune responses are mounted against antigens or substances that the body considers foreign, generally specific portions of the infectious agent. Certain macrophages process these antigens via phagocytes; they interact with T and B lymphocytes, which clonally expand and recognize the antigens, and responses are generated against the invading agent. These responses are of two types. Cell-mediated responses involve activated T lymphocytes, which can act in several ways by either controlling antibody-mediated responses, obliterating infected cells, generating chemicals called lymphokines that activate other cells like phagocytes, or destroying modified host cells (such as malignant ones). There are also antibody-mediated responses in which protein antibodies that specifically recognize and bind to foreign antigens are created utilizing B lymphocytes.

HARMFUL IMMUNE RESPONSES

The main way in which the **immune system causes harmful responses** is through development of allergic diseases. Allergic manifestations can occur in the nose or eyes (hay fever), the respiratory tract (asthma), as skin rashes (hives), or systemically as anaphylactic shock. Most of these reactions are to pollens and other environmental allergens such as pet dander or to foods. Both antibody-mediated responses (elicited by a class of antibody called IgE) and cell-mediated responses to antigens (allergens) can occur. Certain chronic infections can also precipitate cell-mediated allergic responses. Contact dermatitis is a form of cell-mediated allergic reaction to certain chemicals such as the oils from poison ivy, nickel in jewelry, or latex. Allergic responses are generally evaluated by doing skin tests, and there are also immunoassays available measuring IgE in serum. Individuals may overcome their allergies if they develop enough of what are called blocking antibodies to the offending antigen.

Need for Immunization

INFLUENZA INFECTIONS

Influenza respiratory infections are characterized clinically by acute onset, high fever (up to 104 °F), severe headache and other pains, prolonged fatigue, cough, and severe chest discomfort in most cases. Stuffy nose, sneezing, and sore throat are more characteristic of colds, not the flu. Influenza can lead to critical complications such as bronchitis, pneumonia, and even death. The incubation period for the virus is 1 to 4 days, and the virus is maximally shed around the onset of symptoms. The mode of transmission is generally aerosols or droplets, although direct contact is sometimes implicated. There are two types of influenza, types A and B, and variants within those two types. The CDC suggests annual single-dose vaccination with preparations prepared each year to reflect the expected culprits in the hemisphere where administered. There are two kinds of vaccine, an inactivated or killed vaccine that is administered intramuscularly, and a live, attenuated or weakened vaccine (LAIV) given intranasally. The intramuscular, inactivated form is recommended for most people including healthcare workers. LAIV should only be given to non-pregnant individuals ages 5 to 49. There are antiviral medications available, but these are not realistic options.

CONTRAINDICATIONS FOR LAIV VACCINE AND INFLUENZA VACCINES

Some influenza vaccines are prepared using eggs, meaning they may contain trace amounts of egg proteins, but formulations prepared without the use of eggs are now generally available. People with severe allergy to eggs should not receive a formulation made using eggs as they may develop critical anaphylactic hypersensitivity reactions. There are a number of contraindications for the LAIV vaccine as it contains live, albeit weakened, influenza virus and is given in a form (intranasally) quickly accessible to the respiratory tract. Only healthy, nonpregnant individuals between the ages of 5 and 49 should take this vaccine. People outside these age ranges, those with chronic pulmonary or cardiovascular diseases, anyone with underlying medical conditions like diabetes or renal disease, people with known or possible immunodeficiency diseases, those with Guillain-Barré syndrome, and pregnant women should not take the live attenuated influenza vaccine. Children or adolescents who are taking aspirin or calculates should not take the LAIV vaccine either because of its association with the childhood disease called Reye's syndrome, but they should receive the inactivated influenza vaccine. Individuals in intimate contact with immunosuppressed patients, for example certain healthcare workers, should also refrain from receiving the LAIV vaccine.

HEPATITIS B VACCINATION AND IMMUNIZATIONS

New employees should be offered the hepatitis B vaccination series (generally 3 spaced injections) within 10 days of employment and after receiving training. The vaccine should be offered free of charge and administered by a licensed physician or nurse practitioner in an office where the OSHA Bloodborne Pathogens Standard is available. Potential employees need not be prescreened for hepatitis B immunity, and after employment they are not required to accept the vaccination offer. However, if they do not accept at that time, they must sign a vaccination refusal statement. The physician must sign a written confirmation for those employees who are vaccinated. Vaccination also involves testing for effectiveness, measurement of antibody to hepatitis B surface antigen 1 to 2 months after the series. Non-responders should be advised further. There should also be an annual review of employee records to ensure that they are up-to-date on other immunizations that are deemed important.

RECOMMENDED IMMUNIZATIONS FOR HEPATITIS B VIRUS

Hepatitis B virus (HBV) presents a significant occupational hazard for dental health care personnel (DHCP) if they are not vaccinated. The bloodborne virus is quite virulent and stable. It causes both acute and chronic symptoms, including liver cirrhosis, necrotizing vasculitis, and hepatocellular carcinoma. OSHA requirements regarding immunization are discussed elsewhere. Some version of the recombinant Hepatitis B vaccine is recommended for DHCP and other at-risk adults. The administration schedule is 2 doses 4 weeks apart given intramuscularly in the deltoid muscle followed by a third dose 5 months later. The available single antigen vaccines are Recombivax HB and Engerix-B, and there are combination vaccines containing HBV antigens

along with others (Twinrix for adults, Comvax and Pediarix for children). Serologic tests for anti-HBsAg to measure protective effects should be done one to two months after completion of the dose series. Individuals who are exposed to HBV but are not immune should be given hepatitis B immune globulin, 0.6 mL/kg intramuscularly within 7 days of exposure. This should be followed by another round a month later if the HBV vaccine series has not been initiated.

TETANUS IMMUNIZATION

Tetanus is characterized by acute hypertonia and sweeping muscles spasms, usually initially in the jaw and neck area. It is important because even though the incidence is low in the United States, tetanus remains a global problem and can cause death. Tetanus, also called lockjaw, is caused by the toxins released by the bacterium *Clostridium tetani*. Most children are given immunizations with tetanus toxoid, an inactivated form of the toxin, in conjunction with diphtheria and pertussis in a combination DPT vaccine. They are given 3 to 4 doses during the first year of life followed by boosters. The CDC recommends booster shots every 10 years into adulthood to maintain antitoxin levels or earlier if an individual has some sort of traumatic injury. The latter is suggested because *C. tetani* bacilli and spores are transmitted from environments where they flourish (such as soil) to the bloodstream through open cuts and wounds.

CDC RECOMMENDATIONS FOR IMMUNIZATION OF DENTAL HEALTH CARE PERSONNEL

VARICELLA ZOSTER

Varicella zoster virus (VZV or HHV-3) is responsible both for childhood chickenpox and for its adult recurrent form, shingles. The HHV-3 is retained on nerve ganglia and can reactivate in later life. Shingles is characterized by red bumps that evolve into blisters that cause inflammation and pain. It is suggested that dental health care personnel (DHCP) receive varicella zoster live virus vaccine in two 0.5 mL doses given subcutaneously given 4 to 8 weeks apart if they do not have a reliable history of previous infection or laboratory confirmation of immunity. It is cost effective to do serologic tests before vaccinating because the vast majority of people are immune. Vaccination is contraindicated in pregnant women, immunocompromised individuals, and those with history of anaphylactic reactions to gelatin or neomycin. Salicylate (aspirin) should be avoided for 6 weeks post vaccination. DHCP should also receive varicella zoster immune globulin (VZIG) if they are not immune, are susceptible to infection (for example pregnant women), and are in contact with infectious individuals. VZIG is given at a dose of 125 units/10kg up to 625 units.

MEASLES, MUMPS, AND RUBELLA

The available vaccines for **measles, mumps, and rubella** all contain live virus. A combined vaccine called MMR is generally the vaccine of choice if it is felt that the person is susceptible to more than one virus. All are contraindicated during pregnancy, if the person is immunocompromised, or if the individual has shown an allergic, anaphylactic reaction to gelatin, neomycin, or, in the case of measles, immune globulin. The MMR or separate vaccines are given subcutaneously in a single dose with no booster. The exception is measles vaccine, which requires a booster at least a month after the first shot. The decision of whether to receive these vaccines is somewhat dependent on age as anyone who was born before 1957 can be assumed to be immune. Nevertheless, vaccination should be considered if the worker has no documentation of vaccination on or after his or her first birthday, laboratory verification of the diseases, or physician-diagnosed infection. People who were immunized between 1963 and 1967 with the killed measles alone or the killed measles vaccine followed by the live type should be revaccinated. Further if the type of vaccine is unknown, the individual should be revaccinated. Inclusion of live rubella virus can be risky for the fetus of women becoming pregnant within 3 months of immunization.

VACCINATION FOR TUBERCULOSIS

Control of tuberculosis is generally aimed at means other than immunization in the United States. These measures include early detection, treatment with various anti-tuberculosis drugs, or prevention therapy using the agent isoniazid. However, main strains are resistant to various drugs, and there are areas where the likelihood of infection is high. In those instances, vaccination with BCG, bacille Calmette-Guerin, should be

considered for dental personnel. BCG contains a weakened strain of the tubercle bacillus. The suggested administration is a single dose of 0.3 mL given percutaneously under the skin. Pregnant women, or individuals who are immunocompromised, such as those with HIV or various cancers, should not be given the vaccine.

Preventing Adverse Reactions

HARMFUL REACTIONS TO GLOVES

Latex is derived from the rubber tree *Hevea brasiliensis.* The latex goes through quite a bit of processing, and other materials are added to make gloves. Up to 6% of the populace and 12% of regularly exposed healthcare workers may be sensitive to latex. Most reactions to latex gloves are actually to other chemicals in the gloves or put on the hands in the form of irritant contact dermatitis. There are two forms of true allergic reactions to latex possible as well, allergic contact dermatitis and latex allergy. Allergic contact dermatitis is a delayed type IV hypersensitivity reaction to latex in gloves or often the chemicals used during processing of them. It is characterized by itching, erythema, and vesicles a day or two after exposure and later dry skin, cracks, and sores. The other type, latex allergy, is type I hypersensitivity elicited by substances released upon exposure to latex proteins by mast cells to which IgE class anti-latex antibodies are bound. Signs of latex allergy appear rapidly about 20 minutes after exposure and can include hives, erythema, sneezing, and asthma. Allergic individuals with subsequent exposures can go into anaphylactic shock and possibly die. Latex allergy can be elicited by airborne latex proteins from glove powder.

PREVENTING LATEX ALLERGIES

Use of **non-latex gloves** is the best way to prevent dental worker exposure, but powder-free or reduced-protein latex gloves do cut down on potential exposure. It is recommended that the dental office follow the recommendations of the National Institute for Occupational Safety and Health. It is very important to determine whether patients might be allergic to latex or rubber products by including in their medical history a number of relevant questions. The medical history of the patient should include information about allergies to rubber-containing products ranging from balloons to condoms, allergies to certain foods such as bananas and kiwis, possible exposure through surgical procedures at any time in their life, allergic testing results if performed, presence of asthma or hay fever, and current use of rubber gloves or other latex-containing products. Special precautions should be taken for patients with possible latex allergies. They should be treated at the beginning of the day in a room in which latex is excluded before and during treatment. This exclusion includes anything in contact with the patient, anything a dental worker is wearing, and possible airborne latex proteins from glove powder.

NIOSH RECOMMENDATIONS FOR PREVENTION OF LATEX ALLERGIES

The National Institute for Occupational Safety and Health (NIOSH) has issued **recommendations for workers and employers for prevention of latex allergies in the workplace**. The NIOSH recommends that workers use nonlatex gloves when appropriate or at least use latex gloves that are powder-free with reduced protein or refrain from use of oil- or petroleum-based lotions, which degrade the gloves. If latex gloves are used, the worker should wash and dry hands after removal. An office utilizing latex gloves requires frequent cleaning including changing of ventilation filters and vacuum bags. The personnel should be informed about ways to prevent latex allergies and the potential signs. Individuals should refrain from use of latex-containing gloves and other articles if they have symptoms of latex allergy. If they have symptoms of latex allergy, they should confer with a physician. Latex-allergic personnel should wear a medical alert bracelet stating that fact. The employer's responsibilities include provision of non-latex and/or reduced-protein, powder-free gloves, institution of housekeeping procedures that get rid of latex dust, offering education regarding latex allergy, regular evaluation of personnel for latex allergy symptoms, and ongoing quality control.

Hand Hygiene

APPROPRIATE HAND HYGIENE PROCEDURE

The certified dental assistant should carry out **hand hygiene** thoroughly with soap and water for one minute on arrival at work, and thereafter with soap and water (if hands are visibly soiled) or alcohol rub whenever the hands are contaminated, before applying gloves, before and after assisting patients, and after removing gloves. Antimicrobial soaps are only recommended if the hands have had contact with blood or body fluids. Note that any lotions applied to the hands should be compatible with latex. Jewelry and artificial nails should be avoided as they may harbor bacteria. Hand hygiene procedure:

1. Wet hands thoroughly with warm water, apply soap, and rub hands together to massage the soap into the tissue, including between the fingers and about the nails.
2. Rinse hands completely to remove all soap.
3. Dry hands completely with clean towel or air dry.
4. Use a clean towel or foot control to turn off the water.

If using alcohol rub, it should be thoroughly rubbed into all surfaces for at least 15 seconds. Drying time should take at least 15 seconds or insufficient rub was applied.

ANTIMICROBIAL SPECTRUM OF HAND HYGIENE AGENTS

Hand hygiene agents are designed to remove transient skin flora, microorganisms to which an individual is exposed when touching contaminated areas. Transient skin flora differs from normal resident skin flora in that transient flora is less deeply embedded and potentially more dangerous. Alcohol-based hand rubs containing 60 to 90% alcohol are the fastest acting and are quite effective against all potential pathogens, including gram-positive and negative bacteria, mycobacterium, fungi and viruses. Intermediate in terms of speed of action are chlorhexidine (2 or 4%), iodophors, phenolics and triclosan. All of these are fairly effective against bacteria. Of these, chlorhexidine is the reagent with the broadest spectrum of effectiveness against other types of microorganisms, it continues to be effective longer, and it rarely produces allergic reactions. Quaternary ammonium compounds act slowly, are only used in conjunction with alcohols, and are only minimally effective against bacteria and viruses. Mycobacteria and fungi are resistant to triclosan and quaternary ammonium compounds.

ALCOHOL-BASED HAND RUBS

Alcohol-based hand rubs are very effective for hand hygiene and asepsis. Unfortunately, they are also flammable because most contain at least 60% isopropyl or ethyl alcohol. It is the opinion of the American Society of Healthcare Engineering that alcohol-based hand rub dispensers can be located in hallways, suites, or near patient room entries with the following restrictions: The largest single containers of gel/liquid alcohol-based rubs that can be used are 1.2 liters in egress corridors and 2 liters in suites such as dental operatories. The dispensers cannot be mounted anywhere near electric receptacles or other possible ignition sources. If the container extends more than 3.5 inches into a corridor, it should be documented in the fire plan and training program. Alcohol-based hand rub containers being stored must be in an official flammable liquid storage cabinet. Total amounts of alcohol-based hand rubs present in the facility should not surpass amounts indicated by building and fire codes.

HAND HYGIENE PRIOR TO SURGICAL PROCEDURES

Prior to surgical procedures, jewelry is removed and multiple scrub and rinse cycles (from 2 to 6 minutes) using either an antimicrobial surgical scrub product or a non-antimicrobial agent are done. This is followed by rinsing and keeping the hands above the elbow level. The person lets water drip off from the elbows and then dries the hands with sterile towels. If an antimicrobial surgical scrub product, which eliminates soil and transient flora and kills some resident microbes as well, was used, the person then puts on sterile gloves with the aid of an assistant. If a non-antimicrobial agent was used, then an alcohol-based hand rub should be rubbed into the hand before sterile gloves are donned as previously described. In both cases, the gloves must be vigorously inspected for defects and no contaminated surfaces or other items should be touched.

Personal Protective Equipment (PPE)

DONNING AND REMOVING PERSONAL PROTECTIVE EQUIPMENT

There is a suggested sequence for use of personal protective equipment. Protective clothing should be donned before performing activities such as positioning the patient's bib and unpacking instruments and supplies. Then the worker puts on the mask and eyewear. Prior to treatment procedures, the worker should wash his or her hands and don gloves. No contaminated surfaces should be handled once gloves are donned prior to patient contact. When procedures are completed, the suggested sequence of PPE removal is disposable gown if used, then gloves, followed by protective eyewear and the mask. This sequence of removal is performed by pulling the gown off over gloves turning it inside out, taking off the first glove with the other hand by pinching at the wrist and pulling in the direction of the fingers, and then placing the ungloved thumb inside the wrist area of the other glove and pulling it off toward the fingers. Eyewear and the mask are subsequently removed by grasping the ear rests and elastic bands or ties respectively.

GLOVES

Gloves are one aspect of personal protective equipment (PPE). According the **OSHA Bloodborne Pathogens Standard** gloves must be provided in facilities such as dental offices where workers may be exposed to bloodborne pathogens. Gloves used in the dental office protect members of the dental team from infections transmitted by patients, patients from infections spread by the dental team, and patients from infections from other patients. Dentists and other members of the dental team who wear gloves have a barrier to transmission from the patient though cuts in their skin. Gloves also protect dental personnel against irritants like chemicals and dental materials. Certain gloves guard against burns during processing operations. Donning of gloves during patient operations by the dentist and other personnel protects the patient from microorganisms on the worker's hands. Dental workers can be in contact with infectious agents on just about every contaminated surface in the area, and they may harbor bloodborne pathogens that can escape through cuts on the skin. If they are in contact with patient's blood it can be preserved on the hands for days, particularly under fingernails, and spread to other patients if ungloved.

TYPES USED IN DENTISTRY

The two main types of gloves used in dentistry are those for patient care activities and those designed as utility gloves. There are also specialized types such as heat-resistant gloves (for use with sterilizers, etc.) and cotton dermal gloves. No matter what type of patient care gloves are employed, they should be disposable and used for a single patient or until compromised (cuts, tears). Patient care gloves are either **sterile** for surgical procedures or **non-sterile** for all other routines. They can also be categorized according to material. Gloves may be made of latex or some other material. Many people are allergic to latex. Sterile patient care surgical gloves come in latex, reduced-protein latex, neoprene, styrene, and synthetic copolymers. Examination gloves are generally latex, synthetic copolymer, nitrile, styrene-butadiene, or polyurethane. Latex gloves also come in powderless, flavored, and low-protein versions. Utility gloves should be worn during cleaning activities, preparation and use of chemicals, and instrument processing. Utility gloves are heavier, made of materials like heavy latex or nitrile and, in some instances, thin copolymer or plastic. Each worker should have his or her own assigned pair, which should be washed with an antimicrobial agent, rinsed, and dried.

PROTECTIVE EYEWEAR

Protective eyewear is a form of personal protective equipment (PPE). It comes in a variety of forms, including goggles (the best coverage), prescription eyeglasses that have side shields, and protective eyeglasses with shields. There are also masks with attached eye protection and face shields. Protective eyewear serves two purposes. It protects the mucous membranes in the eye from exposure to potentially infectious sprays, splatters, or aerosols. It also offers protection against impact damage to the eyes which can occur during activities such as polishing or grinding, chemical splashes, and ultraviolet irradiation. Therefore, protective eyewear use is suggested for a variety of activities in the dental office, including grinding and polishing materials, cleaning instruments or surfaces, developing radiographs and working in the dental lab.

MASKS

Masks are personal protective equipment (PPE). They are classified according to the level of bacterial or particle filter efficiency as N-series (95%), R-series (99%) or P-series (99.97%). In dentistry, the primary purpose of face masks is to protect the dental worker's nasal and oral mucous membranes against sprays, splatters, or aerosolized particles from the patient that could contain infectious agents. The masks also reduce worker to patient transmission. Masks should be worn and then discarded after single patient use during certain procedures. These procedures include anything involving handpieces, ultrasonic scalers, air/water syringes, and oral irrigators. Face mask use is also suggested during polishing or grinding of potentially contaminated items (for example in the dental lab) and during instrument processing. Since masks are dome shaped or flat covering the bridge of the nose, they can allow some transmission of fluids or aerosols if they are not tight. Thus, respirators instead of masks are indicated in some instances such as when treating patients with potential airborne infections such as SARS (severe acute respiratory syndrome).

PROTECTIVE CLOTHING

Protective clothing should be donned over street clothes by dental workers anytime there is potential for splashing or spraying of blood, saliva, or other potentially infectious materials. Examples of acceptable protective clothing include lab coats, gowns, uniforms, aprons and jackets. Clothing that resists fluids is preferable. Disposable protective gowns are useful; they should be discarded in biohazardous waste daily or when soiled. Reusable protective garments should also be taken off when soiled and anytime the worker leaves the office. OSHA requires that reusable protective clothing be left at the office and be laundered there or through a commercial laundering service. Work shoes to be worn only at the workplace are another form of protective clothing; these are not mandated by law.

INSTRUMENT PROCESSING AREA

The instrument processing area should be distinct from other spaces, yet centrally located. Ideally it should be in a separate room or rooms with no outside doors or windows to let in dust and good ventilation. There should be three separate areas for decontamination, packaging, and sterilizing and storage. There should be a logical work flow within each zone and between zones. Each area should be clearly marked. The **decontamination area** should be equipped with personal protective equipment, a sharps container, tongs, a sink and handwashing dispenser, an ultrasonic cleaner and detergent, waste containers for biohazardous materials and nonregulated waste, facilities to prepare handpieces (cleaners, lubricants, air and vacuum lines for flushing), and a drainer. The **packaging area** should be equipped with rust inhibitors, replacement parts, biologic and chemical indicators, packaging materials, a heat sealer, and autoclave tape. The **sterilizing and storage area** should contain the sterilizer(s), appropriate solutions (water, glutaraldehyde, etc.), a glutaraldehyde monitor if used, lubricant for the handpiece, air and vacuum lines for flushing excess lubricant, an incubator for culturing spore strips/vials, and an enclosed storage space.

Protecting the Patient and the Operator

UNIVERSAL AND STANDARD PRECAUTIONS

Universal precautions are infection control measures needed to prevent exposure to blood and other bodily fluids of patients, who are treated as if they are infectious. **Standard precautions** are more inclusive infection control measures that extend to blood, all bodily fluids such as secretions and excretions (excluding sweat), skin that is not intact, and mucous membranes. All of these are considered as potentially infectious under standard precautions because, even if patients exhibit no symptoms, they can be asymptomatic carriers of disease agents. Wording in the OSHA Bloodborne Pathogens Standard still refers to universal precautions, but the more inclusive standard precautions should be followed in the dental office.

DENTAL DAMS AND EYE SHIELDS

A **dental dam** is a rubber or silicone barrier that is placed in the mouth to separate the site of dental treatment from the rest of the mouth. The dam helps to keep saliva away from the operative site so that it remains clean and dry, allows improved visibility, protects soft tissue in the mouth, and decreases risk of the patient inadvertently swallowing dental debris. For procedures, such as root canals, the use of a dental dam is an infection control procedure. However, the dental dam prevents the patient from communicating while it's in place. Patients are unable to breathe through the mouth with the dam in place, so they must be able to breathe through the nose. Some patients may not be able to tolerate use of the dam because it makes them feel claustrophobic.

Eye shields should be used by both the patient and the operator (who should also wear a facemask) during any drilling procedure in which there may be spray or other aerosolized debris to protect the eyes from contamination and injury.

SALIVA EJECTOR

Saliva ejectors are used to suction saliva and fluids out of the oral cavity during procedures. Studies indicate that there is a great likelihood of a reverse flow in the vacuum line back into the patient's mouth if a seal is created around the saliva ejector. This reverse flow could transmit infectious agents. Therefore, measures to prevent the retraction are suggested. The patient should be instructed to refrain from closing the lips tightly around the ejector. Another way to ensure against creating a seal and inducing retraction is to use disposable saliva ejector tips that have a tiny hole on the side, which reduces pressure and stops reverse flow.

PRE-PROCEDURE MOUTH RINSE

Pre-procedure mouth rinsing by the patient with an antimicrobial mouth rinse greatly reduces the number of microorganisms in the oral cavity. Thus, fewer oral microbes can be transmitted during procedures as aerosols, splatter, or directly through contact to the professional. This should also reduce surface contamination in the area. It is particularly suggested that the patient perform a mouth rinse before procedures involving a prophylaxis cup or ultrasonic scaler as these practices preclude use of other aseptic measures such as a rubber dam and high-volume evacuation. In addition, it is beneficial for dental team members to use a long-lasting antimicrobial mouth rinse, generally containing chlorhexidine gluconate, essential oils, and ionosphere.

MINIMIZING DUST AND MICROORGANISMS

In addition to surface disinfection and sterilization procedures discussed elsewhere, there are general housekeeping considerations. Dusting and sweeping in any patient care locales should be done with a wet cloth or mop to reduce dispersal of microorganism-containing dust. These cloths and mops should be disposable or they should be permitted to dry between uses. The mop water should contain a low-level disinfectant, for example, a quaternary ammonium compound, and it should be changed at least every day. During periods when the office is closed, dust covers might be utilized for surfaces in the operatory and sterilizing rooms. Filters need to be replaced often. Patient care areas should have smooth surface floors (not carpeting) and no cloth upholstery. Other office areas should be kept clean and dust-free.

Infection Control Procedures Upon Completion of Dental Treatment

At the completion of a dental treatment, the dental assistant should remove handpieces and tips for the HVE and air/water syringe while still gloved. He or she should then don overgloves to document information on the patient's chart or in the computer, gather radiographs, and remove the patient's napkin. After dismissing the patient, the assistant while gloved should put the handpiece, HVE, and air/water syringe back on the unit and flush them. Afterwards the handpiece and syringe are placed back on the treatment tray. Sharps are carefully placed into the sharps container, and the chair cover is removed by inversion to create a bag. This bag will contain potential infectious material within. Subsequently barriers and disposables are removed and placed within the bag. The assistant should then carry the treatment tray to the sterilizing area before removing gloves and putting them in the bag, which is properly disposed of. At the end, the assistant should wash his or her hands.

Chapter Quiz

Ready to see how well you retained what you just read? Scan the QR code to go directly to the chapter quiz interface for this study guide. If you're using a computer, simply visit the bonus page at **mometrix.com/bonus948/danbcda** and click the Chapter Quizzes link.

Prevent Cross-Contamination During Procedures (ICE)

Transform passive reading into active learning! After immersing yourself in this chapter, put your comprehension to the test by taking a quiz. The insights you gained will stay with you longer this way. Scan the QR code to go directly to the chapter quiz interface for this study guide. If you're using a computer, simply visit the bonus page at **mometrix.com/bonus948/danbcda** and click the Chapter Quizzes link.

Maintaining Aseptic Conditions

ASEPTIC TECHNIQUES

Aseptic techniques are any procedures that reduce or eliminate the dissemination of pathogens. One of the most basic aseptic techniques is ensuring that one touches as few surfaces as possible with the fingers (gloved or ungloved) that might be coated with blood or saliva. This can be accomplished by making sure that surfaces are covered or cleaned and disinfected. Gloves are used but changed every time they are contaminated or the professional leaves the chair side. The professional should avoid touching his or her person with contaminated, gloved hands. Another important aseptic technique is the reduction of dental aerosols and spatter produced by use of handpieces, ultrasonic scalers and the air/water syringe. This can be accomplished through methods such as the use of high-volume evacuation (HVE) and a rubber dam. The HVE system should also be cleaned by flushing with detergent or detergent-disinfectant combination at the conclusion of each day and emptying the trap periodically. The rubber dam isolates the area being worked on and minimizes saliva. Other techniques include pre-procedure mouth rinsing, use of disposables whenever possible, and effective housekeeping.

GENERAL METHODS AND ASEPTIC TECHNIQUES OF INFECTION CONTROL PROGRAM

Standard precautions should always be followed. Other general methods include proper hand hygiene, avoidance of activities like eating and applying cosmetics in the area, having the patient rinse his or her mouth before a procedure, measures to diminish splattering of blood or saliva, never using disposables for more than one patient, and checking of sterilized instrument packages prior to use. Dental water is an important consideration. It should contain less than 500 CFU/mL of heterotrophic bacteria. It should not be used to irrigate surgical sites. Its anti-retraction valves should always be in order, and all devices connected to it should be flushed for 20 to 30 seconds between patients.

DISINFECTION

Disinfection is the use of chemical agents called disinfectants that can destroy most microorganisms but not the more resistant bacteria or fungal spores. Disinfectants are generally used at room temperature to reduce microbial load on surfaces. Chemicals that are used for disinfection include agents such as iodophors, phenolics, sodium hypochlorite, alcohol, and quaternary ammonium compounds. Some high-level disinfectants such as glutaraldehyde can also be used for liquid chemical sterilization if used for prolonged periods. Unlike some methods of sterilization, there is no way of monitoring the effectiveness of surface disinfection.

DISINFECTION AND CLEANING OF FINAL TREATMENT ROOM

After a patient has been treated and dismissed, and other post-treatment procedures are performed, the dental assistant should wash his or her hands and don utility gloves. Surfaces are then **disinfected** with an intermediate level disinfectant following an established routine. Iodophors, sodium hypochlorite (bleach), and phenolics qualify as intermediate level disinfectants. All necessary solutions, towels, and 4×4 gauze squares

are carried into the area. All surfaces are sprayed with the disinfectant, wiped to get rid of debris, sprayed again and left for about 10 minutes, and then wiped off again. Alternatively, gauze squares can be sprayed with disinfectant and used to wipe down the surfaces. It is important to remember to disinfect surfaces like the chair adjustments, amalgam cradle, view box, and curing light all of which are potentially contaminated.

CLINICAL CONTACT SURFACES AND HOUSEKEEPING SURFACES

Clinical contact surfaces are any surfaces predisposed to contamination during patient care activities. They might be touched with gloved hands during patient care or in some other way become contaminated with potentially infectious materials. Examples of clinical contact surfaces are as follows: various controls and switches, countertops, hoses connected to the handpiece or evacuator or air/water syringe, various parts of the x-ray unit, the chair back or headrest, the handle and tip of the light curing instrument, mirror and faucet handles, and shade guides. Some clinical contact surfaces such as controls, handles, and the light curing tip should be protected with surface covers while others must be precleaned and disinfected.

Housekeeping surfaces are those surfaces that do not generally come in contact with contaminated hands or devices such as floors, walls, and basin. These surfaces can be treated at the conclusion of the day while clinical contact surfaces need to be addressed more immediately.

PRECLEANING AND DISINFECTION SURFACES

Surfaces that are non-electrical, smooth, and easily reached are appropriately treated with precleaning and disinfection as opposed to using surface covers. Precleaning reduces the bioburden. Soap and water or preferably a surface cleaner/disinfectant is used for the precleaning step. There are two accepted methods for precleaning and disinfection. Utility gloves and personal protective equipment should be worn during either process. The first method is the **spray-wipe-spray technique** in which the surface is initially sprayed with cleaning/disinfecting agent, thoroughly wiped with paper towels, resprayed with disinfectant agent, and left moist for about 10 minutes. This method can be done using paper towels or gauze pads saturated with the disinfecting agent instead of spraying. The other method is the **wipe-discard-wipe technique** in which a disinfectant towelette from a dispenser is used to wipe the surface, discarded, another towelette is used to wipe the surface again and discarded, and the surface is allowed to dry. In either case, if the surface is wet when needed for patient care, it can be wiped dry. Disinfectant should be rinsed or wiped off surfaces that will come in contact with the patient's mouth or skin.

INTERMEDIATE-LEVEL DISINFECTANTS

Intermediate-level disinfectants are used for disinfection of clinical contact surfaces and noncritical surfaces laden with visible blood. The most commonly used intermediate-level agents are chlorine compounds, iodophors, alcohols, synthetic phenolics, and quaternary ammonium compounds. Theoretically these should only be used in forms that are EPA-registered and claim to have tuberculocidal activity. The main chloride compound used is sodium hypochlorite as part of an EPA-registered product, or commercial bleach diluted freshly 1:10 to 1:100. Iodophors are iodine-containing compounds. They may be corrosive and/or staining and generally require dilution before use. Ethyl or isopropyl alcohols are usually used in combination these days with phenolics. Phenol or carbolic acid is quite toxic, but synthetic phenolics incorporating phenol are not; they usually come in combination with another phenolic or an alcohol. Quaternary ammonium compounds are cationic detergents and are only tuberculocidal, intermediate-level agents when in combination with alcohol, which augments antimicrobial activity.

DECONTAMINATION OF ALL EQUIPMENT IN PATIENT CARE AREA

First of all, disposables should be used and discarded afterwards whenever possible, regardless of whether or not the equipment penetrates soft tissue or tooth structure. Non-disposable instruments that penetrate soft tissue or tooth structure should be cleaned, packaged, and heat sterilized after use. Non-disposable instruments that are used in the mouth but do not pierce soft teeth tissue or tooth structure should be treated in various ways depending on whether they can be covered and whether they are heat stable. If they can be covered, that is the method of choice. Items such as these include the handle of a mouth mirror or a light-curing tip. If they cannot be covered, the approach depends on whether or not they are heat stable. Items that can withstand high temperatures should be packaged and heat sterilized while those that are heat-sensitive should be sterilized in a liquid sterilant, rinsed, and packaged. Equipment in the area that is susceptible to contamination via splatter or touch but not directly used in the patient's mouth should be heat sterilized if possible. If the equipment cannot be sterilized, it should be covered to thwart contamination or cleaned and disinfected. If there is little chance of contamination of room items, for example the walls, they can simply be cleaned.

Single-Use Devices

Single-use devices, also called disposable devices, are intended to be used once and disposed of immediately after, therefore reprocessing (post-use disinfection/sterilization) is not required. These devices should be labeled as single-use or disposable on their packaging, but in the case that a device does not contain any label, it should be treated as a single-use device. Generally, single-use devices come in sterile packaging. This packaging should be opened onto the sterile dental tray after the dental assistant has performed hand hygiene and donned the proper personal protective equipment. If the item falls to the floor or onto any object outside of the sterile tray, it should be disposed of and replaced with a new device. Single-use devices should then be disposed of after use according to state regulations based on the type of fluid it came in touch with during the procedure, and the nature of its materials (for instance, sharps should be disposed of in a sharps container).

Single Unit Doses

Single unit dose packages contain enough medication for a single use, and are meant to be used as a means of minimizing medication errors and cross-contamination from multiple uses. They also are meant to enhance the efficiency of medication administration. Single unit doses come in sterilized packaging that should be opened onto the sterile tray after performing hand hygiene and donning the appropriate PPE. The medication should then be disposed of according to the disposal instructions on the drug label.

Handpiece Asepsis

The inside and outside of handpieces and their attachments must be cleaned and sterilized between patients as they may contain patient materials. While still attached to the hose after patient treatment, the handpiece should be wiped free of visible debris. High-speed handpieces should also be flushed 20 to 30 seconds into the vacuum line or some receptacle like the sink or a container. The handpiece is then removed from the hose and externally cleaned, rinsed, and dried. Then the internal parts should be cleaned and lubricated per manufacturer's instructions. The handpiece is reconnected to the air/water system for flushing the excess out as before. Surplus lubricant on the outside is wiped off. At that point, the handpiece should be packaged and sterilized as directed by the manufacturer. Note that some handpieces cannot withstand extremely high temperatures such as those used in dry heat sterilizers. The handpiece is then dried, cooled, and retained in the packaging until ready for use. Some handpieces need post-sterilization lubrication; if so, the bag is opened using aseptic technique, lubricant is squirted into it, the hose is attached, and excess lubricant is extruded.

Surface Covers

If surface covers are impermeable to fluids and thick enough to resist tearing, they are appropriate for protection against surface contamination by blood, saliva, or other possibly contaminated fluids. Various types of plastic covers will generally meet the requirements. Specially fitted covers, plastic sheets and plastic bags are used in various combinations. Surface covers should be put on before surfaces are exposed to contamination. Otherwise, the surface must first be precleaned and disinfected while gloved, the gloves discarded, and hands washed before placing the covers. The surface covers should be removed with gloved hands at the end of patient care or other activities. Care should be taken not to touch the surface under the cover during removal, and if the surface is touched, precleaning and disinfection must be done as above. Used covers can be thrown into the standard trash unless local legislation deems them regulated waste. Afterwards, contaminated gloves should be discarded, hands washed, and new surface covers applied before the next patient. Surface covers are not appropriate for some surfaces such as the bracket table, countertops, and mirror hands, all of which are usually precleaned and disinfected.

CONCENTRATIONS AND TYPES OF MICROORGANISMS IN DENTAL UNIT WATER

General **water** is supplied to a dental office by municipal facilities. At the point of origin, the water is non-sterile but low in microbial growth, typically from 0 to 500 CFU/mL. CFU stands for a colony-forming unit, a single or small number of bacteria that can develop further. The same water that is supplied to the rest of the office (faucets, etc.) is also delivered to the dental unit except that the hoses for the latter are narrower inviting microbial growth. Typical dental unit water in untreated systems contains over 100,000 CFU/mL and often much higher levels of microbial growth. Numerous species of bacteria derived from both the water and patient's mouths have been identified in dental unit water. Some of these bacteria are opportunistic and pathogenic. A number of species of fungi and protozoa have also been recognized in dental water, but those identified have low pathogenicity.

MICROORGANISMS IN DENTAL WATER THAT ARE OF MOST CONCERN

The microorganisms found in dental water of most concern are various species of *Pseudomonas, Legionella pneumophila,* and nontuberculous species of *Mycobacterium. Pseudomonas* species often thrive in the water supply and are opportunistic and pathogenic. Two in particular are of concern, **P. aeruginosa**, which can cause urinary tract and wound infection, pneumonia, and possibly septicemia and **P. cepacia**, which causes respiratory problems in patients with cystic fibrosis. *Legionella pneumophila* (as well as other species) is a water-borne bacterium that can cause respiratory issues and to a lesser extent wound infections and Pontiac fever. Other opportunistic pathogens have been identified in dental water units in addition to those mentioned. In addition, studies suggest that the levels of endotoxins, toxic substances released from the cell walls of dead gram-negative bacteria, can be higher than desirable.

BIOFILM

Biofilm is a mass or layer of microorganisms directly attached to a surface with moisture exposure. There are numerous types of biofilm in nature, but the ones of interest in dentistry are dental plaque and biofilm attached to the interior of a dental unit water line. In a water line some bacterial growth is free-floating or planktonic. Those bacteria that affix to a surface, in this case the internal walls of the water line, form cell surface polymers called exopolysaccharides or glycocalyx polymers, which enlarge as new bacterial cells are recruited from the planktonic portion forming a slimy surface biofilm.

FORMATION OF DENTAL UNIT WATER LINE BIOFILM

A number of factors contribute to **formation of dental unit water line biofilm**. Water within the tubing stagnates when the unit is not being used. The tubing feeding the unit is small in diameter which means there is a large surface to volume ratio facilitating bacterial contact and attachment to the surface. Many of these waterborne bacteria have characteristics that encourage surface attachment. They are always present in some concentration, and as they attach to the walls of the line they multiply, increasing the biofilm mass. In addition, other bacteria can enter the dental unit water line from the air, at water line openings, or through retraction through the handpiece or air/water syringe. Water surging past the attached biofilm can acquire bacteria from the biofilm passing it into the handpiece, air/water syringe, and other equipment.

DENTAL UNIT WATER QUALITY
MONITORING QUALITY

If measures are being taken to improve the quality of dental unit water, their effectiveness should be monitored at baseline and at regular intervals. Water samples are taken and either shipped cold to a facility for testing (such as a microbiology laboratory or dental company) or tested in-house. The testing involves neutralizing the water sample in diluted chlorine, inoculating it onto a specific type of agar plate called R2A and then incubating the plate at room temperature for a minimum of a week before determining bacterial counts. Dental unit water quality measures are considered effective if the bacterial counts are less than 500 colony-forming units (CFU)/mL. However, this testing is only approximate because the relationship between the amount of biofilm on the water line and the concentration of bacteria in a particular water sample has not been established.

IMPROVING QUALITY

One approach to improving dental water quality is to disconnect from the municipal water supply and set up an independent water reservoir for delivery of dental treatment water. Another tactic is to use decontaminating and antimicrobial agents in independent water reservoirs. Depending on the agent, they can be flushed periodically thru the water lines or put directly into the treatment water. Municipal water systems use other means of destroying microorganisms such as ultraviolet light or heating. Placing an antimicrobial filter in the line just ahead of where the water enters the handpiece or air/water syringe can filter out free-floating microorganisms and, in some instances, endotoxin. Filters must be changed regularly. All devices used must be FDA-cleared, and all chemicals utilized must be registered by the EPA. FDA-approved sterile water delivery systems, which completely circumvent the dental unit lines, should be used for surgical procedures.

BOIL WATER NOTICE

A boil water notice is a warning issued by authorities to boil municipal water before using it for drinking, bathing, or healthcare-related activities. Boil water notices are released by the water company or health officials because some type of problem has occurred in the municipal water treatment plant or water distribution system. Implications of an issued boil water notice in the dental office are that municipal water should not be used for any sort of patient treatment or handwashing. Offices that use an independent water reservoir for the dental unit can still treat patients but must find some other means of handwashing. If they normally use municipal water for the dental unit, syringe irrigation with other water (for example distilled) must be used or patient care must be suspended. Once the boil water notice has been lifted, the dental water lines must be disinfected and flushed per manufacturer's or local authority's instructions or if unknown for 5 minutes before use.

INDEPENDENT WATER RESERVOIR

Use of an independent water reservoir to deliver treatment water, circumventing the municipal water system, is one way of improving the quality of dental unit water. The unit is disconnected from the municipal water system and the independent water reservoir is attached instead for water delivery. Initially on three consecutive evenings cleaner/disinfectant is added to a bottle, the bottle is connected to the dental water line and pressurized to flush the cleaner through the system. Then it is left that way overnight. The subsequent morning the bottle is taken off, the pickup line rinsed, and another bottle with water is connected and run through the same type of flushing. After three sets of cleaner followed by water flushing, a clean bottle with distilled water is connected to the unit and pressurized for use. Distilled water has been boiled to reduce microbial counts. After each patient day, the water reservoir with distilled water is emptied and put back on the unit and pressurized to blow out excess water. The next morning, a clean bottle with distilled treatment water is attached and pressurized for use. Once a week, flushing with cleaner/disinfectant (as described above) is done once before connecting a new treatment bottle.

BACTERIA THAT CAN BE TRANSMITTED VIA DENTAL UNIT WATER

Dental units and hoses harbor waterborne bacteria and viruses. Some of the bacteria affix to the inside of the water lines forming a biofilm, which can then be discharged upon use. While as many as 40 species of bacteria might be present, the two of most concern are *Legionella pneumophila* and *Pseudomonas aeruginosa*. **L. pneumophila** causes Legionnaires' disease (lung infections characterized by pneumonia) through inhalation of contaminated water or drawing in of bacteria already colonizing the oropharyngeal region. The agent can also produce the flu-like Pontiac fever. The other waterborne bacterium of interest is **P. aeruginosa**, which can generate oral infections in susceptible individuals. Dental units also may have low levels of oral bacteria in their water supply due to retraction. The CDC and the ADA suggest that dental unit water should not be employed for irrigation of exposed surgical sites and that lines should be rinsed out first thing in the morning and between patients.

LABORATORY AND RADIOGRAPHIC ASEPSIS

The primary consideration in terms of **laboratory asepsis** is that any item that has been contaminated with oral fluids should ideally be sterilized; if that is impossible, the item should at least be rinsed and disinfected prior to being sent to the dental laboratory. In turn, items sent from the dental laboratory to the office should be disinfected, rinsed, confirmed as such, and established as being uncontaminated before they are inserted into a patient's mouth. The major tactic in terms of **radiographic asepsis** is the covering of x-ray films and digital x-ray sensors with plastic surface covers before they are inserted into the patient's mouth. If films or sensors are not covered with plastic barriers, then they must be rinsed and disinfected or handled aseptically after removal. Also, if daylight loaders are used, then caution must be exercised to avoid contact between contaminated gloves or films and the loader's sleeves.

INFECTION CONTROL PROCEDURES DURING RADIOGRAPHIC EXPOSURE

The dental assistant should wash his or her hands and place all barriers, which are generally various plastic covers or bags, on all equipment and possibly other surfaces. Alternatively, surfaces could be disinfected if shorting of equipment is not an issue. Barriers such as sandwich bags should be placed on either side of the lead-lined x-ray room door and switches. Often chairs are covered as well. Dental films to be exposed should be placed within FDA-cleared plastic, protective barrier pouches. If digital radiographic sensors are utilized for digital radiography instead of films, they should be protected with disposable plastic covers (preferably FDA-cleared). Generally, complete personal protective equipment is donned when the patient is seated. Disposable or heat-tolerant film holders that can be sterilized between patients should be used. After each x-ray is exposed, it is placed in a disposable cup before transportation for processing. Barriers and gloves are removed after patient procedures are completed; they are generally not considered regulated medical waste but local regulations for disposal should be considered. Exposed surfaces should be disinfected.

INFECTION CONTROL PROCEDURES FOR PROCESSING OF RADIOGRAPHS

Exposed x-ray films should be conveyed to the darkroom in disposable cups or within a paper towel. There the dental assistant (wearing disposable gloves) should drop each film out of its packet onto an uncontaminated, disposable paper towel or into a cup. After all are removed, he or she then discards the packets and gloves, washes hands, and starts the processing procedure. For processing, gloves should be worn anytime films are contaminated. So for manual processing, gloves should be donned if the films were not protected during exposure with removable protective film pouches, but they are also generally necessary because films are dunked into solutions. If automatic processing with a daylight loader is done, films must first be placed inside the loader and unwrapped and dropped into another cup or paper towel inside the loader while gloved (powder-free gloves recommended). The waste is collected in another cup, and the dental assistant then inserts each opened film into the automatic processor with bare hands. Alternatively, he or she might initially use overgloves, which are removed for insertion.

LABORATORY ASEPSIS DURING OPERATION OF DENTAL LATHE

A dental lathe is used in the dental laboratory to grind, polish, and blast prostheses and impressions for proper presentation. Its use creates many opportunities for injuries as well as the spread of microorganisms. Protective eyewear, preferably with a front Plexiglas shield, should always be worn when using a dental lathe. The room should be adequately ventilated, and mask use is suggested as well. The spread of infectious agents can be facilitated by techniques such as the following: use of the lathe through hand holes to create a barrier, sterilization or disinfection of all accessories, disinfection of the unit twice daily, and utilization of new pumice and pan liners for each item. Polishing agents should always be discarded if unused, not returned to their source. Disposable polishing attachments should be used if possible; if not, they should be sterilized or disinfected between uses as directed.

INFECTION CONTROL FOR DIGITAL RADIOGRAPHY

Reusable intraoral sensors are utilized with digital radiography. Infection control depends on the type of sensor used. A CCD or charge-coupled device sensor and its attached cable should be covered with a plastic barrier to prevent contamination. CCD sensors are heat-sensitive and should never be heat sterilized, but they can be disinfected by the spray-wipe-spray method if contamination occurs. Complementary metal-oxide semiconductors with active pixel sensors should be treated similarly. Photostimulable phosphor plate sensors must be covered thoroughly with plastic barriers as they cannot withstand heat sterilization or disinfection. Computers should either be used with clean hands or, if contaminated, swabbed with disinfectant wipes. Cameras cannot be decontaminated and therefore should be covered with plastic or used only with clean hands. Computer-aided design or manufacturing devices (CAD/CAMS) have a small camera and wire that is placed in a patient's mouth; here manufacturer's directions for decontamination should be followed.

Disposing of Biohazard Materials

WASTE GENERATED IN DENTAL OFFICE

Medical waste is any solid waste produced during diagnosis, treatment, or immunization in some type of healthcare facility. Most medical waste is not infectious and is not regulated. Items that have touched blood or other bodily fluids are considered contaminated waste, and wastes that can place a human being or the environment at risk are deemed hazardous. Infectious waste is the portion of medical waste that is capable of inducing an infectious disease. Infectious waste is a regulated medical waste governed by the OSHA Bloodborne Pathogens Standard. There are 5 types of OSHA regulated medical waste, all of which can be found in dentistry. These 5 categories are

- Blood or other potentially infectious material (OPIM) such as saliva in liquid or semiliquid form
- Contaminated items that could discharge blood or OPIM if compressed
- Articles caked with dried blood or OPIM that could liberate infectious materials
- Contaminated sharps
- Pathologic or microbiologic wastes that contain OPIM or blood

MANAGEMENT OF REGULATED WASTE

Regulated waste includes sharps, nonsharps waste, liquids to be disposed of, and human tissues (such as teeth). Each type of waste should be handled, processed, and stored in a proper manner, and containers should be clearly labeled with a biohazard symbol, color coding, and if necessary, name and address. Sharps are a major concern. They should be handled carefully. Sharps containers should be readily available and never overfilled. Specimens containing human tissue or any bodily fluid including blood should be put in appropriate containers and clearly labeled with a biohazard symbol and color coding. Regulations regarding processing of regulated waste should be followed prior to their being discarded or transported to a disposal facility. Records should be kept documenting the treatment, transport, and disposal of regulated waste.

BLOOD IN LIQUID OR SEMILIQUID FORM

Blood in free-flowing liquid or semiliquid form is regarded as an infectious and regulated medical waste. The Centers for Disease Control (CDC) recommends that blood, suctioned fluids, and other liquid waste be decanted carefully down a drain connected to a sanitary sewer system. This method of disposal should only be employed if it is in compliance with local and state regulations as well. There may be restrictions aimed at minimizing the volume of blood in the sewage system. If blood is disposed of in the water system, daily rinsing of sink traps and evacuation lines with a nonbleach disinfectant and water is recommended.

PATHOGENIC WASTE

In the dental office, pathogenic waste consists of biopsy specimens, excised tissues, and most often, extracted teeth that are not returned to the patient. All of these are considered OSHA regulated wastes that are potentially infectious. They should be placed in leakproof, color-coded containers, either biohazard bags or, in the case of teeth, possibly sharps containers. After collection, pathogenic waste should be decontaminated or neutralized in a steam autoclave or chemical vapor sterilizer before boxing and discarding the treated waste according to local regulations. Extracted teeth that contain amalgam restorations should be disinfected with full-strength glutaraldehyde or another sterilizing chemical instead of any type of heat sterilization. CDC recommendations also permit return of extracted teeth to the patient.

SHARPS SAFETY AND DISPOSAL

Sharps (for example, needles, scalpel blades, and broken glass) are regarded as infectious and regulated as medical waste. OSHA mandates that disposable sharps be put in sharps containers directly after use. Sharps containers must be clearly-marked (biohazard symbol, usually color-coded red), leakproof, closable, and puncture-resistant. There are many ways to make sharps use safer. In particular, when using injection needles, one should either use some sort of protective cap-holding contrivance or the cap sheath should be replaced using the one-handed scoop method. Other safety measures include organizing sharp instruments and handpieces with tips or burs pointing away from the operator, filling sharps containers to a maximum of three-quarters full, and use of tongs or pliers to pick up sharps or disengage burs. When sharps containers are full, they can be relayed to waste handlers or, if allowed by state law, decontaminated onsite in a steam sterilizer. In the latter case, "sterilizable" sharps containers should be at most ¾ full. They are placed upright with vents open into the sterilizer and autoclaved for 40 to 60 minutes, cooled, closed, labeled, and disposed of in a manner allowed locally.

Chapter Quiz

Ready to see how well you retained what you just read? Scan the QR code to go directly to the chapter quiz interface for this study guide. If you're using a computer, simply visit the bonus page at **mometrix.com/bonus948/danbcda** and click the Chapter Quizzes link.

Instrument/Device Processing (ICE)

Transform passive reading into active learning! After immersing yourself in this chapter, put your comprehension to the test by taking a quiz. The insights you gained will stay with you longer this way. Scan the QR code to go directly to the chapter quiz interface for this study guide. If you're using a computer, simply visit the bonus page at **mometrix.com/bonus948/danbcda** and click the Chapter Quizzes link.

Processing Reusable Instruments

INSTRUMENT PROCESSING

Instrument processing programs should be instituted in every dental unit using the following guidelines. Reusable sharps should be carefully placed after use in labeled containers (biohazard symbol, color coded) that can be secured for transport. There should be a main instrument processing area with separate sections for cleaning and decontamination, packaging, sterilization, and storage. Handpieces and their attachments and reusable instruments must be sterilized between patients. Contaminated instruments should be mechanically cleaned, rinsed, dried, packaged for sterilization, and sterilized using the appropriate technique. Most instruments should be sterilized in a steam sterilizer or autoclave, but if they are more heat-sensitive, a low-temperature process such as soaking in glutaraldehyde can be used. Sterilizers should undergo spore testing weekly (and records kept) as well as monitored for correct timing and temperature. Packages should have an attached temperature strip that indicates completeness of sterilization, and they should be allowed to dry before handling. If stored, they should be marked with sterilization date.

PROCESSING STEPS

There are seven steps involved in **preparing contaminated instruments to be reused**. They are as follows:

1. Brief holding or presoaking of the contaminated instruments in detergent, water, or enzyme solution to keep attached debris from drying
2. Precleaning to reduce the bioburden, surface microbial or organic material, before decontamination, generally through use of an ultrasonic cleaner
3. Corrosion control measures, drying, and/or lubrication to moderate potential damage to the instrument
4. Packaging of the instruments to preserve sterility after sterilization
5. Sterilization or disinfection with a high-level agent to destroy all microorganisms present
6. Biological, chemical and/or mechanical monitoring of the sterilization process to ensure the sterilizer is performing properly
7. Correct handling of the processed instruments, including procedures like drying and cooling and proper techniques for storage, distribution, and opening of the instrument packages

TRANSPORTING OF CONTAMINATED INSTRUMENTS

Reusable dental instruments that are to be reprocessed must be stored and **transported safely** in order to prevent cross contamination. These instruments include those classified as critical because they penetrate or touch open tissue (such as files, surgical burs, and scaler tips) as well as semicritical items that contact mucous membranes (such as rubber dam frames and mouth props). Procedure trays should be in the operatory, and contaminated instruments placed in the tray. During transport to the area set aside for cleaning, disinfecting, and sterilizing, the container should be covered and taken directly to the receiving area. If the instruments cannot be immediately processed, they are usually placed in a holding solution to prevent body fluids (blood, saliva) from drying on the instruments. Precleaning is a critical step prior to sterilization to removal all bioburden, which may interfere with the sterilization process.

RECEIVING ITEMS IN/FROM DENTAL LABORATORY

All items **received and worked on in the dental laboratory** are to be considered potentially infectious. There should be a specific receiving area for these items. It should be covered with impermeable paper and contain hand washing facilities and good ventilation. All articles received, generally prostheses or impressions, must be disinfected here before any other laboratory work is done. The technician should always wear personal protective equipment and use an EPA-registered intermediate- or high-level disinfectant. The disinfectant method is dependent on the type of material. If prostheses are heavily laden with calculus or adhesive, they can be precleaned before disinfection by placing them in a zippered plastic bag with disinfectant and using the ultrasonic cleaner. Completed prostheses are generally sent from the laboratory in containers containing mouth rinse. They must be disinfected again (at the chairside if possible) before use by rinsing them in tap water followed by a suitable disinfectant. If an impression cannot be immersed, it can be sprayed with disinfectant and wrapped in a saturated paper towel. Items that are heat-tolerant should be sterilized.

CDC CATEGORIZATION OF PATIENT CARE ITEMS

The Centers for Disease Control and Prevention (CDC) places patient care items into one of three categories in terms of how they must be processed after contamination.

- The first category is **critical items**, which are items that pierce soft tissue, touch bone, or come in contact with the bloodstream or normally sterile oral tissue. These include items such as scalers, blades, dental burs, and surgical instruments. The CDC mandates critical items must be cleaned and then sterilized using heat.
- **Semicritical patient care items** are those that come in contact with mucous membranes but do not penetrate them, or that come in contact with bone, the bloodstream, or normally sterile oral tissue. Semicritical items include things like the mouth mirror, reusable impression trays, and handpieces. They should be processed just like critical items, using cleaning followed by heat sterilization unless they are heat-sensitive. With heat-sensitive items, a high-level disinfectant can be used.
- Lastly, **noncritical items** are those that only come in contact with intact skin, such as a blood pressure cuff or stethoscope. These items should be cleaned and disinfected using a low-or intermediate-level disinfectant, depending on whether or not there is visible blood on them.

DECONTAMINATION OF INSTRUMENTS OR OPERATORY SURFACES

Personal protective equipment should be worn during decontamination of instruments or operatory surfaces. Instruments should be decontaminated prior to servicing or shipment, with areas of inadequate decontamination clearly marked. Any surfaces including the operatory that are part of patient treatment should be covered with protective barriers which are changed between patients or cleaned and disinfected after each patient. Any reusable containers in contact with bodily fluids should also be cleaned and disinfected. There should be a written schedule for work area decontamination. The patient care room should not be carpeted or have cloth coverings anywhere. Its floors, walls, and sinks should be cleaned regularly, and window treatments should be cleaned when perceptibly dusty or dirty.

CHEMICALS THAT CAN KILL MICROORGANISMS

There are four types of chemicals that can destroy microorganisms. Two of these types are only effective in or on the body. These are antibiotics, which are effective only systemically or topically, and antiseptics, which are chemicals that effective in killing microorganisms on the skin or other body surfaces but should not be used systemically. The other two types are utilized only on inanimate surfaces, sterilants or disinfectants. A sterilant is a chemical that can kill all microorganisms on inanimate objects including most bacterial spores. Disinfectants are chemicals that can destroy various types of microorganisms on environmental surfaces or inanimate objects but usually not high numbers of bacterial spores.

DISINFECTING OR STERILIZING CHEMICALS

The Centers for Disease Control classifies disinfectants by their **spectrum of activity against microbial agents**. The organization groups sterilants and high-level disinfectants together. Both destroy all microorganisms on submerged, inanimate, heat-sensitive items but only sterilants also destroy most bacterial spores. The chemicals falling into both these categories are glutaraldehyde, glutaraldehyde-phenate, hydrogen peroxide with or without peracetic acid, and peracetic acid. Another chemical, ortho-phthalaldehyde, is strictly a high-level disinfectant. Intermediate-level disinfectants can kill vegetative bacteria, most fungi and viruses, and inactivate *Mycobacterium tuberculosis* var *bovis* on surfaces. EPA-registered hospital disinfectants claiming tuberculocidal activity fall into this category. They contain phenolics, iodophors, and quaternary ammonium compounds plus alcohol, bromides, or chlorides. Low-level disinfectants destroy vegetative bacteria and some fungi and viruses but are not tuberculocidal. Low-level hospital disinfectants are generally quaternary ammonium compounds; they should be used only for housekeeping surfaces unless they claim reactivity against HIV and HBV.

TERMS FOUND ON LABELING FOR ANTIMICROBIAL PRODUCTS

Terms with the suffix "**-cidal**" indicate that the agent has at least some ability to kill a particular type of microorganism. Thus, the terms bactericidal, virucidal, or fungicidal mean the agent can destroy at least some bacteria, viruses, or fungi respectively. More specific activity is indicated by the terms such as "tuberculocidal" or "sporicidal," which refer to the ability to kill *Mycobacterium tuberculosis* var. *bovis* or bacterial spores respectively. An agent that is sporicidal is essentially a sterilant. Labels often specify the genus and species of microorganisms they can kill in addition to other information about the product. If a label brands the product as a hospital disinfectant, it indicates that it has been demonstrated to destroy the bacterial species *Staphylococcus aureus, Salmonella choleraesuis,* and *Pseudomonas aeruginosa.*

WARNING LABELS USED ON POTENTIALLY INFECTIOUS CONTAINERS

Regulated waste, refrigerators, freezers, sharps, or any other containers used for transport must be labeled with the word "**biohazard**" on a fluorescent orange or orange-red label. There is usually also a **biohazard symbol** on the label made up of interconnected circular patterns. Individual unlabeled containers of potentially infectious materials can be placed within labeled ones. If employees are clearly informed, alternatives can include red bags or containers. Contaminated equipment being transported must be labeled as well, including the area of contamination. Contaminated laundry that is sent offsite should generally be bagged and labeled similarly unless the laundry facility is known to use universal precautions (they should still be clearly identified). Contaminated sharps need to be discarded into leak proof, puncture-resistant, closable, and red and/or "biohazard" labeled containers. Other regulated waste that might be infectious should be put in leakproof, closable, color-coded or labeled containers such as biohazard bags.

STERILIZATION

Sterilization is a means of killing all microorganisms present. There are three methods of sterilization applicable to dentistry. These are sterilization using heat, gas, or liquid chemicals. **Heat sterilization** is performed in a steam sterilizer or autoclave at 250-375 °F. **Gas sterilizers** generally use ethylene oxide at a lower temperature of 72-140 °F but for a longer time period; they are uncommon in dental settings. Articles that will not withstand heat are usually subjected to liquid chemical sterilization at room temperature. **Liquid chemical sterilants**, also classified as high-level disinfectants, include agents such as glutaraldehyde and hydrogen peroxide often in combination. Heat sterilization is the most effective method because if the sterilizer is working properly it can kill more resistant microorganisms such as *Mycobacterium* species as well as highly-resistant protein products such as bacterial endospores and fungal spores. The standard for biological monitoring of a sterilizer is whether it in fact can kill bacterial endospores. At present it is difficult to monitor effectiveness of liquid chemical sterilization.

STERILITY ASSURANCE

Sterility assurance is the practice of measures to ensure that sterility of items processed through a sterilizer is achieved and maintained. These measures include suitable instrument packaging, the sterilization process, proper storage of sterilized packages, and use of monitoring procedures. A sterility assurance program can be instituted by selecting the correct procedure(s), developing a detailed written protocol for performance, including these protocols in employee training, and setting up biologic, chemical and mechanical monitoring systems of the performance. It is also advisable to set up a system of measuring results.

PRECLEANING CONTAMINATED INSTRUMENTS PRIOR TO STERILIZATION

Most contaminated instruments are **presoaked** in water, detergent, or enzyme solution directly in the basket in which they will be precleaned. This step removes gross debris. The subsequent precleaning step reduces the bioburden of microbes and organic components. The FDA approves use of ultrasonic cleaners or instrument washers for precleaning. Manual scrubbing of instruments at this juncture is not recommended. **Ultrasonic cleaners** utilize ultrasonic energy, high frequency sound waves, to remove debris. Loose instruments are placed in removable cleaning baskets or cassette racks in the cleaner, covered, and cleaned per manufacturer's instructions. There should be enough cleaning solution to cover the instruments during the process. The cleaning time is variable depending on factors like the types of instruments being cleaned and what is on them; it usually varies from 4 to 16 minutes. Afterwards, the basket or cassette rack is taken out and rinsed with tap water. The cleaning solution should be drained or disposed of daily. In larger settings, FDA-regulated instrument washers are used for precleaning; they come in bench top, floor unit, and large production versions. Utility gloves and personal protective equipment should always be worn.

PACKAGING INSTRUMENTS FOR DRY HEAT STERILIZERS

Instruments that are to be put in dry heat sterilizers can be wrapped in paper wrap, certain nylon plastic tubing, closed containers, wrappers made for perforated cassettes, or aluminum foil. Aluminum foil is not ideal as it can tear or be easily perforated, and if closed containers are used, a biological indicator must be included. Many plastic types of wrapping are unsuitable because they may char or melt. The appropriate types of wrapping for use with an unsaturated chemical sterilizer are paper wrap, paper and plastic peel pouches, and appropriately wrapped perforated cassettes. Closed containers cannot be used for chemical sterilization. Cloth wrapping is unsuitable as it absorbs chemical vapor, and certain plastics are also unsuitable as they can melt. Regardless of the sterilization process to be used, the wrapping material must be FDA-approved.

PACKAGING INSTRUMENTS FOR HEAT STERILIZATION

After presoaking, precleaning, and procedures such as drying to reduce instrument damage, the instruments are packaged for sterilization. All instrument packaging is regulated. Packaged instruments are medical devices and packaging must be FDA-approved. Instruments that are to be heat sterilized in a steam autoclave can be packaged in paper wrap and sealed with autoclave tape, placed within special nylon plastic tubing and heat sealed or taped, or put in self-sealing peel pouches with paper and plastic sides. If functional groups of instruments are being sterilized, the whole cassette can be wrapped. Heat sterilization precludes use of closed containers, cloth, and certain plastics. The envelope wrapping technique is often suggested if heavy paper is used. The instruments are placed in the center of the paper diagonal to the edges, and an envelope is created by folding up the bottom, then each side, and finally a top flap followed by sealing with autoclave tape (a mechanical monitor). All packages should have some form of monitoring included.

TREATMENT OF CONTAMINATED TREATMENT TRAY

At the completion of a dental treatment and associated duties, the dental assistant brings the contaminated treatment tray into the sterilization center. Utility gloves, protective eyewear, and possibly a mask are worn while dealing with the contaminated treatment tray in this area. The contaminated instruments are submerged in a disinfecting holding solution if not sterilized immediately. Sharps and disposables should be properly discarded, including into biohazardous waste if appropriate. When ready to perform sterilization, the assistant first cleans the instruments in an ultrasonic cleaner for approximately 3 to 10 minutes, rinses, dries, and bags

them. The bagged instruments are tagged with indicator tape and placed into a sterilizer (usually steam under pressure). The high-speed handpiece should be rinsed with water or isopropyl alcohol and lubricated before bagging. The tray and many of the other items can simply be disinfected by the spray, wipe, spray again, and leave for 10 minutes rewipe method. The area is cleaned before removing the utility gloves, washing, and drying the hands. When indicated, items in the sterilizer are removed with forceps (as they are hot).

FLASH STERILIZATION

Flash sterilization is the sterilization of unwrapped items at relative short exposure times. It is not recommended by the CDC for routine procedures but can be used in emergency situations requiring short turnaround times. For example, if the dentist drops a critical instrument but still needs it, flash sterilization might be done. When instruments are sterilized unwrapped, they must be handled aseptically afterwards at all points from removal from the sterilizer to patient care use. For example, sterile tongs and transport containers should be used. Procedures for flash sterilization and transport should be carefully outlined in writing, and monitoring practices should be in place.

UNSATURATED CHEMICAL VAPOR STERILIZATION

In unsaturated chemical vapor sterilization, a chemical solution with the active ingredient of 0.23% formaldehyde and other organic compounds is heated in a closed chamber along with the instruments. Once a temperature of about 270 °F (132 °C) and vaporization of the chemical solution is achieved during this heat-up cycle, the sterilizing cycle is initiated and maintained for 20 minutes. These phases are followed by a depressurization and an optional purge cycle. A drying phase is not needed because the chemical solution vaporizes. Another advantage of this method is that instruments will not corrode because the solution contains very little water. A disadvantage is that it is crucial to have adequate ventilation because of chemical vapor smells, which can be alleviated through use of a purge system.

STEAM STERILIZERS

Steam sterilizers kill microorganisms by applying steam under pressure. High temperature is achieved quickly using steam. The three basic types of steam sterilizers or autoclaves are gravity displacement, vacuum pump (type B), and positive steam flush/pressure pulse. Each type forces air out before generating steam. Mechanisms of air removal are via a drain for gravity displacement, a vacuum for type B, and repeated cycles of steam flushes and pressure pulses for the method by the same name. Standard sterilizing conditions are for 20 to 30 minutes once a steam temperature of 250 °F (121.1 °C) is achieved, but shorter times at a higher temperature of 273 °F (134 °C) are also used. Standard small office sterilizers usually have heat-up, sterilizing, depressurization, and drying cycles. Preset sterilizing cycles of 15 or 30 minutes at 250 °F or 3 or 10 minutes at 273 °F are commonly used. Wrapped packages should be inserted on their edge without stacking and unloaded only after drying to avoid wicking, the drawing in of external microbes. Flash sterilization (described elsewhere) should be done only in emergency situations for 3 to 10 minutes at 273 °F. Hospital-type sterilizers are basically larger versions directly connected to a steam line.

DRY HEAT STERILIZATION OF INSTRUMENTS

Dry heat sterilizers heat air to kill microorganisms without generation of steam. This necessitates higher temperatures than other sterilization methods. The biggest advantage of dry heat sterilizers is that they do not corrode instruments. Static air or oven-type dry heat sterilizers have heating coils that generate heat inside through natural convection which is then transmitted to the instruments. Once an internal temperature of 320 °F (160 °C) is achieved, this temperature is maintained for 1 to 2 hours for sterilization. Other dry heat sterilizers use forced air circulation or rapid heat transfer. These sterilizers begin their sterilization cycle once 375 °F or 190 °C is attained. Wrapped or unwrapped instruments should be kept at this temperature for 12 or 6 minutes respectively. Whichever type is utilized, the chamber door must remain closed throughout sterilization to maintain the desired temperature. Timing outlines should be adhered to, and routine spore testing with *Bacillus atrophaeus* is essential.

LESS COMMON STERILIZATION METHODS

Ethylene oxide gas will kill microorganisms at low temperatures (~120 °F) and is useful for sterilizing plastic and rubber items. Its drawbacks are long sterilization times (up to 12 hours), the need for lengthy post-sterilization aeration to get rid of gas molecules, and potential toxicity. Wet items cannot be sterilized with this method.

A new but expensive technique that also uses low temperatures utilizes vaporized hydrogen peroxide gas plasma. So-called **"bead sterilizers"** have been used in the past but are not often recommended, as they are difficult to monitor and deal with aseptically. This type of sterilization involves glass beads heated to about 450 °F. Instruments to be sterilized are briefly plunged into the glass beads. Hot mineral oil baths are another antiquated and unacceptable method of sterilization.

STERILIZING HEAT-LABILE ITEMS

Heat-labile items that do not penetrate tissue (such as rubber dam frames and x-ray collimators) must be sterilized using a liquid sterilant/high-level disinfectant. For example, 2–3.4% glutaraldehyde or 7% hydrogen peroxide may be used as a sterilant/disinfectant. Gloves and other protective equipment should be worn throughout involved procedures. Sterilant solutions often have to be prepared as indicated by the manufacturer before use and may have a restricted life. These solutions should be clearly marked with the chemical name, date, and other useful information and kept in a covered container. They should also be tested for concentration periodically using a chemical test kit and replaced if necessary. The items to be sterilized should be precleaned, rinsed, and dried initially. Then they are placed into the liquid sterilant using a perforated tray or tongs, taking care that they are completely immersed in the solution. The appropriate immersion time should be indicated on the product label. Using aseptic technique (usually sterile tongs), the sterilized items are rinsed with sterile water, dried, and placed in a sterile container until use.

HANDLING INSTRUMENT PACKAGES AFTER STERILIZATION

Instrument packages that have been sterilized must be dried and cooled before use. Most steam sterilizers have some type of incorporated drying cycle, and unsaturated chemical vapor and dry heat sterilizers generate packages that are dry at the end. The drying prevents wicking, the drawing in of microbes through wet wrapping. The packages will be warm and should be cooled gradually. Sterile packages should be stored in enclosed cabinets in dry, relatively low dust areas and away from water sources. Instruments sterilized in FDA-approved packaging should be sterile at least 6 months if stored properly but a shorter turnaround time is suggested. Instruments flash sterilized unwrapped have no storage life. It is suggested that sterile instrument packages be stored away from the patient care area and transmitted to and opened at the chairside when they are needed. Packages should be checked for intactness before opening. They should be opened with clean, ungloved hands after seating the patient. If rearrangement of instruments is needed at that point, sterile tongs should be used.

PROTECTING DENTAL INSTRUMENTS FOR REUSE

One of the biggest concerns regarding protection of dental instruments is **prevention of corrosion**. Stainless steel instruments do not corrode significantly when in contact with moisture and heat, but those containing carbon steel do have this problem. Measures to reduce corrosion include cleaning as promptly as possible, avoiding long storage in water or chloride solutions, use of cleaning solutions specifically designed for cleaning the instruments, and adequate rinsing after cleaning. There are **rust inhibitors** available that can be used on carbon steel instruments before steam sterilization, and alternatively they can be processed using a dry heat or unsaturated chemical vapor sterilizer. For the latter methods, drying the items prior to sterilization also retards corrosion. A general protection method is the avoidance of contact between various instruments during cleaning.

Monitor and Maintain Sterilization Devices

COMPLETE STERILIZATION MONITORING PROGRAM

The CDC advocates that dental offices include as part of a complete sterilization monitoring program a **chemical indicator** on the inside of every package. If the internal chemical indicator is not visible, an external chemical indicator should be placed as well on every package to be processed. Every cycle should also undergo **mechanical monitoring**, which entails observation of all gauges, displays, and readouts. In addition, **biologic monitoring** in the form of spore testing appropriate for the type of sterilizer utilized should be carried out at least weekly. Documentation of each type of monitoring is essential for sterility assurance and should be kept in case problems are identified.

BIOLOGICAL MONITORING

Since it is impossible to directly test each piece of sterilized equipment for effectiveness of sterilization, the process must be monitored by biologic, chemical, and/or mechanical monitoring. Biological monitoring, also termed spore testing, basically involves putting very resistant bacteria spores into the system and later checking to see whether they have been killed. The biological indicators (BIs) generally used are strips (or vials for steam sterilization) of spores of *Geobacillus stearothermophilus* for steam autoclaves and unsaturated chemical vapor chambers, and *Bacillus atrophaeus* spore strips in dry heat or ethylene oxide sterilizers. After each sterilization, the BIs are removed aseptically and incubated in culture medium for 2 to 7 days at 55 °F for *G. stearothermophilus* or 37 °F for *B. atrophaeus*. The growth medium will turn cloudy or change color if spores are present. Vial-type indicators are squeezed or have caps that are pushed down to break an internal ampule and subsequently incubated at 55 °F. Spore testing should be performed minimally once a week. A control strip or vial that was not put in the sterilizer should be cultured similarly for reference.

SPORE TESTING OF SMALL OFFICE STERILIZERS

Biological monitoring or spore testing of small office sterilizers used in a dental office can be done in-house or through a mail-in monitoring service. In-office monitoring is more cumbersome and requires purchase of a number of supplies. Spore testing should be done once a week to confirm that the sterilizer is functioning and being used properly. It should also be performed anytime a new type of packaging material or tray is employed to make sure the sterilizing agent is contacting the surface of instruments. It is also appropriate when initiating use of a new sterilizer for familiarization purposes and initially after a device is repaired to make sure it is functioning correctly. If some change is instituted in the sterilizing procedure, spore testing should be done. Biological monitoring should be done every time sterilization is used for implantable devices to ensure that microorganisms are not implanted; in this case the device should not be installed until results are known. Lastly, spore testing should be done after sterilization runs done by employees undergoing training to make sure they are doing them properly.

BIOLOGIC MONITORING OR SPORE TESTING

The appropriate biological indicator should be inserted into a suitable type of wrapping, placed into the center of a load to be processed in the sterilizer, and treated in exactly the same manner as contaminated instruments in the sterilizing process. The package containing the biological indicator should be clearly marked if necessary, and if a spore strip is utilized, it should not be removed from its blue envelope. The center of the load is usually appropriate for the BI as that is the most difficult area for the sterilization to reach. After processing, the test date, sterilizer type, time and temperature used, type of monitor, and operator should be documented. The biological indicator is removed from the sterilizer. It and an unprocessed control indicator are sent to the sterilization monitoring service or incubated and observed for spores in-house to make certain of test reliability and sterilization success. Monitoring results should be recorded and maintained. If a sterilization failure is indicated, the sterilizer must be removed from service and spore testing done under controlled conditions.

CHEMICAL MONITORING OF STERILIZATION PROCESS

Chemical monitors are indicators that change color or transform physically during the sterilization process. Externally-applied autoclave tape and special markings on certain pouches and bags are examples of chemical monitors that change color once a certain high temperature has been reached. Autoclave tape develops dark stripes and other types of chemical monitors have distinct color changes within a certain region. There are also chemical monitors called **integrated indicators** that are designed to be put inside every wrapped instrument package, where they undergo color changes during sterilization. If these internal indicators are not visible, an external chemical monitor such as autoclave tape should also be applied. After the sterilization process, if external chemical monitors have not changed color indicating a sterilization failure, the processed instruments should not be used and spore testing should be done. Processed instruments should also not be used if it is clear after opening that an internal chemical monitor has not changed color. When internal indicators have not changed color, either no sterilization was performed or the sterilizing agent did not get through the packaging for some reason.

ALUMINUM FOIL TEST

The aluminum foil test is a method of evaluating the functionality of an ultrasonic cleaning unit. A piece of aluminum foil about 1 inch shorter than the length of the chamber by about 1 inch longer than its depth is cut. The foil is dipped vertically into the chamber filled with solution without touching the bottom. The unit is turned on for 20 seconds. The foil is taken out and scrutinized for pebbling or small indentations on the foil. If the ultrasonic unit is operating properly, this pebbling will be uniformly found on the previously submerged portion of the foil. If there are areas with no pebbling, the unit may need to be serviced.

STERILIZATION FAILURE

Sterilization failure is an extremely rare occurrence if sterilization is performed correctly. Sterilization failure can be due to improper precleaning or packaging of the instruments, use of an unacceptable method of sterilization, or improper loading, timing or temperature setting related to the sterilization process. Instruments that are not precleaned properly can still have attached debris that prevents contact between the item and the sterilizing agent. If the wrong packaging material is used, the sterilizing agent might be prevented from contact with the contaminated item or the packaging material might melt. Contact with the sterilizing agent can also be retarded if too much packaging or a closed container is used. Cloth wraps are unacceptable in chemical vapor sterilizers as they absorb chemicals. Method problems are generally related to use of sterilization for heat-sensitive items like plastic or attempts to use chemical vapors or dry heat to sterilize things in solution or water. Overloading or failing to separate packages can impede penetration of the sterilizing agent. Insufficient heat or sterilization time will not kill all microorganisms or spores.

FOLLOW-UP PROCEDURES

The first step in the event of a sterilization failure is the removal of that sterilizer from service and complete re-processing of any instruments sterilized since the previous spore test. Sterilization procedures then need to be scrutinized. This involves review of all chemical monitoring records since the most recent negative spore test. Loading and operating methods should be reviewed to determine if any changes had been made, if anything had been done differently during the failed cycle, or whether new personnel were involved. Any problems identified should be addressed and the sterilizer retested afterwards using the same conditions as during the sterilization failure. All 3 types of monitoring should be included during this cycle, and all gauges and readouts should be observed during the process. If biologic and chemical monitoring tests are negative, the sterilizer can be returned to service at this point, but if the spore test is positive the machine must be repaired or replaced. Later a new or repaired sterilizer must be spore tested three times with negative results before any instruments can be sterilized in it.

Chapter Quiz

Ready to see how well you retained what you just read? Scan the QR code to go directly to the chapter quiz interface for this study guide. If you're using a computer, simply visit the bonus page at **mometrix.com/bonus948/danbcda** and click the Chapter Quizzes link.

Occupational Safety/Administrative Protocols (ICE)

Transform passive reading into active learning! After immersing yourself in this chapter, put your comprehension to the test by taking a quiz. The insights you gained will stay with you longer this way. Scan the QR code to go directly to the chapter quiz interface for this study guide. If you're using a computer, simply visit the bonus page at **mometrix.com/bonus948/danbcda** and click the Chapter Quizzes link.

Occupational Safety Standards and Guidelines

TENETS OF INFECTION CONTROL

The World Health Organization developed three basic tenets of infection control in 2003 in reaction to the SARS or severe acute respiratory syndrome epidemic ensuing at that time. Many now believe that there should be a fourth tenet as well. The first three are to **protect the patient**, the **practitioner**, and **repeat both if necessary**. The newest tenet is to **protect the environment**. It is not enough just to protect the patient in situations where infections can be spread. It is equally as important to safeguard the health care worker and to practice measures, if possible, that will not generate excess waste, bring in potentially dangerous chemicals, or cause adverse tissue reactions.

AVOIDING OR CUTTING DOWN NEGATIVE ENVIRONMENTAL IMPACT

Almost all aspects of infection control in the dental office can be made more eco-friendly and improve upon the generally negative environmental impact they generate. The sterilization process, for example, can be made more eco-friendly by using a large instrument washer to clean multiple cassettes instead of an ultrasonic cleaner over and over, cutting down water and chemical use. Some personal protective equipment can be washed and reused instead of being disposed of. The vast majority of waste is not regulated medical waste and can be flushed down the sink. Use of disinfectant wipes instead of saturated paper towels cuts down on waste. Digital radiography eliminates the need for developer and fixer chemicals used with traditional radiography. Paper use can be diminished through use of digital patient records. These are just some examples of eco-friendly measures.

DEVELOPING PATIENT TRUST

First of all, there should be clear-cut established infection control procedures in the dental office. Employees should be knowledgeable about these procedures. They can give patients written information about the procedures, offer patients tours of the workplace including the sterilizing room, and generally maintain a clean and dust-free environment. Furthermore, the dental worker can directly show the patient that he or she is practicing infection control by making sure the patient sees the dental worker washing his or her hands, putting on new gloves, and unpacking sterile instruments from their sterilizing packages.

REGULATIONS GOVERNING INFECTION CONTROL

The main regulations are dictated by **OSHA**, the Occupational Safety and Health Administration, which is part of the U. S. Department of Labor. OSHA has set up a blood-borne pathogens standard as well as another for protection against hazardous chemicals. These standards must be followed in every state and are monitored. Twenty-eight states have OSHA divisions within their state departments of labor. Additional state and **local regulations** vary regarding dental office infection control, and most are concerned with medical waste management, instrument sterilization, and spore testing. The **Food and Drug Administration (FDA)**, a division of the U. S. Department of Health and Human Services, also affects infection control because it

regulates production and labeling of medical devices (of which there are many used in the dental office), antimicrobial handwashing solutions, and mouth rinses. The **Environmental Protection Agency (EPA)** is also involved in infection control as it regulates medical waste and provides guidelines for disinfectants.

ENFORCEMENT AGENCIES FOR INFECTION CONTROL

The main enforcement agency is OSHA (the Occupational Safety and Health Administration) which also has developed a number of standards to be followed, most notably for the dental office the OSHA Bloodborne Pathogens Standard and the OSHA Hazard Communication Standard. Recommendations are made by the Centers for Disease Control and Prevention (CDC), the Organization for Safety and Asepsis Procedures (OSAP), and the American Dental Association (ADA). The Food and Drug Administration (FDA) regulates manufacturing and labeling of medical devices (for example sterilizers and personal protective equipment) and solutions. The Environmental Protection Agency (EPA) approves things such as disinfecting and sterilizing solutions and also regulates hazardous waste removal.

CDC RECOMMENDATIONS FOR INFECTION CONTROL

The Centers for Disease Control (CDC) issued recommendations for infection control in the dental workplace in 2003. They are similar in many respects to the OSHA Bloodborne Pathogens Standard with the following exceptions. Many of the CDC's recommendations had to do with sterilization and disinfection of patient care items and environmental infection control. For example, the CDC suggests a central instrument processing area with areas for preparation, cleaning and decontamination, sterilization, and storage. The CDC also goes into detail about sterilization and its monitoring. The CDC recommendations cover disinfection of clinical contact surfaces with EPA-registered disinfectants, use of EPA standards for dental unit water and flushing of lines, restrictions against use of water when there are boil-water notices, and adherence to manufacturer's recommendations for decontamination of devices attached to air or water lines. The CDC suggests testing of dental office personnel for anti-HBsAg a month or two after HBV vaccination to determine effectiveness. The CDC also expounds further on hand hygiene and suggests screening for latex allergy.

UNIQUE SITUATIONS

The CDC recommendations also include sections on dental radiology, administration of parenteral medications, oral surgical procedures, disposal of extracted teeth, and practices in the dental laboratory. Dental radiology infection control is covered on the Radiation Health and Safety exam. The CDC recommends use of aseptic technique and, if possible, single-dose vials when administering parenteral medications and utilization of single-use disposable devices. For oral surgical procedures, the CDC recommends hand antisepsis, use of sterile surgical gloves, and use of sterile fluids for cooling or irrigation. The CDC suggests that extracted teeth be considered medical waste, taking note of whether or not they contain amalgam. Personnel working in the dental laboratory should wear PPE and treat objects received as contaminated until appropriate measures have been taken to decontaminate these objects.

CDC RECOMMENDATIONS FOR MICROORGANISMS IN WATER

The Centers for Disease Control and Prevention (CDC) currently recommends that the **dental treatment output water supply** in a dental office meet EPA standards for drinking water, which is less than 500 CFU/mL of heterotrophic waterborne bacteria. The dental office should refer to the dental unit manufacturer's instructions as to suitable ways to maintain and monitor this recommended quality of dental water. The office should use and follow directions related to recommended water treatment products. Personnel should discharge water and air for at least 20 to 30 seconds after each patient from any piece of equipment attached to the dental water line that has been in contact with the patient's mouth. The CDC also recommends that the dental unit manufacturer be consulted regarding regular maintenance of anti-retraction devices. The desired levels of bacteria in dental water expressed above (<500 CFU/mL) are less strict than those advocated by the American Dental Association, which encourages water delivered to patients for nonsurgical procedures to be ≤200 CFU/ml. The CDC also counsels that dental unit water not be used for oral surgical procedures.

CDC GUIDELINES FOR INFECTION CONTROL IN DENTAL HEALTHCARE SETTINGS-2003

The **Centers for Disease Control and Prevention Guidelines for Infection Control in Dental Healthcare Settings-2003** are recommendations for infection control in dental settings. These recommendations are ranked into categories IA, IB, IC, II and unresolved issues based on existing scientific data, theoretical rationale, and/or applicability. Those guidelines ranked Category IC are the most important because they are mandated by law or CDC standard to be implemented. Categories IA and IB items are strongly recommended, and Category II items are suggested. The Guidelines cover personnel health elements of an infection control program, prevention of transmission of bloodborne pathogens, hand hygiene, use of personal protective equipment, contact dermatitis and latex hypersensitivity, sterilization and disinfection of patient-care items, environmental infection control, dental unit waterlines and water quality, and a number of special considerations.

CDC'S BASIC EXPECTATIONS FOR SAFE CARE, 2016

The *CDC Summary of Infection Prevention in Dental Settings: Basic Expectations for Safe Care, 2016* is an interactive online article that offers dental workers the opportunity to refresh their understanding of infection control in the dental office setting while also earning CDE credits toward their recertification. The three main objectives of this article are (1) to provide the basic infection prevention principles and recommendations to dental healthcare settings, (2) to reaffirm standard precautions as the foundation of infection transmission prevention, and (3) to provide links to guidelines and documents as resources for more detailed information and recommendations. The interactive article contains a post-course assessment of 20 questions and costs $30.00. It can be accessed through The Dale Foundation online, amongst other continuing education courses for dental health care providers.

WORKPLACE SAFETY AND HEALTH STANDARDS DEVELOPMENT

The **Occupational Safety and Health Administration** creates advisory committees to evaluate standards that it or other organizations deem important (such as federal or state agencies or the National Institute for Occupational Safety and Health). If OSHA decides to initiate, change or get rid of a standard, it circulates its intention to do so in the Federal Register. The public is given a time period to respond to or provide additional information regarding the proposed new rules as well as notification regarding related hearings. New standards including related clarifications and rationale (or if appropriate notice of no change) are also published ultimately in the Federal Register. If circumstances arise that OSHA deems critical and uncovered by present standards, it can issue a binding emergency temporary standard until it has been reviewed as above.

OSHA

OSHA, the Occupational Safety and Health Administration, was established in 1971 subsequent to the federal Occupational Safety and Health Act of 1970. OSHA's **mission** is the promotion of workplace safety and health through compelling enforcement measures, assistance with outreach and compliance, and affiliations and cooperative programs. OSHA provides a number of **functions** to these ends. These functions include promotion of workplace safety programs, research, outlining responsibilities and rights of workers and employers, acting as a repository for recordkeeping regarding injuries and illnesses, developing training programs, spelling out standards for health and safety, and working with state agencies. Twenty-four states plus two U. S. territories have OSHA-approved programs. OSHA has established standards for a multitude of workplace hazards, including but not limited to hazardous waste, infectious diseases, and toxic substances. Employers are expected to achieve these standards by any combination of acceptable stated means. OSHA also covers circumstances not specifically covered elsewhere in the OSHA General Duty Clause.

OSHA 2018-2022 STRATEGIC MANAGEMENT PLAN GOALS

The overall objective of the OSHA 2018-2022 Strategic Management Plan has been the reduction of deaths, illnesses, and injuries in the workplace. OSHA's goals are in support of the Department of Labor's Strategic

Plan and its goals, which are a prepared and secure workforce and quality workplaces. OSHA broke down its Strategic Management Plan into four underlying goals. They are:

1. **Respect for the Rule of Law**: Promptly and fairly resolve the cases before it, including reducing the average age of review-level cases.
2. **Expanding Transparency and Openness**: To the extent consistent with the agency's statutory authority and responsibilities, see to enhance the transparency of its operations.
3. **Promoting Organizational Excellence**: Including a culture of professionalism, mutual respect, and organizational pride, and ensuring that staff members are adequately trained and developed.
4. **Managing agency resources in a manner that instills public trust**: Including information technology to monitor, evaluate, and improve programs and processes in order to better accomplish the agency's mission.

RELATIONSHIP BETWEEN OSHA AND STATE SAFETY AND HEALTH PROGRAMS

States can and are encouraged by OSHA to work out and enforce their own job safety and health programs. OSHA will fund up to 50% of the working costs of state programs that have been endorsed under the Occupational Safety and Health Act. These state programs must be at least as comprehensive as the federal standards to receive endorsement and funds. State programs may encompass only public sector employees or they may also incorporate private sector workers. All but three of the 26 states with current OSHA plans cover both the public and private sectors. Federal employees still fall under the umbrella of federal OSHA regulations.

FILING AND PROCURING ACTION REGARDING COMPLAINTS

Safety or health hazards occurring at a worksite or by an employee can be reported by anyone to OSHA. The complainant can request that his or her name be withheld from the employer. Complaints can be filed online at osha.gov using form OSHA-7 or by printing out the form, completing it, and then faxing or mailing it to the OSHA Regional Office. Employees who have been discriminated against for exercising their rights or refusing to work under unsafe conditions as outlined by OSHA can file discrimination complaints with the OSHA Regional Office. Then OSHA will stage no inquiry, conduct an inquiry, or perform an onsite inspection of the hazards listed in the complaint. If OSHA decides to conduct an onsite inspection, it is generally done without warning to the employer, who may request a warrant necessitating a return visit. The OSHA inspectors typically hold an explanatory opening conference at the site, carry out a walk-through inspection looking for hazards, and afterwards hold a closing conference at which they discuss hazards observed and possible citations and distribute a copy of *Employer Rights and Responsibilities Following an OSHA Inspection*. An employee representative is present throughout.

INSPECTIONS PERFORMED BY OSHA

OSHA, the Occupation Safety and Health Administration, performs 6 types of inspections, listed below in order of decreasing priority. They are investigations of the following:

1. **Imminent danger**, situations that could result in death or grave physical harm.
2. **Severe injuries or illness**, circumstances that resulted in death or hospitalization. Fatalities must be reported within 8 hours and severe injury or illness within 24 hours.
3. **Worker complaints**, situations in which employees have made official complaints.
4. **Referrals**, inspections on hazards that have been reported by other federal, state, or local agencies in addition to individuals, organizations, or the media.
5. **Targeted inspections**, periodic evaluations at sites identified by OSHA as potentially highly hazardous.
6. **Follow-up inspections**, evaluations done to determine whether an employer has rectified prior violations.

OSHA Standards Eliciting the Most Inspections and/or Citations

By far, the two OSHA standards eliciting the most inspections and/or violation citations in dental offices and laboratories are the OSHA **Bloodborne Pathogens Standard** followed by the OSHA **Hazard Communication Standard**. These are the most often cited in both the Offices and Clinics of Dentists Industry Group and the Medical and Dental Laboratories Industry Group. In 2013, 229 of the total 274 citations issued to dental offices were relating to these two standards.

Potential Outcomes of OSHA Inspection

The OSHA inspector will report his or her observations to the area director who makes a determination regarding violations. OSHA then issues citations to the employer for violations. The employer has 15 days to dispute the terms using the *Notice of Intent to Contest*, sent to the OSHA Review Commission. Violations generally involve some sort of financial penalty issued along with the citation or shortly thereafter. Violations fall into one of six categories. They are considered "willful" if the employer knew of the hazard but made no attempt to eliminate it, "serious" if the danger has potential to cause death or serious physical harm but the employer was unaware of the violation, and "other-than-serious" if the hazard would not cause death or serious illness. Violations can also be classified as "de minimis" or not directly affecting health or safety, "failure to abate" referring to violations previously cited and not dealt with, or "repeated" where the same type of violation recurs over repeated visits.

Exposure Control Plan

OSHA mandates that a **written exposure control plan** be developed and available to all appropriate employees. The exposure control plan should include the following: information about how exposure is determined; the schedules and procedures for compliance, hepatitis B vaccinations, evaluation of exposure episodes, post-exposure medical assessment and follow-up; and methods for communication of biohazards. The plan should contain any recordkeeping concerning the OSHA Bloodborne Pathogens Standard. It should also include information about new safety devices, and the plan should be revised yearly or when new laws, techniques or equipment become available. There should also be a written CDC-compliant tuberculosis infection control plan. In addition, there should be written policies, procedures and records related to health of individual personnel including such features as immunizations received, medical conditions, training, work restrictions, and latex allergies if present.

Office Safety Coordinator

Every dental office should have a **safety officer**, who is generally a dental assistant or hygienist. He or she is responsible for systematizing and supervising office safety and maintaining all related documents. The officer is responsible for tasks such as the following: preparing, reviewing, and revising all procedural manuals and control plans (especially infection control and hazardous materials); training of personnel; monitoring compliance with safety procedures; overseeing hepatitis B vaccination programs; and assessment of exposure incidents. Many of the safety officer's duties are related to overseeing equipment safety, such as spore testing for sterilizers, proper disposal of regulated medical waste, keeping smoke alarms in operating order, and maintaining certification of radiographic equipment.

Office Safety Documents and Records

Office safety documents and records fall into three categories. There are **regulatory documents** that should be available, including the Occupational Safety and Health Administration's (OSHA) Bloodborne Pathogens and Hazard Communications Standards as well as state and local regulations. Next there are **policy documents**, which include written infection exposure control and hazard communication programs for the office, CDC-compliant tuberculosis infection control and personal health plans, and action plans for fires or other emergencies. Safety procedures not encompassed by OSHA standards, such as instrument sterilization, should be included as well. The OSHA poster entitled "Job Safety and Health Protection" is considered a policy document and should be posted. Lastly, there are a whole range of **records that should be kept**, including but

not limited to training records related to bloodborne pathogens and hazards, employee medical records, spore testing, radiographic equipment certification, cataloging of hazardous chemicals, and safety data sheets.

OFFICE STAFF TRAINING

OSHA requires that office staff members who might be exposed to infections be **trained** about infection control when they are first employed and, thereafter, at least annually. The instructor must be conversant about the subjects covered and the dental office setting and should welcome questions during the presentation. The training should include a thorough explanation of causes, signs, epidemiology, transmission and prevention of bloodborne illnesses and tuberculosis. It should also include a rundown of the office's exposure control plan, information about the equipment and supplies that aid in reduction of transmission, facts regarding the offered hepatitis B vaccination, procedures related to exposure incidents, and explanations about biohazard designations and color coding. The audience should be given and made aware of the OSHA Bloodborne Pathogens Standards and other pertinent infection control laws.

OCCUPATIONAL EXPOSURE, POST-EXPOSURE MEDICAL EVALUATION, AND FOLLOW-UP

All occupational exposures to potentially infectious materials such as blood or saliva should be documented and reported. A medical **evaluation and follow-up** must be offered free of charge to the employee by a licensed physician or nurse practitioner in an office where the OSHA Bloodborne Pathogens Standard is available. The physician must counsel the employee about the results and possible scenarios and send a written confirmation to the employer that such events have occurred. In addition, if patients can be identified as the source of transmission, they should be asked to be tested for their hepatitis B and HIV status. Exposure incidents should be reviewed afterwards to see if they might be prevented in the future.

OSHA BLOODBORNE PATHOGENS STANDARD

The **Occupational Safety and Health Administration Bloodborne Pathogens Standard** covers protection measures for exposure to blood and other potentially infectious materials (OPIMS). It states that every facility where such exposure might occur, such as the dental office, must review the standard. The facility must also prepare a written exposure control plan including how it plans to protect and train workers. It must make available appropriate biohazard communications via training and use of signs and labels. Workers must be offered the hepatitis B vaccination series as well as medical evaluations and follow-ups if they are exposed. Medical and training records must be maintained for each employee. Standard precautions must be followed in the facility with respect to blood, all bodily fluids except sweat, nonintact skin, and mucous membranes. This includes both engineering and work practice controls such as use of hand washing and handling of contaminated sharps as well as use and disposal of personal protective equipment. The Standard also covers appropriate housekeeping procedures, management of regulated waste, and procedures for contaminated laundry. It does not address instrument sterilization.

CATEGORIES OF POSSIBLE OCCUPATIONAL EXPOSURE

There are three categories of possible occupational exposure as pertaining to the OSHA Bloodborne Pathogens Standard. They are based on the type of tasks performed and the risk of exposure to blood and other potentially infectious materials (OPIMS).

- **Category 1** applies to all jobs that directly involve exposure to blood and OPIMS; the dentist, dental assistants, hygienists, and dental laboratory technicians fall into this category.
- **Category 2** applies to tasks that generally do not involve blood or OPIM exposure but may occasionally perform unplanned Category 1 chores such as those performed by the receptionist or coordinator.
- **Category 3** tasks are devoid of blood or OPIM exposure, such as those of the bookkeeper or insurance handler.

EXPOSURE CONTROL PLAN

The OSHA Bloodborne Pathogens Standard mandates that facilities to which it applies develop a written exposure control plan. There are 4 major areas that it should include.

1. The first is determination of the probability and types of occupational exposure that might occur to any employee in the office.
2. The employer also must make a schedule of how and when each of the stipulations in the standard will be implemented.
3. The plan should include a means of evaluating the circumstances surrounding exposure incidents in terms of things such as source patient, protective equipment used, and route of exposure.
4. It should also describe the safety devices to be utilized for prevention of sharps injuries, how they are to be evaluated, and why certain ones are selected.

MINIMAL REQUIREMENTS FOR COMPLIANCE

Employers are required to provide an available copy of the standard and free training to any employee with possible occupational exposure. The minimum requirements for this training should include explanations of epidemiology and symptoms of bloodborne diseases, modes of their transmission, an outline of the exposure control plan, and how to recognize means of exposure. The training should also cover ways to prevent and reduce exposure, including engineering controls, work practices, and personal protective equipment. The employees should be informed about the availability of and need for hepatitis B vaccination and post-exposure procedures and evaluations. Biohazards communication should also involve use and clarification of required signs and labels.

HEPATITIS B VACCINATION

Hepatitis B transmission is one of the greatest concerns in healthcare settings and there are effective vaccines for the disease. The OSHA standard addresses this issue. It requires the employer to provide a copy of the standard to each healthcare professional, vaccine-related training, and the option for a free series of the hepatitis B vaccine within 10 days of employment. An employee can either accept or decline the offer for vaccination. If the employee accepts, the vaccine must be administered by a licensed physician or other appropriate healthcare profession (for example, a nurse practitioner). If the employee declines, he/she must sign a declination statement. If, at a later time, the employee wishes to be vaccinated, the employer must provide vaccination free of charge. The healthcare professional evaluates each employee for vaccination, previous protection, or contraindications to vaccination. The health care professional performs the vaccinations and provides a written evaluation to the employee. One copy is to be maintained in the employee's confidential medical file.

OSHA-REQUIRED PROCEDURES FOR POST-EXPOSURE MEDICAL EVALUATION AND FOLLOW-UP

When there is a potentially infectious exposure incident, it is the responsibility of the employer to send the exposed employee to a healthcare professional for testing for hepatitis B virus (HBV) and human immunodeficiency virus (HIV). The only exceptions would be if the employee does not consent or if the employee's viral status to the above agents is already known. Consenting employees are tested and given their results along with an evaluation as to the appropriate course of action by the healthcare professional. The healthcare professional should be provided with an incident report, HBV vaccination status, and other pertinent information by the employer before testing. In turn, the health care professional is required to give the employer a post-evaluation written opinion, which indicates that the employee was informed of results and whether other measures are indicated. This written opinion should be kept confidentially in the employee's medical file.

EMPLOYEE'S RECORDS

Both medical and training records should be included in an employee's record. The OSHA Bloodborne Pathogens Standard indicates that training records should be kept for at least 3 years and includes the dates of training, the topics that were covered, the names and qualifications of the instructors, and the names and job

titles of all present. Medical records must be kept longer, at least 30 years after termination of employment. They must include the employee's name and Social Security number, the employee's hepatitis B vaccination status and all associated documentation, and any occupational exposure incidents including the healthcare professional's post-exposure written opinion.

OSHA-REQUIRED ENGINEERING AND WORK PRACTICE CONTROLS

The OSHA Bloodborne Pathogens Standard mandates a number of engineering and work practice controls to minimize exposure to infectious agents. An **engineering control** is something that can impact the hazard itself such as use of puncture-resistant sharps containers or retractable scalpels. For example, both disposable and reusable contaminated sharps should be placed directly into sharps containers (the latter for later processing). **Work practice controls** are measures taken during a task that reduce the likelihood of exposure. These include things such as thorough handwashing practices after removal of gloves or personal protective equipment, flushing of mucous membranes if exposed, minimizing splatter of blood or saliva (for example with use of a rubber dam and/or evacuation), and limiting activities such as drinking and eating in the work area.

PERSONAL PROTECTIVE EQUIPMENT

The OSHA Bloodborne Pathogens Standard states that an employer must provide **free of charge personal protective equipment (PPE)** to employees with the potential for occupational exposure. The employer must also make sure that the employee uses the PPE, that a range of suitable sizes is available in the office, that provisions are made for cleaning and/or disposal of PPE, and that it will be repaired or replaced to preserve effectiveness if necessary. PPE falls into several categories. The first category is gloves, which should be donned any time the employee may be in contact with blood, saliva, mucous membranes, broken skin, or contaminated surfaces. The next type of personal protective equipment is anything that shields the face. This category of PPE includes masks covering the nose and mouth and protective eyewear, such as goggles or glasses. Protective clothing must be worn as an outer garment to protect against exposure, taken off afterwards, and laundered at the office or by a service. The type of protective clothing (for example lab coats, aprons, gowns, etc.) depends on expected exposure. PPE penetrated by blood or saliva should be replaced immediately.

HAZARDOUS CHEMICAL

A hazardous chemical is one that presents either a physical or health hazard. A physical hazard is any chemical for which there is scientific verification that it is unstable in some way. This can mean it is a combustible liquid, a compressed gas, unstable or water reactive, flammable, explosive, can ignite spontaneously, or is an organic peroxide and oxidizer. Basically, physical hazards fall into two categories, those that are flammable and those that are reactive. Flammable chemicals are those that can quickly or thoroughly vaporize at atmospheric pressure and room temperature or that burn easily. Reactive or unstable chemicals are those that are susceptible to release of energy, including ones that are normally unstable chemically but do not explode or materials that are reactive with water. A health hazard is any material that can cause major health damage or death quickly despite prompt medical attention. Health hazards must have warning labels indicating the specific health hazard, including the target organ affected.

OSHA HAZARD COMMUNICATION STANDARD

Hazard communication ranks second in number of citations issued by the Occupational Safety and Health Administration in dental settings. The OSHA Hazard Communication Standard (also known as the **HazCom Standard** and the "Employee Right to Know") applies to any workplace setting in which chemicals are used. This standard is designed to prevent employee exposures to hazardous chemicals. It mandates that chemical manufacturers evaluate and provide information to employers (who must in turn convey this to employees) about the hazards associated with their chemicals. It is comprehensive, meaning it covers all hazardous chemicals that might be encountered in a variety of workplaces while excluding things generally for private consumption such as drugs, tobacco, alcohol, and consumer products. The scope of the HazCom standard includes setting up a written HazCom Program (WHCP) in affected workplaces, provision of Safety Data Sheets

(SDS) by the manufacturer, use of special protective equipment when using hazardous chemicals, and engineering and workplace controls.

NFPA's Method of Labeling Chemicals

The **National Fire Protection Association (NFPA)** suggests chemical labels be colored as follows: red for fire hazards, yellow for reactivity, and blue for health hazards. Containers for chemicals are often labeled with a diamond-shaped area on the front with 4 subdivisions. At the apex is a red **fire** hazard classification with numbering system as follows: 0 for non-combustible, 1 and 2 for caution for combustible when heated or a combustible liquid, 3 for a flammable liquid, and 4 for danger due to a flammable gas or very flammable liquid. Below the red diamond are blue and yellow ones for **health** and **reactivity** hazards respectively. For blue health hazards, the numbering system is as follows: 0 for no unusual hazard, 1 for possible irritation, 2 and 3 for harmful if inhaled and corrosive or toxic respectively, and 4 for danger and the possibility of fatality. For yellow reactivity ratings, the numbering system is as follows: 0 for stable, 1 for caution of possible reactivity if heated or mixed with water, 2 for instability under the same conditions, 3 for dangerous around sparks or heating under confinement, and 4 for explosive at room temperature. The label has a white diamond on the bottom indicating appropriate **personal protective equipment** (designated A to G).

Written Hazard Communication Program for the Workplace

Workplaces utilizing hazardous chemicals (including dental offices) are required under the OSHA HazCom Standard to develop a custom-made written hazard communication program (WHCP) for compliance. Initially copies of the HazCom Standard should be given to each employee for familiarization. A HazCom compliance officer and a backup officer (generally the dentist) should be internally identified. A list should be compiled of all the chemicals used or manufactured at the workplace including their locations. Methods for use of hazardous chemicals in situations like performance of nonroutine tasks or while employing part-time or contract workers should be described in the WHCP. Methods of labeling containers should be clearly defined. Safety Data Sheets (SDSs) should be obtained for each hazardous chemical and maintained in an organized manner. A training coordinator should be named and details of a training program regarding the HazCom described. In addition, if chemical formulas are trade secrets the manufacturer or supplier still has the responsibility of indicating the appropriate protective measures, which should be included in the WHCP.

Safety Data Sheets

Safety Data Sheets (SDSs) are information sheets that must be conveyed by chemical manufacturers and importers with any product containing hazardous chemicals. Official SDS forms are issued by the U. S. Department of Labor and OSHA for compliance with the OSHA HazCom Standard. They should be kept in a central organized location as well as available near where the chemical is used. There are 16 sections on a SDS which contain information about the manufacturer, the hazardous ingredients in the preparation and identity information (including the NFPA Hazard rating), the physical and chemical characteristics of the chemical, fire and explosion hazard data, reactivity data, health hazard data, applicable precautions for safe handling and use, any additional information, and control measures (such as personal protective equipment) required. Other SDS sections also have information regarding special precautions required and/or emergency and first aid procedures.

Chemical Inventory Forms and Hazardous Chemical Labels

A chemical inventory form should include the inventory date and name of the dental office. Each chemical that is utilized in the office should be listed by its chemical name. The hazard classification from 0 to 4 should be listed for each possible distinction as a health hazard, fire hazard, or a possible reactivity. For each chemical, the appropriate personal protective equipment to use should also be listed, the physical state (for example gas, liquid or solid) should be indicated, and the manufacturer should be recorded. It is helpful to leave space for comments as well. A challenge in the dental office is the fact that hazardous chemicals may be part of dental materials kits without proper labeling, making it difficult to correctly inventory them. Not all manufacturers follow the National Fire Protection Association labeling recommendations. The minimum requirements according to the HazCom Standard regarding labeling of hazardous chemicals are inclusion of the identity of

the hazardous chemical(s), the appropriate hazard warning including target organs if a health hazard, and information about the manufacturer or other responsible party.

PROBLEMS REGARDING HAZARDOUS CHEMICALS IN THE OFFICE

Employees often feel that there may be a problem regarding hazardous chemicals in the office. For example, they may be getting headaches or dermatitis. The first step should be to actually ascertain whether there is a problem. Some problems can be detected through use of monitoring equipment, for example badges or air samplers that undergo color changes in the presence of certain chemicals. The employer may need to seek advice from authorities such as an industrial hygienist or health or air quality departments. If there appears to be an issue, engineering controls, work practice controls, and/or personal protective equipment (PPE) can be changed to potentially eliminate the problem. Engineering controls (the most effective) are any procedures or materials that can reduce hazardous chemical exposure, for example use of sterilization rather than glutaraldehyde. Work practice controls are any procedural changes that can diminish the likelihood of exposure, for example, use of a fume hood for ventilation. Alterations in PPE use are generally the least effective means of dealing with these issues.

TRAINING REGARDING THE HAZCOM STANDARD

Any employee who might come in contact with hazardous chemicals, even non-routinely, must be trained regarding the OSHA HazCom Standard. This training must occur at the time of employment, every time a new hazard is presented, and once a year for all continuing employees. Training can be done by the designated HazCom compliance officer. The essential elements of the training are five-fold. First, employees must be shown the ways in which the Standard is generally carried out, such as labeling methods, warning signs, and use of Safety Data Sheets (SDSs). They must all be made aware of the health and physical hazards linked to hazardous chemicals and how they are indicated on the above. Employees must be educated in the use of appropriate personal protective equipment. The trainer must also acquaint the employee with site-specific details such as where SDSs are located, emergency procedures, protection of certain equipment, and engineering and work practice controls. Lastly, the training should include a portion where the employee observes things like the smells and appearances of specific hazardous reagents.

CHEMICAL HYGIENE PLAN

A written chemical hygiene plan, as required by the OSHA Occupational Exposure to Hazardous Chemicals in Laboratories Standard, should cover a variety of topics. The plan should list procedures for procurement, allocation, and storage of chemicals. It should address environmental monitoring if required or in the case of problems. It should also specify housekeeping procedures such as frequency of monitoring of safety equipment (e.g., eye-face wash stations), maintenance of egress to emergency equipment, and general procedures for cleanliness. The plan should address the use of personal protective equipment and emergency equipment. PPE for chemical use is not necessarily the same as for infection control, and additional items like eye-face washes, fire extinguishers, and ventilation fume hoods are needed. The plan should address how spills and accidents are to be dealt with and evaluated thereafter. There should be a medical program in place that deals with medical surveillance, exposure outcomes, and provision of first aid. The plan should address maintenance of accident, chemical, and medical records; pertinent signage (like emergency phone numbers); and labeling, training of employees, and waste disposal methods.

OSHA OCCUPATIONAL EXPOSURE TO HAZARDOUS CHEMICALS IN LABORATORIES STANDARD

The OSHA Occupational Exposure to Hazardous Chemicals in Laboratories Standard is designed to safeguard employees using hazards in a laboratory setting. It is applicable to dental offices as well as dental laboratories because there are many opportunities for exposure to a hazardous chemical, defined as any chemical scientifically proven to cause acute or chronic health issues. This standard calls for designation of a chemical hygiene officer to oversee compliance, including responsibilities such as familiarity with exposure limits, ensuring that employees use chemicals in an appropriate manner, and monitoring all facets of chemical use. It also calls for development of a written site-specific chemical hygiene plan that covers ways to protect

employees against hazardous chemicals and applies the principles of prudent practices for safety and use of chemicals.

OSHA Fire Safety Standard

The OSHA Fire Safety Standard mandates that a fire safety and prevention plan be developed for the office. New employees must be informed of the components of the fire safety plan. In offices with less than 10 employees this information can be transmitted verbally, but it is suggested that a written plan be developed as is required for larger offices. The written fire safety plan should minimally include the following: an inventory of major fire hazards in the workplace; information about how possible ignition sources are used, stored, and disposed of; fire protection equipment available in the office; ways that flammables and combustibles are kept to a minimum; safeguards in place on instruments that produce heat; names or job classifications of individuals responsible for upkeep of equipment and control of fuel source hazards; housekeeping duties related to potential fire hazards; and components of employee training. An emergency notification and evacuation plan in case of fire should be outlined, which could also be part of an emergency action plan (discussed elsewhere). Two or more separated fire exit routes should be identified and other measures such as sprinkler systems are suggested.

Office Emergency Action Plan

A number of OSHA standards, such as the Fire Safety Standard and the HazCom Standard, require development of a written **emergency action plan (EAP)**. Minimally, the EAP should address the practices for informing authorities about a fire or other emergency, evacuation procedures and escape routes, methods of accounting for all employees after evacuation such as a designated meeting place, responsibilities of employees who might be able to perform rescue procedures such as resuscitation, and names or job classifications for contacts knowledgeable about the plan. An EAP might also include procedures for employees who stay longer than others to shut off equipment or utilities if necessary. The EAP should be gone over with each new employee. It should be available for ongoing perusal. Just as with a fire prevention plan, the EAP may be communicated verbally if there are fewer than 10 employees, but a written plan is required for larger offices.

Evacuation Policies and Procedures

As part of an emergency action plan (EAP), there are essential elements that should be included in the actual evacuation policies and procedures. The EAP should clearly single out situations that warrant evacuation (and its scope), such as fire, certain natural disasters, or chemical spills. It should identify the emergency plan coordinator and further chain of command in evacuation or shutdown situations. It should spell out how different types of emergencies should be handled. It may designate someone to shut down critical operations. It should include a map posted prominently that delineates evacuation routes and exits. It is helpful, particularly in larger workplaces, to appoint a number of employees to assist at various points during evacuations or to help visitors, people with disabilities, or those who are non-English speaking. It is also important to identify in the plan at least one assembly place after evacuation to do a head count of employees.

Issues Addressed in Emergency Action Plan

It is essential to make sure that an emergency action plan (EAP) addresses all potential natural or man-made emergencies, including things such as fires, natural disasters, toxic materials release, radiological and biological accidents, and interpersonal disruptions. It should also identify all potential chemical hazards and other situations that could cause emergencies. The EAP should address how emergencies might impact office operations and measures to deal with such. It should talk about the procedures for rescue operations that might be needed, such as the local fire department, and provision of necessary medical care. To the latter point, if there are not extremely close medical facilities for treatment, then personnel should receive formal first aid training. The plan should include contact information for key employees, local emergency responders, and personnel with responsibilities related to emergency action, as well as contact and medical information for all employees.

EAP FOR ALERTING EMPLOYEES, REPORTING EMERGENCIES, AND TRAINING EMPLOYEES

An emergency action plan (EAP) should detail procedures for alerting employees in the event of an emergency. Appropriate types of alert systems include distinctive **alarm systems**, announcement over a **public address system**, and use of **floor wardens** to notify and direct employees. Usually fires and other emergencies are reported to authorities by dialing "911." There may be internal **methods of reporting** in addition to or in lieu of calling "911," such as coded intercom systems, manual pull stations, or certain alarms. In terms of **employee training** regarding the EAP, training should be given to new employees and everyone when the plan is initially developed, when it is altered, and annually for retraining. The training should address the following: individual responsibilities; potential hazards and appropriate actions; procedures for alerting, emergency response, evacuation, and accountability; the location of emergency equipment; and shutdown procedures if appropriate. Provisions for periodic emergency drills are also suggested.

Documentation

EXPOSURE CONTROL PLAN

An exposure control plan evaluates the exposure risk of each employee according to the person's duties and establishes safety measures to prevent exposure. These measures may include the use of safety-engineered devices, such as syringes with retractable needles. The plan must also outline the types of personal protective equipment necessary for different procedures and types of possible exposure. The plan should include measures to minimize exposure to blood and body fluids. Additionally, the plan must address protocols for post-exposure prophylaxis for occupational exposure to bloodborne pathogens, including any necessary follow-up monitoring or treatment, the name of the person responsible for directing the care of the individual, the place where testing will be carried out, and the information necessary to ensure adequate assessment of the exposure. The exposure control plan should also include tuberculosis control measures, such as TB screening, and should address the issue of pregnancy and exposures that may pose a risk to the pregnancy or the developing fetus.

BREACHES

According to the CDC, the steps for assessing a breach of infection control include:

1. **Identifying the type of breach**: Determine how the breach occurred and what risk of exposure exists. Take corrective action as soon as possible to prevent further breaches and review techniques.
2. **Gathering additional data**: Determine when breach occurred and who was exposed, and carry out a literature review and/or consult with experts.
3. **Notifying key stakeholders**: These may include infection control professionals, health departments, government agencies, accreditation agencies, risk management, and all those who risk exposure.
4. **Assessing the breach**: Classify as category A breach (gross error with high risk of exposure) or category B (lesser risk of exposure).
5. **Making a decision about patient testing/notification**: Classify as category A if notification and testing is necessary or as category B if the need to notify is balanced against low risk.
6. **Communicating**: Materials to communicate are developed.
7. **Post-exposure prophylaxis**: Outline logistical matters—who, where, when, how.
8. **Media and legal issues**: Make media announcement if indicated and consult legal representatives for liability issues.

STERILIZATION LOGS AND TRAINING RECORDS

Sterilization logs may vary somewhat but are used to monitor sterilization and provide evidence that the process was carried out correctly. Elements of a log often include the date, the identification number of the item, the contents, the beginning and ending times or the duration, the temperature, the pressure (PSI), the results of the chemical indicator, the spore count, and the signature of the person responsible. These records may be reviewed when sterilization fails in order to try to determine the cause or when products are recalled. The log and dating of the sterilized items also helps to ensure proper rotation of supplies.

Training records provide documented evidence that infection control training was carried out, the type of training, and the participants. Dental health care personnel should receive training regarding infection control principle, employment-associated risk factors, preventive measures, and post-exposure protocols. Training should be appropriate for the individual's duties and responsibilities.

Chapter Quiz

Ready to see how well you retained what you just read? Scan the QR code to go directly to the chapter quiz interface for this study guide. If you're using a computer, simply visit the bonus page at **mometrix.com/bonus948/danbcda** and click the Chapter Quizzes link.

DANB Practice Test

Want to take this practice test in an online interactive format?
Check out the bonus page, which includes interactive practice questions and much more: **mometrix.com/bonus948/danbcda**

General Chairside

1. When a patient needing orthodontic care bites in centric occlusion, the maxillary anterior teeth are positioned lingually to the mandibular anterior teeth, leaving an excessive space between the facial aspect of their maxillary anterior teeth, and the lingual aspect of their mandibular anterior teeth. What is the name of the orthodontic condition present in this patient?

    a. Underjet.
    b. Overbite.
    c. Overjet.
    d. Open bite.

2. Which of the following directly leads to the body going into anaphylactic shock?

    a. A spinal injury experienced by the patient.
    b. A severe infection in the body.
    c. A severe allergic response to a substance foreign to the body.
    d. A severe drop in a patient's blood sugar.

3. What type of bur is used to make undercuts in a tooth preparation?

    a. A round bur.
    b. An inverted cone bur.
    c. An end-cutting bur.
    d. A plain fissure straight bur.

4. What is a significant feature of the electric hand piece?

    a. The electric handpiece has a self-contained water reservoir separate from the dental unit.
    b. The electric hand piece is only used for endodontic procedures.
    c. The electric hand piece can operate as either a high speed or low speed hand piece.
    d. Anesthesia is usually not needed while using the electric hand piece.

5. When properly brushing the teeth, all areas of the mouth will be cleaned EXCEPT:

    a. the lingual area.
    b. the buccal area.
    c. the occlusal area.
    d. the interproximal area.

6. Which of the following statements best defines a reorder point used in inventory management systems in a dental office?

a. The determination of the maximum amount of supplies that need to be on hand after an order is placed.
b. The location in which the dental office manager and the sales member will meet to order supplies.
c. The minimum number of supplies that can be available for a given product prior to more being ordered.
d. The point in the week where all supply orders are placed.

7. Which of the following dental products would NOT be used for a final impression?

a. Alginate
b. Polysulfide
c. Polyether
d. Silicone

8. How does an assistant retrieve the locking cotton pliers during instrument transfer?

a. At the working end.
b. Using a palm thumb grasp.
c. Using a reverse palm thumb grasp.
d. At the hinged end.

9. When a patient is experiencing a local anesthesia overdose, he may experience all of the following symptoms EXCEPT:

a. decreased heart rate.
b. twitching.
c. increased apprehension.
d. slurred speech.

10. When an alginate impression is stored in a moist environment, it may absorb or take up additional water. What is the name of this process?

a. Exothermic release.
b. Imbibition.
c. Calcimining.
d. Syneresis.

11. When documenting progress notes into a patient's chart, which of the following is correct?

a. The patient must sign the progress notes after they have been completed.
b. The entry must be signed and dated by the dental team member who recorded the entry.
c. The entry may be entered in blue ink only, according to national guidelines.
d. If a mistake is made, it must be erased and re-recorded by the dental team member.

12. When having a procedure performed on the maxillary arch, how should the patient be positioned?

a. The mandibular arch needs to be parallel to the floor when the patient's mouth is halfway open.
b. The maxillary arch should be parallel to the floor.
c. With the chair as low as possible, and with the patient's back at a 45-degree angle.
d. In the supine position.

13. During a frenectomy, which structure(s) are removed?

a. The complete frenum and the attachment of the frenum to the underlying bone.
b. The complete frenum only.
c. The marginal gingiva and marginal sulcus.
d. The cortical bone.

14. Formocresol is used in which of the following procedures?

    a. A non-vital pulpotomy.
    b. A vital pulpotomy.
    c. A non-vital pulpectomy.
    d. A vital pulpectomy.

15. When selecting an impression tray for a patient, which of the following should be avoided?

    a. The impression tray needs to be deep enough to allow for impression material to flow between the tray and the occlusal surface.
    b. The tray should be two sizes larger than the size of the mouth to allow for adequate impression material to be loaded onto the tray.
    c. The tray should extend behind the last erupted tooth on both arches.
    d. The tray should extend slightly beyond the facial surfaces of the teeth.

16. What is the most likely reason for a permanent tooth to have a "chalky" appearance located in the enamel?

    a. Deep carious lesions are present.
    b. The tooth is necrotic.
    c. The tooth has periodontal disease.
    d. The tooth has incipient caries.

17. Which of the following materials serves as a permanent root canal sealer used during an endodontic procedure?

    a. RC Prep cream.
    b. Densfil.
    c. Tubli-Seal.
    d. Formocresol.

18. During a subjective examination of a tooth, what type of information should be given?

    a. Problems or symptoms that the patient is experiencing.
    b. The periodontal condition surrounding the tooth.
    c. The mobility of the tooth.
    d. The type of restoration present in the tooth.

19. Which of the following is not true about the state Dental Practice Act?

    a. The act provides requirements for licensure and renewal of licenses.
    b. It specifies the duties that may be performed by a dental assistant or a dental hygienist.
    c. It specifies regulations and requirements surrounding infection control and radiation use.
    d. The act is the same from state to state but is enforced by individual state dental boards

20. A dental patient who is experiencing xerostomia can be given_____ to help reduce or eliminate the symptoms of this condition.

    a. bleaching solutions
    b. topical fluoride treatments
    c. home impression materials
    d. saliva substitutes

21. When charting during an oral exam, a ___ line is placed within the root(s), parallel to the long axis of the root(s), to indicate that a root canal needs to be performed.

a. yellow
b. red
c. blue
d. green

22. What type of gypsum is used to produce study models?

a. Impression plaster.
b. Class I stone.
c. Class II stone.
d. Lab plaster.

23. As a healthcare professional, the dental assistant is a mandated reporter and is required by most states to report all of the following types of abuse EXCEPT:

a. suspected child abuse.
b. suspected bullying or verbal abuse.
c. suspected elderly adult abuse.
d. injuries or abuse from stabbing, assault, or rape.

24. When considering the placement of dental sealants, the dental assistant should avoid placing sealants on which type of teeth?

a. A tooth next to a tooth that needs occlusal restorations.
b. A newly erupted tooth.
c. A fully erupted permanent tooth.
d. A primary tooth that has roots that are partially resorbed.

25. When referring to the classification of dental cavities, Class I decay involves all of the following EXCEPT:

a. fissures on premolars.
b. fissures on molars.
c. occlusal pits on premolars.
d. occlusal pits on incisors.

26. Which of the following products is used as a cavity liner due to its ability to protect the pulp from irritation and its compatibility with various types of restorative materials?

a. Copalite.
b. Mizzy Flecks.
c. Zinc phosphate.
d. Calcium hydroxide.

27. Which gland does mumps, a viral infection, most often affect?

a. Submandibular salivary gland.
b. Parotid salivary gland.
c. Sublingual salivary gland.
d. Wharton's duct.

28. A patient requires a xenograft. Where is the grafted tissue to be taken from?

a. Other areas of the patient's mouth.
b. Other members of the family.
c. Different animal species.
d. Plants.

29. What is the normal, healthy amount of blood usually present in an adult body?

   a. 2 to 3 pints.
   b. 5 to 6 quarts.
   c. 3 gallons.
   d. 25 ounces.

30. Which statement is correct regarding the working end of an instrument?

   a. The working end of the instrument performs the intended function of the instrument.
   b. The working end of the instrument is the area that will be held in the hand.
   c. The working end of the instrument contains a rubber area that allows for the instrument to be gripped for ease of use.
   d. The working end of the instrument connects the handle to the shaft.

31. When working with dental waxes, which of the following is the best way to prevent distortion of the wax?

   a. Avoid extreme temperature changes during manipulation and storage.
   b. Manipulate the wax as often as possible to break the wax in.
   c. Ensure the wax is in its soft state for a long period of time.
   d. After the wax has been used, place it in a warm, dark place for storage.

32. Which of the following statements best describes a scheduling matrix?

   a. The routine review of patients' charts and placement in an order according to the last scheduled appointment.
   b. The layout of a dental office's schedule accounting for the office hours and all days the office will be open and closed.
   c. An appointment scheduling system that allows for the longest appointments to have priority over shorter appointments during early-morning time slots.
   d. A way in which the dental software schedules patients based on account status.

33. When using the Universal numbering system, the maxillary left first molar is tooth number

   a. 30.
   b. 3.
   c. 14.
   d. 19.

34. Which of the following statements best describes how luting cement is applied to an item?

   a. A thin layer of cement is applied to the item prior to placing it in the mouth.
   b. This type of cement is formed into a ball and placed into the base of a restoration prior to placement.
   c. A restorative item is filled with this type of cement to allow for better adhesion.
   d. A viscous layer is applied to an item, light cured, and then placed onto the tooth.

35. What is the most common cause of corrosion and staining on sterilized instruments, after autoclaving is complete?

   a. Instruments were not completely dried when placed in storage.
   b. Instruments were disinfected rather than autoclaved.
   c. Instruments were placed in a cassette prior to sterilization.
   d. Instruments were washed with soap and water, rinsed, and dried, before entering the autoclave.

36. What is the difference between a hemostat and a needle holder in a dental surgical setting?

a. They hold surgical supplies during a surgical procedure.
b. They are both able to be autoclaved.
c. A hemostat has shorter beaks than does the needle holder.
d. A needle holder has shorter beaks than does the hemostat.

37. When using the Federation Dentaire Internationale (FDI) System for identifying a specific tooth, the _____ number is written first.

a. tooth
b. sextant
c. quadrant
d. maxillary arch

38. When identifying a contra-angle high-speed hand piece, which of the following is correct about the angle of the head of the hand piece?

a. The head of the hand piece is slightly angled to the fiber optics of the hand piece.
b. The head of the hand piece is slightly angled to the shank of the hand piece.
c. The head of the hand piece is slightly angled to the chuck of the hand piece.
d. The head of the hand piece is slightly angled to the rheostat.

39. When working with a patient receiving treatment on the maxillary arch, how should the dental assistant adjust the operatory light?

a. Lowering the light and directing the beam downward.
b. Raising the light and directing the beam downward.
c. Raising the light and directing the beam upward.
d. Lowering the light and directing the beam upward.

40. Which of the following vitamins or minerals is not directly related to tooth formation?

a. Vitamin D
b. Phosphorus
c. Folic acid
d. Magnesium

41. What is the main goal of a plaque control program?

a. To have the patient come into the office once per month to disclose the teeth and see the progress of personal oral hygiene.
b. To develop a technique to thoroughly remove plaque from the teeth at least once per day.
c. To experiment with different interdental cleansing aids to determine what best removes plaque from patient's teeth.
d. To design a brushing and flossing schedule to prevent the build-up of calculus.

42. Which type of bone grafting has the best rate of success in dentistry?

a. Alloplastic.
b. Xenogeneic.
c. Allogeneic.
d. Autologous.

43. ZOE paste mixed with a drop of formocresol is used on what type of tooth?

a. Permanent canines.
b. Primary bicuspids.
c. Permanent molars.
d. Primary molars.

44. What would be the appropriate type of wax to select for setting denture teeth?

   a. Casting wax

   b. Baseplate wax

   c. Inlay casting wax

   d. Utility wax

45. Which of the following instruments is used to measure the sulcus depths of the teeth in the dentition?

   a. Periodontal probe.

   b. U-15 scaler.

   c. Gingival curette.

   d. Periodontal explorer.

46. What is the one piece of information that is NOT included on a packing slip?

   a. The quantity ordered.

   b. The name of the product.

   c. The price information.

   d. The manufacturer's name.

47. Which of the following is the last step in the preparation and application of a composite resin material?

   a. Have the liquid bonding resin available for use by the dentist

   b. Use the cure light

   c. Apply final carving touches

   d. Select the appropriate shade of composite

48. Which of the following best describes how patient fees and treatment plan options should be discussed with the patient?

   a. These should be discussed after the insurance company has been billed and the patient has an account balance.

   b. These should be discussed in the operatory after the treatment has been performed.

   c. These should be discussed in the waiting room as the patient is waiting for his appointment.

   d. These should be discussed in a private counseling room in the dental office.

49. Edema is most often the first symptom in which emergency condition?

   a. A stroke.

   b. Hyperventilation.

   c. An allergic reaction.

   d. Epilepsy.

50. What type of final restoration should be placed with the use of type II glass ionomer materials?

   a. An occlusal restoration.

   b. An MOD restoration.

   c. An MODBL restoration.

   d. A class V restoration.

51. What is type II zinc oxide also referred to as?

   a. A resin cement.

   b. An intermediate restorative material.

   c. An endodontic cleaning solution.

   d. A permanent cement.

52. Which of the following vital signs would be cause for concern during dental treatment?

   a. Blood pressure of 140/90 mm Hg
   b. Respiratory rate of 18 breaths per minute
   c. Pulse of 70 beats per minute in an adult
   d. Oral temperature of 99 °F

53. Complete the following sentence correctly. When coronal polishing with an abrasive, the type of abrasive used determines the _____.

   a. length of the appointment.
   b. pressure to be used.
   c. rate of abrasion.
   d. quality of the coronal polishing.

54. Which of the following would not be the first choice for managing a reluctant child during a routine cleaning appointment?

   a. Ask the child to hold and assist with the saliva ejector
   b. Involve the child in the procedure such as selecting the flavor of fluoride or toothpaste
   c. Use a papoose board
   d. Allow the parent to stay in the room to help keep the child calm

55. After polishing a partial denture following an adjustment, what should be done with the used laboratory rag wheel?

   a. It should be disposed of.
   b. It should be sprayed with disinfecting solution.
   c. It should be covered with a plastic barrier.
   d. It should be removed, rinsed, and autoclaved.

56. Which of the following conditions is a result of ingesting too much fluoride?

   a. Mulberry molars.
   b. Mottled enamel.
   c. Hypodontia.
   d. Macroglossia.

57. A patient with type 1 diabetes is receiving dental care. The patient is complaining of dry mouth and a headache. You notice a fruity, acetone odor on the patient's breath. What is the appropriate action?

   a. Provide a source of concentrated sugar such as orange juice or a sugar packet to help raise blood sugar level.
   b. You determine that the patient has skipped the morning insulin dose and assist the patient with insulin administration
   c. Call 911 immediately
   d. Call the patient's emergency contact

58. Which statement is FALSE in regards to the properties of condensable composites?

   a. Condensable composites contain low amounts of filler particles.
   b. Condensable composites are "putty like" in consistency.
   c. Condensable composites are highly viscous.
   d. Condensable composites are stiffer in consistency than other composites.

59. Sickle scalers are primarily used for which of the following reasons?
   a. To remove supragingival calculus.
   b. To remove subgingival calculus.
   c. To remove interproximal calculus.
   d. To remove lingual calculus.

60. *Gelfoam*, used to induce clotting in a tooth socket after extraction, is what type of drug?
   a. Nitrate.
   b. Anti-inflammatory.
   c. Hemostatic.
   d. Antifungal.

61. Dental office employees may be at risk for certain types of occupational exposures to certain diseases. What type of hepatitis vaccination is required by OSHA to be offered to these employees within 10 days of initial job assignment?
   a. Hepatitis A
   b. Hepatitis B
   c. Hepatitis C
   d. Hepatitis D

62. When instructing a patient on how to care for dentures, which of the following must be avoided in order to prevent damage to the new dentures?
   a. Remove the dentures at least once per day and rinse the oral cavity.
   b. Use a denture brush to clean all areas of the denture.
   c. Use hot water to soak the denture for one hour per day to allow for proper disinfection.
   d. Store the dentures in a moist container to prevent them from drying out.

63. Which of the following actions should be avoided by the dental assistant during the preparation and placement of a periodontal dressing following periodontal surgery?
   a. Place the dressing over the crown of the tooth and the surrounding gingival tissue.
   b. Extrude equal lengths of the base and catalyst material onto a mixing pad.
   c. Lubricate gloved fingers for ease of manipulation prior to handling the product.
   d. Apply gentle pressure to allow for the dressing to adhere to the tissue.

64. When assisting with an amalgam procedure, which of the following steps comes first?
   a. Place the amalgam into the amalgam well.
   b. Place the amalgam capsule into the amalgamator.
   c. Twist open the amalgam capsule and discard the scrap amalgam.
   d. Load the amalgam onto the amalgam carrier.

65. A patient experiencing difficulty speaking, paralysis, vision impairment, or sudden headache may be experiencing a(n):
   a. myocardial infarction.
   b. migraine.
   c. cerebrovascular accident.
   d. seizure.

66. When evaluating an alginate impression, which of the following is NOT a desirable characteristic for the impression to have?

a. The impression will be free from rips or tears.
b. The impression demonstrates the required anatomical structures and features.
c. The impression needs to contain only the teeth undergoing restorative procedures.
d. The impression tray should not be visible through the impression material.

67. During which stage of tooth development do the teeth and the dental tissues fully mineralize into their final forms?

a. Bud stage.
b. Maturation stage.
c. Apposition stage.
d. Cap stage.

68. Which of the following is the most accurate term used to describe the complete removal of a tooth?

a. Restoration.
b. Gingivectomy.
c. Extraction.
d. Sealant.

69. When evacuating during a restorative procedure, where should the bevel of the evacuation tip be placed?

a. Parallel to the mesial surface of the teeth.
b. Parallel to the distal surface of the teeth.
c. Parallel to the buccal or lingual surfaces of the teeth.
d. Parallel to the occlusal surface of the teeth.

70. What should the dental assistant do when the dentist is using the amalgam carver to carve in the anatomical features of the tooth?

a. Use the high-volume evacuator to remove excess amalgam from the patient's mouth.
b. Keep the area dry with air.
c. Provide the dentist with gauze to place the excess amalgam.
d. Prepare the calcium hydroxide for application.

71. When assisting chairside during an amalgam procedure, which of the following products is placed first into the prepared tooth?

a. Dycal.
b. Desensitizer.
c. Varnish.
d. Amalgam material.

72. Dry angles, used for moisture control, are primarily used to control the ducts of which salivary glands?

a. Submandibular.
b. Parotid.
c. Sublingual.
d. Parathyroid.

73. A pregnant patient receiving dental treatment may experience which of the following after sitting up quickly in the chair?

 a. Postural hypertension
 b. Hypoglycemia
 c. Postural hypotension
 d. Syncope

74. What type of instrument is used to remove enamel during the placement of a veneer?

 a. Condenser
 b. Diamond bur
 c. Evacuator
 d. Carver

75. When transferring a new instrument to the dentist, which finger does the dental assistant use to collect the used instrument?

 a. Ring finger.
 b. Little finger.
 c. Middle finger.
 d. Index finger.

76. Where would you palpate the cervical lymph nodes during an oral dental exam?

 a. Bilaterally, along the sides of the tongue.
 b. Bilaterally, along the internal jugular vein.
 c. Bilaterally, along the region of the temporomandibular joint.
 d. Bilaterally, along the ramus of the mandible.

77. What does amalgamation refer to?

 a. The actual chemical reaction that takes place when the alloy particles and mercury are mixed.
 b. The process of rapidly triturating the alloy and mercury.
 c. The separation of the mercury from the alloy.
 d. The separation of the alloy from the mercury.

78. When performing suture removal, what is the final thing that the dental assistant must do?

 a. Irrigate the surgical site with warm saline solution if there is bleeding.
 b. Count the number of sutures that have been removed and compare this number with the number that were indicated on the patient's chart.
 c. Swab the site to remove any debris from the area.
 d. Place a non-eugenol periodontal dressing over the surgical site where the sutures were placed.

79. What is the name given to the surface of each tooth that is found furthest from the patient's midline?

 a. Buccal.
 b. Mesial.
 c. Distal.
 d. Lingual.

80. Which of the following does the manufacturer issue if an item ordered is not available at the time of placing the order?

 a. A credit slip.
 b. A replacement of greater value.
 c. A back order slip.
 d. A replacement of lesser value.

81. How often should a review of the dental patient's medical health history be completed?

    a. At each dental office visit.
    b. At every other dental office visit.
    c. At every six month "check-up" visit.
    d. At every prophy appointment only.

82. What type of instrument is a burnisher?

    a. Restorative
    b. Accessory
    c. Basic
    d. Hand cutting

83. Which of the following supplies would most likely NOT be used for taking a mandibular preliminary impression?

    a. Wide-blade spatula
    b. Biohazard bag
    c. Alginate measure scoop
    d. Polycarboxylate

84. When storing any item shipped from the manufacturer, where should the new item be stored?

    a. The new item should be stored behind the current item, allowing for the current item to be used first.
    b. The new item should be stored in front of the current item, allowing for the new item to be used first.
    c. The new item should be stored in a new location.
    d. The new item should remain in the box it was shipped in, until needed.

85. Which of the following terms is used to describe a written agreement formed by the dentist and the patient receiving care outlining and agreeing to the treatment to be performed?

    a. Implied consent.
    b. Informed consent.
    c. Nonmaleficence consent.
    d. Beneficence contract.

86. A patient undergoing a procedure of approximately 30 minutes will most likely require which of the following types of anesthetics?

    a. Bupivacaine
    b. Prilocaine HCl block
    c. Novocain
    d. Lidocaine HCl

87. Which of the following interdental items is used to clean areas in the oral cavity that are difficult to reach with a toothbrush?

    a. End-tuft brush
    b. Bridge threaders
    c. Perio-Aid
    d. Rubber-tipped stimulator

88. An excisional biopsy involves the removal of which of the following?

    a. The entire lesion with the addition of a small amount of adjacent tissue.
    b. A portion of the suspicious lesion with the addition of a small amount of adjacent tissue.
    c. The entire lesion without removal of the adjacent tissue.
    d. A small sample of the lesion for analysis.

89. What is the name of the instrument that includes the following types: straight, binangle, Wedelstaedt, and angle-former?

a. Excavator
b. Hatchet
c. Gingival trimmer
d. Chisel

90. In reference to a dental office's inventory supply system, the term, "lead time" is best described as:

a. the quantity of a disposable item used in a given time.
b. the amount of time between when an order was placed and when it was received.
c. the time allowed for ordering before the final item is used.
d. how long an item can remain not in use before it expires.

91. Where are frontal sinuses located?

a. Under the chin in the soft tissue of the throat.
b. Beneath the zygomatic arches in the forehead.
c. Beneath the left and right eyes in the forehead.
d. Just above the left and right eyes in the forehead.

92. When referring to the five classifications of range of motion for the dental assistant, which of the following describes the motion of the entire arm and shoulder?

a. Class II.
b. Class III.
c. Class IV.
d. Class V.

93. When working chairside, which of the following ergonomic positions should be avoided?

a. Keeping a bend in the wrist during all procedures while holding the high-volume evacuator to allow for easier access.
b. Sitting six inches above the dentist to allow for adequate vision of the procedure.
c. Keeping the back straight and supported by the backrest to ensure proper posture.
d. Sitting in the middle of the dental-assisting chair with the feet on the foot rest allowing for maximum stability.

94. Where is fluoride primarily absorbed in the body?

a. Gastrointestinal tract.
b. The lungs.
c. The stomach.
d. The liver.

95. The vitality test is used to measure the health of:

a. enamel.
b. dentin.
c. pulp.
d. root.

Infection Control

1. What is the initial step for instrument cleaning?

    a. Rinse instruments, scrub them with a brush, and place into a holding solution.

    b. Place instruments in an ultrasonic cleaner for processing.

    c. Rinse instruments and wrap them for processing in an autoclave.

    d. Wrap instruments in an approved sterilization wrap.

2. When handling biopsy specimens, what should the dental healthcare worker do to decrease the chance of cross-contamination?

    a. Label the container with a hazard sticker during storage.

    b. Transfer the specimen in a sturdy container with a secure lid.

    c. Keep the specimen stored in the refrigerator until it is ready to ship.

    d. Return the container to circulation for future specimens after the lab has performed the required testing and returned the container and results.

3. Latex or non-latex gloves are a barrier for the hands of all dental professionals. Which of the following must be considered to retain the integrity of the gloves?

    a. Washing with detergents can cause "wicking" to occur.

    b. The length of a person's nails should not be considered in determining size.

    c. Gloves should be kept in a cool storage place no more than two months.

    d. None of these are concerns.

4. What is the correct protocol to follow when considering decontamination procedures for digital x-ray sensors?

    a. After use, the sensor should be immersed in a high-level disinfectant for the time specified by the manufacturer for sterilization.

    b. The sensor should be covered during use with a barrier and then removed from the cable cord and placed in the autoclave for sterilization.

    c. The sensors should be covered with barriers during use and then disinfected with an intermediate-level disinfectant.

    d. The sensors should be placed in the autoclave sterilizer on the flash cycle after being wiped down with an intermediate-level disinfectant.

5. Digital x-ray sensors are used on multiple patients per day. How are these kept in aseptic condition?

    a. Providing continuous wipe downs with alcohol.

    b. Replacing sensors 2-3 times per year to prevent bioburden.

    c. Soaking the sensors in a tuberculocidal solution overnight once per week.

    d. Covering the sensors with a plastic sleeve during each patient use.

6. What type(s) of personal protective equipment should be worn when the dental auxiliary is working with alginate impression material?

    a. Mask.

    b. Mask and eyewear.

    c. Mask, eyewear, and gloves.

    d. No personal protective equipment is needed, as this is harmless when in powder form.

7. Which of the following is NOT included in the bloodborne pathogens exposure control plan that should be implemented at each dental office?

   a. Hepatitis B vaccination requirements.
   b. Exposure determinations.
   c. Hazardous waste disposal.
   d. Exposure incident protocols.

8. Unsaturated chemical vapor, used in some sterilizers, consists of what components?

   a. Isopropyl alcohol and ethylene glycol.
   b. Sodium sulfate and denatured water.
   c. Water and isopropyl alcohol.
   d. Formaldehyde and alcohol.

9. What is the basic concept that Universal or Standard Precautions is based on?

   a. Standard precautions only apply to those individuals who have a history of infectious disease
   b. Standard precautions only apply to those individuals who have a history of high-risk behavior such as drug abuse or sexual orientation
   c. Standard precautions apply to all patients and all bodily fluids should be treated as if infectious
   d. Standard precautions only apply to blood and saliva based on the patient's history

10. Which of the following is a semi-critical instrument?

   a. Scalpel.
   b. Bone chisel.
   c. Extraction forceps.
   d. Dental handpiece.

11. When the pre-cleaning of hard surfaces is performed, what technique is best for removing bioburden?

   a. Wipe with disinfectant wipes, allow it to dry, and then repeat.
   b. Spray with disinfectant and wipe with paper towels.
   c. Wipe with a paper towel and spray if still visibly soiled.
   d. Clean with alcohol wipes, then allow to air dry.

12. How long is a dental employer required to keep the records of employees?

   a. The length of employment
   b. The length of employment plus 10 years
   c. The length of employment plus 20 years
   d. The length of employment plus 30 years

13. In order to assure patients that instrumentation is sterilized, it is important:

   a. to open instrument packs and do a thorough hand washing after the patient is seated.
   b. to use a new pair of gloves when recording patient notes.
   c. to change amalgam separator filtration once or twice per year.
   d. to display licenses and certification near patient operatories.

14. A needlestick injury has resulted in exposure to hepatitis C. Which of the following is not a recommendation for the first 6 months?

   a. Restriction from sexual activity
   b. Leave of absence from work
   c. Defer plans for starting a family
   d. Blood donation

15. The dental assistant is preparing for the use of an alcohol-based hand rub prior to an amalgam procedure. Which one of the following should be avoided during the hand cleaning process?

    a. Use a hand rub that is 100% alcohol to provide the greatest ability to kill all microbes present.

    b. Rub the hands together, making sure to reach all areas including the fingertips, between the fingers, the palms, and the back sides of the hands.

    c. Use the amount recommended by the manufacturer, not more or less.

    d. Only use the product if the hands are free of physical debris, which can decrease the ability of the hand rub to work.

16. Prions were discovered through the research of Dr. Stanley Prusiner who was studying Creutzfeldt-Jakob disease. What is a prion?

    a. A strain of DNA that has been damaged by radiation treatments.

    b. A proteinaceous infectious particle.

    c. A form of spirochete that thrives in dental water lines.

    d. A particularly strong viral strain that causes flu-like symptoms.

17. Which of the following methods of sterilization uses low temperatures to sterilize items and requires 4-12 hours for sterilization and up to 16 hours for post-sterilization aeration?

    a. Stem under pressure.

    b. Dry heat.

    c. Unsaturated chemical vapor.

    d. Ethylene oxide.

18. According to the bloodborne pathogens standard, following a baseline blood collection after an exposure incident at the dental office with the employee not giving consent to test for HIV, how long should the exposed employee's blood be preserved by the testing laboratory?

    a. 40 days.

    b. 75 days.

    c. 90 days.

    d. 125 days.

19. Which of the following is a correct statement regarding pre-procedural mouth rinses?

    a. Pre-procedural rinses are to be used both before and after the procedure for maximum effectiveness.

    b. There is a large amount of scientific evidence that supports the use and effectiveness of pre-procedural mouth rinses in preventing oral infections in patients.

    c. Pre-procedural mouth rinses are recommended by the CDC prior to prophylaxis procedures.

    d. The intent of pre-procedural mouth rinses is to reduce the amount of microbes found in the oral cavity and to prevent them from being released into the air during a procedure.

20. Which type of hard surface disinfectant is broad spectrum, intermediate level, and must be prepared daily?

    a. Glutaraldehyde.

    b. Synthetic phenol compounds.

    c. Iodophors.

    d. Chlorine dioxide.

21. How many employees in a dental office will necessitate a written emergency action plan?

    a. 2 or more.

    b. 5 or more.

    c. 11 or more.

    d. 20 or more.

22. Surgical instruments require _____ to insure they are not corroded by thorough and constant sterilization under high heat and pressure.

    a. soaking for at least an hour in detergent
    b. placement in a surgical milk bath before packaging for the autoclave
    c. thorough scrubbing with brushes
    d. extra rinsing with hot water

23. Which of the following terms can be defined as a person who is infected with a disease but does not show any recognizable symptoms of that disease?

    a. Pathogenic carrier.
    b. Microbial carrier.
    c. Communicable carrier.
    d. Asymptomatic carrier.

24. The Centers for Disease Control and Prevention (CDC) Guidelines for Infection Control in Dental Health-Care Settings were developed for which category of employees?

    a. Office support
    b. Clinical employees
    c. Insurance companies
    d. Dental accreditation bodies

25. Which level of disinfection is required for counter tops in the dental operatory?

    a. Glutaraldehyde spray.
    b. Household degreaser spray.
    c. Alcohol wipes.
    d. Surface disinfectant with tuberculocidal capability.

26. Who is covered by the OSHA bloodborne pathogens standard?

    a. All employees who are occupationally exposed to blood or other potentially infectious materials.
    b. Anyone in any type of job, as it is a multifaceted standard.
    c. Physicians and dentists are covered and have the option to delegate duties of this standard to their employees.
    d. Clinical dental workers only.

27. When working on a patient who is infected with syphilis, the dental assistant must ensure that they are adequately protected by personal protective equipment in order to prevent which of the following that is associated with this infection?

    a. An infectious ulcerating sore called a chancre.
    b. Inhalation of highly infectious viral particles known as *Treponema pallidum*.
    c. Exposure to bacteria that will lead to an infection causing lockjaw.
    d. An infectious lesion on the tongue called herpes.

28. Which is correct regarding the hepatitis B vaccination?

    a. If an employee refuses the vaccination, they are required to obtain counseling regarding the benefits of the vaccination.
    b. The employee is responsible for the cost of the vaccination if they initially decline, but change their mind in the future.
    c. If an employee starts the series but does not finish it, they are not required to because of the immunity that has been built up in their body from the initial doses of the vaccine.
    d. The employer must offer the vaccination to all employees at no cost within 10 days of initial employment.

29. What type of hypersensitivity allergy can be caused by repeated exposure to the many chemicals used in the production of gloves and PPE as well as the chemicals used in dentistry?

    a. Type I hypersensitivity allergy
    b. Type II hypersensitivity allergy
    c. Type III hypersensitivity allergy
    d. Type IV hypersensitivity allergy

30. What type of biological particulate is used in a biologic monitoring strip?

    a. Paramecia.
    b. Endospores.
    c. Methicillin-resistant *Staphylococcus aureus* (MRSA).
    d. Influenza B virus.

31. When a chemical spill has occurred in the dental office, it is important to remember to:

    a. use protective eyewear and utility gloves and to keep neutralizing agents on hand.
    b. notify all staff and keep a record of the incident.
    c. dispose of all hazardous materials immediately.
    d. All of these are correct.

32. When considering the disinfection of housekeeping surfaces in the dental office, which of the following is correct?

    a. The dental assistant must ensure that walls and drapes are included in the disinfection process as well as the floors and countertops.
    b. If blood or body fluids are present, the dental assistant must use a high-level disinfectant to decontaminate the area.
    c. An EPA-registered hospital disinfectant or low-level disinfectant is recommended to clean these surfaces.
    d. Mops and cloths can be used for 3 days before they need to be cleaned and allowed to dry for reuse.

33. All of the following are reasons for a sterilizer to fail a spore test, except when:

    a. the sterilizer becomes overloaded with cassettes and instruments.
    b. cloth wrap is in the chemical vapor sterilizer.
    c. there is a sterilizer timer malfunction.
    d. liquids (not water) were placed in a dry heat sterilizer.

34. Which of the following would NOT be considered an advantage to using surface barriers in the dental office?

    a. Efficient use of time
    b. Environmentally friendly
    c. Protection of hard to clean surfaces
    d. Provides a positive image of cleanliness to the patient

35. Which of the following is an example of a noncritical instrument?

    a. Stethoscope.
    b. Dental mouth mirror.
    c. Impression trays.
    d. Amalgam condenser.

36. Aseptic technique can be maintained while making notations in patient charts. How is this accomplished?

a. Spraying paper charts with antiseptic mist.
b. Using barrier protection on writing implements.
c. Changing gloves after writing notes.
d. None of these are true.

37. What temperature is required for dry heat sterilization?

a. 350-400 °F
b. 320-375 °F
c. 375-450 °F
d. 400-500 °F

38. When the dental assistant is considering hand hygiene and infection control practices, which one of the following is correct?

a. The hands must be washed with soap and water before placing new gloves prior to the start of a procedure.
b. Gloves are produced without defects from the manufacturer, meaning there is no risk in clinical glove usage.
c. Bacteria will multiply in dark, moist conditions, such as occurs when the hands are not dried prior to donning a pair of gloves before a procedure.
d. Bar soap can be used during handwashing as long as it has antimicrobial properties.

39. Which of the following statements is LEAST accurate regarding dental unit water lines (DUWL)?

a. The primary source for any microorganisms present in the DUWL originates from the public water supply
b. Water from DUWL can be used for all dental procedures
c. Anti-retraction devices can be installed in DUWL to help prevent saliva from entering the waterline during patient care
d. The tubing that connects the DUWL to the handpieces can become colonized with many different types of bacteria or other microorganisms

40. Why is it important to have heavy-duty utility gloves in the sterilization area?

a. Water used to rinse instruments is quite hot and could cause burns.
b. To protect healthcare workers' hands from puncture injuries during cleaning.
c. In case an inspection team needs to see where they are kept.
d. They are used for window washing and floor cleaning.

41. Which one of the following is NOT representative of best practices by the dental team for minimizing the risk of spreading disease in the dental office?

a. Ensuring that natural fingernail tips are shorter than 1 inch in length
b. Avoiding chipped nail polish
c. Removing transient flora during hand cleaning procedures
d. Determining the hand cleaning method based on the procedure being completed

42. What is the main purpose of the holding solution?

a. The holding solution serves as an intermediate-level disinfectant required prior to processing.
b. It provides a method of pre-cleaning prior to instrument sterilization.
c. To prevent debris from hardening onto the surface of the dental instrument.
d. It is used as a disinfectant for the dental instruments.

43. After an evaluation following an exposure incident at work, how long does the evaluating healthcare professional have to provide the exposed employee with a written opinion of the results?
   a. 10 days.
   b. 15 days.
   c. 20 days.
   d. 25 days.

44. According to the OSHA occupational exposure categories, which one of the following is an accurate statement about category 1 employees in dentistry?
   a. Category 1 employees may occasionally be exposed to body fluids during patient care.
   b. Category 1 employees are never exposed to blood or body fluids during patient care.
   c. Category 1 employees are occasionally responsible for cleaning dental operatories and patient care areas.
   d. Dental assistants are an example of category 1 employees.

45. What is the first step in treating a needle stick injury to a finger?
   a. Apply antibacterial ointment
   b. Apply surgical disinfectant soap
   c. Use soap and water to wash affected area as soon as possible following injury
   d. Wash with soap and water, then apply an antiseptic ointment

46. According to the bloodborne pathogens standard, which of the following is a correct requirement of the employer and/or employee?
   a. The employer must replace personal protective equipment used by the employees as needed at no cost to the employees.
   b. If an employee damages utility gloves due to incorrect cleaning procedures, they are required to replace the gloves in a reasonable time.
   c. The employee is responsible for laundering their personal uniforms.
   d. The employee must provide their own gloves if they are experiencing dermatitis reactions due to the gloves currently provided by the employer.

47. Which of the following infections may occur when dental healthcare workers are exposed to infected dental unit waterlines and aerosolized water?
   a. Tetanus.
   b. Legionnaires' disease.
   c. Methicillin-resistant *Staphylococcus aureus* (MRSA).
   d. Hepatitis B.

48. During an amalgam procedure, the dental assistant's glove and skin are perforated by an explorer during an instrument transfer. Upon removal of the gloves, it is noticed that the area is bleeding. Which one of the following describes a correct component of appropriate management of this exposure?
   a. Identify what led to the exposure in the exposure incident report while avoiding sharing details about the incident to the patient to protect the dental assistant.
   b. Offer the dental assistant the opportunity to provide an immediate sample for a baseline blood test in order to identify the presence of infectious diseases including the hepatitis B virus (HBV) and human immunodeficiency virus (HIV).
   c. Determine who was at fault for the incident, and document that in the employee's credentialing file.
   d. The dental assistant should don new gloves and finish the procedure. Following the procedure, the dental assistant should work with office management to complete an incident report.

49. Which of the following is an example of regulated biohazardous waste?

    a. A used Band-Aid.
    b. A piece of 2x2 gauze that has dried blood flaking off of it.
    c. Used fixer solution.
    d. A used patient napkin with a small amount of blood.

50. What vaccination protects against lockjaw?

    a. MMR
    b. H1N1
    c. Varicella
    d. Td

51. How should cloth wrapping be fastened when used for sterilizing cassettes?

    a. Safety pins.
    b. Indicator tape.
    c. Stapler.
    d. Any of these.

52. What type of information is not found on a Safety Data Sheet?

    a. Information on the physical or chemical characteristics of a material used in a dental practice.
    b. Fire and explosion hazard data.
    c. Boiling point of a given chemical or material.
    d. Dental procedure protocols.

53. Which of the following is not correct regarding hepatitis B?

    a. Hepatitis B can cause serious illness involving the liver including cirrhosis, liver cancer, or liver failure
    b. Only individuals who are symptomatic can transmit the virus
    c. More than one-third of all hepatitis cases are due to hepatitis B
    d. Hepatitis B is transmitted through blood and saliva

54. What items cannot protect patients from aerosolized spray during treatment?

    a. Safety goggles.
    b. High volume evacuators.
    c. Rubber dams.
    d. Mask.

55. Which of the following terms best describes physical devices or items that should be used by the dental auxiliary to prevent occupational exposures to bloodborne pathogens and aid dental auxiliaries in providing safe dental care while at work?

    a. Engineering controls.
    b. Work practice controls.
    c. Hazardous waste controls.
    d. Contamination controls.

56. Which of the following provides the best description of disease transmission by indirect contact?

    a. Performing a procedure where blood accidently splashes into the eyes of the dental healthcare worker.
    b. Using a contaminated object that was not sterilized properly on a new patient.
    c. Breathing in aerosols suspended in the air, which are attached to infectious microbes.
    d. Being exposed to spray or spatter containing infectious microorganisms.

57. A low-level EPA registered disinfectant is not effective against which of the following?

a. HIV
b. HBV
c. Influenza
d. Aspergillus

58. The dental assistant is cleaning out one of the dental operatories and finds that the sharps container in the cupboard is overflowing and sharps items are falling out onto the cupboard floor. Which one of the following is the correct action to take?

a. The dental assistant should remove the cover of the overflowing sharps container, gently shake the container to allow for the contents to settle, and carefully place the cover back on the container.
b. The dental assistant should carefully remove the items that do not fit into the container and place them into a new sharps container. The full container should then be sealed and disposed of according to standard practices.
c. The dental assistant should leave the container and call the sharps disposal company to come and pick up the overflowing sharps container.
d. The overflowing sharps container should be placed in an additional and separate larger leakproof sharps container that can be securely closed, containing the same required labels as the original sharps container.

59. Which is an example of a chronic condition that affects the liver and is spread by blood transfusions and organ transplants?

a. Shingles.
b. Herpes type 1.
c. Hepatitis A.
d. Hepatitis C.

60. The OSHA Needlestick Safety and Prevention Act was expanded to include sharps with engineered sharps injury protection. This can best be described as:

a. Sharps that contain a standard produced that must be reviewed with the dental team and used in every procedure
b. Sharps that are paired with a separate form of an engineering control that must be assembled and combined prior to use
c. Sharps that are provided from the manufacturer with a built-in safety mechanism that will help keep the user of the sharps item safe from injury during manipulation
d. Sharps that have been engineered in a way that changes the functionality and purpose of the sharps item, but maintains operator safety

61. An instrument that penetrates bone or soft tissue is classified by the CDC as:

a. noncritical.
b. semicritical.
c. critical.
d. hazardous.

62. What is the required amount of time a dental practice must retain an employee's medical record regarding immunization and post-exposure medical evaluation?

a. 5 years.
b. 10 years.
c. 7 years past the termination of employment.
d. 30 years past the termination of employment.

63. What is a second name given to biological indicators?

a. Microbe monitoring devices.
b. Physical indicator strips.
c. Autoclave tapes.
d. Spore tests.

64. Which of these statements is TRUE about surface covers in the dental operatory?

a. They can be reused if the item was untouched during the procedure.
b. They are too costly to be used to cover all potentially exposed items.
c. All surfaces that cannot be repeatedly pre-cleaned and disinfected must have barriers.
d. None of these are true.

65. Which level of disinfectants is capable of sterilization?

a. Maximum-level.
b. High-level.
c. Intermediate-level.
d. Low-level.

66. How often should biologic monitoring be performed in the dental practice?

a. At least once per week.
b. Every 3 weeks.
c. Quarterly.
d. Biannually.

67. Which of the following is a requirement set in place by the OSHA Hazard Communications Standard?

a. SDS forms only come with products that are considered biologically hazardous in the dental office.
b. When a new SDS form is received by a dental office, it must be presented to all affected staff and reviewed before the product can be used.
c. SDS forms are optional safety documents that are provided by most manufacturing companies regarding the components of the specific product.
d. Employers must ensure that any SDS forms that come in with products are maintained and readily accessible to employees.

68. How often does the exposure control plan need to be updated?

a. Biannually
b. Annually
c. Every 3 years
d. Every 5 years

69. Which of the following should the dental healthcare worker avoid when handling sharps items in the dental office?

a. If the sharps container is nearing full capacity, continue to fill it only until sharps items are even with the top brim of the container.
b. Be sure to keep sharps containers at the point of use, in each operatory, and in the sterilization center.
c. Ensure that sharps items are placed in a puncture resistant container labeled with a biohazard label.
d. Never break or bend sharps prior to placing them into the sharps container.

70. What would be an appropriate alternative for a high-level disinfectant with low odor?

    a. Isopropyl alcohol
    b. Chlorine Dioxide
    c. Glutaraldehyde
    d. Ortho-phthalaldehyde

71. Which of the following safety protocols should be followed in the event of a mercury spill in a dental office?

    a. The mercury should be absorbed by paper towels and thrown in the trash receptacle, and the area should be decontaminated with a high-level disinfectant.
    b. A mercury spill kit should be used to clean and decontaminate the area.
    c. The spill should be diluted with a basic cleaning compound and then the area should be wiped down with an intermediate-level disinfectant.
    d. Mercury specific sand should be placed over the mercury, swept up, and placed in the biohazardous waste container.

72. When decontaminating an area on the floor in a treatment room after a blood spill, which of the following should be used?

    a. A low-level disinfectant.
    b. Detergent and water.
    c. A hospital disinfectant that has a HBV and HIV claim.
    d. An intermediate-level disinfectant that has a tuberculocidal claim.

73. Which of the following disinfectants are the best choices to use on alginate impressions?

    a. Complex phenols and chlorine dioxide.
    b. Quaternary ammoniums and glutaraldehyde.
    c. Iodophors and diluted sodium hypochlorite.
    d. Phenols and iodophors.

74. How often should disposable plastic suction traps be changed in the dental office?

    a. Once a week.
    b. Once a month.
    c. Quarterly.
    d. Twice each year.

75. When instruments are emerging from the ultrasonic unit with visible debris left on them, what is the likely problem?

    a. Cold water was used to fill the unit.
    b. There is a clog in the filter.
    c. The enzymatic solution was not mixed properly.
    d. The unit is malfunctioning.

76. Which one of the following is a regulation that contains standards that dental workers must follow to protect against the spread of infectious diseases?

    a. OSHA Hazard Communications Standard
    b. CDC Morbidity and Mortality Weekly Report
    c. OSHA Bloodborne Pathogens Standard
    d. NIOSH Infection Control in Dentistry

77. Which of the following techniques should be utilized during surgical procedures in dentistry?

   a. The solutions being used must be decontaminated with an antibacterial tablet prior to use.

   b. The dental auxiliary must use distilled water when assisting in surgical procedures.

   c. The office must use a filtering system to remove bacteria and microbes in the solutions used during surgery.

   d. The office must use a sterile water delivery system or device to deliver solutions during surgery.

78. When handling contaminated laundry, which of the following protocols needs to be followed by the dental staff member?

   a. Employees who handle the contaminated laundry should wear protective gloves and other appropriate personal protective equipment when necessary.

   b. If there is wet laundry, this should avoid contact with any type of bag due to the potential of soak-through and should be placed immediately into the washing machine.

   c. All laundry generated by a dental office must be shipped to an off-site secondary facility in order to prevent cross-contamination.

   d. The dentist is the only staff member that is able to process or handle contaminated laundry due to the liabilities that can occur if there was an occupational exposure from items found in the laundry area.

79. Which of the following would be an inappropriate action regarding the use of PPE that requires laundering?

   a. Placing contaminated items that need laundering in a biohazardous waste container

   b. Taking contaminated surgical gown home for laundering following Universal Precautions

   c. Changing a gown throughout the day whenever it becomes visibly soiled

   d. Carefully removing the gown by pulling it off but keeping the gown inside out so it does not touch the clothing underneath

80. The dental assistant is reviewing the medical history of a new patient in the dental office. The patient has disclosed a history of tuberculosis infection. Why is it essential for the dental assistant to discuss this disease history with the patient prior to any treatment?

   a. Per standard precautions, patients with a history of tuberculosis cannot be treated at a dental office and must obtain their dental care from medical facilities.

   b. Due to the high transmissibility of tuberculosis, the dental team must know if the disease is in an active state and, if so, whether the patient is currently taking the prescribed medications for this condition.

   c. If a patient has a history of infection with tuberculosis, he or she is likely to have infections with bloodborne pathogens, and the dental team would need to conduct further screenings for these infections.

   d. Patients with a history of tuberculosis must undergo a blood test administered by the dentist to identify an active disease state prior to receiving further dental treatment.

Radiation Health and Safety

1. The amount of radiation absorbed per gram of tissue is referred to as a:

  a. rad.
  b. rem.
  c. mrem.
  d. Roentgen.

2. When referring to imaging in dentistry, what does CBCT stand for?

  a. Central-beam classification technology
  b. Cone-beam computed tomography
  c. Center-balanced computer technology
  d. Coronal-beam central topography

3. When the kilovoltage or kV setting in the tubehead is increased:

  a. Electrons move from the anode to the cathode with more speed.
  b. X-rays move from the anode to the cathode with more speed.
  c. Electrons move from the cathode to the anode with more speed.
  d. X-rays move from the cathode to the anode with more speed.

4. When exposing dental images in a dental operatory, what is the purpose of using barriers and disinfecting the treatment room following each patient?

  a. To reduce the susceptibility of the dental patient's immune system in order to lessen disease transmission potential
  b. To limit the types of portals or openings that exist for a pathogen to enter the dental patient and cause an infectious disease
  c. To improve time management for the dental team by allowing for shorter dental operatory turnover times between patients
  d. To eliminate or reduce the number of pathogens that are present due to aerosols of oral and respiratory fluids produced during dental imaging

5. Which of the following are correct in regard to the different wavelengths produced in dentistry?

  a. X-rays with longer wavelength have less penetrating power.
  b. X-rays with shorter wavelength have less penetrating power.
  c. X-rays with shorter wavelengths are more likely to be absorbed by matter prior to striking the image receptor.
  d. X-rays with longer wavelengths can be referred to as hard rays.

6. Using the proper _____ assists in controlling the amount of radiation emitted to the patient.

  a. exposure factors
  b. size film
  c. monitoring device
  d. time management

7. Which of the following types of radiation is also known as "useful radiation?"

  a. Secondary radiation.
  b. Primary radiation.
  c. Tertiary radiation.
  d. Scattered radiation.

8. According to the National Council on Radiation Protection and Measurements, what is the maximum permissible dose of radiation that a dental auxiliary can receive in 1 year?

a. 4 rems.
b. 5 rems.
c. 6 rems.
d. 7 rems.

9. A cone-shaped radiopaque image on a panoramic x-ray is likely caused by:

a. Use of a thyroid collar during imaging
b. Earrings
c. Orthodontic retainer
d. Tongue piercing

10. Which one of the following is an advantage of the paralleling technique?

a. Receptor placement is simple and easy to duplicate.
b. Patient discomfort is minimal during dental imaging.
c. The paralleling technique can be done without the use of any receptor placement tool, thereby reducing infection control requirements.
d. The paralleling technique is easy to use with patients who have a low roof of the mouth or bony growths in the mouth.

11. When exposing periapical images on a young child, what size image receptor should the dental auxiliary choose?

a. Size 0.
b. Size 1.
c. Size 2.
d. Size 3.

12. What is the correct way for a dental assistant to wear a dosimeter?

a. Only when he/she is taking x-rays
b. All day, every day
c. Just during normal business hours for the practice
d. Only when he/she is at the dental office

13. Which of the following images needs to show the entire tooth from 2-3 mm beyond the apex to the entire occlusal or incisal edge?

a. Occlusal image.
b. Bitewing image.
c. Periapical image.
d. Panoramic image.

14. Which of the following is not an effective way that the "as low as reasonably achievable" (ALARA) principle can be achieved in the dental office for the protection of the patient?

a. Use of lead aprons and thyroid collars
b. Use of D film
c. Minimize the time of exposure
d. Use of digital radiographs

15. When the bisecting technique is used, which of the following angles is bisected?

   a. The angle formed by the image receptor and the long axis of the tooth.
   b. The angle formed by the central ray and the tooth
   c. The angle formed by the central ray and the image receptor.
   d. The angle that is perpendicular to the image receptor.

16. Which of the following is a direct result when an image receptor is exposed with a high milliamperage or mA setting?

   a. High contrast.
   b. Low contrast.
   c. High density.
   d. Low density.

17. When classifying patient care items based on their potential to spread infection due to their intended use, which classification is the Snap-A-Ray?

   a. Critical instrument
   b. Semicritical instrument
   c. Noncritical instrument
   d. Due to its use in dental imaging and the minimal risk of it transmitting disease, it is not classified into one of these classifications.

18. Determine which of the following statements is TRUE:

   a. Patients must have a complete series of x-rays taken once a year.
   b. Dental images should not be taken on a "routine basis."
   c. Multiple attempts at obtaining a diagnostically acceptable radiograph should be made until an attempt is successful.
   d. Informed consent is not needed for exposing routine dental x-rays.

19. During production of dental x-rays inside the dental tube, which component is responsible for creating thermionic emission?

   a. The tungsten target.
   b. The filament circuit.
   c. The step-up transformer.
   d. The cathode.

20. Which of the following is correct regarding a radiation monitoring badge?

   a. It is a device that can measure the amount of radiation that reaches the body of the radiographer.
   b. It consists of calcium tungstate crystals that are sensitive to secondary radiation.
   c. It is worn by the dental assistant for a minimum of 4 months and then sent in for processing.
   d. The badge should be stored in the dental operatory where the radiation exposures take place.

21. When the bisecting technique is used, foreshortening will occur if the central ray is directed perpendicular to the:

   a. plane of the image receptor.
   b. imaginary bisector.
   c. long axis of the tooth on the same arch.
   d. long axis of the tooth in the opposite arch.

22. Which of the following images has the purpose of demonstrating the buccal-lingual and anterior-posterior relationships of structures on an image receptor?

  a. Lateral cephalometric image.
  b. Occlusal image.
  c. Periapical image.
  d. Waters projection.

23. During extraoral panoramic dental radiography, if the chin is positioned too high or tipped inward:

  a. the Curve of Spee will be correctly aligned.
  b. the Frankfort plane is positioned too high.
  c. the Frankfort plane is positioned too low and is tipped in a downward direction.
  d. the final processed panoramic will have increased definition in the area of the maxillary teeth.

24. Which of the following best describes cone beam computed tomography (CBCT)?

  a. The smallest element of three-dimensional imaging, also known as a volume element pixel.
  b. A term used to describe computer-assisted digital imaging in dentistry.
  c. A technique that uses a cone-shaped x-ray beam to gather information and present it in three dimensions on a computer screen.
  d. The reconstruction of raw data into images when imported into a specific viewing software.

25. Which of the following choices is NOT a type of somatic cell?

  a. Brain cells.
  b. Kidney cells.
  c. Reproductive cells.
  d. Liver cells.

26. Indicate which of the following statements is TRUE:

  a. All dental x-rays pass through the patient's skin and reach the dental film.
  b. The skin tissues of the patient being radiographed absorb all x-rays.
  c. The skin tissues of the patient being radiographed absorb some x-rays.
  d. No dental x-rays pass through the patient's skin and reach the dental film.

27. A patient is being prepared for a panoramic exposure. The patient is wearing an earring in the left ear only. The exposure is made and the panoramic radiograph is processed. Where will the earring artifact be seen on the panoramic film?

  a. The earring will be seen on the right side of the film, slightly higher than the real object.
  b. The earring will be seen on the left side of the film, slightly higher than the real object.
  c. The earring will be seen in the area of the anterior mandibular teeth.
  d. The earring will be seen on the right side of the film, slightly lower than the real object.

28. Which type of x-rays is removed by the aluminum disks found within the x-ray tube head?

  a. Low energy, short wavelength.
  b. Low energy, long wavelength.
  c. High energy, long wavelength.
  d. High energy, short wavelength.

29. Under state laws, the *respondeat superior* doctrine states that:

  a. the employee is responsible for his or her own actions when taking a dental radiograph.
  b. the employer is responsible for the actions of the radiographer when taking a dental radiograph.
  c. the patient is responsible for the actions of the dental radiographer.
  d. the state is responsible for the actions of the dental radiographer.

30. Which of the following is worn by the dental auxiliary in order to measure radiation exposure?

    a. Particulate monitor.
    b. Dosimeter.
    c. Radiation shield.
    d. Ionization badge.

31. When considering hand hygiene practices that may be used during dental imaging, which one of the following is the most accurate?

    a. A routine hand washing should include using water and nonantimicrobial soap, washing the hands for 20–30 seconds followed by a long rinse with water from the fingertips to the wrists.
    b. An alcohol-based hand rub should be used and rubbed between the hands and fingers, covering all areas until the hands are completely dry.
    c. A soap product should be selected that has antimicrobial properties and is used with water for 10 seconds of hand washing.
    d. A routine hand wash should be performed for 20–30 seconds followed by an alcohol-based hand rub until the hands are completely dry.

32. Determine which of the following statements is TRUE regarding the standard of care that is provided by a dentist:

    a. Documentation signed by the patient, releasing the dental provider from liability, protects the dentist when treating a patient who refuses dental x-rays.
    b. Dentists are allowed to treat a patient even though the patient refuses necessary dental x-rays.
    c. Legally, a patient cannot consent to negligent care.
    d. Legally, a patient can consent to negligent care.

33. How far does the dental auxiliary need to stand from the source of radiation in order to prevent exposure to secondary radiation?

    a. 3 feet.
    b. 4 feet.
    c. 5 feet.
    d. 6 feet.

34. Characteristics of x-rays include all of the following EXCEPT:

    a. X-rays are not visible or apparent to any of the senses
    b. X-rays travel at half the speed of light
    c. X-rays travel in a straight line but can easily be deflected
    d. Shorter x-rays are more useful in dental radiographs

35. Which one of the following is the name of the infection precaution measure used in dentistry to ensure that all patients are treated in the same manner for infection control practices?

    a. Standard precautions
    b. Universal precautions
    c. Medical precautions
    d. Contact precautions

36. When capturing dental images, which one of the following is an example of how infectious diseases can be spread directly from patient to patient?

    a. Using a contaminated XCP device for sensor placement
    b. Glove puncture in the dental assistant's gloves during placement of the sensor
    c. The dental assistant wearing a mask below the nose when capturing images
    d. Failing to have the patient wear protective eyewear during image exposure

37. Which one of the following statements describes the correct infection control guidelines to follow when capturing dental images with a wired sensor?

    a. After using the wired sensor to capture digital images, the first step in processing the sensor is to place it in the ultrasonic machine for a minimum of 10 minutes.

    b. The wired sensors do not require the use of a barrier because they can be sterilized with the autoclave and/or chemiclave.

    c. When using a wired sensor during digital imaging, a barrier covering the sensor and the wired connection is required along with disinfection of the wired sensor after use.

    d. Avoid the use of a plastic finger cot when using wired sensors due to the compression that the finger cot places on the sensor.

38. When taking which of the following images does the dental radiographer need to ensure that the interproximal areas and the bone levels are adequately captured and demonstrated along with the coronal surfaces of the teeth?

    a. Reverse Towne image.

    b. Posteroanterior image.

    c. Bitewing image.

    d. Periapical image.

39. Which one of the following best describes the purpose of the panoramic digital image?

    a. To look at the length of the back teeth

    b. To look at the upper and lower jaws and teeth

    c. To view the inner areas of the ear

    d. To look for dental decay

40. All of the following apply to the lead apron EXCEPT:

    a. It is recommended for both intraoral and extraoral image receptors.

    b. It is intended to protect the reproductive and blood-forming organs.

    c. It is a device that prevents radiation from reaching radiosensitive organs.

    d. It was developed with the main purpose of shielding the patient from leakage and stray radiation.

41. Which one of the following agencies developed and released the 2003 Guidelines for Infection Control in Dental Health-Care Settings that apply to dental radiography and include paid and unpaid dental professionals?

    a. Occupational Safety and Health Administration (OSHA)

    b. Centers for Disease Control and Prevention (CDC)

    c. Organization for Safety, Asepsis, and Prevention (OSAP)

    d. American Dental Association (ADA)

42. A dental assistant is seeing a patient who is having pain in a front tooth. The patient states that it is a throbbing and aching pain that prevents sleep at night. Which one of the following techniques is most effective at capturing all of the areas that the dentist will need to view in the correct dimensions?

    a. Bisecting

    b. Occlusal

    c. Bitewing

    d. Paralleling

43. When using the bisecting technique, which one of the following is correct?

    a. The digital receptor is placed on the facial surface of the tooth to allow for optimal patient comfort.

    b. The digital receptor must be placed parallel to the tooth.

    c. The dental assistant must visualize and use an imaginary angle.

    d. The dental assistant must use a bisecting digital system when performing this technique.

44. Which one of the following is considered the most important infection control law in dentistry and exists to protect employees from occupational exposure to blood and other potentially infectious materials?

    a. Morbidity and Mortality Weekly Report infection control guidelines
    b. Hazard Communication Standard
    c. Employee Right-to-Know Law
    d. Bloodborne Pathogens Standard

45. Which of the following is considered secondary radiation?

    a. Radiation that goes through the collimator and position-indicating device (PID)
    b. Radiation that reflects off the patient's face
    c. Radiation that leaks from the tubehead
    d. Radiation directed at an area for cancer treatment

46. If the milliamp (mA) setting is increased on the dental radiograph x-ray control panel, what will the overall effect be on the density of the processed dental film?

    a. The processed dental film will have decreased density.
    b. The processed dental film will have increased density.
    c. The processed dental film will have decreased contrast.
    d. The processed dental film will have increased contrast.

47. When positioning the patient for panoramic exposure, the Frankfort plane should be positioned:

    a. perpendicular to the floor.
    b. parallel to the floor.
    c. perpendicular to the cassette.
    d. parallel to the cassette.

48. Which of the following structures will appear as a radiolucent area on a dental radiograph?

    a. Coronoid process.
    b. Incisive foramen.
    c. Genial tubercles.
    d. Zygomatic process.

49. When considering personal protective equipment (PPE) and dental imaging, which one of the following practices must be followed to limit the risk of disease transmission?

    a. When spatter and aerosols are likely, the dental assistant must wear a surgical mask and protective eyewear or a chin-length face shield.
    b. It is not required to wash face shields and dental eyewear after dental imaging or patient treatment because these PPE items are not directly touched and have no ability to spread infection.
    c. An N95 respirator face mask should be worn for all dental imaging procedures due to the proximity of the dental assistant to the patient's oral cavity.
    d. Protective clothing is not required for the process of capturing dental images because minimal spatter is generated.

50. What type of radiograph is used by an orthodontist to assist with treatment planning?

    a. Tomography
    b. Sialography
    c. Cephalometric
    d. Occlusal

51. Which of the following can be defined as tiny particles of matter that possess mass and travel in straight lines and at high speeds?
   a. Electromagnetic radiation.
   b. Radioactive radiation matter.
   c. Particulate radiation.
   d. X-radiation.

52. Short teeth with blunted roots appear on the image receptor when:
   a. the horizontal angulation is incorrect.
   b. the occlusal plane is misaligned.
   c. there is collimator cutoff.
   d. the vertical angulation is excessive.

53. The best radiograph to obtain for diagnosis of temporomandibular joint (TMJ) is:
   a. Panoramic
   b. Periapical
   c. Sialography
   d. Arthrography

54. Which of the following is controlled by the milliamperage or mA setting found on the control panel of a dental tubehead?
   a. The speed of the x-rays that hit the image receptor.
   b. The size of the x-rays that hit the image receptor.
   c. The shape of the x-rays that hit the image receptor.
   d. The number of x-rays that hit the image receptor.

55. A critical organ(s) affected by cumulative radiation exposure is/are:
   a. the mucosa of the mouth.
   b. the bones of the hand.
   c. the lens of the eye.
   d. the nostrils.

56. When using the paralleling technique during periapical exposure:
   a. the central ray of the beam is perpendicular to the tooth and film.
   b. the central ray of the beam is parallel to the long axis of the tooth and film.
   c. the central ray of the beam is at a 45-degree angle to the tooth and film.
   d. the central ray of the beam is at a 65-degree angle to the tooth and film.

57. During a patient exam, the dentist requests that the dental assistant capture an image that will show the complete apices and the full crowns of teeth #8 and #9 to evaluate pain that the patient is experiencing. Which dental image should the dental assistant capture?
   a. Occlusal
   b. Bitewing
   c. Periapical
   d. Panoramic

58. A bitewing radiograph is useful in diagnosing all of the following EXCEPT:
   a. An impacted tooth
   b. Tooth decay
   c. Periodontal bone loss
   d. Gum disease

59. All of the following are part of the panoramic head positioning device EXCEPT:

   a. notched bite block.
   b. forehead rest.
   c. lateral head guides.
   d. the cassette.

60. Which one of the following is correct regarding the object-receptor distance in dental imaging?

   a. The object-receptor distance is the space between the tooth and the imaging sensor used by the dental staff.
   b. The object-receptor distance should always be as small as possible.
   c. When using this distance as a guide in digital imaging, it is referred to as the long-cone technique.
   d. The object-receptor distance is only considered when taking panoramic images.

61. What is NOT an advantage of the paralleling technique?

   a. Structures on the image will have sharp detail.
   b. Minimal enlargement of teeth structures.
   c. Images will have increased clarity and contrast.
   d. Comfortable for the patient and easy to place the image receptor for operator.

62. When considering the use of surface barriers in the treatment room during dental imaging, which one of the following is correct?

   a. Surface barriers are required for use in dentistry and must be present in every patient treatment to prevent the spread of aerosolized pathogens.
   b. Smooth, hard surfaces including countertops, dental imaging trays, light handles and supply containers should always be covered with barriers due to their proximity to patient care.
   c. The electrical switches of the imaging exposure button and the dental tubehead should be covered with barriers, when possible, to prevent contamination.
   d. When surface barriers are used and remain intact during a procedure, the dental assistant must disinfect all areas under the barriers after the procedure is complete.

63. Which federal law requires that all persons who operate x-ray machinery to produce dental radiographs are properly trained and certified?

   a. OSHA.
   b. JADA.
   c. FDA.
   d. The Consumer-Patient Radiation Health and Safety Act.

64. Which of the following statements is TRUE regarding the use of cotton rolls and image receptor holding devices during the placement of the image receptor and radiation exposure?

   a. Plastic image receptor holding devices are not advised during radiation exposure due to the radiopaque distortion they create on the resulting image.
   b. Cotton roll holders should be used in all cases where cotton rolls are placed in the mouth in order to prevent shifting during radiation exposure.
   c. Cotton roll can be placed in an edentulous area to aid in stabilizing the image receptor during exposure.
   d. Styrofoam image receptor holding devices are outdated and should no longer be used during radiation exposure.

65. Which one of the following is an effective method of sterilizing patient care items used in dental imaging, uses water steam under pressure, prevents corrosion, and produces dry patient care items once the cycle is complete?

   a. Unsaturated chemical vapor
   b. Static air sterilizer
   c. Forced air sterilizer
   d. Steam autoclave

66. Who of the following would be the most sensitive to the effects of radiation?

   a. 2-year-old child.
   b. 15-year-old teenager.
   c. 25-year-old man.
   d. Developing fetus.

67. An XCP device is an example of what type of control used in dentistry that can be described as equipment or a device used to minimize employee exposure?

   a. Work practice control
   b. Engineering control
   c. Administrative control
   d. Sensor placement control

68. What is the function of the collimator?

   a. It directs the x-ray beam to the appropriate place
   b. It allows the electrons to cross over the cathode to reach the anode
   c. It forms the shape and size of the x-ray beam upon leaving the tubehead
   d. It filters out the wavelengths that are unusable

69. The American Academy of Oral and Maxillofacial Radiology recommends using the _____ technique, which will provide the dentist with the most accurate image with the least amount of distortion.

   a. bitewing
   b. paralleling
   c. bisecting angle
   d. extraoral

70. When identifying anatomical structures and dental materials on radiograph, which of the following is TRUE?

   a. The enamel is radiolucent and located at the crown of the tooth
   b. The root canals are radiopaque and extend from the pulp chamber to the apex of the tooth
   c. The periodontal ligament can be visualized as radiopaque
   d. The dentin is not as radiopaque as enamel

71. Which one of the following best defines microorganisms that can be spread during dental imaging and are capable of causing disease?

   a. Bacteria
   b. Pathogens
   c. Protozoa
   d. Biofilms

72. Legally, dental images, as part of the patient's dental record, are the property of:

a. the patient.
b. the patient's caretaker.
c. the dentist.
d. the insurance company.

73. All of the following would appear radiolucent on a processed dental periapical x-ray EXCEPT:

a. the orbit of the eye.
b. the nasal septum.
c. the mucosa of the cheek.
d. dentin.

74. When processing an XCP device after patient use, which one of the following is an acceptable method of precleaning that works by using high-frequency sound waves to loosen and remove debris?

a. Holding solution
b. Ultrasonic cleaning
c. Hand scrubbing
d. Instrument washing machine

75. Under what circumstances may the dental auxiliary hold a digital receptor in a patient's mouth during exposure?

a. The dental auxiliary should never hold an image receptor in a patient's mouth during exposure.
b. When the child is a minor and the parent is not present.
c. When the patient is physically handicapped and is unable to keep the image receptor in their mouth.
d. During emergency surgeries when the patient is unconscious.

76. What disinfectant level should be used for the disinfection of clinical contact surfaces, including the dental tubehead and dental operatory where images are captured?

a. Sterilant level
b. High level
c. Intermediate level
d. Low level

77. When mounting processed radiographs, which anatomical landmark can assist you in mounting the mandibular premolar periapical?

a. The mental foramen.
b. The genial tubercles.
c. The lingual foramen.
d. The maxillary sinus.

78. Disproportionate changes in the size of an image on a processed radiograph are caused by:

a. improper placement of the film prior to exposure.
b. too large of a film size having been used.
c. excessive or insufficient horizontal angulation.
d. excessive or insufficient vertical angulation.

79. Which of the following is used to control the degree of penetration of the x-ray beam?

a. Exposure button
b. Kilovoltage peak selector
c. Milliamperage selector
d. Master switch

80. Which of the following projections are used to evaluate facial growth and development, trauma, and disease, and developmental abnormalities that may occur in the cranium?

    a.   Waters projection.
    b.   Submentovertex projection.
    c.   Transcranial projection.
    d.   Lateral cephalometric projection.

Answer Key and Explanations

General Chairside

1. A: Underjet occurs when a patient bites in centric occlusion and the maxillary anterior teeth are positioned lingually to their mandibular anterior teeth. This leaves an excessive space between the facial of their maxillary anterior teeth, and the lingual of their mandibular anterior teeth.

2. C: A patient who is severely allergic to something may experience anaphylactic shock if accidently exposed to that substance. When this type of shock is induced in the body, it can lead to the throat swelling shut, the tongue swelling out of the mouth, and the eyes swelling shut. If proper medical attention is not given to the patient suffering from anaphylactic shock, it may result in death due to lack of ability to get oxygen into the body.

3. B: Burs are dental instruments used to cut away tooth enamel. Different shaped burs are used for different procedures, and according to clinician preference. The type of bur used to make undercuts in a preparation is the inverted cone.

4. C: A significant feature of the electric hand piece is that the electric hand piece can operate as either a high speed or low speed hand piece. This gives the dentist greater control over how much enamel to remove and how precise the cuts need to be.

5. D: The interproximal areas of the mouth cannot be reached while brushing the teeth with a toothbrush. The interproximal areas can only be reached by flossing; however, all other surfaces of the teeth can be reached by brushing.

6. C: Every inventory management system should have a reorder point associated with inventory levels. This reorder point is the minimum number of products that can be on hand before an order must be placed. Utilizing a reorder point will prevent the dental office from running out of essential products needed for patient care.

7. A: Alginate is an irreversible hydrocolloid used to make preliminary impressions. Two types are available, normal set and fast set. The fast set can be used for patients with an extreme gag reflex or if there is only one person working to take the impression. Elastomeric materials are used to make final impressions. The available types include polyether, silicone, polysulfide, and polysiloxane. Each material is slightly different from the other. These materials have three forms: light, regular, or heavy bodied. The light bodied is used first followed by the heavy bodied. After the material has gone through initial set and final set, it is removed from the mouth. Final cure occurs between 1 and 24 hours. Properties include dimensional stability (the ability of the impression to stay intact after removal from the mouth), deformation (the ability of the impression to stay intact during removal from the mouth), and permanent deformation (the impression will remain in the shape after it changes).

8. A: When an assistant receives the locking cotton pliers during instrument transfer, she/he receives the cotton pliers at the working end. The locking cotton pliers do not have a hinged end.

9. A: When a patient is experiencing a local anesthesia overdose, he may experience twitching, talkativeness, increased apprehension, slurred speech, and even stuttering. Many times, local anesthetic contains epinephrine, which will speed up the heart rate, causing the patient to feel very uncomfortable and complain of a very rapid heart rate. The emergency response team should be called and the patient should be kept lying down in the supine position until the response team arrives.

10. B: During storage, if an alginate impression is around anything moist, including a wet paper towel or excess water, it may actually absorb this fluid, causing the alginate impression to swell (imbibition). The opposite of this is syneresis, which is the process of the alginate impression drying out due to moisture being pulled from the impression and causing it to distort.

11. B: When recording progress notes into a patient's chart, the dental team member who wrote the notes must always sign and date after his entry. If this person is a dental assistant or dental hygienist, the dentist must also add her signature and date to the entry as well. The patient is not required to sign the progress notes. If a mistake is made in a patient's chart, it should be crossed out by a single line, initialed, and then the correct statement should be made. This can be made in any color that the dental team member chooses to use.

12. D: When having a procedure performed on the maxillary arch, the patient should be placed in the supine position. This position involves lowering the entire dental chair to thigh level and then lowering the patient's back so it is parallel to the floor, allowing the maxillary arch to be perpendicular with the floor.

13. A: A frenectomy is the surgical removal of the frenum, a piece of tissue that connects the lip to the gums covering the maxilla or the tongue to the floor of the mouth. The complete frenum and the attachment of the frenum to the underlying bone are removed.

14. B: Formocresol is used in dentistry to "mummify" a tooth's remaining vitality in the event that part of it has been damaged. The use of formocresol during a non-vital pulpotomy or pulpectomy procedure has no benefit, as the pulp is already non-vital. Formocresol should not be used during vital pulpectomy procedures as it is the intent to do no further harm to the pulp. The hope is to enable the pulp to heal itself through the process of generating reparative dentin.

15. B: When selecting impression trays to be used during patient procedures, the dental assistant needs to be sure that the tray fits the patient's mouth and is not too big or too small, as this may produce discomfort for the patient. The tray must be deep enough to allow for the occlusal surfaces of the teeth to show up in the impression, and it must cover all areas of the mouth including the retro molar pad and the tuberosity when applicable.

16. D: The chalky appearance of the enamel on a tooth may indicate the presence of incipient caries. Teeth having this appearance often are experiencing a demineralization of the enamel, meaning that the enamel is no longer as strong as it once had been. The chalky appearance signifies an area of porosity that is on microscopic level and unable to be detected by the dental explorer.

17. C: Tubli-Seal is a material that is used as a permanent root canal sealant. RC Prep cream is a material that is used to help clean and shape the pulp canal space, formocresol serves as a bactericidal agent to help resolve infection from the tooth, and Densfil is a system that uses obturators to fill root canal chambers.

18. A: A subjective examination includes information as provided by the patient. It includes: pain, sensitivity, and complaints of bleeding. After discussing this information with the patient, the provider will then complete the objective examination, which includes clinical data about the tooth in question.

19. D: The state Dental Practice Act is a set of laws enacted by individual states to protect the public from dental providers who may not be fully qualified to practice. The legal requirements vary between each state but typically cover many of the same issues. It is important for dental assistants to be very familiar with the law in the state where they are practicing. Most of the state's Dental Practice Act is available for review on the internet. The Dental Practice Act typically includes requirements surrounding licensure and renewal of licenses. It sets the guidelines for appropriate level of continuing education that must be done over a specified time. It will specify the specific responsibilities that can be covered by dental assistants and dental hygienists. It will include rules and regulations surrounding the use of radiation and infection control.

20. D: A patient who was diagnosed with xerostomia experiences dry mouth and a reduction in the amount of saliva produced by the mouth. There are saliva substitutes that the patient can use at home that will assist in the production of saliva.

21. B: A red line(s) should be drawn running parallel to the long axis of each of the roots needing endodontic therapy. Yellow and green ink of any kind, is not permitted in the charting area. Blue ink can be used to identify any previous restorations that have been completed. Progress notes are to be completed in black ink only.

22. D: Lab plaster is the gypsum product that should be used when constructing study models in dentistry. Impression plaster is a product that is not widely used today, and would be used to take an impression on an edentulous patient. Class I stone is commonly used to produce working casts to make dentures and partials, and class II stone is used to make exact replicas of teeth that are being prepared for crowns and other restorative materials.

23. B: When working as a dental assistant, one is required to report suspected cases of child abuse, older adult abuse, and any form of violence or injuries including assaults, rapes, and gunshots. It is not required to report verbal abuse or bullying to state officials although there may be information and literature on resources that can be given to patients regarding these subjects.

24. D: When considering the placement of dental sealants, the dental assistant needs to avoid placing sealants on primary teeth that have roots that are partially resorbed. The reason is that these teeth will fall out in a short period of time and may not need sealants at this point. It is best to place sealants on a tooth when it first comes into the mouth to ensure that future decay can be avoided.

25. D: Decay is classified in six categories depending on the location and extent of the decay. Class I decay is designated when there are pits and fissures present on posterior teeth but not on the incisal edge of the anterior teeth. If there are occlusal pits on the incisors, the decay would be designated as Class III.

26. D: Calcium hydroxide, otherwise known by its brand name Dycal, is a type of cavity liner that is commonly used during amalgam restorative procedures due to its ability to prevent pulp irritation, its compatibility with many types of restorative materials, and its ability to aid in the production of secondary dentin.

27. B: Mumps is a viral infection that spreads through the saliva and most infects the parotid salivary glands. The infection can cause the glands to swell to a large size and become quite painful. Mumps isn't seen very often because of the high rate of childhood vaccination against this infection.

28. C: An autologous graft involves taking tissue from one area of a patient's mouth and transplanting it to another part. When tissue is taken from a living donor, regardless of whether they are family or unrelated, this is called an allogenic graft. A xenograft is when tissue is transplanted from one species of animal to another. Grafted tissue is generally not taken from plants.

29. B: The healthy human body will have an average of 5 to 6 quarts of blood in the body. This may vary slightly if there is a condition where blood loss occurs, but if the body is able to replace the blood on its own, the patient will be able to recuperate quickly. If too much is lost, the patient may need a blood transfusion to make up for the lost blood.

30. A: The working end of the instrument performs the intended function of the instrument. The dentist or assistant holds the handle, which is attached to the working end of the instrument by the shank. Sometimes, there is a grip or rubber area on the handle to make it easier for the dentist to hold the instrument.

31. A: To avoid distortion when handling wax, avoid extreme temperature changes during the manipulation and storage of wax products. The more a wax product is handled and manipulated, the more the wax is stressed, and the chances of distortion are higher. It is important to know what you want to do with the wax, and perform the task with as little manipulation as possible. Do not store wax in warm places with direct sunlight as this may cause the waxes to soften and distort.

32. B: A schedule matrix is an outline of the dental office's schedule. This matrix will have the days in which the dental office is open and closed and can be made available up to a year in the future. Any employee meetings, days off, or holidays can be listed in this schedule matrix, allowing for the scheduling staff to know when to make appointments for patients calling the office.

33. C: When using the Universal numbering system, the maxillary left first molar is tooth number 14, the maxillary right first molar is tooth number 3, the mandibular left first molar is tooth number 19, and the mandibular right first molar is tooth number 30.

34. A: When a luting type of cement is used in the oral cavity, it is typically used to cement a restoration onto a tooth. It is important to use only a thin layer of this type of cement. The dental assistant should lightly coat the restoration, place it onto the tooth, and then remove any excess cement. A large amount of luting cement does not need to be used as this will cause the dental assistant to have more cement to remove from the tooth and restoration, and does not enhance the adhesion of the cement.

35. A: Corrosion and staining occurs after sterilization because the initial instruments were not completely dried before being placed in storage. The pooled moisture from the autoclaving process is not allowed to evaporate through the drying cycle, and it collects near the instrument. This causes the instrument to steep in the pooled water, causing the corrosion and staining.

36. D: A common difference, when comparing a needle holder and a hemostat, is noted when comparing the beaks of each instrument. The needle holder has beaks that are significantly shorter than those of the hemostat.

37. C: When referring to the use of the Federation Dentaire Internationale (FDI) system for identifying a specific tooth, the quadrant number is written first. When using the Universal/National System, the tooth number is written first. If required to identify an entire arch of teeth, either maxillary or mandibular, double digits would be used (according to the Federation Dentaire Internationale System).

38. B: A high-speed handpiece is a cutting tool that operates at very high speeds, usually above 12,000 rpm. When identifying a contra-angle high-speed hand piece, look for the head of the hand piece to be slightly angled to the shank of the hand piece. This allows the dentist to reach difficult to reach areas of the tooth or mouth.

39. D: The maxillary arch is the upper jaw of the patient. When assisting the dentist with a patient receiving treatment on the maxillary arch, the light should be lowered and the beam directed up toward the upper jaw to best visualize the entire arch.

40. C: The main vitamins and minerals that are involved in tooth formation are vitamin D, calcium, phosphorus, magnesium, and fluorine. Vitamins A, C, and E are also important for healthy gums. Sources of vitamin D include fortified milk, eggs, and fish. The body can also produce vitamin D with sun exposure. Vitamin D deficiency is becoming more and more common and has a significant impact on enamel formation, leading to an increase in cavities. Sources of calcium include dairy products, soy products, and green leafy vegetables. Sources of phosphorus include dairy products, meat, eggs, and whole grain products. Sources of magnesium include leafy green vegetables, nuts, grains, seafood, and bananas. Good nutrition is important to healthy teeth and gums. It is best for vitamins and minerals to be obtained through natural food sources instead of supplementation whenever possible. The exception is vitamin D, which may require over-the-counter supplementation with medical guidance.

41. B: There are many different aspects to a plaque control program, including evaluating how a patient brushes and flosses and developing new techniques and schedules, but the main goal of a plaque control program is to remove plaque from the teeth at least once every 24 hours due to the fact that it takes 24 hours for plaque to form on the teeth. If patients can keep up this cycle, they may greatly reduce the amount of plaque, tartar, and decay that they normally experience.

42. D: The type of bone grafting that has the best rate of success in dentistry is autologous bone grafting. In this procedure, bone is taken from the patient's own body and used in another area of the mouth.

43. D: ZOE paste, mixed with a drop of formocresol is used during a pulpotomy procedure of the primary dentition. The formocresol in the mixture will mummify the primary tooth's remaining vital pulp, but will allow the tooth to remain in the mouth for permanent eruption spacing purposes.

44. B: Dental wax is made from natural products including beeswax or fatty acids. It can also be made from synthetic materials to provide the necessary qualities needed for certain dental procedures. Each type of dental wax has a specific function in a dental laboratory. Baseplate wax is used for setting denture teeth. It is also used in initial arch form molds for the recording of the occlusal rim. Inlay casting wax is a harder type of wax used for producing a pattern of the indirect restoration from a model. Casting wax is used when concentrating on a single tooth for indirect restorations, a fixed bridge, or the metal portion of partial denture plate. Utility wax is used for comfort in orthodontic treatment by covering a bracket that may be irritating to gums during treatment. Boxing wax is used for in making preliminary impressions by surrounding the wall of the model to make a cleaner model without as much trimming required.

45. A: A periodontal probe is used to measure the depth of the sulcus area around each tooth, commonly referred to as the periodontal pocket. Each tooth is measured in six different locations. These measurements by the periodontal probe will allow the dental staff to assess the health of the patient's periodontium and determine if any further treatment measures are necessary.

46. C: The price information of the product ordered is not included on a packing slip. All of the other answers, including the quantity ordered, name of the product and name of the manufacturer should be included, however.

47. B: Composite resins are more commonly used in dentistry for anterior teeth as well as some posterior teeth. Class I through V restorations can be completed with this product as well as the closing of diastema (space between front teeth) or restoration of abrasions or surface defects due to attrition or hypocalcification. The first step in the procedure for preparing and applying composite resin materials is to select the appropriate shade. Next the syringe is prepared and moved into the transfer zone for the dentist. The dentist applies the resin to the appropriate tooth and the curing light is then used for final setting of the resin. After the material is applied and set, there is a finishing and polishing stage. Finishing burs and any abrasive materials are contraindicated. A white stone or finishing diamond is used to gently reduce the resin followed by the use of diamond burs or other superfine burs to polish the resin. Polishing paste is used last to finish the process.

48. D: It is good practice to discuss treatment plans and patient fees with a patient prior to any treatment being performed. This allows patients to be educated about what will be done and what it may cost them, regardless of whether they carry insurance or not. This should be discussed in a private setting at the dental office to avoid other patients from hearing what is covered in that conversation.

49. C: Edema or swelling is most often the first symptom of an allergic reaction. During a stroke, there are several symptoms that a patient might display, including difficulty speaking and paralysis of one half of their face or body. Anxiety and rapid breathing are the first signs in a patient who is hyperventilating. Symptoms of epilepsy include muscle rigidity and uncontrolled body movements.

50. D: Type II glass ionomer cement is used to fill cavities in areas that are not stress-bearing. It is typically used during the final restoration. A buccal class V restoration is a good example of when type II glass ionomer cement should be used.

51. B: Type II zinc oxide is referred to as an intermediate restorative material. The monomer that is mixed with the zinc oxide polymer is eugenol. Eugenol is an obtundent monomer, known for its soothing effect on dentin. Rarely is Type II zinc oxide used as an endodontic cleaning solution, as the properties of the material do not suggest that any form of cleaning or disinfecting occurs when using this product. Zinc oxide is not used during a procedure as a composite or resin cement.

52. A: Dental procedures may affect a person's vital signs. It is important to know how to check vital signs when needed in order to help make an assessment of whether to continue treatment. The 4 vital signs are temperature, pulse, respiration, and blood pressure. A normal oral temperature can range from 97.6 to 99 °F. An increased temperature may indicate an infection and dental treatment may need to be postponed. A normal pulse or heart rate for an adult is 60-100 beats per minute at rest and 70-120 beats per minute for a child. A normal respiratory rate is 10-20 breaths per minute for an adult and 18-30 breaths per minute for a child or teen. Increases in pulse or respiratory rate may reflect stress, age, medications, or other reasons. A normal blood pressure is a systolic reading less than 120 mm Hg and a diastolic less than 80 mm Hg. Elevated blood pressure at the time of a dental exam may also require postponement.

53. C: Coronal polishing is a procedure that, in some states, dental assistants are allowed to perform. The procedure removes surface plaque and external stains on the enamel of the tooth. When performing a coronal polishing with an abrasive on a patient, the specific abrasive selected by the dental assistant determines the rate of abrasion.

54. C: Developing a positive relationship with a child is very important in establishing good dental habits and a good attitude about dental visits. Many dentists will use the Frankl scale, which rates the child's behavior on a scale from 1 to 4 in order to track behavior over time. Simple steps can be taken to make the dental visit a pleasant experience. The child can be involved in the visit by holding the saliva ejector, choosing the flavor of toothpaste or fluoride, and helping select where to start the procedure. Explanations should be given to the child in simple terms, followed by showing the child what will be done and then doing exactly what you have told the child. Positive reinforcement is always helpful, such as a reward at the end of the visit. Parents can be allowed to stay in the room to help calm a patient but sometimes this can make the situation worse. A papoose board is not typically a choice during cleanings.

55. D: Polishing wheels in the dental laboratory are primarily made of a muslin fabric. This muslin traps polishing mediums and sporadically dispenses it onto the appliance as it spins on the dental lathe. Cross contamination of the used laboratory rag wheel occurs when the wheel is not properly sterilized. Rag wheels should be removed after use, rinsed and dried, and sterilized according to the manufacturer's instructions. Plastic barriers will inhibit the rag wheel from properly polishing the surface of the desired appliance. Complete disinfection cannot occur if the rag wheel is simply sprayed with a disinfecting solution because the rag wheel has multiple layers of muslin and not all layers of the fabric may be reached by the solution. Immersion of the rag wheel in a sterilization solution should not be attempted, as the strength of the solution will break down the strength of the muslin fabric.

56. B: When too much fluoride is ingested into the body during tooth formation, a condition called dental fluorosis or mottled enamel may occur. This can cause the teeth to appear pitted and stained, with colors ranging from thick white spots to dark brown areas on the teeth. These stains are intrinsic and cannot be removed by a prophylaxis.

57. B: Dry mouth, headache, and a fruity, acetone breath odor are all signs of hyperglycemia or elevated blood sugar. Other signs include excessive urination, blurred vision, rapid pulse, and decreased blood pressure. If untreated, it can lead to loss of consciousness. Type 1 diabetes is always treated with insulin. These patients are at risk for hyperglycemia as well as hypoglycemia. It is important to determine if the patient has eaten recently and if insulin was taken as ordered by his or her physician. In this case, the patient has not taken insulin and insulin administration is required immediately. If the patient has access to his or her insulin, assistance should be provided. Otherwise, alternative arrangements must be made to obtain insulin immediately, including calling the patient's emergency contact or 911 if necessary. Untreated short-term hyperglycemia can lead to serious complications that may require hospitalization.

58. A: A condensable composite is used primarily to be compressed into an area of a tooth preparation. With this thickened consistency, the operator is able to use specific instruments that can be pressed against the composite with some resistance, enabling the material to be "stacked." The condensable composite is putty-like, has a high viscosity and is stiffer than other composites. Condensable composites contain high amount of fillers, which gives them their thick consistency.

59. A: Sickle scalers are primarily used to remove supragingival calculus. Hoe scalers are used for removing buccal and lingual calculus on posterior teeth. Subgingival calculus is removed by the use of a curette.

60. C: *Gelfoam* is a hemostatic drug. This type of drug is used to initiate clotting in the socket of the extraction. Nitrates are drugs that are used to treat chest pain by dilating blood vessels. Anti-inflammatory drugs are used to reduce inflammation, swelling and pain. Antifungals are prescribed to treat fungal infections.

61. B: Hepatitis B virus (HBV) is the cause of 34% of all acute viral hepatitis illnesses. Some people can be exposed to HBV but do not become ill. They can be carriers of this disease and unknowingly pass it along to others. Transmission is through blood and other types of bodily fluids including saliva. The Occupational Safety and Health Administration (OSHA) mandates that any employee who is starting a job that increases the chances of occupational exposure to HBV be offered the HBV vaccination within 10 days. The employee does not have to take advantage of this vaccination but must sign a release stating the vaccination was offered and the risks are understood. Other types of hepatitis include hepatitis A virus (HAV), which can infect anyone. It is spread through the fecal-oral route. Good handwashing is essential to prevent transmission of HAV. Hepatitis C virus (HCV) is mainly transmitted through blood and is generally contracted through use of contaminated needles.

62. C: When caring for dentures, hot water should be avoided for soaking or disinfecting. The hot water may allow for the denture to become distorted and may affect how it fits into the owner's mouth. Cool water and cleaning products designed specifically for dentures should be used when caring for these items.

63. A: When the dental assistant places the periodontal dressing following periodontal surgery, the dressing should only cover the surgical site and a small portion of the coronal surface of each tooth near that site. Placing the dressing over the entire crowns of the surrounding teeth should be avoided as this may cause the dressing to fall off prior to complete healing of the surgical site.

64. B: When completing an amalgam restoration, the dental assistant must first place the amalgam capsule into the amalgamator to allow this device to mix together the different components that are found in this capsule. The dental assistant then places the mixed amalgam into the amalgam well, loads the amalgam carrier, and transfers this along with the amalgam condenser to the dentist for placement.

65. C: Difficulty speaking, paralysis on one side of the body, sudden change in vision, or a sudden onset of a headache may be signs of a cerebrovascular accident or stroke. Other symptoms may include difficulty with walking, loss of coordination, or trouble finding words. Patients with a history of heart disease or uncontrolled hypertension are at risk. A simple test called FAST can be done to determine if this is a possibility. F is for face, A is for arms, S is for speech, and T is for time. Ask the patient to smile (does one side of the face droop?), ask them to raise both arms over their head (does one arm slowly fall back down?), ask the patient to speak (is the speech slurred?), and call 911 immediately if any of these signs occur. Time is extremely important in stroke treatment. The best outcomes occur if treatment is given within the first 60 minutes of symptom occurrence.

66. C: When taking an impression, it should be free from any rips or tears, contain the correct anatomical features, and the tray should not be visible through the impression material. The impression should also contain all of the teeth on the arch it was taken on, not simply the teeth that are having restorative work done.

The presence of other teeth is required to allow for the proper occlusion relationships to be determined to ensure the new restoration fits the patient correctly.

67. B: It is during the maturation stage, or the final stage in a tooth's development cycle, that it fully mineralizes into its final structure, turning into a mature tooth. During the bud stage a tooth is simply growing and turning into a tooth bud, during the apposition stage, a tooth is developing in different layers, and during the cap stage a tooth is forming its cap from a mass of tissues that surround the tooth bud.

68. C: The most accurate term used to describe the complete removal of a tooth is extraction. A sealant provides the occlusal surface of a tooth with a composite- based material to seal any deep pits or fissures located on the occlusal table. A gingivectomy is a surgical procedure in which the gingiva is surgically altered. This procedure is not associated with the removal of a tooth. A restoration is placed within a tooth, after a portion of the tooth has been removed. This is needed because of a fracture, caries, or any other anomaly.

69. C: When evacuating during a restorative procedure, the bevel of the evacuation tip should be placed parallel to the buccal or lingual surfaces of the teeth.

70. A: When the dentist is carving an amalgam restoration, the dental assistant should be using the high-volume evacuator to remove any excess amalgam that falls into the patient's mouth, to prevent the patient from swallowing this material.

71. B: When completing an amalgam restoration along with a dentist, the dental assistant will use the desensitizing agent first after the tooth has been prepped. The Dycal will come next, and the varnish material will follow. Once all of this has been applied, the dentist will place the Tofflemire and follow by placing the amalgam material.

72. B: Dry angles, used for moisture control, are primarily used to control the parotid salivary gland. This gland's duct is located in the mucosa of the cheek, directly opposite the maxillary first molars. Covering this duct diminishes the amount of saliva that contaminates the area while the dentist is working. The dry angle is specifically designed to absorb the saliva coming from this duct, and gather it within the dry angle.

73. C: Postural hypotension is also known as orthostatic hypotension. It is a form of low blood pressure. This condition may occur when moving into an upright position too quickly. The person may experience dizziness, lightheadedness, nausea, confusion, or blurred vision. Fainting may occur. This condition is usually mild and may only last for a few minutes. Treatment is not required if this happens only occasionally. If the patient becomes unconscious for more than a few minutes, emergency medical treatment should be instituted. This may occur because of pregnancy, dehydration, heart issues, or diabetes. Pregnant women may experience a similar reaction when seated in the chair in a supine position because the uterus may be pressing on the abdominal veins. The woman should be positioned on her left side to allow improved blood flow.

74. B: A veneer is a coating of tooth-colored material (to match the rest of the teeth) over a tooth that has been discolored, darkened, eroded, or chipped. Veneers are also used to help with alignment and lengthening. A diamond bur is used by the dentist to remove a specified amount of enamel in order to prepare the tooth for the placement of the veneer. The surrounding teeth are protected with celluloid matrix strips before the dental materials are applied. The dental assistant may help with transferring tools, curing the veneer, and communicating with the patient.

75. B: When the dental assistant is transferring a new instrument to the dentist, the little finger should be used to collect the used instrument, which allows for the new instrument to be easily placed into the dentist's hands.

76. B: Cervical lymph nodes, which are palpated during an extra oral dental exam, are located bilaterally along the internal jugular vein. During an extra oral dental examination, the exterior area of the head and neck regions are observed and palpated. The dentist is looking to see if the lymph nodes are normal in size or enlarged.

77. A: The term "amalgamation" refers to the actual chemical reaction that takes place when the alloy particles and mercury are mixed together to become silver amalgam. They are separated during the manufacturing process by a small "contact lens" type of barrier directly inside of the capsule. This keeps the alloy particles and liquid amalgam separate until the dental assistant activates the capsule in the amalgamator. Trituration is defined as the actual process of the capsule containing the silver particles and liquid mercury being rapidly shaken back and forth. This action causes the components of the capsule to come into contact with each other.

78. B: It is very important after suture removal has been performed that the dental assistant take the time to count the number of sutures that have been removed and then compare this number to the amount of sutures that were placed (number should be located in the patient's chart). This will ensure that there are no sutures left behind in the oral cavity, which could produce infection and other complications.

79. C: The surface found on each tooth that is furthest from the patient's midline is called the distal surface. The mesial surface is one that is closest to the midline on each tooth, the buccal surface is closest to the cheek on posterior teeth, and the lingual surface is closest to the tongue on all teeth.

80. C: A manufacturer issues a backorder slip if an item ordered is not available at the time the order was placed. A credit slip will not be issued if the item ordered is unavailable because the account should not have been charged. Replacements or greater or lesser value are usually not submitted without the approval from the ordering staff.

81. A: A review of the dental patient's medical health history should take place at every dental office visit, whether it is with the dentist or dental hygienist. A patient may have had significant changes to their medical history or started taking new medication since their last visit. These changes may require the use of different anesthetics or medications as a result.

82. A: Restorative instruments are used in the placement of dental materials such as amalgam within the anatomy of the tooth. These instruments also help to shape the dental material into the correct position on the tooth. Types of restorative instruments include amalgam carrier, condensers, burnisher, carvers, composite placement instrument, and the Woodson. A burnisher is used for smoothing the surface after the amalgam is placed. A carver is used to take away any excess dental material or to make the appropriate indentations in the amalgam to fit the tooth's anatomy before it hardens. A condenser is used to push the dental material into the tooth so it is appropriately packed. The Woodson is the tool used for bringing the dental materials over to the tooth.

83. D: Alginate powder is the type of dental material used for taking mandibular or maxillary impressions. Polycarboxylate is a type of cement used for other dental procedures. Other equipment required for taking impressions is the scoop and water measure that are provided by the manufacturer for preparing the alginate. Water that is at room temperature should be available. The powder is mixed in a rubber bowl using a wide-blade spatula. The material is then spread onto the sterile impression tray and pressed upon with the spatula in order to remove air bubbles that may interfere with the quality of the impression.

84. A: When storing an item shipped from the manufacturer, the new item should be placed on the shelf behind the current inventory. This ensures that items that have expiration dates are used first, rather than newer items. Allowing the current inventory to expire before being used can cause a significant amount of wasted product and the practice to lose money.

85. B: Informed consent is a written agreement that is formed between a dentist and the patient who is to be receiving care. This agreement outlines the treatment to be performed as well as the financial responsibilities that come along with that treatment. This consent demonstrates that the patient is in agreement with the work that needs to be done as well as agreeing to the financial responsibility of paying for that work.

86. D: The most commonly used anesthetic in dentistry is lidocaine HCl. It is a type of short-duration anesthetic used for procedures expecting to last approximately 30 minutes. For procedures that will last about an hour, an intermediate-duration anesthetic will most likely be selected by the dentist. This would include lidocaine with epinephrine, mepivacaine with epinephrine, prilocaine HCl (with and without epinephrine), and articaine with epinephrine. Long-duration anesthetic such as bupivacaine with epinephrine is used for procedures that will last 90 minutes or more. Procaine (*Novocain*) is not used as frequently as a short-duration anesthetic since the introduction of lidocaine.

87. A: An end-tuft brush is a device that can be used to reach hard-to-access areas in the mouth. These can be areas that are too small for a traditional toothbrush to reach and may include the very posterior area of the mouth, the area around orthodontic brackets, and areas between and underneath fixed bridges. These can be used in conjunction with flossing aids and a traditional toothbrush to obtain the greatest outcome possible.

88. A: If there is a suspicious lesion on the gum, tongue or buccal tissue, the dentist may take a biopsy to determine what the lesion is and if it is cancerous. An excisional biopsy involves the removal of the entire lesion with the addition of a small amount of adjacent tissue.

89. D: Hand-cutting instruments are used to allow the dentist to easily remove the parts of the tooth that are decayed. These instruments are positioned next to the basic setup on the tray. Types of hand-cutting instruments include the excavator, hoe, chisel, hatchet, and gingival margin trimmer. Many types of chisels are available, all with a slightly different function. Straight, binangle, Wedelstaedt, and angle-former are all types of chisels. Chisels are used to get through the enamel part of the tooth or to make straight lines. Most dentists will have their personal preference as to what type of chisels they use most often.

90. B: "Lead time," when referring to a dental office's inventory supply means the amount of time between when an order was placed and when it is received.

91. D: The frontal sinuses are one pair of the paranasal sinuses. They are located behind the forehead, just above the left and right eyes. Mucus production is one of the important functions of the frontal sinuses; this mucus helps to trap bacteria and dirt/debris, preventing it from entering the respiratory tract.

92. C: There are five categories of motion for the dental assistant. Class I involves the fingers only. Class II uses the fingers and hands. Class III involves the movement of the fingers, wrist and arm. Motion that involves the entire arm and shoulder of the dental assistant is designated as Class IV. Movement of the arm and body (such as twisting in your chair) is designated as Class V.

93. A: The dental assistant should be sitting six inches above the dentist to allow for adequate vision during a procedure, feet should be kept on the foot rest, and the back should be straight. The dental assistant should avoid bending or stressing the wrist for long periods of time as this can lead to damage of the carpal tendon and cause wrist damage.

94. A: Fluoride is absorbed through the intestines. The lungs are responsible for the exchange of inhaled oxygen and exhaled carbon dioxide. The stomach is responsible for processing food that is eaten, by breaking it down into nutrients that can be used by the body systems. The liver is responsible for removing excess sugar from the bloodstream and storing this excess as starch.

95. C: The vitality test in dentistry is used to evaluate the health of the pulp, which is the tissue or nerve located inside the tooth. This test can provide valuable information for diagnostic and treatment planning purposes. The vitality test checks to see if there is a nerve issue. This is typically done on teeth that have undergone some sort of trauma. A root canal removes the pulp from the tooth, so the vitality test would provide no information for this tooth. The following techniques can be used to check the pulp: palpation of the area above the root, apply cold or heat to the tooth, or use the electric pulp test (EPT). The dental assistant would typically assist the dentist with this procedure and record results of the testing.

Infection Control

1. B: Place instruments in an ultrasonic cleaner for processing. This initial step in sterilization processing can include the use of a holding solution to prevent blood from drying on instruments. Hand scrubbing with a brush or sponge is never ideal because of the risk of puncture injuries to dental staff. Instruments cannot be wrapped for the autoclave until they have had debris removed, washed, and rinsed off.

2. B: When handling biopsy specimens, the items need to be in a container that is leak-proof, sturdy, and has a secure lid. This container must have a biohazard symbol on it as well during storage, transport, and disposal. The specimen should not be automatically kept in a refrigerator during storage unless indicated by the medical lab that is contracted with the dentist. Once a container has been used, it should be properly disposed of to avoid the potential of cross-contamination if that container were to be reused.

3. A: Washing with detergents can cause "wicking" to occur. There are inherent defects in the natural material of gloves that can be exploited by opportunistic bacteria seeking a host. A dental staff member must be careful not to let her nails grow too long or wear any kind of jewelry that may puncture or cause micro-tears in the gloves.

4. C: The best and most effective way for a dental auxiliary to prevent cross-contamination from occurring during the use of digital radiographic sensors is to place the sensor(s) in barriers during use, and afterwards, wipe down the sensor(s) with an intermediate-level disinfectant. These sensors are unable to be sterilized, as the heat, steam, and/or chemicals will damage the delicate parts, nor can these items be submerged in any type of liquid.

5. D: Covering the sensors with a plastic sleeve during each patient use. Sensors should never be wiped with alcohol since this can cause cracking in the cords and damage to the sensor itself. They should never be soaked in any type of solution for disinfection. These digital components are very costly to replace and most practices must train every staff member to handle them with care.

6. C: When working with alginate material, the dental auxiliary must wear a mask, eyewear, and gloves to protect themselves from the fine powders that may be released as they are preparing the alginate material for use. It is good practice to always wear gloves when working with dental products to prevent these products from being absorbed into the skin, and also to wear eyewear to prevent anything from splashing into the eyes.

7. C: A bloodborne pathogens exposure control plan should include exposure determinations, methods of compliance with the plan, hepatitis B vaccination records and any other vaccination records, engineering controls, and work practice controls. Hazardous waste disposal is not part of the bloodborne pathogens standard and therefore is not included in this plan. This type of waste disposal includes used and outdated chemicals and is discussed and covered under the hazard communications standard, as it does not involve infectious waste disposal.

8. D: Formaldehyde and alcohol. These components make up the unsaturated chemical vapors used in this type of sterilization. Unsaturated chemical vapors are used in place of water to sterilize instruments and the instruments then dry quickly following processing.

9. C: The Centers for Disease Control and Prevention (CDC) developed Standard Precautions to help prevent the spread of disease. Standard Precautions and Universal Precautions are used interchangeably. The basic concept for Universal or Standard Precautions is that all blood and bodily fluids should be treated as infectious. It is not possible to determine which patients may have an infectious illness even with the patient's history available for review. Some patients do not tell the truth and some patients might not know about a condition. Universal or Standard Precautions should apply to all patients. Bodily fluids that may spread disease include blood, secretions, saliva, skin, mucous membranes, and products of excretion. Standard Precautions consist of handwashing, the use of personal protective equipment, treatment of patient care equipment and environmental surfaces, and prevention of injury.

10. D: A dental handpiece is an example of a semi-critical level instrument. The description of this category of instruments is that they come into contact with the mucosa in the oral cavity, but they do not penetrate bone. The bur that is placed in the dental handpiece would be considered a critical level instrument, but the handpiece itself is an example of a semi-critical level instrument.

11. A: Wipe with disinfectant wipes, allow it to dry, and then repeat. The steps of operatory sanitation and disinfection must be consistently followed in order to assure that instruments are sterile and to facilitate the training of new office staff.

12. D: The dental office employer must keep records for each employee for the length of employment plus 30 years. The records must be confidential and kept in a locked location. The records include medical information, including accidental injuries or accidents that occurred at the worksite. The records also must contain immunization records. Employee records also contain a history of earnings, tax information, workers compensation information, and other types of information. This is an OSHA requirement. If the dental practice is sold, all employee records become the legal property of the new owner.

13. A: To open instrument packs and do a thorough hand washing after the patient is seated. Patient surveys often return with comments pertaining to the value of actually seeing the instrument pack opened in front of them and watching the healthcare workers perform thorough hand washings. All jewelry should be removed and the nails should be cleaned as part of this process. A patient's sense of comfort and peace of mind is enhanced when he feels that the staff truly cares for his best health outcomes.

14. D: The last step in the Post-Exposure Prophylaxis is follow-up. If exposed to hepatitis C, follow-up testing for hepatitis C virus and liver function tests will need to be done at approximately 4-6 months. A test for HCV RNA can be done sooner at 4-6 weeks; however, this test can sometimes yield a false-positive. During the follow-up period, the affected employee should be asked not to donate blood, plasma, any organs, or semen. Changes in daily activities do not need to be made, such as restriction from sexual activity. Plans for breastfeeding or pregnancy can continue as desired. Mental health counseling can be offered for those that may be having a hard time dealing with the situation.

15. A: Hand rubs are very effective at reducing the amount of pathogens and microbes present on the dental assistant's hands. There are very specific instructions to follow for optimal effectiveness. The dental team should not use hand rubs that have an alcohol concentration of greater than 95% because these are actually less effective and do not kill as many microbes as hand rubs having lower concentrations. When the correct concentrations of ingredients are used and when the hand rubs are applied to all areas of the hands, they are a great alternative to handwashing.

16. B: A proteinaceous infectious particle. Prions are composed entirely of proteins that lack nucleic acids (DNA or RNA). It was discovered that proteins alone can transmit diseases like spongiform encephalopathy (mad cow disease). A prion is not a spirochete and is highly resistant to heat, chemical agents, and irradiation. There is no treatment for the diseases caused by prions, so the best prevention is not to eat contaminated foods, especially those that contain nerve tissue.

17. D: Ethylene oxide is a gas that is capable of sterilization using low temperatures, and is commonly used in large hospital settings. This method of sterilization works well for items that would melt in heat sterilization machines, but due to the large time requirement for this method, it is rarely found in a smaller dental practice setting. The ethylene oxide gas can take 4-12 hours to sterilize and then the instruments must be allowed to go through an aeration cycle to avoid burning patient tissue; this time period can range from 4-12 hours.

18. C: After a baseline blood collection is taken, if the employee does not give consent to test his blood for HIV, the sample should be preserved for at least 90 days. If the employee changes his mind and decides to have the baseline sample tested, the blood will be available.

19. D: Pre-procedural mouth rinses have the purpose of reducing the number of microbes present in the mouth prior to a procedure being performed. This will then decrease the volume of microbes that have the potential to be released from the patient's mouth and into the air. According to the CDC, there is no substantial evidence indicating that pre-procedural mouth rinses reduce the prevalence of clinical infections, and therefore, they are not recommended for use at this time to prevent clinical infections among patients or dental healthcare workers.

20. B: Synthetic phenol compounds. These types of surface disinfectants are prepared daily and are classified as intermediate-level hospital disinfectants. Since they leave a chemical residue on some surfaces, it is best to use synthetic phenol compounds on rubber or plastic items, rather than metals.

21. C: 11 or more. According to OSHA, a written plan must be kept in office records if the office employs 11 or more people. This is the size where OSHA mandates have decreed the need for certain documentation, which must be enacted and maintained.

22. B: Placement in a surgical milk bath before packaging for the autoclave. Detergents may remove some of the surface sheen on surgical tools and contribute to the oxidizing formation of rust. It is acceptable to use regular dish washing soap as a holding solution for oral surgery instruments, but they should be dipped in surgical milk (without subsequent rinsing) to coat them before packaging for the autoclave. This will protect their longevity.

23. D: An asymptomatic carrier is an individual that is infected with a disease but who does not show any symptoms. This type of individual poses a danger to dental healthcare workers and the general public, due to the fact that he or she is infected with a contagious disease and has the capability to spread that infection. However, the person may not show any signs or symptoms of an infection and may not even know about the infection.

24. B: In 2003, the CDC developed a very detailed list of infection control guidelines for all healthcare workers (or clinical employees) who may be exposed to blood or other body fluids. In dentistry, these clinical employees include the dentist, dental hygienist, dental assistant, and anyone else who may provide direct or indirect care and have potential exposure. The CDC does not enforce these guidelines; it only collaborates with experts in the field of infection control and dentistry to develop them. The Occupational Safety and Health Administration (OSHA) enforces the guidelines. Every clinical team member must be aware of and abide by these guidelines.

25. D: Surface disinfectant with tuberculocidal capability. It is necessary to use a surface disinfectant that contains tuberculocidal additives on any counter tops within three feet of the dental chair. These surfaces are near enough to the patient's mouth to be contaminated by aerosol back spray.

26. A: The bloodborne pathogens standard is set in place to help protect all employees who are exposed to blood or other potentially infectious materials. This standard has many areas of coverage that relate to different fields in which workers may come into contact with blood, including nursing, dentistry, and mortuary science. All individuals in these fields are expected to abide by and follow the guidelines in this standard.

27. A: When an individual is infected with syphilis, he has a bacterial infection that is caused by the *Treponema pallidum* spirochete bacteria. The bacteria enter the body through an open sore, through blood, or through body fluids. Once the infection starts, it can be divided into three stages. During the first stage, the infected individual may develop an ulcerating infectious sore called a chancre. The dental healthcare worker must prevent fluids from this lesion from contacting her skin or mucous membranes in order to prevent the spread of this infection. During the second stage, the infected individual may demonstrate mucous patches and measles-type rashes on the body. The third stage is typically fatal and does not show itself until 20 years after the initial infection, due to remaining dormant in the body for so many years.

28. D: Upon initial employment at a dental office, the employer must offer the new employee the hepatitis B vaccination at no cost to the employee within 10 days. If the employee initially declines the series, they may change their mind at a later date with the employer still being responsible for the cost of the series. If an employee declines to receive the vaccination, they must sign a declination form, which will become part of their permanent medical record; there is no required counseling if this were to occur.

29. D: There are many types of allergies that can result due to repeated use of a product. In dentistry, type IV hypersensitivity can result from exposure to the chemicals that are found in the production of gloves as well as common products in the dental office. This type of allergy is an immune response to repeated exposures to a specific chemical that can cause a rash-type reaction.

30. B: Endospores. The bacteria found in biological monitoring strips are a harmless strain of heat-resistant spores. These are the toughest organisms to kill; therefore, they are a great test of an autoclave's sterilization capabilities.

31. D: All of these are correct. All of the listed answers are important to know and to have in a written plan in case of spills in the dental office. The hazardous spill should always be cleaned immediately, and care should be taken not to allow the incident to happen again. There is no limit to the number of reports that can be submitted, but it is the duty of all healthcare personnel to use standard precautions to prevent accidental spills.

32. C: When considering the cleaning and disinfection of housekeeping surfaces, is it important to know that these are the areas in the dental office that pose little risk in the transmission of disease. These areas need to only be cleaned with a hospital-grade disinfectant or a low-level disinfectant. Walls and drapery items do not need to be cleaned unless they are visibly contaminated. If mops and cloths are used to disinfect any areas, they should immediately be cleaned and allowed to dry prior to use to prevent any cross-contamination between areas.

33. D: Liquids (not water) were placed in a dry heat sterilizer. All of the answers are correct reasons for sterilization failure except for the last one. Liquids cannot be placed in the chemical vapor because sterilizing agents cannot penetrate solutions and in the dry heat sterilizer, solutions will boil over and evaporate (Miller, 2010).

34. B: Many surfaces in the operatory are difficult to clean. The invention of surface barrier protection has improved the ability to protect and maintain surfaces, such as knobs, handles for certain dental instruments, light switches, touch pads on equipment, and computer keyboards. These areas must continue to be cleaned and disinfected at the start and end of the workday even with the use of barriers. Barriers must be changed between patients. Advantages include a reduction in time spent cleaning and disinfecting the operatory between patients, reduction in the use of chemicals, and less damage to equipment due to moisture and chemicals. It also provides the patient with the visualization of a clean area during dental treatment. Surface barriers are not environmentally friendly because they are not able to be recycled and must be discarded in the appropriate waste container (typically unregulated unless visibly soiled with blood).

35. A: A stethoscope is an example of a noncritical level instrument. This level of instrument can be described as one that comes into contact with intact skin and includes other items such as blood pressure cuffs and pulse oximeters. These items can be processed using an intermediate to low-level disinfectant.

36. B: Using barrier protection on writing implements. All surfaces that cannot be repeatedly pre-cleaned and disinfected must have barriers. Barrier protection can be used on writing utensils as a method of maintaining aseptic technique.

37. B: Dry heat sterilization is another type of sterilization process that is commonly used in dental offices. Air is heated to a temperature between 320 and 375 °F. The exact temperature depends upon the length of the sterilization cycle. There are 2 types of dry heat sterilizers, static air and forced air. Static air works like a convection oven while the forced air sterilizer works by circulating hot air at a high rate of speed throughout the heat chamber. Items to be sterilized must be cleaned and dried before being wrapped. If the items are not dry before using dry heat sterilization, the instruments will rust. Any instrument with a hinge, such as scissors or forceps, should be in the open position. The heat chamber is loaded and the temperature and time controls are set according to manufacturer's directions. Cooling must take placed before any of the wrapped packages are handled because of the risk of serious burn injury.

38. C: When considering hand hygiene practices, it is important to understand that bacteria will multiply in the dark, moist conditions that are present when the hands are not dried completely before donning a new pair of gloves. There are various hand hygiene practices that can be used, including more than just liquid hand soap and the use of alcohol-based hand rubs. It is important to note that bar soap is not allowed in dentistry because it can transmit bacteria and other microbes among users.

39. B: The contamination of dental unit water lines (DUWL) can be an issue in dental offices. This is of particular concern because immunocompromised patients may become ill from contaminated water. The source of contamination can be from both the public water supply entering the DUWL and from the patient's mouth during dental care. Colonization can also occur in the tubing. Installation of anti-retraction devices can help reduce contamination as well as flushing the DUWL between patients. The public water supply is usually safe and must adhere to specific standards; however, when this water enters the DUWL, it mixes with other microorganisms and these can begin to multiply. DUWL can be used during most dental procedures except for surgical procedures involving the mouth. Sterile water should be used in this case. Occasionally, a boil water advisory will be issued for a public water supply and the DUWL should not be used in this situation. There are a couple different ways that DUWL can be tested and monitored for safety, including in-office test kits.

40. B: To protect healthcare workers' hands from puncture injuries during cleaning. This is an OSHA safety regulation that must be practiced in all dental offices. It does not matter if an inspector is there to check or not. All contaminated instruments should be treated as potentially hazardous while in the sterilization area. Typically, heavy-duty utility gloves are not used for cleaning floors and windows; standard rubber household gloves are acceptable for these chores.

41. A: When considering the various ways that each dental team member can minimize the spread of infection at the dental office, fingernail length is an important factor. Dental team members involved in patient care should keep their fingernail tip length at less than a quarter inch long. This will prevent tears that may occur when wearing gloves with long fingernails, something that can decrease the integrity of the gloves. It also minimizes the space for bacteria to be harbored beneath the nails. The dental team should also avoid nail polish that is uneven and unkempt as well as strive to remove transient flora from the hands and make sure to select the correct method of hand cleaning based on the dental procedure being performed.

42. C: The main purpose of the holding solution used in a dental sterilization area is to prevent the organic debris, the bioburden, from drying onto the instruments. If this material does dry onto the instruments, it can interfere with the sterilization process by creating a shelter for the microbes to hide in and preventing the sterilization machine from producing steam, heat, or a chemical vapor that can reach these microbes, rendering the item unsterile and leading to cross-contamination during patient care.

43. B: Following an exposure incident at the dental office, the exposed employee will be sent to a physician for post-exposure follow-up and testing. The employer must obtain and provide those results to the affected employee within 15 days of the completion of the evaluation. This is set in place to ensure that results are given within a timely manner and to aid in the event that additional steps are required due to an acquired infection from an occupational exposure at work.

44. D: Category 1 employees include dental assistants and employees who are routinely directly exposed to patient body fluids and blood during procedures. Others in this category include the dental hygienist and the dentist. This category of staff is required to wear personal protective equipment (PPE), including gloves, eye protection, and masks, due to the risk of exposure.

45. C: The first step in treating a needlestick injury is to thoroughly wash the affected area with soap and water. If the injury was to the eye, the eye should be flushed with water or saline. Antiseptic products or disinfectants should not be applied. After the injury has been cleaned, it must be reported and documented. The report must detail the date and time of exposure and how the incident occurred. Details regarding the amount of fluid exposed and severity should also be documented. The third step is to evaluate the exposure for risk of contraction of HBV, HCV, or HIV. A needlestick injury would involve blood. The fourth step is to evaluate the exposure source. If the source patient is known, request permission to screen for bloodborne pathogens. The final step is disease-specific management. For example, if the source patient tests positive for any bloodborne pathogen, then the affected employee should be treated accordingly.

46. A: The employer is responsible for providing personal protective equipment to the employees at no cost. This includes gloves, masks, eye protection, and smocks, gowns, or scrubs. The employer is not able to charge the employee if they experience an allergic reaction to certain protective devices; instead, the employer must provide an alternative form of protection to the employee. If a piece of personal protective equipment is damaged due to incorrect cleaning procedures, the employee should be counseled on how to use that item properly, but is not responsible for replacing the item.

47. B: Legionnaires' disease is a disease that is caused by an individual being exposed to the *Legionella pneumophila* bacteria. It can only be spread by aerosolization and aspiration of contaminated water. The disease was named after an outbreak that occurred in Philadelphia during an American Legion convention. Tetanus is a bacterial infection that is introduced into the body by a break in the skin or a wound. MRSA is also a bacterial infection that is caused by the *S. aureus* bacterium, which is commonly carried on the skin. This can get inside the body through a break in the skin and cause infection or may even cause infection on the outer surfaces of the skin. Hepatitis B is a blood-borne virus that attacks the liver, commonly introduced into the body by infected blood and/or body fluids.

48. B: Following an injury during a procedure in which the skin is perforated by a contaminated instrument or needle, the dental team should stop the procedure and complete basic first aid by flushing the puncture site and stopping any bleeding. The next step is to complete an incident exposure report to document the details of the incident without any designation of blame. The patient should be informed of what happened, and the dental assistant and the patient should be requested to provide a blood sample to test for infectious diseases including HIV and HBV so that they have a baseline blood test on file in the event that an infectious disease that may be attributed to the exposure develops in the future. This may also allow for prophylactic treatment to avoid the spread of disease in case either party tests positive for an infectious disease.

49. B: Regulated biohazardous waste is the type of waste that is produced in the dental office and must be disposed of in a special manner due to the ability of this type of waste to spread infection. Examples of regulated biohazardous waste include blood-soaked items, items with dried blood that is flaking off, items saturated with other body fluids, and extracted teeth.

50. D: Tetanus is a type of bacterial spore that is found in dirt, dust, or human waste. It is very dangerous and can be fatal if not treated. Tetanus can cause lockjaw. The symptoms of lockjaw include muscle stiffness that initially involve the jaw and neck but then progress to other parts of the body. It is very important for all health care workers to remain current on vaccinations. Td vaccination is for tetanus and diphtheria prevention in adults. Children receive this vaccination as part of the DTaP vaccination. If an adult has not received primary vaccination, this must be done by administering 3 shots on a predetermined schedule over a 6-month period. A tetanus booster must be given every 10 years.

51. B: Indicator tape. This type of tape is specifically designed to withstand the heat of the sterilization process and contains a color-changing medium that allows for verification of the cycle. It is never acceptable to use metal staples, paper clips, or safety pins in the wrapping of instruments due to the concern for sharp objects that could potentially penetrate the packaging or cloth material.

52. D: Health hazards, flammability, and reactivity of the chemical, as well as its boiling point, are all contained within the Safety Data Sheets. The hazardous ingredients and the health hazard data of the chemical or material are also listed on an SDS. Dental procedure protocols are not included in Safety Data Sheets.

53. B: Hepatitis B virus (HBV) is an inflammation of the liver caused by a virus. HBV is spread through direct contact with blood, saliva, or other bodily fluids from a person infected with HBV. It can also be passed to an infant during childbirth. Initial infection with HBV may not cause any symptoms or may cause a prolonged illness for a few weeks before diagnosis is made. Symptoms of HBV include loss of appetite, low-grade fever, muscle pain, nausea, and vomiting. Some individuals will develop jaundice or yellowing of the skin. Even if symptoms are not present, the disease can progress and cause liver damage. Health care workers including dental assistants are at risk for contracting HBV and should give serious consideration to receiving the vaccination because of exposure to blood and saliva. The vaccination consists of 3 shots over a period of 5 months. Once the vaccination is completed, the blood can be tested to ensure antibodies are present for immunity to HBV.

54. D: Safety goggles, high volume evacuators, and rubber dams are all ways to protect the patient from aerosolized spray, which can contain bloodborne pathogens that transmit disease. Masks cannot be used during treatment.

55. A: Engineering controls are pieces of equipment or devices that need to be used in dental offices in order to prevent exposure to items that may be contaminated with bloodborne pathogens. These controls make procedures safer for dental team members and decrease the chances that a dental team worker sustains any type of percutaneous injury. Examples include handwashing stations, sharps containers, eye washing stations, and needle recapping devices.

56. B: Cross-contamination is also known as indirect contact or indirect disease transmission. This occurs when a patient or dental healthcare worker is exposed to a contaminated instrument or any other contaminated item that was improperly processed and/or sterilized. It is important that the dental healthcare worker know the proper disinfection and sterilization protocols to follow in the dental setting to prevent indirect disease transmission from occurring.

57. D: Low-level disinfectants registered with the EPA include products such as quaternary ammonium compounds. These products are able to inactivate certain types of bacteria, fungi, and viruses. Types would include HIV, herpes simplex virus, and hepatitis B and C. It would also be effective against *Staphylococcus*, *Pseudomonas*, and *Salmonella* species. *Aspergillus* and *Candida*, both types of fungi, would require an intermediate-level disinfectant, as would polio, Coxsackie virus, and rhinovirus. Research has not demonstrated that floors or walls play a significant role in disease transmission; however, these surfaces need to be effectively cleaned. It is important to make fresh cleaning solution daily to prevent microorganisms from multiplying in dirty buckets.

58. D: An overflowing sharps container can be a dangerous situation to encounter in the dental office due to its purpose and how the items within the container are used. The dental team should take great care to only fill the sharps container to the indicated line and then replace the container with a new one. In the event this does not happen and the container overflows, the dental team must not manipulate the container in any way and should refrain from opening it, shaking it, or trying to pack sharps into it. The correct step would be to obtain a larger container and place the overflowing sharps container into it. It can then be disposed of according to standard sharps disposal procedures.

59. D: Hepatitis C is a virus that can lead to chronic liver infections in 80% of the people that become infected. Chronic infections with hepatitis C may lead to cirrhosis of the liver and liver cancer with the potential for liver failure. This virus is spread by contact with contaminated blood and may be transmitted through childbirth from an infected mother, blood transfusions, organ transplants, and sexual intercourse. Hepatitis A is a virus that causes acute infections of the liver, rarely ever turning into chronic conditions and is caused by fecal contamination in the food and/or water supply. Shingles is a form of the herpes virus that leads to a very painful rash; and herpes type 1 is a virus that causes herpetic lesions, commonly known as cold sores on the oral mucosa and lips.

60. C: The OSHA Needlestick Safety and Prevention Act is an important regulation that provides additional protection to healthcare workers who handle sharps during their workday. One addition to this regulation was injury protection from what is termed "sharps with engineered sharps." This terms describes sharps that are provided from the manufacturer with a built-in safety mechanism that will serve to keep the user free from injury when used properly. This is not something that the dental staff needs to add to the sharps item before it is used, nor is it a procedure that they must follow, but it is an engineered item that serves to keep them safe.

61. C: Critical. This type of instrument requires sterilization due to its very high risk of disease transmission. Examples of critical items include scalpels, bone chisels, and burs. Commonly used plastic items, which cannot be sterilized, should be purchased in disposable form to facilitate disease prevention in the office. This classification means that items must be treated with the utmost care and autoclaved on the longest cycle.

62. D: 30 years past the termination of employment. The rationale behind this is so that if a person contracts a disease later found to be caused by the chemicals found in a particular dental office, legal records can be located to see if the former staff member was vaccinated or treated at the time of exposure.

63. D: Biological indicators are also referred to as spore tests. This is because these items contain spores, which are very resistant forms of microbes, and if these spores can be destroyed by the tested method of sterilization, then all weaker forms of microbes that may be present on the instruments will be destroyed as well.

64. C: All surfaces that cannot be repeatedly pre-cleaned and disinfected must have barriers. This is a standard practice for all dental offices. Reduction of bioburden (a microscopic build-up of patient blood and saliva on hard surfaces that are often difficult to clean) is always a concern in order to prevent cross contamination in the dental operatory.

65. B: High-level disinfectants are those disinfectants that are capable of sterilization when the submersion time is greatly increased. Glutaraldehyde and chlorine dioxide are examples of chemicals that can be used as methods of sterilization when items are submerged in these solutions for 6-10 hours, depending on the manufacturer's instructions. These items can also be used as disinfectants when needed.

66. A: At least once per week. This type of monitoring is essential to prove that a sterilization system is performing properly. Some types are read in the office, while others can be sent out for testing in an offsite location. There are several other reasons for biological monitoring: after an electrical or power outage, after changing packaging materials (to verify that items are sterilized), after training new employees, and once a week to verify proper functioning of the autoclave. It is perfectly acceptable to use biological monitoring more often than once per week to check that patient items are sterile.

67. D: According to the hazard communications standard, employers must ensure that any SDS forms that come in with products are maintained and readily accessible to employees. This is important in the event that there was a chemical spill or exposure, in that these forms could be easily accessed to aid in guiding clean-up or decontamination procedures. SDS forms are required for each product and as long as the product is in the office, the SDS form must be kept on hand, either electronically or physically. When new SDS forms arrive, they can be uploaded or filed and reviewed as needed by employees; there is no need to alert all employees of a new form.

68. B: Title 29 of the Code of Federal Regulations requires that an exposure control plan be established to protect workers who may be occupationally exposed to blood or other potentially infectious materials (OPIM).

The plan details how the employer plans to minimize the risks for exposure. The plan also details who may be at risk within the workplace and what tasks or procedures may result in an exposure. The plan must be updated every year. The update should encompass any changes in procedures or tasks that may directly affect occupational exposure. The employer also needs to have documentation that safer medical devices have been researched that may reduce the risk of occupational exposure. The update must also show that input has been obtained from employees who are at risk for occupational exposure in terms of any changes that are needed to the exposure control plan.

69. A: A sharps container should never be filled past capacity; the dental healthcare worker needs to remove the sharps container from use prior to the items filling the entire container. If this is allowed to happen, the chances of the dental healthcare worker obtaining a percutaneous injury increase. When the sharps container is nearing full capacity, the container should be closed and removed from the operatory for final disposal.

70. D: A high-level disinfectant registered with the EPA is required for semi-critical dental instruments that are not heat tolerant. This would include items such as mirrors, amalgam condensers, and reusable trays. A high-level disinfectant must be capable of killing spores. Glutaraldehyde is the most commonly used high-level disinfectant; however, many people are sensitive to the fumes. The amount of time required for disinfection is up to 90 minutes. Chlorine dioxide is another high-level disinfectant; however, it must also be used with good ventilation because of its odorous fumes. Ortho-phthalaldehyde is an appropriate alternative. This product will disinfect within 12 minutes and has a low odor. The disadvantage is that this product is more expensive than other high-level disinfectants.

71. B: In the event of a mercury spill in a dental office, the dental auxiliary should use the mercury spill kit, which every dental office should have on hand to clean and decontaminate the area. This spill kit should include items that are specific to cleaning this hazardous chemical, including mercury-absorbing powder, mercury-absorbing sponges, and a disposal bag for the waste. The dental auxiliary must always wear eye protection, a mask, and utility gloves when cleaning a mercury spill.

72. D: When decontaminating an area on the floor in a treatment room after a blood spill, the dental auxiliary must use a disinfectant that has a tuberculocidal time. Therefore, intermediate or high-level disinfectants must be used, as low-level disinfectants are not capable of killing tuberculosis. These intermediate-level disinfectants need to be used on clinical contact surfaces with or without visible blood.

73. C: There are many different types of disinfectant choices to consider when deciding how to disinfect impression materials. The best choices for alginate impressions are iodophors and dilute sodium hypochlorite solution. There are many products available that contain these chemicals, so the dental office can decide as a team which product works best for their office.

74. B: Once a month. Changing disposable suction traps once a month is a minimum amount of time since the traps tend to fill up with the removal of many amalgam fillings or old crowns. If this is not done regularly, the suction hoses can back up and their waste materials start to come out, even when turned on.

75. D: The unit is malfunctioning. Ultrasonic units clean the gross debris from instruments through the use of sound waves, which create bubbles in the water. The bubbles burst and the implosions result in a percussive effect on the soiled instruments. Holding a piece of aluminium foil in the water for 20 seconds will show if the bubbles are capable of removing debris as desired. The temperature of the water is not important, and the enzymatic solution should not cloud the water.

76. C: The OSHA Bloodborne Pathogens Standard is an important regulation that was developed by OSHA, the federal agency in charge of protecting workers throughout the United States. There are many standards that OSHA has developed specific to various industries in the US. The focus of the Bloodborne Pathogens Standard is practices and protocols that will keep healthcare workers, and other workers who may be exposed to infectious diseases, safe. It also gives workers an understanding of their rights when it comes to this protection and what their employers are responsible for providing in the work environment.

77. D: It is very important that when performing surgical procedures, the dental team uses sterile water if needed during the procedures. In order to prevent infection, the dental team also must ensure that this sterile water is reaching the surgical site in a sterile manner and is not being contaminated by bioburden, biofilms, or other microbial sources.

78. A: When handling the contaminated laundry that is generated by a dental office, the team member or dental auxiliary must wear protective gloves and other appropriate personal protective equipment when necessary to protect themselves against blood or other potentially infectious material. If the laundry is wet, it must be placed and transported in bags or containers that prevent soak-through from occurring. If it is laundered on site, any team member is capable of assisting in washing items, it is not solely the responsibility of the dentist.

79. B: The OSHA BBP regulations prohibit any contaminated laundry from being removed from the dental office for cleaning in the home setting. Contaminated laundry may include surgical nondisposable gowns, cloths or towels, or washcloths. Contaminated laundry needs to be bagged in a leak-proof bag that has the biohazard label affixed to the bag. Protective clothing should never be worn outside of the dental office because of the risk of cross contamination. Protective clothing should be changed whenever an item becomes visibly soiled with blood, saliva, etc. Protective clothing should not be changed around others who are eating or working. Gowns should be removed and turned inside out while removing so the clothing underneath does not get contaminated.

80. B: Tuberculosis is caused by bacteria that is spread easily through the air. This means that it can be spread from the patient to the dental assistant and dental team during dental treatment. If a patient has active tuberculosis, he or she must be currently taking the prescribed medications before dental care can be delivered; this is a way to reduce the chances of transmission to the dental team members. If the patient is unsure of his or her status and has any signs or symptoms of active tuberculosis, the dental team should refer the patient to a medical provider for testing.

Radiation Health and Safety

1. A: A rad stands for radiation absorbed dose and can be defined as the amount of radiation that is absorbed by the tissue following an exposure. Rem stands for roentgen equivalent man, and measures the biological effect radiation may have on a patient. A roentgen measures the quantity of radiation that produces an electrical charge in the air.

2. B: CBCT stands for cone-beam computed tomography. This type of imaging is now common in dentistry for viewing parts of the face and mouth that was not possible in the past. It involves the use of various equipment ranging from a machine to take the picture, a computer to view the images, and a keyboard and software to edit and send the images to specialty providers when needed.

3. C: The kilovolt setting in the dental tubehead controls how fast the electrons and resulting x-rays travel. When this setting is increased, the electrons move from the negative side of the tubehead, the cathode side, to the positive side of the tubehead, the anode, at a greater speed and therefore exit the tubehead at a greater speed. This causes the resulting image to have a lower contrast as the x-rays are able to penetrate more objects in the oral cavity.

4. D: The use of barriers when disinfecting treatment rooms following each patient is a required step in infection control in each dental office. When barriers are properly used and maintained during image exposure, they prevent microbes and pathogens from reaching the dental equipment that they are covering, eliminating the risk of disease transmission. In areas where barriers are not used, or if barriers are compromised during dental treatment, the added process of properly disinfecting each treatment room is required in order to reduce the number of pathogens present on the dental equipment before the next patient can be seen. Time management should not be considered in the implementation of infection control practices because patient safety comes first. Barrier use and the use of disinfectants do not reduce the susceptibility of a patient's immune system nor do they limit the types of portals or openings that exist for microbes to enter a patient.

5. A: Different types of x-rays can be produced by the dental tubehead. X-rays with longer wavelengths have less penetrating power due to the longer wavelengths, and are commonly referred to as soft waves. X-rays with shorter wavelengths that are moving faster and therefore have greater penetrating power are known as hard waves due to how they interact with the objects they strike.

6. A: Using the proper exposure factors assists in controlling the amount of radiation emitted to the patient. The monitoring device is a tool used to measure the possibility of radiation exposure to the employee. Time management is a useful tool to accomplish tasks with efficiency and quality.

7. B: Primary radiation is known as "useful radiation," which produces the latent image needed. All other radiation that is produced by the exposure is not beneficial to the radiograph, the radiographer, or the patient. Much of this non-beneficial radiation is filtered out by the aluminum disks even before the primary bean is emitted from the PID.

8. B: The dental auxiliary, or anyone who may be occupationally exposed to radiation, has a maximum amount of radiation that they should be exposed to. The National Council on Radiation Protection and Measurements has deemed that a dental auxiliary should not be exposed to more than 5 rem in a 1-year time period. Anything beyond this increases the chances that biological damage may occur, and has been labeled as unsafe.

9. A: Incorrect placement of a lead apron or thyroid collar use during panoramic x-rays will likely cause a radiopaque image of a cone that will likely block the mandible. A lead apron without a thyroid collar should always be used for proper imaging. Ghost images seen on the panoramic radiograph can be caused by earrings, glasses, removable dentures, or retainers. Hearing aids and any other type of metallic objects can also cause a ghost image. A ghost image is a whitish looking image of the item that appears on the opposite side of the film. The image usually appears blurry and is larger than the actual item. Any of the aforementioned items should be removed, if possible, prior to the panoramic x-ray being taken.

10. A: The paralleling technique is one that is easy for the dental radiographer to do again and again. It does not involve complex rules and angles and simply involves placing the digital sensor next to the tooth on the inside of the mouth so the two are in the same plane. Other techniques require the use of stricter procedures and protocols that must be practiced before they can be implemented.

11. A: When the dental auxiliary is exposing radiographs on a young child, both periapical or bitewing images, a size 0 imaging receptor should be used due to how small a young child's mouth may be. If a larger size is used, the child may be unable to close properly, causing possible distortion to the image.

12. D: A dosimeter is a radiation monitoring device that is used to measure occupational exposure to radiation. The most common types are film badges or pocket dosimeters. A dental assistant will most likely be assigned a dosimeter to wear. The correct procedure is to wear the device only when at the dental office. It should be removed when leaving the building because sunshine can alter the results. The purpose of the device is to measure occupational exposure, not all radiation exposure during everyday living. The device is turned into the monitoring company at the end of the reporting period, which is typically about 3-4 weeks. The company keeps track of the accumulated radiation exposure for employees quarterly, annually, and over the course of their lifetimes.

13. C: When the dentist needs to view the entire occlusal or incisal edge as well as the apex of a tooth, they will request that a periapical image be taken on the patient. This image requires that, along with the required structures or teeth, that the entire tooth is shown, including the occlusal or incisal edge as well as 2-3 mm beyond the apex in order to determine if there is any periapical lesion in that area.

14. B: Dental radiographs are important but they are a source of radiation exposure to the patient and should be used appropriately. A 2-4 bitewing x-ray will provide about 0.005 mSv. This is not much considering that the average person may be exposed to 3.2 mSv over the course of a year from everyday sources. The ALARA ("as low as reasonably achievable") principle should be followed in dental offices. This incorporates trying to minimize the amount of radiation exposure within the dental office. For patients, the use of lead apron and thyroid collar helps to cut down on exposure. Using an F film speed also helps because this is the fastest speed and it reduces exposure by up to 60%. A reduction in the size of the x-ray beam is important for reducing radiation exposure. The beam should only be as large as the image receptor. Proper processing procedures are also important.

15. A: When the bisecting technique is used, the dental auxiliary must determine what angle they are going to use to aim their central ray at during exposure. This angle is determined by bisecting or dividing in half the angle formed by the long axis of the tooth and the image receptor. This angle is called the imaginary bisecting angle because it does not physically exist, but is created by the dental auxiliary. When the central ray is aimed at this imaginary bisector angle, the end result will be an image receptor with adequate diagnostic capabilities.

16. C: When a high milliamperage (mA) setting is used, the direct effect is an image that will demonstrate high density. This is due to more electrons being created at the tungsten filament, which directly results in more x-rays being created. When there are more x-rays, more are allowed to strike the image receptor and the image will be darker.

17. B: Snap-A-Rays are sensor-holding devices used in dental imaging and are classified as semicritical instruments. These devices hold a digital sensor during placement into the oral cavity during dental imaging. They touch the mucous membranes of the oral tissue but do not penetrate soft tissue or bone; therefore, they have a lower risk for disease transmission. Most brands of sensor holders are heat tolerant—as semicritical instruments, they should be sterilized by heat. Other examples of semicritical instruments used in dental imaging include the XCP device and other reusable receptor-holding items.

18. B: The only true statement is as follows: "Dental images should not be taken on a 'routine basis.'" The rationale for this statement being true is that dental radiographic imaging should only be used as a tool of diagnosis when pathology is considered. To further explain this statement, we must remember that as healthcare professionals, we are to follow the "as low as reasonably achievable" (ALARA) concept. Radiographic images should not be taken on a routine basis as indicated by an insurance policy or as a means of generating office revenue. Images should be taken only when a defined measure is needed to maintain the health of the patient.

19. B: During production of the dental x-rays inside the dental tube, the filament circuit is responsible for creating thermionic emission. The step-up transformer is directly associated with the source of electrical flow into the dental tube. This energy created by the electrical circuit from the wall outlet immediately charges the filament circuit, making charged electrons available to be emitted as x-rays through the position-indicating device (PID).

20. A: A radiation monitoring badge, commonly referred to as a dosimeter, is a device that is worn at waist level by a dental auxiliary during their time at the dental office. This device measures the amount of radiation that they are exposed to. It contains a piece of film inside of a plastic case that is sensitive to radiation. After a specified amount of time, this device is sent in for analysis and a report is generated and sent back to the dental auxiliary describing the results.

21. A: When using the bisecting technique, the dental auxiliary needs to aim the central ray at the imaginary bisecting line that is created by the long axis of the tooth and the plane of the image receptor. If the central ray is instead aimed at the plane of the image receptor itself, the resulting image will have foreshortening and may need to be retaken in order to reduce the vertical angulations used.

22. B: The occlusal image is taken when the dentist needs to view structures using the third dimension or needs to see things using the buccal-lingual relationships. This image allows the dentist to determine depth when looking at structures, compared with periapical images, which do not allow for adequate depth perception of oral structures.

23. B: During extraoral panoramic dental radiography, if the chin is positioned too high or tipped inward, the Frankfort plane is too high. With this improper positioning of the chin, a reverse smile line may be seen on the processed radiograph. The patient should be positioned so that the Frankfort plane is parallel to the floor to avoid numerous negative effects that may result on the processed radiograph.

24. C: Cone beam computer tomography (CBCT) is a technique that is increasing in popularity in the medical and dental fields. This type of imaging works by using a cone-shaped x-ray beam to expose a patient. This information is then gathered and interpreted by a computer system, resulting in an image that is presented in three dimensions on a computer screen.

25. C: Somatic cells are all cells found in the body except the reproductive cells. The female ova and the male sperm are examples of the reproductive cells, with brain cells, kidney cells, and liver cells being examples of somatic cells.

26. C: The following statement is the only statement that is TRUE: The skin tissues of the patient being radiographed absorb some x-rays. Not all of the x-rays completed come in contact with the patient. Scattered x-rays may immediately diverge from the position-indicating device (PID) and never reach the patient. But those x-rays that are directed at the patient do come in contact with the patient's skin.

27. A: The earring, worn in the left ear, will appear as an artifact in the right side of the film, and it will be slightly higher than the real object. This image is often known as a ghost image.

28. B: Low-energy, long-wavelength x-rays are removed by the aluminum disks found within the x-ray tube head. These long, low-energy wavelengths provide no benefit to the x-ray beam that exits the tube head via the position-indicating device (PID).

29. B: Under state laws, the *respondeat superior* doctrine states that the employer is responsible for the actions of the dental radiographer. Ultimately, the employer is responsible for a person working in his or her office under his or her direction. An employee has the responsibility of following the directions of the employer and must understand that his or her work in taking radiographs is basically an extension of the provider's work. Providers will hold the dental staff responsible for their work, but ultimately, if there is a legal situation pertaining to the care of a patient, it is the employer that would be responsible. It must be noted that this varies from state to state because many states require dental radiographers to be licensed.

30. B: A radiation monitoring badge, commonly referred to as a dosimeter, is a device that is worn by the dental auxiliary during the traditional workday at a dental clinic. This is a device that measures any amounts of radiation that the dental auxiliary may be exposed to. This is something that should not be worn outside of the dental office as it may capture other sources of radiation and distort the final amounts. After the specified time period, a week, a month, or a quarter, this device is then sent in for a final analysis, and the results are then sent to the dental auxiliary for interpretation.

31. B: Hand hygiene is the most important component of minimizing disease transmission from patient to patient. Using an alcohol-based hand rub and rubbing it into the hands until they are completely dry is required before donning and after doffing gloves for dental imaging. It is the rubbing motion that helps make the product effective; it is important to continue the rubbing action until the hands are dry. When the skin has come in contact with bodily fluid such as that in the oral cavity, a hand wash with soap is required. A routine hand wash with nonantimicrobial soap is acceptable, but the length of time for that hand wash must be 40–60 seconds. The use of antimicrobial soaps and products is acceptable for a minimal of 15 seconds in order to be effective.

32. C: Regarding the standard of care that is provided by a dentist, a patient cannot consent to negligent care. The statement, "Documentation signed by the patient, releasing the dental provider from liability, protects the dentist when treating a patient who refuses dental x-rays," is a false statement because the dentist providing treatment will/can be liable for any negligence should a procedure result in a negative outcome. The statement "Dentists are allowed to treat a patient even though the patient refuses necessary dental x-rays" is also false because an ethical practicing dentist will not attempt to treat a patient who refuses dental x-rays because dental x-rays are a vital tool in the proper diagnosis and treatment of every patient.

33. D: In order to prevent any secondary or scatter radiation from striking the dental auxiliary, they should stand at least 6 feet away from the source of radiation or the tubehead during any type of radiation exposure, both intraoral and extraoral.

34. B: X-rays are a type of energy that are able to penetrate matter. They are classified as electromagnetic radiation. Other types of electromagnetic radiation include television waves, radio, radar, and light. Shorter x-rays are more useful in dental radiographs because the penetrate structures more easily than longer wavelengths. X-rays travel at the speed of light. They are not detectable by any of the senses. X-rays do not contain mass or weight and do not contain a charge. X-rays travel in a straight line but are easily deflected to other areas. X-rays are either absorbed by matter or scattered and can cause damage due to secondary radiation exposure.

35. A: Standard precautions refer to the general infection prevention measures that should be used with all patients in dentistry and in medicine. Using standard precautions ensures that even in relatively low infection risk patients, standardized measures are used to protect the patient and dental team from disease transmission. These include the proper use of hand hygiene and personal protective equipment (PPE).

36. A: When capturing dental images, it is essential that the dental team use properly sterilized instruments and receptor holders. The extension cone paralleling (XCP) device (often referred to as a Rinn device, after one manufacturer) is a common dental instrument that is used to position a digital sensor in the patient's oral cavity when capturing dental images. This item must be properly precleaned and heat sterilized between patients. If this does not happen, or if the sterilization process is ineffective or done incorrectly, it will render the dental item unsterile. This can directly cause the spread of infectious diseases from one patient to another because the pathogens may still be on the item when it is used on the next patient. If the dental assistant has a glove puncture or is improperly wearing their personal protective equipment (PPE), this can lead to disease transmission from the dental assistant to the patient or from the patient to the dental assistant. Eye protection is not required nor does it serve any purpose for the patient during image production.

37. C: Wired sensors cannot be placed into an autoclave, chemiclave, or dry heat; they should be processed by other forms of submersion, heat, or pressure sterilization methods. When used, wired sensors must be covered completely with a barrier that extends past the area where the sensor and the wire connect. After use, the barrier should be removed and the sensor needs to be disinfected according to the manufacturer's directions. Wired sensors cannot be placed in the ultrasonic machine because they are electronic devices and will be damaged. Plastic barriers can tear or leak after a few exposures; therefore, finger cots are recommended to provide extra support and will not compromise the wired sensor.

38. C: Bitewing images are the images of choice when the dentist needs to view the interproximal areas of the teeth or when the dentist or dental hygienist needs to view the bone levels in the mouth. When taken with correct vertical and horizontal angulations, these images provide the most accurate view of these structures.

39. B: The panoramic dental digital picture is one that will show the upper and lower portions of the mouth in one image. Not only will bone be in the picture, it will also include parts of the jaw and the eye sockets; the dental radiographer may even see parts of the spine.

40. D: Lead aprons may be required for use in some states and optional in others. Regardless of the requirement to wear a lead apron, they can be worn for both intraoral and extraoral images. They are intended to protect the reproductive and blood-producing cells in the body and to prevent radiation from reaching radiosensitive organs. They are also used to prevent primary and secondary radiation from striking the patients.

41. B: The CDC created the 2003 Guidelines for Infection Control in Dental Health-Care Settings in collaboration with other agencies involved with patient and worker safety. Although these guidelines are from 2003, they are still applicable and referenced today. They contain recommendations that apply to dentistry that are upheld by state boards and authoritative agencies and serve as the best practices for dental care. OSHA is a regulatory agency that serves to protect workers in the United States. The ADA is a national agency composed of dentists across the United States. OSAP is an agency composed of dental professionals, researchers, consultants, and other staff who serve with the goal of providing evidence-based practices on infection control and safety.

42. D: The dental assistant should always use the paralleling technique when needing to view the entire tooth. This is the technique that will show the tooth in the most realistic dimensions possible when viewing a single tooth This will allow the dentist to have a realistic picture to view the dental anatomy and develop a treatment plan that is best for the patient and will provide the most relief for his or her discomfort.

43. C: When using the bisecting technique, the dental assistant will use angles that must be visualized as abstract angles versus the angles that are created when placing the sensor in the mouth. This is because, when using this technique, the mouth is preventing the sensor from being placed at a right angle, which is needed to produce images that are dimensionally accurate.

44. D: The OSHA Bloodborne Pathogens Standard is used to help protect employees from exposure to microbes that can lead to disease. Employers have a duty to provide a safe working environment for staff and are required to implement safety practices that are listed in this standard. The OSHA Hazard Communication Standard, also known as the Employee Right-to-Know Law, is another important standard that protects employees from hazardous chemicals. The CDC's Morbidity and Mortality Weekly Report infection control guidelines have been developed as recommendations for safety in dentistry and are best practices.

45. B: A dental assistant can be exposed to 3 types of radiation. Primary radiation can be received directly from the x-ray machine; the beam that originates from the x-ray tube and goes through the collimator and position-indicating device (PID) is used for obtaining dental radiographs. Secondary radiation is that received because of scatter radiation, which is deflected away. This can occur when radiation hits the patient's face and bounces off. Leakage radiation is received if the tubehead seal is not properly secured. The goal for any dental employee is zero radiation exposure, which can be attainable if proper procedures and safety guidelines are followed.

46. B: If the milliamp (mA) setting is increased on the dental radiograph x-ray control panel, the processed film will have increased density. The mA settings on the control panel are directly related to controlling the amount of density that will be seen on the resulting radiograph. Factors including exposure time, technique used, length of the PID used, and kilovolt peak (kVp) settings will also have an effect on the density of the processed film.

47. B: When positioning the patient for panoramic exposure, the Frankfort plane should be parallel to the floor. If the Frankfort plane were to be positioned perpendicular to the floor, the patient's head would have to be on its side, as if the patient were lying down on his or her side. Because the cassette of the panoramic unit is constantly rotating during the exposure, the patient's Frankfort plane cannot be positioned parallel or perpendicular to the cassette because it is not a fixed object.

48. B: The incisive foramen will appear as a radiolucent area found on the maxillary central periapical image receptor. This anatomical structure appears radiolucent because a foramen is a hole or opening that allows for the passageway of nerves and vessels. The coronoid process, genial tubercles, and zygomatic process are all structures that are made from bone, and will appear radiopaque on a dental radiograph.

49. A: The dental assistant must wear a mask and eye protection or a chin-length face shield when spatter or aerosols are likely. This will provide protection from pathogens entering the eyes or the mucous membranes of the nasal cavity. The dental assistant is not required to use an N95 mask during the capturing of dental images. The Occupational Safety and Health Administration (OSHA) requires these masks to be used if treating patients who may be potentially infected with COVID-19 or other airborne diseases. These masks are available in many dental offices, but they are not required for imaging. Per OSHA guidelines, protective clothing must be worn by the dental assistant during image capturing regardless of the amount of spatter and aerosols anticipated.

50. C: An orthodontist typically uses 2 types of radiographs for treatment planning proposes. The panoramic radiograph is used to visualize the positioning of primary and permanent teeth as well as to visualize the amount of space available for emerging teeth to erupt. The cephalometric radiograph is also used. This is a type of extraoral radiograph that shows the whole side of the head including all the bones, the skull, and soft tissues. This type of x-ray allows the orthodontist to monitor for changes in the jaw as well positioning of the teeth to track treatment progress. Cephalometric radiographs are also used by otolaryngologists to visualize the airway in a patient with sleep apnea.

51. C: Particulate radiation is a type of radiation that can be defined as tiny particles of matter that do have mass or weight and travel in straight lines at high speeds. This type of radiation differs from electromagnetic radiation, which is what is produced in dentistry. Electromagnetic radiation does not possess weight or mass and cannot be seen with the naked eye.

52. D: When an image receptor is taken and appears to have short, blunted root tips, the error is foreshortening. This is caused by excessive vertical angulations and, in order to be corrected, the dental auxiliary needs to retake the image and reduce the amount of vertical angulation that were used.

53. D: The temporomandibular joint (TMJ) is located at the jaw joint. TMJ disorders can cause a range of symptoms including clicking sounds, locked jaw, headaches, and ear pain. TMJ can be quite debilitating for many patients. TMJ disorders can be caused by trauma to the TMJ, aging, grinding, or clenching of the teeth, or misalignment of the teeth that causes issues with proper bite. There is no single diagnostic test for TMJ disorders. Regular dental x-rays do not diagnose TMJ. Transcranial radiographs are sometimes used to show changes in bone structure. The patient's history of symptoms along with possible arthrography, MRI, or CAT scan may be required. Arthrography involves the use of radiographic contrast injected into the temporomandibular joint. This makes the area being visualized turn opaque to highlight the structure of the area.

54. D: The milliamperage setting (mA setting) controls the number of electrons generated by the tungsten filament, which directly controls how many x-rays will be created at the tungsten target. The mA setting does not control how fast the electrons move inside the tubehead and does not control the size or the shape of the resulting x-ray beam.

55. C: A critical organ affected by cumulative radiation exposure is the lens of the eye. Although every organ can be affected by cumulative radiation exposure, the lens of the eye is much more sensitive to this exposure than the others listed. A critical organ is one that does not have an immediate source of protection to absorb the radiation exposure. The lens of the eye does not have this protection, whereas many other organs do. The layers of skin, for example, are protective layers that must be penetrated before the radiation can reach deep internal organs.

56. A: When using the paralleling technique during periapical exposure, the central ray of the beam is perpendicular to the long axis of the tooth and film. The central ray, if positioned correctly, will be positioned at a 90-degree angle. This 90-degree angle is formed by the position-indicating device (PID) placement, perpendicular to the long axis of the tooth and the film parallel to the long axis of the tooth.

57. C: The dental assistant should expose a periapical image, which is the best choice when the dentist needs to see the entire tooth structure. The sensor is placed behind the tooth for this type of image, which will go from the tip of the tooth to the tip of the root, providing the view that the dentist will need for a correct diagnosis.

58. A: A bitewing x-ray is a type of intraoral radiograph. This type of x-ray shows the upper and lower teeth in one portion of the mouth. The range of the x-ray extends from the tooth to the crown up to the bone. It does not include the roots. Bitewing x-rays will detect tooth decay and show changes in bone density related to gum disease. Bitewings are also used to check crown placement and fillings. In order to obtain a proper bitewing radiograph, the patient must be in an upright position in the dental chair, covered with a lead apron and thyroid collar. The x-ray film is placed in the patient's mouth using a special device for film holding. The film is positioned between the upper and lower teeth of the area to be x-rayed. The patient is instructed to bite down on the film and the x-ray beam is directed towards the film. The patient should remain still during the procedure. An impacted tooth is generally diagnosed using an extraoral x-ray.

59. D: The cassette is not a part of the panoramic head-positioning device. The cassette is what is used to contain the panoramic film as it rotates around the patient during exposure. The notched bite stick, the lateral head guides, and the forehead rest are all components of the head-positioning device that help the dental assistant to correctly position the patient's head prior to exposure.

60. A: The object-receptor distance is the distance between the tooth and the sensor or receptor. Ideally, the dental radiographer should insert the sensor in a way that allows it to get as close to the tooth as possible, which will provide an image that limits the amount of size expansion or minimization of a tooth.

61. D: While the paralleling technique has many advantages, patient comfort is not one of them. In this technique, the dental auxiliary must place the image receptor parallel to the long axis of the tooth, which can create substantial patient discomfort as the image receptor may impinge upon patient tissues and oral structures.

62. C: When considering the use of surface barriers in dentistry, it is recommended to place them over hard-to-clean areas and surfaces as a way to minimize aerosols and pathogens from reaching those areas, including the exposure button used in dental imaging. Surface barriers are not required for use in dentistry; each office determines its use/nonuse of surface barriers and what types of surface barriers to use or if they prefer to use disinfectants in the operatories after patient care instead. When surface barriers are used and remain intact during a dental procedure, the dental staff is not required to disinfect the area under the barriers because it was not exposed to aerosols due to the protection that the surface barrier provides.

63. D: The federal Consumer-Patient Radiation Health and Safety Act requires that all persons who operate x-ray machinery to produce dental radiographs are properly trained and certified. The *Journal of the American Dental Association* (JADA) is filled with useful information regarding the practice of dentistry in the United States. The Occupational Safety and Health Administration (OSHA) is a federal agency that regulates workplace safety and health. The Food and Drug Administration (FDA) is a regulating agency in the United States that promotes proper health and human services through laws and state regulations.

64. C: Cotton rolls can aid in the placement of an image receptor when the patient has edentulous areas in their oral cavity. If teeth are missing on one arch during a bitewing image, the cotton rolls can serve as a device to help hold the bitewing tab into place, allowing for maximum stability of the image receptor. The dental auxiliary does not need to use cotton roll holders when placing cotton rolls in a patient's oral cavity because the metal from the holder may distort the image.

65. D: There are several methods that can be used to sterilize patient care items used in dental imaging with the steam autoclave being the method that, when used correctly, can provide sterilization of items using water steam under pressure. This method can also prevent corrosion of patient care items, and when the cycle is run to completion, it will produce items that are dry in their packaging and are ready for storage. Unsaturated chemical vapor sterilization methods use a chemical vapor to sterilize instruments under pressure.

Instruments must be dry prior to using this method; otherwise, corrosion may occur. Both forced air and rapid transfer are types of dry heat sterilization that use dry environments to sterilize items and produce items that are dry after each cycle.

66. D: A developing fetus would be the most sensitive to the effects of radiation because a fetus is an accumulation of cells that are constantly undergoing cellular division and replication. If these cells are damaged at this stage, they may produce other damaged cells that will affect the developing fetus. More radiation damage occurs in cells that are sensitive to radiation and are rapidly dividing, such as those of a developing fetus.

67. B: The XCP device, used in dentistry as a beam alignment device and a receptor holder, is an example of an engineering control because it is a physical piece of equipment used to provide operator safety. This device can save the dental provider from unnecessary radiation as well as prevent risks of exposure that can occur when the dental provider must manipulate an imaging sensor inside a patient's mouth during dental imaging. The practice of using an XCP device in dental imaging is an example of a work practice control that may be required in some dental practices but optional in others.

68. C: The collimator is a part of the tubehead. It is a metal disc made out of lead located near the position-indicating device (PID). The x-ray beam passes through the collimator. It allows the beam to exit through a 2-inch opening. It forms the size and the shape of the x-ray beam. A rectangular shape helps to limit the amount of radiation exposure the patient receives. There is a filter located within the PID that filters out the unusable wavelengths, such as the longer waves that are not used for dental radiographs.

69. B: The American Academy of Oral and Maxillofacial Radiology recommends using the paralleling technique, which provides the dentist with the most accurate image with the least amount of distortion. This recommendation stems from the theory that if the dental film is placed parallel to the long axis of the tooth during exposure, this will provide the least possible means of distortion of the tooth being radiographed.

70. D: As a dental assistant, it is important to be able to interpret radiographs and identify structures appropriately. Structures that are visualized as radiopaque are dense structures that block the x-rays from passing through them. There may be a range of radiopacity; they may be seen as white to light gray on the film. Structures that will be viewed as radiopaque include enamel, dentin, cementum, lamina dura, interradicular bone, and interdental bone. Other radiopaque areas will include the hard palate, nasal septum, and maxillary tuberosity. Radiolucent areas on dental radiographs will appear within the range of dark gray to black. The structures are not as dense as the radiopaque structures and the x-rays are able to penetrate the structures to some degree. Structures that will be viewed as radiolucent include the pulp chamber, pulp canals, periodontal ligament, mandibular canal, lingual foramen, and mandibular foramen.

71. B: A pathogen is a type of microorganism that is capable of causing disease. Bacteria and protozoa can be pathogenic in nature, but not always. For instance, there are healthy types of bacteria found in our food or in the normal flora of our gastrointestinal tract. There are not healthy types of pathogens that exist—all pathogens can cause disease. A biofilm is a type of layer composed of bacterial colonies that form together. A biofilm may be found within dental unit water lines and is composed of a variety of different microbes including pathogens but is not pathogenic itself.

72. C: Legally, dental images, as part of the patient's dental record, are the property of the dentist. The patient, patient's authorized caretaker, and the insurance company are able to review, or have a copy of, the dental images, once authorized for release by the patient. Although the patient or the insurance company has paid for the services to have the images taken, the images legally belong to the provider.

73. B: All of the following would appear radiolucent on a processed dental periapical x-ray EXCEPT the nasal septum. This anatomical landmark would appear more radiopaque than radiolucent. The nasal septum is composed of dense bone that prohibits the x-ray beam from successfully going through the film completely due to the thickness of the bone. An image would be created by the exposure in this area, but the resulting radiograph will indicate a radiopacity in the area of this anatomical landmark rather than a radiolucency.

74. B: When possible, an XCP device should be precleaned using the ultrasonic machine, which uses high-frequency sound waves to efficiently and effectively vibrate bioburden off of instruments. This, along with the use of ultrasonic products that have enzymatic or antimicrobial activity, is the best option for precleaning instruments in dentistry. The holding solution is used to prevent bioburden from drying onto instruments and is not a method of precleaning. Hand scrubbing is the least desirable cleaning method due to the risk of occupational injury when scrubbing sharp instruments. The instrument washing machine works similarly to a household dishwasher and serves as a thermal disinfector for instruments; it does not use high-frequency sound waves to loosen and remove debris.

75. A: It is not acceptable for the dental auxiliary to hold an image receptor in a patient's mouth under any circumstances. This is because this action may result in unnecessary exposure to both primary and secondary or scatter radiation to the dental auxiliary, which does not follow the ALARA principle.

76. C: Intermediate-level disinfectants are used when disinfecting clinical contact surfaces, including the dental tubehead and dental operatory after dental imaging. This level of disinfectant has the ability to destroy a wide range of microbes while having the ability to prevent extensive damage to dental equipment, making it very common in dentistry. A high-level disinfectant is not required for use when disinfecting clinical contact surfaces, and a sterilant is recommended for use only for reusable heat-sensitive items and by immersion only. Low-level disinfectants are recommended for cleaning and disinfecting floors, walls, and other noncritical surfaces.

77. A: When mounting processed radiographs, the anatomical landmark that can assist you in mounting the mandibular premolar periapical is the mental foramen. The genial tubercles and the lingual foramen are anatomical landmarks located in the lingual mandibular anterior area. The premolar is considered a posterior tooth and would not be associated with any of the mandibular anterior landmarks for proper identification or mounting. The maxillary sinus is an anatomical landmark that is associated with mounting the maxillary anterior and posterior periapicals.

78. D: Disproportionate changes in the size of an image on a processed radiograph are caused by excessive or insufficient vertical angulation. The inability to see between the contacts of the teeth is the result of improper horizontal angulation. The size of the film will only directly relate to disproportionate changes in the processed radiograph if too small of a film was used to perhaps see the apex of a tooth.

79. B: The function of the kilovoltage (kVp) peak selector is to control the degree of penetration from the x-ray beam. The normal kVp of a dental radiograph machine is 60-90 kVp. The 90 kVp setting is used for an image with a lower degree of contrast. This image will contain more gray shades and has a lower exposure time. A 60 kVp is used for an image with a higher degree of contrast. It has fewer gray shades in the image and more definitive light and dark areas. The exposure time is slightly longer. Dentists will have their own individual preferences for the kilovoltage peak selector that is used for most images.

80. D: When considering what image to take in order to obtain the best view of facial growth, facial trauma and disease, or developmental abnormalities that may occur in the oral cavity or cranium, the lateral cephalometric projection is the top choice. This is due to the large 8 x 10 cassette that is used to capture this image and also how the vertical and horizontal angulations are set up when exposing this image. This image is commonly taken in orthodontic offices and used to allow the dentist to trace the anticipated growth of the mandible and maxilla as braces are considered for a patient.

How to Overcome Test Anxiety

Just the thought of taking a test is enough to make most people a little nervous. A test is an important event that can have a long-term impact on your future, so it's important to take it seriously and it's natural to feel anxious about performing well. But just because anxiety is normal, that doesn't mean that it's helpful in test taking, or that you should simply accept it as part of your life. Anxiety can have a variety of effects. These effects can be mild, like making you feel slightly nervous, or severe, like blocking your ability to focus or remember even a simple detail.

If you experience test anxiety—whether severe or mild—it's important to know how to beat it. To discover this, first you need to understand what causes test anxiety.

Causes of Test Anxiety

While we often think of anxiety as an uncontrollable emotional state, it can actually be caused by simple, practical things. One of the most common causes of test anxiety is that a person does not feel adequately prepared for their test. This feeling can be the result of many different issues such as poor study habits or lack of organization, but the most common culprit is time management. Starting to study too late, failing to organize your study time to cover all of the material, or being distracted while you study will mean that you're not well prepared for the test. This may lead to cramming the night before, which will cause you to be physically and mentally exhausted for the test. Poor time management also contributes to feelings of stress, fear, and hopelessness as you realize you are not well prepared but don't know what to do about it.

Other times, test anxiety is not related to your preparation for the test but comes from unresolved fear. This may be a past failure on a test, or poor performance on tests in general. It may come from comparing yourself to others who seem to be performing better or from the stress of living up to expectations. Anxiety may be driven by fears of the future—how failure on this test would affect your educational and career goals. These fears are often completely irrational, but they can still negatively impact your test performance.

Elements of Test Anxiety

As mentioned earlier, test anxiety is considered to be an emotional state, but it has physical and mental components as well. Sometimes you may not even realize that you are suffering from test anxiety until you notice the physical symptoms. These can include trembling hands, rapid heartbeat, sweating, nausea, and tense muscles. Extreme anxiety may lead to fainting or vomiting. Obviously, any of these symptoms can have a negative impact on testing. It is important to recognize them as soon as they begin to occur so that you can address the problem before it damages your performance.

The mental components of test anxiety include trouble focusing and inability to remember learned information. During a test, your mind is on high alert, which can help you recall information and stay focused for an extended period of time. However, anxiety interferes with your mind's natural processes, causing you to blank out, even on the questions you know well. The strain of testing during anxiety makes it difficult to stay focused, especially on a test that may take several hours. Extreme anxiety can take a huge mental toll, making it difficult not only to recall test information but even to understand the test questions or pull your thoughts together.

Effects of Test Anxiety

Test anxiety is like a disease—if left untreated, it will get progressively worse. Anxiety leads to poor performance, and this reinforces the feelings of fear and failure, which in turn lead to poor performances on subsequent tests. It can grow from a mild nervousness to a crippling condition. If allowed to progress, test anxiety can have a big impact on your schooling, and consequently on your future.

Test anxiety can spread to other parts of your life. Anxiety on tests can become anxiety in any stressful situation, and blanking on a test can turn into panicking in a job situation. But fortunately, you don't have to let anxiety rule your testing and determine your grades. There are a number of relatively simple steps you can take to move past anxiety and function normally on a test and in the rest of life.

Physical Steps for Beating Test Anxiety

While test anxiety is a serious problem, the good news is that it can be overcome. It doesn't have to control your ability to think and remember information. While it may take time, you can begin taking steps today to beat anxiety.

Just as your first hint that you may be struggling with anxiety comes from the physical symptoms, the first step to treating it is also physical. Rest is crucial for having a clear, strong mind. If you are tired, it is much easier to give in to anxiety. But if you establish good sleep habits, your body and mind will be ready to perform optimally, without the strain of exhaustion. Additionally, sleeping well helps you to retain information better, so you're more likely to recall the answers when you see the test questions.

Getting good sleep means more than going to bed on time. It's important to allow your brain time to relax. Take study breaks from time to time so it doesn't get overworked, and don't study right before bed. Take time to rest your mind before trying to rest your body, or you may find it difficult to fall asleep.

Along with sleep, other aspects of physical health are important in preparing for a test. Good nutrition is vital for good brain function. Sugary foods and drinks may give a burst of energy but this burst is followed by a crash, both physically and emotionally. Instead, fuel your body with protein and vitamin-rich foods.

Also, drink plenty of water. Dehydration can lead to headaches and exhaustion, especially if your brain is already under stress from the rigors of the test. Particularly if your test is a long one, drink water during the breaks. And if possible, take an energy-boosting snack to eat between sections.

Along with sleep and diet, a third important part of physical health is exercise. Maintaining a steady workout schedule is helpful, but even taking 5-minute study breaks to walk can help get your blood pumping faster and clear your head. Exercise also releases endorphins, which contribute to a positive feeling and can help combat test anxiety.

When you nurture your physical health, you are also contributing to your mental health. If your body is healthy, your mind is much more likely to be healthy as well. So take time to rest, nourish your body with healthy food and water, and get moving as much as possible. Taking these physical steps will make you stronger and more able to take the mental steps necessary to overcome test anxiety.

Mental Steps for Beating Test Anxiety

Working on the mental side of test anxiety can be more challenging, but as with the physical side, there are clear steps you can take to overcome it. As mentioned earlier, test anxiety often stems from lack of preparation, so the obvious solution is to prepare for the test. Effective studying may be the most important weapon you have for beating test anxiety, but you can and should employ several other mental tools to combat fear.

First, boost your confidence by reminding yourself of past success—tests or projects that you aced. If you're putting as much effort into preparing for this test as you did for those, there's no reason you should expect to fail here. Work hard to prepare; then trust your preparation.

Second, surround yourself with encouraging people. It can be helpful to find a study group, but be sure that the people you're around will encourage a positive attitude. If you spend time with others who are anxious or cynical, this will only contribute to your own anxiety. Look for others who are motivated to study hard from a desire to succeed, not from a fear of failure.

Third, reward yourself. A test is physically and mentally tiring, even without anxiety, and it can be helpful to have something to look forward to. Plan an activity following the test, regardless of the outcome, such as going to a movie or getting ice cream.

When you are taking the test, if you find yourself beginning to feel anxious, remind yourself that you know the material. Visualize successfully completing the test. Then take a few deep, relaxing breaths and return to it. Work through the questions carefully but with confidence, knowing that you are capable of succeeding.

Developing a healthy mental approach to test taking will also aid in other areas of life. Test anxiety affects more than just the actual test—it can be damaging to your mental health and even contribute to depression. It's important to beat test anxiety before it becomes a problem for more than testing.

Study Strategy

Being prepared for the test is necessary to combat anxiety, but what does being prepared look like? You may study for hours on end and still not feel prepared. What you need is a strategy for test prep. The next few pages outline our recommended steps to help you plan out and conquer the challenge of preparation.

STEP 1: SCOPE OUT THE TEST

Learn everything you can about the format (multiple choice, essay, etc.) and what will be on the test. Gather any study materials, course outlines, or sample exams that may be available. Not only will this help you to prepare, but knowing what to expect can help to alleviate test anxiety.

STEP 2: MAP OUT THE MATERIAL

Look through the textbook or study guide and make note of how many chapters or sections it has. Then divide these over the time you have. For example, if a book has 15 chapters and you have five days to study, you need to cover three chapters each day. Even better, if you have the time, leave an extra day at the end for overall review after you have gone through the material in depth.

If time is limited, you may need to prioritize the material. Look through it and make note of which sections you think you already have a good grasp on, and which need review. While you are studying, skim quickly through the familiar sections and take more time on the challenging parts. Write out your plan so you don't get lost as you go. Having a written plan also helps you feel more in control of the study, so anxiety is less likely to arise from feeling overwhelmed at the amount to cover.

STEP 3: GATHER YOUR TOOLS

Decide what study method works best for you. Do you prefer to highlight in the book as you study and then go back over the highlighted portions? Or do you type out notes of the important information? Or is it helpful to make flashcards that you can carry with you? Assemble the pens, index cards, highlighters, post-it notes, and any other materials you may need so you won't be distracted by getting up to find things while you study.

If you're having a hard time retaining the information or organizing your notes, experiment with different methods. For example, try color-coding by subject with colored pens, highlighters, or post-it notes. If you learn better by hearing, try recording yourself reading your notes so you can listen while in the car, working out, or simply sitting at your desk. Ask a friend to quiz you from your flashcards, or try teaching someone the material to solidify it in your mind.

STEP 4: CREATE YOUR ENVIRONMENT

It's important to avoid distractions while you study. This includes both the obvious distractions like visitors and the subtle distractions like an uncomfortable chair (or a too-comfortable couch that makes you want to fall asleep). Set up the best study environment possible: good lighting and a comfortable work area. If background music helps you focus, you may want to turn it on, but otherwise keep the room quiet. If you are using a computer to take notes, be sure you don't have any other windows open, especially applications like social media, games, or anything else that could distract you. Silence your phone and turn off notifications. Be sure to keep water close by so you stay hydrated while you study (but avoid unhealthy drinks and snacks).

Also, take into account the best time of day to study. Are you freshest first thing in the morning? Try to set aside some time then to work through the material. Is your mind clearer in the afternoon or evening? Schedule your study session then. Another method is to study at the same time of day that you will take the test, so that your brain gets used to working on the material at that time and will be ready to focus at test time.

STEP 5: STUDY!

Once you have done all the study preparation, it's time to settle into the actual studying. Sit down, take a few moments to settle your mind so you can focus, and begin to follow your study plan. Don't give in to distractions or let yourself procrastinate. This is your time to prepare so you'll be ready to fearlessly approach the test. Make the most of the time and stay focused.

Of course, you don't want to burn out. If you study too long you may find that you're not retaining the information very well. Take regular study breaks. For example, taking five minutes out of every hour to walk briskly, breathing deeply and swinging your arms, can help your mind stay fresh.

As you get to the end of each chapter or section, it's a good idea to do a quick review. Remind yourself of what you learned and work on any difficult parts. When you feel that you've mastered the material, move on to the next part. At the end of your study session, briefly skim through your notes again.

But while review is helpful, cramming last minute is NOT. If at all possible, work ahead so that you won't need to fit all your study into the last day. Cramming overloads your brain with more information than it can process and retain, and your tired mind may struggle to recall even previously learned information when it is overwhelmed with last-minute study. Also, the urgent nature of cramming and the stress placed on your brain contribute to anxiety. You'll be more likely to go to the test feeling unprepared and having trouble thinking clearly.

So don't cram, and don't stay up late before the test, even just to review your notes at a leisurely pace. Your brain needs rest more than it needs to go over the information again. In fact, plan to finish your studies by noon or early afternoon the day before the test. Give your brain the rest of the day to relax or focus on other things, and get a good night's sleep. Then you will be fresh for the test and better able to recall what you've studied.

STEP 6: TAKE A PRACTICE TEST

Many courses offer sample tests, either online or in the study materials. This is an excellent resource to check whether you have mastered the material, as well as to prepare for the test format and environment.

Check the test format ahead of time: the number of questions, the type (multiple choice, free response, etc.), and the time limit. Then create a plan for working through them. For example, if you have 30 minutes to take a 60-question test, your limit is 30 seconds per question. Spend less time on the questions you know well so that you can take more time on the difficult ones.

If you have time to take several practice tests, take the first one open book, with no time limit. Work through the questions at your own pace and make sure you fully understand them. Gradually work up to taking a test under test conditions: sit at a desk with all study materials put away and set a timer. Pace yourself to make sure you finish the test with time to spare and go back to check your answers if you have time.

After each test, check your answers. On the questions you missed, be sure you understand why you missed them. Did you misread the question (tests can use tricky wording)? Did you forget the information? Or was it something you hadn't learned? Go back and study any shaky areas that the practice tests reveal.

Taking these tests not only helps with your grade, but also aids in combating test anxiety. If you're already used to the test conditions, you're less likely to worry about it, and working through tests until you're scoring well gives you a confidence boost. Go through the practice tests until you feel comfortable, and then you can go into the test knowing that you're ready for it.

Test Tips

On test day, you should be confident, knowing that you've prepared well and are ready to answer the questions. But aside from preparation, there are several test day strategies you can employ to maximize your performance.

First, as stated before, get a good night's sleep the night before the test (and for several nights before that, if possible). Go into the test with a fresh, alert mind rather than staying up late to study.

Try not to change too much about your normal routine on the day of the test. It's important to eat a nutritious breakfast, but if you normally don't eat breakfast at all, consider eating just a protein bar. If you're a coffee drinker, go ahead and have your normal coffee. Just make sure you time it so that the caffeine doesn't wear off right in the middle of your test. Avoid sugary beverages, and drink enough water to stay hydrated but not so much that you need a restroom break 10 minutes into the test. If your test isn't first thing in the morning, consider going for a walk or doing a light workout before the test to get your blood flowing.

Allow yourself enough time to get ready, and leave for the test with plenty of time to spare so you won't have the anxiety of scrambling to arrive in time. Another reason to be early is to select a good seat. It's helpful to sit away from doors and windows, which can be distracting. Find a good seat, get out your supplies, and settle your mind before the test begins.

When the test begins, start by going over the instructions carefully, even if you already know what to expect. Make sure you avoid any careless mistakes by following the directions.

Then begin working through the questions, pacing yourself as you've practiced. If you're not sure on an answer, don't spend too much time on it, and don't let it shake your confidence. Either skip it and come back later, or eliminate as many wrong answers as possible and guess among the remaining ones. Don't dwell on these questions as you continue—put them out of your mind and focus on what lies ahead.

Be sure to read all of the answer choices, even if you're sure the first one is the right answer. Sometimes you'll find a better one if you keep reading. But don't second-guess yourself if you do immediately know the answer. Your gut instinct is usually right. Don't let test anxiety rob you of the information you know.

If you have time at the end of the test (and if the test format allows), go back and review your answers. Be cautious about changing any, since your first instinct tends to be correct, but make sure you didn't misread any of the questions or accidentally mark the wrong answer choice. Look over any you skipped and make an educated guess.

At the end, leave the test feeling confident. You've done your best, so don't waste time worrying about your performance or wishing you could change anything. Instead, celebrate the successful completion of this test. And finally, use this test to learn how to deal with anxiety even better next time.

> **Review Video: Test Anxiety**
> Visit mometrix.com/academy and enter code: 100340

Important Qualification

Not all anxiety is created equal. If your test anxiety is causing major issues in your life beyond the classroom or testing center, or if you are experiencing troubling physical symptoms related to your anxiety, it may be a sign of a serious physiological or psychological condition. If this sounds like your situation, we strongly encourage you to seek professional help.

Additional Bonus Material

Due to our efforts to try to keep this book to a manageable length, we've created a link that will give you access to all of your additional bonus material:

mometrix.com/bonus948/danbcda